MW00988708

In PURSUIT *of* FAITHFULNESS

"In this narrative of how Goshen became Goshen, Preheim tells fascinating stories about conflict over education, same-sex marriage, clothing, and vain amusements like birthday parties. These agonies were redeemed, however, by a resolute dedication to discipleship and peace, even if that peace was sometimes difficult to achieve. This terrific book is both an accomplishment of historical recovery and a testimony to the faithfulness of God."
—*David R. Swartz, associate professor of history, Asbury University*

"Preheim tells a powerful story—my story, our story, the story of our beloved church. Like the Mennonite church today, *In Pursuit of Faithfulness* shimmers with tension and hope, flawed and faith-filled believers, amazing advances and perplexing problems. With each chapter, my sense of God's patient leading kept growing."
—*Lois Johns Kaufmann, conference minister, Central District Conference*

"Through its history, Rich Preheim notes, the Indiana-Michigan Conference has been situated at the geographical and theological crossroads of the Mennonite church. The metaphor works perfectly. In this fine narrative history, Preheim presents in microcosm much of the Mennonite story in America for the past hundred years. It is an important and illuminating book."
—*Perry Bush, professor of history, Bluffton University*

"In this volume, Preheim demonstrates the qualities of an energetic journalist and judicious historian. Uncovering multiple expressions of conviction, conflict, compromise, he makes the 170 years of Indiana-Michigan Mennonite Conference come alive in the dynamic interplay of the Word repeatedly becoming flesh and dwelling among us. Readers will also discover germane, delightful sidebars."
—*John A. Lapp, executive secretary emeritus, Mennonite Central Committee*

"A good read requires conflict in subject matter and a lively writing style, both of which abound in *In Pursuit of Faithfulness*. The conflict comes from the many changes that this history documents, especially since 1955, when J. C. Wenger's history was published, and intensifying in 2016 on the release of this book. Lay members in the Indiana-Michigan Mennonite Conference will be particularly well served by Preheim's work, which traces the origins of many resolved, and some major unresolved, issues. It also highlights the work of individuals who emerge from the margins, whether because of their gender, ethnicity, or special interests that challenged their community's orthodoxy."
—*Ervin Beck, president, Michiana Anabaptist Historians*

In PURSUIT *of* FAITHFULNESS

Conviction, Conflict, and Compromise in Indiana-Michigan Mennonite Conference

Rich Preheim

Herald Press

Harrisonburg, Virginia
Kitchener, Ontario

Library of Congress Cataloging-in-Publication Data
Names: Preheim, Rich, 1967- author.
Title: In pursuit of faithfulness : conviction, conflict, and compromise in
    Indiana-Michigan Mennonite Conference / Rich Preheim.
Description: Harrisonburg : Herald Press, 2016. | Series: Studies in
    Anabaptist and Mennonite history series ; 50 | Includes bibliographical
    references and index.
Identifiers: LCCN 2015049446| ISBN 9780836199994 (pbk. : alk. paper) | ISBN
    9781513800356 (hardcover : alk. paper)
Subjects: LCSH: Indiana-Michigan Mennonite Conference--History.
Classification: LCC BX8129.I53 P74 2016 | DDC 289.7/772--dc23 LC record
available at http://lccn.loc.gov/2015049446

IN PURSUIT OF FAITHFULNESS
© 2016 by Herald Press, Harrisonburg, Virginia 22802
    Released simultaneously in Canada by Herald Press,
    Kitchener, Ontario N2G 3R1. All rights reserved.
Library of Congress Control Number: 2015049446
International Standard Book Number: 978-0-8361-9999-4 (paper);
    978-1-5138-0035-6 (hardcover)
Printed in United States of America
Cover and interior design by Reuben Graham
Cover photo courtesy of Mennonite Church USA Archives–Goshen

All rights reserved. This publication may not be reproduced, stored in a retrieval system, or transmitted in whole or in part, in any form, by any means, electronic, mechanical, photocopying, recording, or otherwise without prior permission of the copyright owners.

Unless otherwise noted, Scripture text is quoted, with permission, from the *New Revised Standard Version*, © 1989, Division of Christian Education of the National Council of Churches of Christ in the United States of America.

For orders or information, call 800-245-7894 or visit HeraldPress.com.

20 19 18 17 16   10 9 8 7 6 5 4 3 2 1

To Leanne,
who brought me here

Contents

Foreword

Mennonite life in the Indiana-Michigan Conference has displayed a colorful and flourishing faith on the sharp edge of persistent conflict. As Christians who traced their European origins to the Anabaptist branch of the great sixteenth-century splintering of Western Christendom called the Reformation, Indiana-Michigan Mennonites accepted that controversy is intrinsic to discipleship. They understood from their faith ancestors that bearing the cross of Jesus Christ involved both persecution from without and contention from within the church. They also recognized that Christ's call to unity and reconciliation persists amid the disagreements of church life. And so they sought, again and again, to heal past divisions and to join together in new networks of mission and accountability.

For example, leaders of scattered Amish groups across North America began gathering together in the mid-nineteenth century for the *Diener-Versammlungen*—annual meetings that sought to achieve unity amid growing diversity of practice in Amish churches, including contentious differences among Indiana Amish Mennonites about matters of proper Christian attire and the location of worship. At the same time, Mennonite leaders were increasingly influenced by an Indiana Mennonite entrepreneur and publisher by the name of John Fretz Funk to gather regional Mennonite conferences into a new denomination in 1898—the Mennonite Church General Conference—whose denominational agencies and seminary would be located in Goshen and Elkhart, Indiana.

Meanwhile, one of the area conferences that emerged from the Amish *Diener-Versammlungen* was the Indiana-Michigan Amish Mennonite Conference, which in 1916 joined together with the Indiana-Michigan Mennonite Conference. The merger of these two conferences contributed to a concentration of Mennonite leadership and influence in northern Indiana that reverberated across North American Mennonite life. Eventually, when the Mennonite Church's seminary joined with the seminary of another Mennonite denomination to form Associated Mennonite Biblical Seminaries in Elkhart, the momentum was strengthened toward the 2002 denominational merger of the Mennonite Church with the General Conference Mennonite Church into what is now called Mennonite Church USA.

Yet all of these discoveries of unity in Christ also drove Amish and Mennonites apart from each other. The *Diener-Versammlungen* led to both the Old Order Amish division and the organization of the Egly Amish into a separate denomination—the Evangelical Mennonite Church (now known as the Fellowship of Evangelical Churches) with headquarters in Fort Wayne, Indiana. As Indiana-Michigan Mennonites moved toward denominational cooperation, the conservative Jacob Wisler escalated a confrontation with conference leaders that led eventually to the formation of a separate Old Order Mennonite community. About the same time, the revivalist leader Daniel Brenneman led another cluster of churches out of the conference to form what became known as the Mennonite Brethren in Christ—one stream that fed into today's Missionary Church denomination. More recently, the struggle over denominational polity in the Mennonite Church USA has led to the formation of a new group—the Evana Network—with many leadership ties to Indiana-Michigan Conference and an uncertain future relationship to the conference.

Amid the churning of conflict and the challenge of mission, the spiritual life of the conference was renewed again and again as its sons and daughters prophesied and its elders dreamed dreams. Barbara Stutzman had a vision of Jesus Christ and offered a prophetic critique of Protestant influences such as Sunday schools and church buildings in the late nineteenth century. Harold Bender had an Anabaptist vision of discipleship, brotherhood, and peace that advanced Mennonite convictions after the Second World War. Wilma Bailey found the spiritual authority to challenge the constraints of gender and race when she became the first woman to be credentialed as a pastor by the conference in 1980.

Because of the conference's leadership role at the midwestern crossroads of the Mennonite Church, its visions and divisions were amplified in broader Mennonite denominational life. Thus, this conference history is a valuable resource not only for historians who seek knowledge of the Mennonite past but also for any person of faith who strives to understand how Anabaptist convictions are expressed in real human communities of faith. To be sure, this history is indispensable for anyone—church leaders, members, onlookers—who are working to grasp the origins and dynamics of the present-day polity conflicts in Mennonite Church USA.

This story of deep Christian conviction, fostered in close-knit communities of earnest believers whose unity is constantly tested by conflict, is ably told by Rich Preheim, a skilled journalist who loves the church and its history. Preheim's narrative craft shines with the intriguing details of church strife while celebrating the achievements of faithfulness in a plotline that keeps moving through the changes and challenges of congregational and conference life over a century and three-quarters. Preheim does not shy away from the controversies and traumas of church history, seeing them rather as evidence of dynamism and strength of conviction.

The gift offered by this book, then, is a gift not only of a competent journalist and scrupulous historian, but even more of a faithful seer—one who observes with the eyes of faith. What Rich Preheim sees and helps us to see in the history of Indiana-Michigan Mennonite Conference is a story not only of human faith and failure, but even more of God's faithfulness and unfailing love. For this lively and inspiring story of tenacious Mennonite witness to the God of Jesus Christ, we give thanks.

Gerald J. Mast, Series Editor
Studies in Anabaptist and Mennonite History

Introduction:
Crossroads of Faithfulness

Since 1937, Indiana's official motto has been "The Crossroads of America," a commemoration of the state's importance in American culture and commerce. It's not difficult to understand why. The National Road, the first federal highway, was constructed across the state in the 1830s, just a few years before Mennonites and Amish Mennonites started arriving. The fabled Lincoln Highway, the first paved transcontinental road, literally came to them in 1913, running through Fort Wayne, Ligonier, Goshen, and Elkhart and their church communities on its way from New York to San Francisco. By the 1970s, the interstate highway system, the backbone of American overland travel, radiated from Indianapolis throughout the Midwest to Chicago, Columbus, Louisville, Saint Louis, and beyond. More than 120 years earlier, Indianapolis was the hub of seven rail lines, leading it to proclaim itself "The City of Railroads." To serve them all, the first union railroad station in the United States was built in Indianapolis in 1853.[1]

Farther north and well before the invention of automobiles and trains, what is now Michigan had already been a crossroads, albeit a nautical one. Bounded on three sides by the Great Lakes, the region was first visited by whites in 1622, when French explorers sought a water route to the Orient. While no such passage was ever discovered, Michigan became an important location for trapping beaver for fur, as the pelts were in demand for Europe's sartorial fashions. England took control of Michigan in 1763 after defeating the French in the French and Indian War, and then the colonists won the region in the American Revolution. The 1830s saw ships bringing in throngs of settlers to Michigan, by then a state, and hauling out tons of lumber, copper, and later iron ore. The first locks at Sault Ste. Marie opened in 1855, safely

13

linking Lake Superior, the westernmost lake, with Lake Huron and the rest of the Great Lakes to the east. More than a century and a half later, Sault Ste. Marie had become the world's busiest locks.[2]

But Indiana and Michigan have been more than just central connections for moving goods and people across the country. The Hoosier State is also the birthplace of Indiana-Michigan Mennonite Conference, an area conference of Mennonite Church USA that has been an intersection of ideas and innovations that have profoundly shaped Mennonite faith and practice in North America and around the world since the nineteenth century.[3] Higher education, missions, publishing, and other initiatives that would become common in the church are rooted in what would become Indiana-Michigan. The conference has also been at the fore of some of the most contentious conflicts North American Mennonites have faced. Starkly divergent views on issues such as Sunday schools, Christian fundamentalism, the charismatic movement, and sexuality have collided in highly visible, dramatic, and often painful ways in Indiana-Michigan. The ramifications, good and bad, often went far beyond the conference's boundaries, like all those roads, rails, and freighters. Thus what has happened in Indiana-Michigan usually hasn't stayed in Indiana-Michigan, resulting in a legacy of influence that is unsurpassed in the Mennonite church.

Subsequently, a purported history of the conference is much more than that. It is even more than a history of a critical part of Mennonite Church USA or its predecessor denominations, the Mennonite Church and General Conference Mennonite Church. Other bodies such as the Mennonite Brethren, Missionary Church, Old Order Amish, and Old Order Mennonites all have, to various degrees, distinct and important connections to Indiana-Michigan Mennonite Conference. The conference story can't be told without theirs, and vice versa. Indiana-Michigan's history is an inextricable part of the history of the Mennonite and Amish Mennonite church in the United States and Canada and even the entire global Anabaptist fellowship.

That alone made this project invigorating. But writing it was also an unexpected engagement with my own history, even though it has no straight coats, prayer coverings, bishops, or any of the other stereotypical characteristics of the Mennonite Church. A descendant of ethnically Germanic Mennonite immigrants from the Ukraine to the United

States in the mid-1870s, I grew up in a General Conference Mennonite Church congregation and community in southeastern South Dakota and later lived and worked in a similar setting in south central Kansas.[4] All that didn't prevent Indiana-Michigan from asking me to research and write a new conference history. I had recently moved to Indiana from Kansas, and I readily accepted the conference's invitation, thinking it would be a great way to learn more about my new faith environment. It proved to be that—and so much more.

I came to a greater understanding of my own Amish Mennonite heritage when I discovered that representatives from my home community attended sessions of the *Diener-Versammlungen*, the crucial Amish Mennonite ministers' meetings of the 1860s and '70s that resulted in the development of separate Old Order Amish and more progressive Amish Mennonite groups.[5] I was generally aware of John F. Funk's role in facilitating the Russian Mennonites' immigration to North America in the mid-1870s, but it became much more relevant when, while going through his *Herald of Truth* periodical, I found references to familiar names and places on the Great Plains, where the immigrants settled and which were largely outside traditional Swiss Mennonite regions in the United States. In another revelation, I was astonished to discover that the Mennonite mutual aid organization based in my home community was actually started in Indiana by Funk. I learned more about the genius of Anabaptist Mennonite Biblical Seminary, the Elkhart school that has educated people from my home community and many of the pastors that ministered to them and me. All of this made an enjoyable—dare I say fun?—project even more rewarding.

But there is a certain irony to all this Midwest traffic and all these connections. At the same time that so many roads were leading to and from Indiana-Michigan, some church members tried—repeatedly, even desperately—to erect fences to protect themselves from external forces they considered incompatible with their understandings of what it means to be a disciple of Jesus Christ. The Mennonites and Amish Mennonites who settled in Indiana and Michigan in the 1800s carried with them the centuries-old legacy of their Anabaptist forebears, born out of a fresh reading of Scripture and followed by intense state-sponsored persecution across Europe. The world—that is, everything that wasn't the church as they defined it—was considered a potential threat to the faithful. That's why Indiana-Michigan Mennonite Conference in 1864 declared its opposition to political involvement, the use of violence and force, swearing oaths, and "all needless ornaments, hoops, laces, jewelry, artificial flowers, and other things which tend to pride, such as wearing the hair after the fashions of the world and all its idle and useless follies."[6] It was just one of many declarations against what was feared could lead church members to compromise their steadfastness in the Lord. As the world changed, Indiana-Michigan's leadership took firm stands not to be swayed. Those attempts naturally led to powerful struggles between the resisters and proponents of change, as both groups earnestly sought religious devotion in their own ways.

As agonizing as it may be, it is imperative that we do not shy away from such conflicts and difficulties when recounting the past. Human shortcomings are inevitable, and they do as much as human achievement in determining who we are, what we do, and what we believe. Understanding Indiana-Michigan requires understanding the missteps, misconceptions, and disagreements that have produced rancorous debates, schisms, and withdrawals as well as opportunities to practice grace and forgiveness. To gloss over or ignore them would result in a history lacking honesty and integrity. Even the Bible includes negative accounts about some of the greatest individuals in Christian history, such as the inebriated and naked Noah and the apostle Peter, who denied knowing Jesus.[7] They have lessons for us, and so do Indiana-Michigan's struggles as well as its successes.

What's in a Name

Speaking of struggles, telling the Indiana-Michigan story presented some nomenclature challenges. It's always important to be attentive to names, but particularly when dealing with Amish and Mennonites, which are two words that can be used haphazardly and inconsistently, even by those who claim those identities. Here is how I am using them and other terms in this book.

Mennonites are members of a sixteenth-century Anabaptist group named after Menno Simons, the Dutch Catholic priest who became one of the movement's preeminent leaders in the 1530s. In the late 1600s, *Amish Mennonites*, under the leadership of Jakob Ammann, separated from the larger Mennonite fellowship in Switzerland, southern

Germany, and the Alsace. By the early twentieth century, North American Amish Mennonites had developed into a variety of groups, such as Old Order Amish and Beachy Amish, or had joined the more mainstream Mennonite Church. *Old Mennonites* is an admittedly imprecise term, but is used here to refer to the Mennonite and Amish Mennonite groups that would compose the Mennonite Church, which was formed in 1898. Old Mennonite can also include groups, particularly Lancaster Mennonite Conference and Franconia Mennonite Conference, that never officially joined the Mennonite Church until 1971, when the denomination was restructured, but practically had been members as they participated in much of the work of the Mennonite Church. A number of other denominations and organizations are mentioned throughout the book and are further described in the endnotes.

One of the most overused words in the Mennonite lexicon is *conference* because it can denote both an organization and an event. As a result, a conference can hold an annual conference. For clarity's sake, I use *assembly* or a synonym to refer to the event where business is conducted by authorized delegates; *conference* is reserved for the association of congregations convening the assembly. There is, however, one exception: I also use *conference* for gatherings other than delegate assemblies, such as academic or study conferences. Another problematic word is *church*, which can mean a body of believers or the building in which they meet. Again attempting to be as clear and precise as possible, I use *congregation* as the name of the local, organized gathering and *church* for the meetinghouse. I also sporadically employ *church* to describe the often informal or loosely organized fellowship of adherents of a faith, such as the global Mennonite church that transcends specific Mennonite denominations.

It is also quite easy to confuse denominations, especially the two most prominent in Indiana-Michigan history: the *Mennonite Church General Conference* and the *General Conference Mennonite Church*. The former was the name adopted by the Old Mennonites when they started holding biennial delegate assemblies in 1898. It will usually be lowercase—*general conference*—unless the full formal name is used. The general conference was replaced by a *general assembly* as part of the Mennonite Church's 1971 denominational reorganization. The General Conference Mennonite Church, meanwhile, was a denomination founded in 1860 and would become home for many former Indiana-Michigan members. The name will always be uppercase, and shortened to *GCMC* when possible.

In Mennonite Church USA, *minister* and *pastor* are often used interchangeably—and not inaccurately. But there are notable differences between the two. A pastor has congregational responsibilities, such as preaching and visitation, for which he or she may be ordained by the congregation's area conference. An ordained pastor is called a minister. While the vast majority of pastors, but not all, are ministers, not all ministers are pastors. They can also be missionaries or administrators, or serve in other church-related positions. They can also be retired. In short, pastor is an occupation and minister is a credential not limited by occupation. That's an important distinction, as the understanding of leadership within Indiana-Michigan, as well as the rest of the church, has been transformed, particularly with the growing acceptance of the professional pastorate and theological education.[8]

Progressive and *conservative* are among the most troublesome identifiers, because they are relative. Someone or something can be progressive in one context but conservative in another. In the case of Indiana-Michigan, nineteenth-century progressives were supporters of innovations such as Sunday schools and preaching in English rather than German. In contrast were the *traditionalists*, who generally opposed change and wanted to continue the ways of their forebears. In the twentieth century, some of the progressives became conservatives, not because they wanted to go back to traditionalism, but because they wanted to use progressive means to maintain key beliefs and practices they saw as endangered.

The names of many Indiana-Michigan congregations and conference-related organizations have changed through the years. As much as possible, I have used the names in use at the time of this writing. For example, the first Mennonite congregation in Elkhart, Indiana, is always called Prairie Street Mennonite Church in this book, although initially it was simply referred to as Elkhart Mennonite Church. Nevertheless, there will be exceptions, particularly with more well-known organizations. These will be noted as appropriate, either in the body of the text or in the endnotes.

I've strived for honesty and accuracy in all facets of my research and writing. So I must note that on occasions I have forgone accuracy for the sake of readability. Some minor errors in quoted materials, such as misspellings or punctuation errors, have been silently corrected in order to limit distractions for the reader.

Acknowledgments

One of the hallmarks of Anabaptism since its inception was, in the words of the *Mennonite Encyclopedia*, "the obligation of a brother to help his brethren in need."[9] *In Pursuit of Faithfulness* demonstrates that it is still practiced, as I was in need of much help during the research, writing, and revising of the manuscript. It was commissioned by Indiana-Michigan Mennonite Conference and overseen by a conference committee. Its members provided counsel and feedback and also worked hard to keep the book's author on track during the project, which took much longer than it really should have. Recognition and appreciation is due to committee chair Mary Swartley, who was the driving force in initiating this project, and members Warren Bontrager, Leonard Gross, Janeen Bertsche Johnson, Tim Lichti, and Rachel Nolt. Others providing particularly valuable assistance and insights were Wilma Bailey, John Bender, Jane Stoltzfus Buller, Esther Farmwald, Leanne Farmwald, Leon Farmwald, Carolyn Holderread Heggen, Dan Hochstetler, Gerlof Homan, Nelson Kraybill, John A. Lapp, and Jose Ortiz. My deepest thanks to them for their willingness to take the time to read and critique all or portions of the manuscript in its various stages.

Thanks are also due to those indispensable folks responsible for turning the manuscript into an actual book: Gerald Mast, editor of the Studies in Anabaptist and Mennonite History (a distinguished series that I'm honored to be included in), and Amy Gingerich, Valerie Weaver-Zercher, and the rest of the staff at Herald Press. Their patience in dealing with my neophyte questions and concerns exemplified going the extra mile.

But before there was a manuscript or book there was research. That process would have been much more difficult, much less productive, and much less pleasant if not for the abilities of the staffs of the Mennonite Church USA Archives in Goshen, Indiana, and North Newton, Kansas; Mennonite Historical Library, Goshen; Bluffton (Ohio) University archives; Elkhart (Ind.) County Historical Society; Anabaptist

Mennonite Biblical Seminary library, Elkhart; and the public libraries in Elkhart and Goshen. Genealogist par excellence Thelma Martin repeatedly provided wonderful assistance and with good humor. And I count it a great privilege that historian and scholar Theron Schlabach allowed me to repeatedly pick his brain. Others deserving specific mention for their help at crucial points are David R. Graber, Andy Brubacher Kaethler, and Steve Nolt. I am also grateful for the many other individuals, too numerous to list here, who gave of their time to be interviewed or otherwise answer my questions, not to mention my questions about their answers to my questions. What they imparted was not only informative but often inspirational as well.

Additionally, I need to credit the work of J. C. Wenger and his *The Mennonites in Indiana and Michigan*, published in 1961. It was the first history of Indiana-Michigan Mennonite Conference, and *In Pursuit of Faithfulness* neither replaces nor updates it. I made great use of Wenger's book, and it remains a fine resource, particularly for the histories of individual congregations and biographical sketches of all the ordained men through the 1950s. Thanks to volunteer Vernard Guengerich for helping compile the appendices. I also need to extend my sincerest, deepest gratitude to Jim Juhnke and Keith Sprunger, my history professors at Bethel College in North Newton, Kansas. While they had no direct participation in the creation of this book, their passion for history, high standards of scholarship, and commitment to the church are an inspiration that grows greater as I grow older. I pray that *In Pursuit of Faithfulness* reflects well of them.

While Indiana-Michigan Mennonite Conference funded this project, I received a very welcome research grant from the Mennonite Historical Society and funding from Michiana Anabaptist Historians to interview Indiana-Michigan members in Michigan's Upper Peninsula.

Finally, I can't thank enough all the family and friends who encouraged me with their interest in what I was doing, even when they couldn't understand my enthusiasm over the most arcane discoveries. The most important person was my wife, Leanne Farmwald, without whom this book never would have been started or completed. Her presence in my life is the greatest earthly gift I have received. As with any sizable endeavor, I was at various times delighted, excited, relaxed, stressed, and frustrated during the course of researching and writing. But I was never alone.

1
Beginnings, Both Anabaptist and American

After traveling 1,300 miles west from the shadow of the Allegheny Mountains to the other side of the Mississippi River, the Amish Mennonite scouting party from Pennsylvania was finally on the return trip home. It was the summer of 1840, and brothers Daniel S. Miller and Joseph Miller plus Nathan Smeily and Joseph Speicher had left their Somerset County community in the southwestern part of the state in search of new and cheaper lands where church members could live, work, and worship.[1] The four men had traveled the Ohio and Mississippi Rivers as well as overland as far as southeastern Iowa, where the rich, rolling countryside made a favorable impression on them. But on the way back to Pennsylvania, the group decided to also investigate the possibilities in Indiana. It had become the nation's nineteenth state only twenty-four years earlier, and the last of the region's Native American population was still being removed to accommodate the increasing demand for territory for white settlers. The Millers, Smeily, and Speicher went east from Iowa to the town of Chicago, Illinois (population 4,500), where they crossed Lake Michigan to northern Indiana and made their way to Goshen, the county seat and largest town in Elkhart County with some six hundred citizens. It was located on a stretch of prairie that broke up the forested and occasionally swampy lands that covered much of the area. The scouting party returned home to Pennsylvania with glowing reports of a fertile region and contented inhabitants.[2] While Iowa may have been good, Indiana was deemed very good.

The next year, on June 3, four families—twenty-four people in all—departed Somerset County in seven horse-drawn wagons bound for the Hoosier State. The group comprised the Miller scouts and their families—Barbara and Daniel and their five children and minister Joseph and Elizabeth and their four children—and two Borntreger brothers and their families—deacon Joseph ("Sep") and Barbara and their five children and Christian and Elizabeth and their two children. The Borntreger and Miller brothers were cousins. Winding their way through Ohio and Michigan, the travelers reached Goshen on June 29, 1841, and soon took up residence three miles south of town in existing cabins.[3] After several months, however, they forsook the lush but expensive prairie and bought cheaper, forested land about ten miles to the northeast, where Elkhart County abutted LaGrange County to the east. Joseph Miller and Joseph Borntreger each purchased eighty acres in Elkhart's Clinton Township, while their brothers moved east just across the county line into LaGrange. Five more families, including another minister, moved to the area in the fall of 1841. They met at least once for worship that fall, at the home of Barbara and Daniel Miller.[4]

A more formal and permanent worshiping fellowship emerged the following spring, after the harshness of winter had passed. Fourteen baptized adults and their families gathered in the Clinton Township home of minister Joseph and Elizabeth Miller on Easter Sunday, March 27, 1842. So on the day celebrating Jesus Christ's resurrection, a day associated with new beginnings, a congregation was born. It was the first worship service in the life of what would become Indiana-Michigan Mennonite Conference and eventually bring together Amish Mennonites and Mennonites who would settle in the region.[5]

The two groups were part of the Anabaptist movement, a radical stream flowing out from the Protestant Reformation.[6] The Reformation emerged out of European social, economic, political, and spiritual strife. The political and spiritual arenas were largely controlled by the Roman Catholic Church, and attempts at reform had been squelched through the centuries; by the early 1500s discontent had long been brewing. German monk Martin Luther famously issued his "Ninety-Five Theses" in 1517, and he was soon joined by others in challenging the church. In Zurich, Switzerland, another priest, Ulrich Zwingli, was also preaching reform. But some followers thought he didn't go far enough. Zwingli, as well as Luther, still accepted a church controlled by the state, which required parents to have their infants baptized. It was an act of both civic and religious responsibility. The group dissatisfied with the reformers believed in the church as a voluntary association, composed of those individuals who freely chose to accept the eternal salvation provided by Jesus Christ. Only adults, not babies or children, could make that decision. On January 21, 1525, members of a group gathered for Bible study in a Zurich apartment decided to rebaptize themselves, thus repudiating their baptism as infants and committing themselves to a new, separate Christian fellowship. They were soon called Anabaptists, or "rebaptizers."

For the Anabaptists, Jesus Christ was not only their Savior but also their model for daily living. Their earnest attempts to emulate Christ earned them a reputation as good, devout, and honest people, even as many of Europe's Protestant and Catholic authorities doggedly tried to eradicate the movement because of its threats to the religious and civil order. Thousands of Anabaptists were imprisoned, exiled, and executed. That did not stop Anabaptism's growth, but it did foster a deep, foundational belief that the world, including other Christians, was wicked. Members' experiences gave testimony to biblical admonitions, such as 1 Corinthians 10:21 and Romans 12:2, for believers to distance themselves from temporal corruption and immorality in order to lead righteous lives.[7] The first Anabaptist confession of faith, written in 1527, declared: "Now there is nothing else in the world and all creation than good or evil, believing and unbelieving, darkness and light, the world and those who are [come] out of the world, God's temple and idols. Christ and Belial, and none will have part with the other. . . . From all this we should learn that everything which has not been united with our God in Christ is nothing but an abomination which we should shun."[8]

For the first several decades of its existence, Anabaptism was hardly a unified movement. Members held a wide range of beliefs on matters such as the use of violence, Christ's second coming, and relations with those who sympathized with the movement but never joined it. Much-needed leadership soon came from Menno Simons, a disenchanted Dutch priest who left Catholicism and affiliated with the Anabaptists in 1536. His influence, through his many writings and extensive travels, was so great that adherents would become known as Mennonites.

By the late 1600s, tensions were emerging among church members in the region of South Germany, Switzerland, and the Alsace.[9] Jakob Ammann, elder of a group of Anabaptists that originated from a relatively new community south of Bern, saw a church diluted by earthly compromises. He set out on a campaign of renewal, advocating for commemorating the Lord's Supper twice a year instead of once and for more strict discipline to limit interactions between church and world. The latter was resisted by Hans Reist, the more moderate leader of the Mennonites in the Emmental region east of Bern.[10] The Emmental had been home to Anabaptists since the early years of the movement. Subsequently, authorities had repeatedly tried to rid the area of the religious rebels. Aiding in Mennonites' survival were local citizens who interceded on their behalf, hid them, and provided other forms of support. They were called *Halbtäufer*, or "Half Anabaptists," because they were sympathetic but never joined the faith. To Ammann, they were not saved and thus were to be avoided. Reist, however, refused to condemn people who had assisted them. Ammann also criticized Reist and his flock for agreeing to leave the Emmental when threatened at various times, only to return when opportunities presented themselves. They were liars, according to Ammann, acting contrary to God's teachings. For the Emmentalers, however, they were simply doing what they felt they needed to for their own security.

Ammann and Reist formally broke fellowship in 1693, and the split spread during the next year, with those following Ammann becoming known as Amish Mennonites. Over the next several years, they tried several times to repair the breach with their Mennonite brothers and sisters but were always rebuffed. Despite the formal division, however, the two groups remained connected with each other. After their arrival in North America, they found themselves living in proximity to each other in places such as Lancaster and Bucks Counties in eastern Pennsylvania and Holmes County, Ohio. They worked together in Pennsylvania for exemptions from military service during the American Revolution, and members of one group periodically joined the other. Nevertheless, they remained separate fellowships with their own means of discernment and discipline.

By the time of the founding of the Clinton Amish Mennonite settlement, another community, this one Mennonite, was developing west of Goshen along the Yellow Creek, so named because of the color it reflected in the sunshine.[11] Most of the newcomers were from Ohio, plus a few from Ontario. But the Yellow Creek Mennonites wouldn't hold their first worship service until 1848, nearly a decade after the first arrivals, because they had no active minister or bishop. The first ordained man in the group was aged bishop Martin Hoover, who moved from Medina County, Ohio, in 1845. He had ministered at Markham, Ontario, for thirty-three years before relocating to Ohio in 1837. There he was elevated to bishop before leaving for Indiana, giving him authority to conduct baptism and communion services for the fledgling flock.[12] They were two essential rites in the life of the church. Baptism ushered new believers into the fellowship, while communion was a corporate exercise, commemorating members' commitment to God and to one another. Both ordinances could be conducted only by a bishop. But there was little churchly activity under the feeble Hoover, who was in his eighties. By 1848, however, ministers Jacob Wisler and Jacob Christophel had arrived from Columbiana County, Ohio. They led the first Mennonite worship service in the county on June 1, 1848, Ascension Day, an important holiday in the church, celebrating the conclusion of Christ's earthly ministry and his ascent into heaven. Sixteen adults were in attendance for the service, held in a schoolhouse not far from where they would build their first meetinghouse the next year.[13] Wisler delivered the sermon, and Hoover offered a few remarks but remained seated. Despite the traditional Mennonite emphasis on congregational singing, no hymns were sung, because no one was present who could lead the little congregation in singing.[14]

Both Amish Mennonites and Mennonites were already living in Indiana before the arrival of the Clinton and Yellow Creek groups.[15] The first Mennonite congregation in the state was founded in 1839 in Adams County in eastern Indiana, a year after immigrants from Switzerland started arriving in the area.[16] Also in 1838, Mennonites from Virginia's Shenandoah Valley and Pennsylvania's Lancaster County began moving to Arcadia in Hamilton County in central Indiana. But no congregation was organized there until the 1860s. At Nappanee in southwestern Elkhart County, a new Amish Mennonite settlement was emerging in the 1840s with transplants from Holmes County, Ohio. Some members of the Elkhart-LaGrange community would later join them. The Arcadia Mennonites and some of the Nappanee Amish Mennonites would affiliate with their brothers and sisters farther north in formal fellowship, although Arcadia would die out around the turn of the twentieth century. No relations were established, however, with the Adams County congregation, which was of different cultural and ethnic stock. An exception was a small splinter group under the leadership of minister Christian Augsburger, which joined the northern Indiana Mennonites in 1871. Regular worship services ceased when Augsburger died in 1903. Meanwhile, the rest of the area Mennonites would start First Mennonite Church in Berne and join the General Conference Mennonite Church.

The migration of Amish Mennonites and Mennonites that would spawn Indiana-Michigan Mennonite Conference was both typically Anabaptist and distinctly American. In Europe, many Anabaptists were repeatedly forced to move in order to avoid persecution, so they wandered throughout the continent and some eventually sailed to North America. They found their haven in Pennsylvania, the colony of English Quaker leader William Penn. He had received the land from King Charles II in 1681 as repayment of a debt owed to Penn's father. The colony was soon providing religious sanctuary to European Quakers, Catholics, Lutherans, and Jews, as well as Mennonites and Amish Mennonites. The first permanent Mennonite settlement and congregation in the New World was established in 1683 at Germantown. Thousands more Anabaptists would soon follow, including the first Amish Mennonites, who landed in the early eighteenth century and also settled in eastern Pennsylvania.

But arrival in the New World did not necessarily end their travels. Disagreements with fellow church members prompted some church members to look elsewhere to live. More often, however, it was increasingly crowded communities in the East, large families requiring more room and resources, the prospects of better economic fortunes, and even a sense of adventure that beckoned Amish Mennonites and Mennonites westward.[17] Such treks made them like hundreds of thousands of Americans. Between 1833 and 1860, the percentage of the nation's population living west of the Appalachian Mountains jumped from a quarter to half.[18] When the Millers and Borntregers left for Indiana in 1841, their Somerset County community, started by Amish Mennonites from eastern Pennsylvania, was less than seventy years old, yet some members had even left as early as 1809 to settle in Ohio.[19] That pattern was repeated in the young Yellow Creek Mennonite community, where about a third of the settlers had moved on by 1850, just two years after their first worship service.[20]

The imminent tide of white people started trickling into Indiana after the American Revolution.[21] Before the war, the area had been the home of the Miamis, Potawatomis, and other, smaller Native tribes, even as it had been claimed at various times by the English, French, and Spanish. The Europeans, however, did little to directly threaten the indigenous ways of life, as their presence was generally limited to trappers, traders, and soldiers. In fact, the British in 1763 barred whites from moving west of the Appalachians. Instead of Europeans, newer Indiana inhabitants were other tribes forced west by whites taking over their longtime lands in the east. That began to change after the 1783 Treaty of Paris, which ended the American colonists' successful revolt against the British crown and gave the new nation virtually all territory west to the Mississippi River. The U.S. government quickly opened the newly acquired region to white settlers by creating the Northwest Territory in 1787, which would become the states of Ohio, Michigan, Indiana, Illinois, Wisconsin, and part of Minnesota. The next step was securing the area. That was accomplished through military force and treaties, in which the Native residents gave up their land in exchange for territory farther west. Although frequently messy and morally questionable, the federal strategies succeeded in their objectives. In 1820, 120,000 Native Americans lived east of the Mississippi River; that number was reduced to 30,000 by 1844.[22] By the time Indiana was granted statehood in 1816, seven treaties had already been reached with the region's tribes, opening the southern part of the state to settlement. When Indiana's first Mennonites arrived at Berne and Arcadia in the late 1830s, those lands had been in white control for some two decades. With ten more treaties, Native Americans in Indiana would officially relinquish their claims on the rest of the state by 1840. The well-traveled roads into the state had resulted in the involuntary use of roads going out.

In northern Indiana, the last of the Potawatomi—the largest tribe in the region—was removed to Kansas and Oklahoma in 1838, two years before the Pennsylvania Amish Mennonite scout party arrived in Elkhart and LaGrange Counties.[23] While most Potawatomi agreed to relocate, one group resisted. In Marshall County, just west of Nappanee, Chief Menominee argued that he had not consented to any move. Impatient white settlers overran Menominee's village, and the Potawatomi responded by destroying a squatter's hut and threatening his life. Whites retaliated by burning down a dozen Native cabins, and soldiers were soon dispatched to evict the remaining tribe members. They surrounded Menominee's village, jailed the chief, and then, at gunpoint, forced everyone to start west on September 4, 1838, on what would become known as the "Trail of Death," due to typhoid and poor food. By the time the Potawatomi arrived in Kansas, two months after departing Indiana, forty-two people had died and were buried along the way. Some sixty more escaped.[24]

The last Indiana lands to be opened for settlement included the neighboring counties of Howard and Miami in the central part of the state. The Miami gave up their claims in 1840, but some tribal members were still in the vicinity when Ohio Amish Mennonites started arriving in the spring of 1848. One of the settlers, Peter Stineman, acquired eighty acres adjacent to his property from another settler by the name of John Smith.[25] Smith had earlier corralled some Miami ponies that had been running loose and destroying crops. Shortly afterward, his cabin, with him and his family inside, was attacked by Miamis who left deep tomahawk marks and bullet holes in the front door. Fearing for his life and the lives of his family, Smith the next day sold his property, crops, and livestock for $450 to Stineman, who obviously wasn't as worried about his safety.

With the Native American population largely and forcibly eliminated, white settlement could grow unfettered. Indiana's population doubled, to 686,000 residents, between 1830 and 1840, then doubled again, to 1.37 million, by 1860. Amish Mennonites and Mennonites from Europe and the eastern United States were part of the influx. An Amish Mennonite community had been started in Miami County in 1843, but it was short lived and no congregation ever developed. The settlement of which Stineman was a member was started five years

While all early settlers contributed to the development of the northern Indiana Mennonite community, none left a greater legacy than Christiana Buzzard Holdeman, the pioneer grande dame of Indiana-Michigan Mennonite Conference. Born in 1788 in eastern Pennsylvania, she was a great-granddaughter of Jacob Gottschalk, the first Mennonite bishop in North America, who oversaw Germantown Mennonite Church from 1708 to 1713. Christiana was also a descendant of Gerhard Hendricks, who was one of the signatories of the first statement against slavery in the New World, drafted in 1688 by Germantown Mennonites and Quakers.[1]

Christiana married Christian Holdeman of Bucks County, Pennsylvania, and they farmed there until 1825, when they moved to Columbiana County, Ohio. By then the family had grown to include eight children, and five more were added over the next nine years. The Holdemans relocated again two years later, this time to Wayne County, Ohio. Tragedy struck in 1846 when Christian was killed while working with a team of horses, leaving Christiana a widow with five children still at home. That prompted her to leave Ohio in 1849, at age sixty-one, for yet another new home, this time in Elkhart County, Indiana. She went with her son John and family and a nephew, Christian Shaum. Christiana's son George and daughter Catharine Landis had moved there a year earlier. By 1852, all of Christiana's children except the oldest, Amos, had settled in western Elkhart County.[2]

The entire clan in Indiana would form the nucleus of a new congregation near Wakarusa that would be named Holdeman Mennonite Church. Of the congregation's first sixteen families, fourteen were Holdemans. The first meetinghouse was located on George Holdeman's property and built under the direction of another son, Joseph, who would also serve the congregation as trustee.[3]

Christiana died on March 11, 1865, at the age of seventy-six. By then she had been preceded in death by her husband, three children, thirty-three grandchildren, and seventeen great-grandchildren. She was survived by 152 descendants. "[W]e have the hope that God, in taking her from us, has only called her home, to join the angel-throng and enjoy endless glory and happiness," said the report of Christiana's death in the *Herald of Truth*.[4]

1. Edwin L. Weaver, *Holdeman Descendants: A Compilation and Biographical Record of the Descendants of Christian Holdeman, 1786–1846* (Nappanee, IN: E. V. Publishing House, 1937), 17–18.
2. After a spiritual awakening, Amos's son John founded the Church of God in Christ, Mennonite, more commonly known as the Holdeman Mennonites, in Ohio in 1859. The new movement found little receptivity among the Old Mennonites in the East, but John Holdeman developed a significant following among Russian Mennonite immigrants in Kansas and Manitoba in the 1870s and 1880s. They are a moderately plain people, and by the late twentieth century had become strict disciplinarians and active in missionary work.
3. Rufus and Thelma Martin, *They Had a Vision: A Guide to Some of the Early Mennonite Pioneers in the Yellow Creek Area, Elkhart County, Indiana* (Goshen, IN: privately published, 1995), n.p.
4. C. S., *Herald of Truth*, May 1865, 40.

earlier farther south along the Howard-Miami county line. That group held its first worship service in 1849. In the northeast part of the state, a handful of Amish Mennonites from Europe arrived in Allen County via Ohio in November 1852, followed by a larger group of fifty-two the following April. A small group of Mennonites moved to the area the next year and started worshiping at the village of Gar Creek. They never had a resident minister, however, and services led by visiting ministers were discontinued about 1910.

Mennonite Organization

While the Amish Mennonite communities continued to grow, the Yellow Creek Mennonites were also swelling in numbers, adding twenty-four families from Ohio in 1848 alone.[26] The growing settlement spread south and west, making travel to the Yellow Creek meetinghouse increasingly prohibitive in the days of horse-drawn transportation, when it could take an hour to go six miles, depending on the horse and road conditions. So new worship sites were established as extensions of the Yellow Creek congregation. By the early 1850s, services were being held in a log cabin six miles southeast of the Yellow Creek church, on the farm of preacher Jacob M. Christophel, and five miles west of the church, near Wakarusa, in the home of Anna and George Holdeman. Another preaching outpost was formed nine miles northwest of Yellow Creek, first in a log cabin and then a mile south in a meetinghouse built on the farm of Jacob and Mary Shaum. Yellow Creek completed a new meetinghouse in 1861, and the twelve-year-old log cabin that had served the congregation was moved four miles south to the farm of Enos Blosser for members in that area. In 1867, the conference decided to make each outpost a stand-alone congregation with its own minister.[27] The result was the establishment of Holdeman Mennonite Church and Shaum Mennonite Church (later renamed Olive Mennonite Church). The Blosser and Christophel groups, however, never grew, and in 1889 they merged to form Salem Mennonite Church near New Paris.

Because the outposts were originally considered part of Yellow Creek Mennonite Church, the second official Mennonite congregation was Clinton Brick Mennonite Church, begun in 1854 east of Goshen in Clinton Township, near the Amish Mennonite community. Yellow Creek Mennonites started settling in the area in the mid-1840s, and

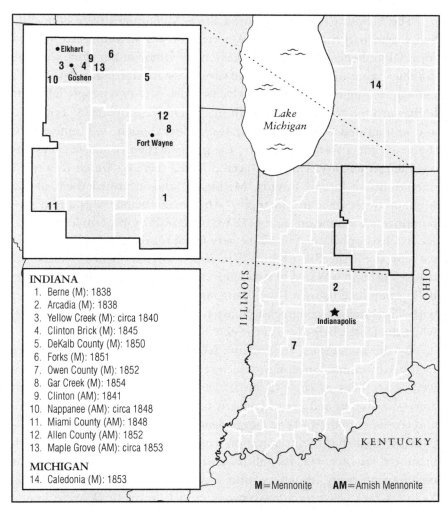

• Elkhart

3 • 4 9 13 6

10 Goshen 5

12

8

Fort Wayne

1

11

INDIANA
1. Berne (M): 1838
2. Arcadia (M): 1838
3. Yellow Creek (M): circa 1840
4. Clinton Brick (M): 1845
5. DeKalb County (M): 1850
6. Forks (M): 1851
7. Owen County (M): 1852
8. Gar Creek (M): 1854
9. Clinton (AM): 1841
10. Nappanee (AM): circa 1848
11. Miami County (AM): 1848
12. Allen County (AM): 1852
13. Maple Grove (AM): circa 1853

MICHIGAN
14. Caledonia (M): 1853

Lake Michigan

14

ILLINOIS

OHIO

2

Indianapolis

7

KENTUCKY

M = Mennonite   **AM** = Amish Mennonite

Earliest Mennonite and Amish Mennonite settlements in Indiana and Michigan. Reuben Graham.

worship services commenced in 1850 under ministerial leadership from Yellow Creek. The first permanent meetinghouse, a log cabin, was built four years later. The first resident minister, Switzerland native John Nussbaum, came from Ohio in 1860. The cabin was replaced in 1880, using materials from a nearby brickyard. As a result, the congregation was called Clinton Brick, to distinguish it from the Amish Mennonite church three miles away that would become known as Clinton Frame because of its wood construction.[28]

The Yellow Creek and Clinton Brick Mennonites were ethnically Swiss who had been in North America for years, coming to Indiana from Ohio, Pennsylvania, and occasionally Ontario. But there was one notable exception. In the course of several waves starting in April 1853 and continuing over the next twelve months, fifty-two people left their homes around the village of Balk in the Dutch province of Friesland and immigrated to the United States.[29] Even though only nineteen of the newcomers were Mennonite, the group settled en masse in southern Elkhart County. They had been directed there by Dutch Reformed immigrants in Grand Rapids, Michigan, who informed them of the Mennonite presence in Indiana.[30] "After many wanderings and disappointments we came on June 4 [1853] to an old Doopsgezinde Preacher, Jacob Christophel, who has done very much for us, and in whose house we stayed till the 8th of June," recorded Greitja Jacobs Symensma, whose husband was one of two ministers among the immigrants.[31] The Balk group held its own Dutch-language worship services but also met with Christophel's congregation, a pattern that continued until 1889, when the Dutch helped form the new Salem congregation.

By the mid-1850s, the Indiana Mennonites were gathering every October for annual meetings, which served two functions.[32] First, they were assemblies of the ordained men—bishops, ministers, and deacons—to discuss matters of concern facing the fellowship and to give and receive support and encouragement. At the 1864 gathering, participants strengthened their separation from the world by opposing church members' involvement in politics and affirming traditional positions on nonconformity, shunning, and conflict resolution.[33] By this time, Yellow Creek, its preaching stations, and Clinton Brick were joined by a third party, Bower Mennonite Church, formed when Mennonites from Ohio and Virginia moved to Owen County in southern Indiana. The Indiana ordained men, however, were not the only ones at the annual deliberations. The conference sessions were usually attended by ordained Mennonites from elsewhere, ranging from Pennsylvania to Kansas (which at the time was home of the westernmost church members), who would have the same rights as their Hoosier brethren. Of course, the privileges were reciprocal, as ordained men from Indiana would attend other conference assemblies. The second major function of the annual gatherings was to bring together church members for the important ordinances of communion and baptism. Symensma recorded in her diary that on Saturday, October 27, 1855, baptism was conducted "by the Wisselar" (bishop Jacob Wisler) and that nine candidates were baptized in the meetinghouse and one in the creek. The next day communion was observed in "jellekreek" (Yellow Creek Mennonite Church).[34] The eventual pattern was for the bishops, ministers, and deacons to meet on Friday, with baptisms on Saturday and communion on Sunday. Every assembly was held at Yellow Creek until 1882, when it was hosted by Holdeman.

As a fledgling fellowship, albeit one with its own name and identity as Indiana Mennonite Conference, it practically functioned with neighboring Ohio Mennonite Conference as one body meeting semiannually, in Ohio each spring and then in Indiana each fall.[35] Founded in 1843, Ohio was on the organized church's western frontier at the time and so assumed responsibility for the spiritual well-being of the far-flung and unaffiliated Mennonite communities springing up as settlers pushed toward the Mississippi River and beyond. Many Ohio leaders, particularly bishop John M. Brenneman of Elida, regularly traveled to Illinois, Iowa, and Missouri, as well as to Indiana and Michigan, to visit and minister to the distant church members. Brenneman served as Indiana's moderator in 1864 and attended conference sessions through the end of the decade. Ohio Conference decisions were considered authoritative in Indiana as late as 1890.[36] Even after Indiana reached maturity and the joint meetings were discontinued, Ohio and Indiana-Michigan representatives would continue to actively participate in each other's annual meetings into the twentieth century. For example, Elkhart bishop and publisher John F. Funk, one of three men from Indiana-Michigan in attendance, chaired the 1893 Ohio assembly. The last Ohio person to have a leadership role in Indiana-Michigan was minister N. O. Blosser of New Stark, who was on the 1895 conference resolutions committee.

Indiana eventually assumed much of Ohio's ministerial mantle and became increasingly responsible for overseeing distant and isolated pockets of Mennonites. The 1864 Indiana assembly recommended "active visitation of brethren living in localities where churches have not yet been established" and of "weak congregations."[37] Ordained men from the conference journeyed to Illinois, Michigan, Missouri, and Tennessee, as well as throughout Indiana, holding worship and communion services, baptizing new members, and encouraging lonely Mennonites far removed from established congregations and communities. In the 1870s, Indiana spun off new area conferences in Illinois and Missouri, while the Tennessee settlements soon died out. The Mennonites in Michigan, however, remained connected with their sisters and brothers south of the state line, and their association was rechristened Indiana-Michigan Mennonite Conference by 1895.

What became the state of Michigan had been home to Huron, Miami, Ojibway, Potawatomi, and other Native Americans. As in Indiana, French and British explorers, traders, and soldiers traversed the region during the eighteenth century. Even after the American Revolution, Great Britain continued to occupy parts of Michigan until 1796, when the United States was able to wrest away control through military and diplomatic means. The region's Native Americans sided with the British during the War of 1812, after which the tribes were forced to relinquish their claims to the Michigan lands. Most were moved west in the 1820s, and white settlement began to mushroom. Statehood was granted in 1837.[38] Mennonites were living in the state by 1853, when a handful moved from Ontario to Kent County in western Michigan. In the fall of 1863, Ontario minister David Sherk went to Michigan and visited "one brother and three sisters from our neighborhood." Reporting in the *Herald of Truth*, a new periodical aiming to serve all North American Mennonites and Amish Mennonites, Sherk said he was only the second Mennonite minister to visit in the ten years since the group had arrived. "Thus the joy it gave them to hear, that one of their own long-known Ministers was on the way to visit them, may be better imagined than described," he wrote. Sherk served communion, baptized two people, and restored to full membership one who had been under church discipline.[39] The 1860s saw an influx of more Mennonites and the appearance of two more worshiping bodies: Bowne Mennonite Church, also in Kent County, with members from Pennsylvania and Ontario, and Pleasant Hill Mennonite Church in Branch County in southern Michigan, made up of Ohioans and Virginians. Indiana and Ohio leaders ministered to these new groups, and by the 1870s, Indiana was acting on Michigan ordination requests and mediating congregational disputes.

Amish Mennonite Innovation

Unlike their Mennonite cousins, the Amish Mennonites did not initially create area conferences but maintained a long-standing Anabaptist style of polity that emphasized the centrality of the congregation. Each congregation made and exercised its own statutes for faithful living and selected its own leaders. Churchwide ministers' meetings were held periodically to address specific issues, but they were only advisory and not authoritative.[40] By the 1860s, however, it was evident that something more was needed, as unrest between burgeoning progressive groups and the more

Isaac Schmucker. MCUSAA–Goshen.

tradition-minded members was afflicting Amish Mennonite communities throughout North America. The long-established boundaries that had separated the church from the world were becoming increasingly porous, and members had to grapple with the effects of growing acculturation. The tensions were particularly acute in Indiana's Elkhart and LaGrange Counties. The settlement was split in 1845 by disagreements over unspecified "rules and regulations" between conservative members, mostly former Pennsylvanians who settled in LaGrange, and those who were more progressive, mostly Elkhart residents who came from Ohio.[41] Matters were resolved two years later when, spurred by continued growth in numbers, the group divided into two separate congregations, each with its own bishop, which allowed them to maintain their own variations in belief and practice while remaining in fellowship with each other.

But peace lasted less than a decade before it began to unravel. The catalyst was Isaac Schmucker, a change-minded minister who came to the Clinton Amish Mennonite community from Ohio in 1841. He was one of the officiating ministers at the first worship service the following

spring, and in 1843 he was ordained the first Amish Mennonite bishop
in Indiana. Schmucker moved to central Illinois in 1851, where he associated with the progressive Rock Creek Amish Mennonites.[42] In 1853
they built one of the first Amish Mennonite meetinghouses in North
America, breaking from the traditional practice of worshiping in members' homes. Schmucker had moved back to Indiana the previous year,
settling in southwestern LaGrange County in the area known as Haw
Patch, so named because of the preponderance of "haws," or fruit of
the hawthorn bush.[43] While bishop Schmucker did not initially oversee
any congregation, his return added to the church's stresses and strains.
A new Amish Mennonite community was born in Haw Patch in 1853
with the arrival of church members from Fairfield County, Ohio, and
the next year Schmucker organized them as Haw Patch Amish Mennonite Church (later renamed Maple Grove Mennonite Church) at
Topeka with eighteen members.[44]

Also in 1854, a progressive contingent, including four ministers,
left the original Clinton group and created what would be called Clinton Frame Amish Mennonite Church. At the request of the new congregation, Schmucker ordained for them a bishop, Jonas P. Troyer, who
had recently arrived from Ohio. A third progressive Amish Mennonite
congregation, Forks, was established in LaGrange County in 1857.
Hansi Borntreger, a conservative member and chronicler of the Elkhart-
LaGrange Amish Mennonite community who witnessed the division,
charged the progressives with "four things which Christ cannot toler-
ate in His church" as especially egregious: wearing worldly clothing,
holding political office, engaging in questionable business practices,
and pursuing the "wisdom of this world," a reference to formal education. Also contributing to the unrest were disagreements over mode of
baptism and building meetinghouses.[45]

Other Indiana Amish Mennonite communities were experiencing
similar problems. The Nappanee and Howard-Miami communities split
in the 1850s over issues including dress, church buildings, and discipline.
But the progressive groups in each place nearly died out when their ministers departed. At Nappanee, minister John Ringenberg died in 1871
at the age of fifty-six, and his flock floundered for several years. Then in
1875 Jonathan P. Smucker, son of Haw Patch bishop Isaac Schmucker,
moved to the area and assumed leadership of the congregation, which

became West Market Street Amish Mennonite Church.[46] Farther south in the Howard-Miami community, the progressives discontinued services when, less than a decade after the settlement's founding in 1848, minister Benjamin Schrock tired of the ongoing local church turmoil and relocated to Elkhart County. But Mary Keck Schrock (whose husband, J. Benjamin, was a cousin to minister Schrock) resurrected the congregation when she started inviting young people to her home for Sunday hymn sings. They began meeting regularly and soon attracted some of the older members. Bible readings were added, leading to the resumption of formal worship services. A new minister was ordained for the group in 1860.[47] Also splintering was the Amish Mennonite community in Allen County in northeastern Indiana, which had been founded by European immigrants in the early 1850s.[48] A progressive faction left in 1861 to form future conference member Leo Amish Mennonite Church. The next year more members withdrew to join the Apostolic Christian Church, an Anabaptist-influenced body that included controversial tenets such as an identifiable conversion experience and sanctification.[49] A third schism came in 1867 when yet another breakaway group joined a fledgling renewal movement led by Amish Mennonite bishop Henry Egly from Berne, who emphasized a more experiential spiritual faith and looser regulations, such as in regard to attire.[50] The remaining Allen County Amish Mennonites would identify themselves as Old Order Amish.

Many splits, however, were hoped to not be permanent. The troubles in Indiana, as well as in Amish Mennonite communities across Ohio and Pennsylvania, prompted the creation of the *Diener-Versammlungen*, translated as "ministers' meetings," a series of annual churchwide gatherings of ordained men to address issues, discern direction, and try to preserve harmony among the members. It was not a new idea, as such meetings had been held occasionally to discuss specific matters as they arose,[51] but now there was a new urgency. The growing volatility and complexity of problems throughout the church finally made it necessary for as many bishops, ministers, and deacons as possible to meet together for careful consideration. It would prove to be a watershed experience that would dramatically reshape North American Amish Mennonitism.

Barn in Wayne County, Ohio, site of the first Diener-Versammlung, 1862. MCUSAA–Goshen.

The first *Diener-Versammlung* (singular of *Diener-Versammlungen*) was held in 1862 in a Wayne County, Ohio, barn with more than seventy participants from six states plus an audience of several hundred more people. Organizers recognized the seriousness of the division in the Elkhart-LaGrange community, making it the first order of business. Almost immediately, a seven-member committee was appointed to investigate the situation. By the end of the first day, the committee reported that the ministers on both sides had forgiven each other "concerning the misunderstandings" between the two congregations.[52] But forgiveness didn't repair the breach, as the conservative LaGrange ministers, according to their traditional congregational polity, wanted to go back to their members for further discernment. The 1863 *Diener-Versammlung* was held in Mifflin County, Pennsylvania, prompted by difficulties there, but the next year's meeting was in Elkhart County, with the focus returning to Elkhart-LaGrange relations. The prospects for resolution seemed bright, with both sides apparently ready to "set a day on which they would come together and try to get united," according to the minutes.[53]

Whether such a meeting was held is unknown, but the two groups never reconciled, and the issue never returned to the

Diener-Versammlungen. While the 1864 gathering had left the impression of progress on the difficulties in northern Indiana, Amish Mennonite conservatives in general were feeling marginalized. The assemblies took no firm action on two issues of particular importance to them: support of shunning and prohibition of political participation. The suggested way to resolve discord was seemingly always for the conservatives to be more tolerant of their progressive brethren.[54] So the more tradition-minded bloc made a concerted effort to draw attention to their concerns. Shortly before the 1865 meeting, again in Wayne County, thirty-four leaders, including nine from Indiana, met to draft a major document outlining their positions for consideration by the *Diener-Versammlung.* Among their concerns were worldly fashions, business practices, household decorations, insurance policies, lightning rods, and attendance at fairs. Signatories said those in agreement "are willing to recognize [one another] as brethren and sisters and resume fellowship . . . and to maintain spiritual unity with them."[55] But their petition received scant attention at the meeting, marking a turning point in internal Amish Mennonite relations. Feeling slighted, few conservatives attended gatherings after 1865. The Amish Mennonites would gradually part ways, not just in Indiana but throughout North America. Those members most resistant to change became known as the Old Order Amish because they wanted to maintain the "old order." The progressive Amish Mennonites continued to regularly meet through 1878. The *Diener-Versammlungen* ceased with the 1878 assembly amid growing tensions among the leadership.[56]

In the wake of the demise of the *Diener-Versammlungen* came Amish Mennonite area conferences. While the Old Order Amish kept the traditional local polity, the progressives sought to continue the broader connections and conversations of the *Diener-Versammlungen* by creating conferences like their Mennonite neighbors.[57] The idea of local or regional bodies had even surfaced during the *Diener-Versammlungen,* but the first one wasn't formed until 1888.[58] On April 7 of that year, representatives from five northern Indiana congregations plus other ordained men from the area and from other states met at the Maple Grove church near Topeka for the inaugural meeting of the "District Conference for the State of Indiana of the Amish Mennonite Church."[59] Indiana conference participants discussed ministerial responsibilities, evangelism, discipline, and divorce and remarriage, and moderator Jonathan Smucker of Nappanee delivered an address on church governance.[60] Congregations not represented at the gathering were Barker Street, just north of the Indiana-Michigan state line, Townline in LaGrange County, and Howard-Miami near Kokomo. The Barker Street bishop had recently moved away, Townline was drifting away, and Howard-Miami was too far away.[61]

Townline was started in 1876 under the leadership of Joseph J. Bontrager, a minister at Forks Amish Mennonite Church. He, along with other Forks members, started a new congregation south of Shipshewana, where they were joined by some Old Order Amish. Taking its name from its location on a township boundary, Townline would move more cautiously than its neighboring congregations and never join the Indiana-Michigan Amish Mennonite Conference. Rather, it would become a member of the Conservative Amish Mennonite Conference, organized in 1910 to navigate the post-*Diener-Versammlung* territory between the Old Order Amish and more mainstream Amish Mennonites. Barker Street, meanwhile, would emerge as one of the more liberal congregations in the conference. Until the twentieth century, it would also be the only Amish Mennonite congregation in Michigan. Barker Street further distinguished itself by bringing Mennonites and Amish Mennonites into one worshiping body. In 1863, Amish Mennonites started to settle in Saint Joseph County, Michigan, on the border with Indiana, and met for worship in homes and a schoolhouse. Mennonites arrived in the area in the 1880s and were initially served by ministers from Elkhart County and sometimes used the same schoolhouse as the Amish Mennonites. But it wasn't long until the two small groups came together.[62] The churchwide periodical *Herald of Truth*, noting that Barker Street had a forty-member Sunday school but no minister, reported in 1891, "Although this little community of believers is partly of old Mennonite and partly of Amish Mennonite extraction, the members work harmoniously for the cause of Christ."[63] The next year, Harvey Friesner relocated from Pleasant Hill Mennonite Church in Branch County, Michigan, to serve Barker Street, becoming its first Mennonite minister after years of Amish Mennonite leadership.[64]

Barker Street, however, was not the first congregation outside Indiana to be included in the conference. Despite its Indiana-Michigan name, as the conference would eventually be called, it stretched across the United States. A charter member in 1888 was a small congregation at West Liberty, Ohio, which was a splinter group formed five years earlier from two other Amish Mennonite congregations. For leadership, it had turned to Clinton Frame bishop Eli Miller, who ordained a minister to lead the congregation. In 1899, the conference adopted a resolution encouraging the West Liberty members to pursue reconciliation with three Ohio brothers and sisters and join the Eastern Amish Mennonite Conference, which had been organized six years earlier.[65] Like its Mennonite counterpart, Indiana-Michigan Amish Mennonite Conference also assumed responsibility for the western congregations where there was no established conference. As a result, a new congregation near Chappell in the Nebraska panhandle was received into membership in 1890.[66] Started by transplanted Amish Mennonites from Ohio, the Nebraskans soon transferred to the Western Amish Mennonite Conference. In 1891, an Oregon congregation that comprised many settlers from Indiana or had other Indiana connections joined Indiana-Michigan.[67] Bishop Jonathan P. Smucker of Nappanee, who had visited Oregon several times in the 1880s, was given oversight of the group.[68] From the other side of the continent, the conference in 1894 accepted Long Green Amish Mennonite Church in eastern Maryland with the proviso that it unite with a closer conference when it became possible. The congregation joined the Eastern conference in 1899.[69]

Parallel Conferences

The two autonomous conferences hardly existed in isolation from each other, since they overlapped in the same geographic region and recognized each other as spiritual kin. Nappanee Amish Mennonite minister John Ringenberg wrote to the *Herald of Truth* in 1864, "I take this opportunity to write to you a few lines, and to address you as a brother, although we do not bear the same name, as I am called an Amonite and you a Mennonite; but Jesus says: Whoever shall do the will of God, the same is my brother and my sister." Ringenberg urged Amish Mennonites and Mennonites to "lay aside all party spirit (or sectarianism) and reach forward to the prize that is before us."[70] It wasn't just a noble sentiment for Ringenberg but was one he put into practice. David Burkholder, longtime minister of the Nappanee Mennonite congregation, had moved back to his native Ohio for a time. When he decided to return to Indiana in the summer of 1863, Ringenberg helped transport his household goods. When they arrived at Burkholder's farm, he discovered that Ringenberg had cleared ten acres and planted wheat. That good deed in Mennonite-Amish Mennonite relations was reciprocated six years later when three Mennonite ministers officiated at the funeral of Ringenberg's wife, Barbara.[71] At their 1864 assembly, after Ringenberg's plea in the *Herald of Truth*, the Indiana Mennonites invited the Amish Mennonites into fellowship, with their ministers expressly welcome to participate in their conference sessions.

Isaac Schmucker, the Amish Mennonite bishop at Haw Patch, publicly favored merger exploration in 1866. That year he hosted a group of Mennonite ministers, then later led an Amish Mennonite delegation to Yellow Creek, where he preached in German.[72] The 1888 Mennonite conference assembly, attended by "a number of the Amish ministers and brethren present and taking part in the work of the conference," declared its support for a churchwide conference to join together "the different conferences of the Mennonite and Amish churches who stand in the evangelical order of the gospel."[73] After the 1889 Amish Mennonite gathering, well-known Mennonite evangelist John S. Coffman of Elkhart noted that it was well attended by both groups. "We recognize that we are one family," he wrote in his diary.[74] During that assembly, Coffman was appointed English-language secretary; two years later he would be named moderator of Indiana-Michigan Mennonite Conference. He was one of twenty-three men who would hold elected or appointed positions in both conferences. At the local level, Barker Street was not the only instance of a Mennonite-Amish Mennonite union. In the mid-1880s, Mennonites and Amish Mennonites in Antrim County, Michigan, were "willing to join hand in hand, and be united as one body in the Lord," according to the *Herald of Truth*.[75] No congregation ever developed, however, although they conducted Sunday school for a while.

Despite all the similarities, however, there was one huge difference between the Mennonites and Amish Mennonites: church organization and governance. Those variations in how each group operated as a fellowship of faith were obscured by their common understandings of the tenets of that faith. Mennonites had long gathered themselves into regional conferences, such as Indiana-Michigan. The first American Mennonites, in eastern Pennsylvania, naturally had the first conferences, Franconia in 1725 and Lancaster in 1740. Four more had been organized by the time the Indiana Mennonites began meeting in the mid-nineteenth century. Each conference, with decisions made corporately by its bishops, ministers, and deacons, had the responsibility of defining and enforcing orthodoxy for its members, which could vary from conference to conference. In 1876, the Indiana Mennonite Conference "strongly maintained that ministers should according to the word of God teach the same thing," according to the minutes of the meeting.[76] Rationale and implications were more explicitly articulated in 1896 when the assembly declared, "Christ is the head of the Church and has given authority of Church Government to the Church. Conference is the representative of this authority and gives expression to the faith and practices taught in the Bible and maintained by the Church." Subsequently, all members were "subject to the decisions of conference."[77]

That was in stark contrast to the Amish Mennonites' emphasis on the congregation as the place for teaching, nurture, and discipline. There was no centralized authority, which didn't substantively change even when church members in Indiana organized their conference in 1888. Congregations still held the power to accept or reject any action taken at the conference level.[78] In 1891, at the conference's third annual meeting, moderator D. J. Johns from the Clinton Frame congregation declared that the conference's function "was not to make commandments but to confer ideas and to get a better understanding of the Word of God and to work in greater harmony."[79] Three years later, moderator John K. Yoder, a prominent Ohio bishop, told the Hoosier assembly that all Amish Mennonite congregations could not be "brought exactly under the same order. Yet we want to be together in love regardless of this, and help each other in the work as much as possible. We should not get 'order of the church' and Faith mixed."[80] The Amish Mennonite structure explicitly deemphasized hierarchy. "No one, whether bishop, minister or deacon or lay member has individual authority over another, but the authority is vested in the church collectively," the conference asserted.[81]

The differing approaches to authority were evident in the way each conference handled the contentious issue of divorce. As early as 1868, the Mennonite conference declared that church membership was incompatible with divorce and remarriage. Their Amish Mennonite brethren, meanwhile, at their first conference addressed a question from the Nappanee congregation about whether a divorced person who came to faith before marrying again could join the church. The majority of the assembly favored allowing membership but didn't make a ruling. Rather, it returned the matter to the "hands of the Nappanee ministers, it being their case."[82] The conference later took its congregational approach a step further by considering allowing lay members to participate in conference sessions, although the measure was never adopted.[83]

Regardless of differences in polity, both the Mennonite and Amish Mennonite conferences saw their purpose as maintaining the boundaries of community and faith in a world that threatened them. Their spiritual forebears in Europe were imprisoned, tortured, executed, and in a number of other ways persecuted by powers and principalities into the eighteenth century. By the mid-nineteenth century in the United States, however, Amish Mennonites and Mennonites were almost entirely free from any governmental infringements on their beliefs and ways of life. But that didn't mean they were immune from other undermining influences, which they usually categorized as "worldly" and contrary to the ways of God. At the second annual Indiana Amish Mennonite meeting, the ministers in attendance urged "that our Churches be not swallowed up in worldliness allowed by many around us in calling themselves Christian," and all seemed to be "of one heart and mind to maintain a doctrine that leads souls to a pure, holy life, separated from the world, and wholly consecrated to God."[84]

To lead such a life, both Amish Mennonites and Mennonites opposed military service, tobacco and alcohol use, jury service, and insurance policies. Secret societies such as the Masons and Odd Fellows, civic and professional organizations, and labor unions were also off-limits because they could result in church members being unequally yoked with people of differing faiths.[85] But particularly targeted were "vain amusements." By the turn of the twentieth century, the Mennonite conference had taken positions against playing baseball, croquet, checkers, and chess. Also issued were prohibitions on fairs, theatrical productions, and dances. Members' time was better spent reading the Bible, praying, and visiting the sick.[86] The Amish Mennonites agreed. In 1902 they came out against "ball games, street fairs, social parties, Sunday excursions and all similar modern amusements" because they rob "the Christian of his spiritual life, and has a tendency to lead others into sin because of his inconsistent living."[87] Even birthday parties and family reunions were suspect.

Amish Mennonites and Mennonites drew such lines to separate themselves not only from the secular world but from other Christians as well. Amish Mennonites and Mennonites practiced close communion—that is, observances of the Lord's Supper in which only church members could participate. The Mennonites barred involvement with YMCAs and Christian Endeavor, a nondenominational youth program, while the Amish Mennonites discouraged the use of literature from Christian sources other than Mennonite. Thirteen years after urging members to use "good judgment" when worshiping with others, the Mennonites in 1909 explicitly forbade sharing meetinghouses with other denominations. The Amish Mennonites in 1916 decided to avoid associating with other denominations unless sanctioned by the conference. Both groups repeatedly forbade their young people from marrying outside the church and their ministers from officiating such ceremonies. Marriage would be a thorny matter for decades. Facing a lack of marriage candidates because of the small size of its member communities, the Mennonite conference in 1873 backtracked on its two-year-old injunction against the marriage of first cousins and declared that because Scripture does not prohibit it, "each one should act according to the conviction of his or her own conscience," provided they did not violate state law.[88] The situation did not improve, however, so in 1915 the conference appointed a committee to investigate the "marriage problem." The committee's recommendations included encouraging young people to attend church events in other communities so as to meet potential spouses.[89]

Through the nineteenth century, Mennonites and Amish Mennonites built their religious beliefs and their various expressions on two pillars: the Bible and history. The Bible was assumed to be completely trustworthy and authoritative, with specific emphasis on Jesus Christ as revealed in the New Testament.[90] Since Anabaptism's sixteenth-century origins, Christ was held up as the ultimate example of faithful life and thought. But he didn't specifically address everything, so the way something was done or believed in the past was an important guide for the present, sometimes to the point of stifling new insights. In 1891, the Indiana-Michigan Mennonite Conference was drawn into a dispute at Caledonia, Michigan, where for several years women had been allowed to wear a "plain veil" or "common handkerchief" rather than the regulation "cap."[91] But bishop John Speicher said women could not partake of communion unless they agreed to wear the cap. Minister Christian Wenger, meanwhile, argued that neither Scripture nor the conference specified the type of head covering to be worn and that Speicher's expectations were based solely on tradition. The conference interceded and sided with the bishop, unanimously deciding that women members were to abide by the "established custom." Tradition trumped Scripture.

For some church members, the possibility of any sort of change was considered a worldly threat. One of the harshest critics was Barbara Stutzman of Clinton Frame Amish Mennonite Church.[92] In the days preceding her death in 1888 at the age of forty, she saw visions of Jesus Christ and began rebuking the church. She condemned Clinton Frame for its new meetinghouse, which she called "an abomination before the Lord," and for singing "those abominable modern tunes." She declared that "Sunday school does not accomplish anything good" and criticized her neighbors and relatives for offenses such as "grand music" and "showy things" in their homes. Stutzman said she "must speak thus by the power of the Almighty God" and warned, "You shall make manifest all what I have told you, and if you do not do so, you shall not die happily, but if you do, you shall die in happiness."[93] Her admonitions were dismissed by progressives—the ministers conducting her funeral did not mention them, as she had directed—but became popular among the traditionalists, who recorded her words and distributed them in pamphlet form. She had specifically identified the Old Order Amish as "nearest to the right."[94]

From the world's perspective, Amish Mennonite and Mennonite efforts to maintain their separation were successful. An early history of Elkhart County noted that the local Mennonites "are peculiarly interesting, since they take very little interest in the military or political worlds, merely contenting themselves with whatever the earth offers, and serving God quietly and perhaps unobtrusively."[95] But in actuality the lines of separation were blurring. Despite counsel against it, some Mennonites voted in the 1876 elections, prompting the conference to admonish the violators and instruct every minister to preach against political participation. In 1894, a number of church members attended the World's Fair in Chicago, again contrary to instructions from both conferences. Among the fairgoers were notable individuals from northern Indiana such as Mennonite bishop and publisher John F. Funk, who went to the World's Peace Congress as a delegate of the Quaker-influenced Christian Arbitration and Peace Society (a questionable affiliation given Mennonite and Amish Mennonite stances on ecumenical relations); well-traveled evangelist John S. Coffman, who went to hear famous preachers; and mission worker William B. Page, who with two friends opened a restaurant to serve fairgoers.[96]

Despite efforts to stay the long-held course of separation, the Indiana-Michigan Amish Mennonite and Mennonite fellowships were increasingly struggling with acculturation. Some members believed that the careful adoption of some "worldly" methods would strengthen the church, but others saw any hint of accommodation as undermining it. The cracks of those disagreements would quickly become full-blown chasms in both conferences.

2
The John F. Funk Era

Mennonites and Amish Mennonites had been venturing west to northern Indiana since the late 1830s, moving from settlements in Ohio, Ontario, Pennsylvania, and Virginia. But John F. Funk bucked the trend. After ten eventful years in Chicago, Illinois, Funk, a successful businessman turned publisher of religious materials, went east to Elkhart in April 1867. He had already risen to prominence with the creation of two periodicals, the *Herald of Truth* and its German-language counterpart, *Herold der Wahrheit*, which Funk had started three years earlier to foster fidelity and fellowship among Mennonites and Amish Mennonites in the United States and Canada. Now, he told his readers, the Lord beckoned him from his distant land to a place with more of his fellow church members and that was more suitable for his ministry. "We hope our efforts in the vineyard of the Lord, in this place, however feeble and imperfect they may be, will not be altogether in vain," Funk wrote.[1] He spent the first day of April busily concluding his Chicago affairs, and he finished loading his train car by 10 p.m. The next day he set up his new printing press in a rented building in downtown Elkhart.

But Funk didn't just bring a publishing company to Indiana. He also came with fresh, innovative ideas that would drastically and dramatically set a new direction for the church. Enterprising, educated, and ecumenically experienced, yet loyally Mennonite, Funk would become the most influential individual among North America's Amish Mennonites and Mennonites in the nineteenth century, a visionary catalyst for revolutionary changes that would turn northern Indiana into the nexus of church life and thought. In doing so he also contributed to simmering unrest in a fledgling regional fellowship that, like the readers of his publications, was struggling with churchly and secular pressures.

Funk would become the primary force that turned Indiana-Michigan Mennonite Conference into a churchwide crossroads that challenged the boundaries erected by its insular members.

The North American Mennonite and Amish Mennonite churches were floundering in the mid-1800s. Other Protestants of the eighteenth and nineteenth centuries had experienced the Great Awakenings: several periods of emotional, explosive religious revival that infused American Christianity with commitment, vitality, and initiative. That was expressed in many ways, including missionary organizations, Sunday schools, evangelistic meetings, Christian colleges and seminaries, spirited hymnody, and social activism.[2] But the cautious, insular, and change-averse Amish Mennonites and Mennonites resisted the Great Awakenings. The movements were of "worldly" origin, from outside of Anabaptism, and so were automatically suspect.[3] For them, revivalism's emphasis on personal conversion and experiential faith, along with its exuberant worship style, promoted pride. It placed what a person thought and felt above the wisdom and counsel of the community or congregation. Humility before God and the church was crucial to the spiritual descendants of Menno Simons and Jakob Ammann. They called it *Gelassenheit* in German, or yieldedness to God's will, which was determined not by the individual alone but by the individual as part of a larger body of discerning believers. Efforts to withstand worldly, pride-inducing newness, however, left much of the Amish Mennonite and Mennonite fellowship spiritually moribund, particularly as proponents of change within the church were often marginalized and forced out, taking their gifts elsewhere and leaving the church constrained by tradition, unable and unwilling to adapt.

In Indiana, Yellow Creek bishop Jacob Wisler, the first active Mennonite bishop in the state, was the champion of tradition. Ordained to the office in 1851, three years after moving to Elkhart County from Ohio, he sought to keep the church on the separatist course set by those who came before him. Wisler staunchly opposed the introduction of Sunday schools, revival meetings, prayer meetings, use of English in worship, even Funk's *Herald of Truth* and *Herold der Wahrheit*. An early challenge to his leadership came from Joseph Rohrer, a Yellow Creek minister prone to exuberant preaching who was ousted in 1867.[4] At the next year's assembly, the conference approved a warning that baptisms not be done "too hastily."[5] That was another strike against revival and prayer meetings. Their supercharged, emotional atmosphere could lead participants to make snap decisions to accept Jesus Christ as their Savior, resulting in a shallow faith that often failed to consider the implications of a choice that could lead to suffering and even death.

But Rohrer's departure was only a temporary triumph. Daniel Brenneman, an ordained minister, had arrived in Elkhart County from Ohio in 1865 and began serving at Yellow Creek, where he soon became a popular preacher with some members. A younger brother to the highly regarded Ohio Mennonite bishop John M. Brenneman, he encouraged Funk in his publishing efforts, preached in English as well as German, advocated prayer meetings, and became a leading proponent of revival meetings. He was also a music lover. Brenneman had instruments at home, in violation of the church's teaching that they were worldly intrusions used for entertainment and not for uplifting purposes, and he delighted singing in four-part harmony rather than in the customary unison. Brenneman's unorthodox ways shook up the community. He was once given a ride by a fellow Mennonite who did not know the identity of his passenger. The driver asked him what he thought of Daniel Brenneman. Brenneman evaded the question and instead asked the opinion of his companion, who responded, "He speaks English and sings bass."[6] That was all Brenneman's driver needed to say to convey his dissatisfaction with the minister and the threat he posed. And for traditionalists, Brenneman wouldn't be the only perceived source of danger to the long-accepted order.

But not all turmoil was of internal origin. The U.S. Civil War of 1861–65 drew the Indiana Amish Mennonite and Mennonite communities further into worldly affairs, and not everyone was in agreement with the historic opposition to military involvement.[7] Often citing the moral necessity of eliminating slavery in the Confederate states, some in the church declared themselves patriotic Union backers.[8] Indiana was one of the strongest contributors to the cause, with nearly two-thirds of the state's three hundred thousand men of draftable age taking up arms.[9] Among them were thirteen members of the Christiana Buzzard Holdeman family, the namesakes of Holdeman Mennonite Church of Wakarusa.[10] Before the first meetinghouse was erected in 1851, services were held in the home of Christiana's son George, who would be drafted and wounded in battle. Two of George's sons and a son-in-law also fought in the war. John, another of Christiana's sons and one of the congregation's first two trustees, was drafted in early 1865 but saw no action before the war's conclusion. The third of Christiana's sons to serve, and the only one not to return home, was Jonas. He enlisted in 1864 after the death of his eldest son, Frederick, who had been captured and died of starvation in a Confederate prison camp. Incensed at the treatment Frederick received from the rebels, forty-year-old Jonas went to war and was killed in Tennessee just seven weeks later. Two other members of the extended Holdeman family also died as a result of taking up arms against the South.

Nevertheless, nonresistance and peace continued to be officially upheld. Sermons encouraged Mennonites and Amish Mennonites to be steadfast. September 26, 1861, was designated as a day of prayer in the Yellow Creek community,[11] and the next year six church members signed a petition against the war.[12] Conscientious objectors could purchase exemptions to military service, and congregations raised money to buy their boys out of the army. But not everyone chose that option. In the Howard-Miami Amish Mennonite congregation near Kokomo, Indiana, brothers Daniel, Christian, and Noah Eash hid for a time to avoid conscription, with their father setting out a basket of food every evening to provide for his nonresistant sons.[13] Meanwhile, in Bower Mennonite Church in southern Indiana, four young men were drafted but permitted to attend to the sick and wounded in hospitals, which a congregational member described as "not contrary to the dictates of our conscience, and no violation of the Gospel or the principles of our church."[14] Most Mennonites and Amish Mennonites, however, paid the "equivalency fee" for exemptions from service or hired substitutes to go in their place.

Chicago Mennonite

In the midst of all this midcentury discord, John Fretz Funk of Chicago appeared on the churchwide stage. Dismayed at the number of Amish Mennonites and Mennonites who were going off to battle, he wrote and published a peace booklet, *Warfare: Its Evils, Our Duty*, in July 1863. He was encouraged in the project by Ohio bishop John M. Brenneman, who had a long visit with Funk during a stop in Chicago on his way to visit western Mennonites. In his booklet, Funk argued against war's "legalized murder and robbery" and for Christian discipleship, including forgiveness and love of enemies. "If I bear the sword of destruction of my enemy, I cannot love him," he wrote, "and hence can be no child of God, and have no salvation, and no heirship with Christ, who died to save me."[15] Later that summer Brenneman submitted to Funk his own manuscript on nonresistance, *Christianity and War*, which Funk also had printed. Like *Warfare: Its Evils, Our Duty*, Brenneman's treatise was also widely distributed and well received.

Funk had taken a roundabout path to faith, religious publishing, and Indiana. A native of Bucks County in eastern Pennsylvania, he was raised in an ostensibly typical Mennonite setting but exhibited an early broad-mindedness. Even though Mennonites resisted Sunday schools, Funk attended one run by local Baptists and later taught in another one. He took courses at Freeland Seminary near Collegeville, Pennsylvania, a school started in 1848 by Abraham Hunsicker, a liberal and former Franconia Mennonite Conference minister.[16] In 1857, after two years of teaching school, Funk, then twenty-two years old, left Pennsylvania when his brother-in-law Jacob Beidler invited him to work at his lumber business in Chicago. With Beidler's support, Funk formed his own lumber company in 1861, which thrived as Chicago grew. But Funk's interests went well beyond business as he enjoyed the benefits of life in

Business card for John F. Funk's lumberyard. MCUSAA–Goshen.

a bustling urban setting. He attended lectures on topics ranging from phrenology to temperance, joined a debate society, closely followed political developments, and, as a fervent abolitionist, campaigned for Republican presidential candidate Abraham Lincoln.

Funk also accepted Jesus Christ as Lord and Savior in Chicago. Despite his upbringing and earlier church involvements, he had never become a Christian, at least in the evangelical understanding of the faith, until January 1858, when a spiritual revival swept the city. But, true to Mennonite aversion to quick decisions, he didn't immediately affiliate with a church. As there was no Mennonite congregation in Chicago, Funk's primary church home was Third Presbyterian Church, which he attended with his sister and brother-in-law. But he was not bound by any sectarianism. Funk grew up in Line Lexington Mennonite Church, a Franconia congregation, but he also worshiped with Congregational, Dunkard, Episcopal, and Reformed congregations.[17] In Chicago, his partner in the lumber business was Jim McMullen, an Irish Catholic whose brother, John, would become a noted priest, bishop, and writer and a good friend of Funk's.[18] Funk was also introduced to Dwight L. Moody, who, like Funk, went to Chicago to work and found his life's calling in service to Christ's church. Moody would become a key shaper of American evangelicalism, with its emphases on conversion and activism. Funk was absorbed into that world. One form of outreach vigorously promoted by Moody was the growing Sunday school movement, which drew Funk's enthusiastic participation, to the point that at one time he was involved in three Sunday schools: one as a student, one as a teacher, and one as a superintendent.[19] He was also a charter member of the Chicago YMCA, where Moody started his career in ministry.

Although exposed to a wide range of other expressions of Christian faith, Funk found that his Mennonite heritage still beckoned. He seriously considered becoming a Presbyterian but was troubled by the church's beliefs about predestination and infant baptism and its acceptance of war. An even greater issue was Third Presbyterian Church's new meetinghouse, which Funk considered opulent and made him long for the simpler Mennonite places of worship.[20] So a year after his conversion, he returned to Line Lexington for instruction and baptism. (An additional factor was that Funk was courting Salome Kratz, a young Mennonite woman in his home community. They were married in 1864.) Now a confirmed and committed Mennonite in Chicago, Funk wanted to join other church members in the important communal ritual of sharing the Lord's Supper, which church members could do only with other Old Mennonites. He first inquired at a Mennonite congregation at Sterling, more than one hundred miles west of Chicago. Funk was told, however, that strife at Sterling made communion highly unlikely in the foreseeable future, since congregational harmony was a prerequisite for its observance,

John F. Funk, circa 1875. MCUSAA–Goshen.

and he was directed to Elkhart County in the other direction. Funk contacted the brethren there and was invited by Yellow Creek Mennonite Church deacon David Good to join them in sharing the bread and the cup at Indiana Mennonite Conference's annual assembly in the fall.

So on Thursday, October 9, 1862, Funk took the train from Chicago to Elkhart, paid one dollar for lodging that night and breakfast the next morning, and then hired a carriage to take him to the home of minister Daniel Moyer, six miles southwest of Elkhart. No one was home, as everyone had already gone to the assembly at the Yellow Creek meetinghouse, so Funk walked seven miles to Good's home. On Saturday he accompanied the deacon to the church, where John M. Brenneman preached and forty-eight people were baptized. Communion was on Sunday morning, which Funk called a "most solemn thing." "Partook for the first time in my life of the Emblems of the Broken Body and the Shed Blood of our Saviour for which purpose I came to this place," he recorded in his diary that day. He spent the night at the home of bishop Wisler and on Monday afternoon took the train from Elkhart back to Chicago.[21]

Funk returned to his workaday world knowing he had found something special in Elkhart County. None of his religious associations in Chicago had fully resonated with him. In Indiana, however, he witnessed a large, vibrant, earnest group of believers daily pursuing Christian discipleship. For Funk, going to the conference assembly was a sort of spiritual homecoming, a rejoining of his people. Indeed, some of the Yellow Creek community came from Funk's native Bucks County. He maintained contacts with church members in Elkhart County and would make the yearly trek back for the assembly. But he didn't remain simply a lay participant for long. Funk had learned of a small Mennonite congregation near Gardner in Grundy County, just south of Chicago, and Brenneman ordained him in 1865 to serve the group. Funk later helped start a Mennonite congregation in Chicago, which was destroyed by the city's great fire of 1871.

Bolstered by the success of *Warfare: Its Evils, Our Duty* and *Christianity and War*, Funk pursued religious publishing on the side while still operating his lumber business. Especially close to his heart was the dream of a churchwide periodical. He had seen such publications effectively serve other denominations by teaching the faith and keeping members connected across the miles, and Funk believed Mennonites and Amish Mennonites would also benefit from their own journal. The idea had been tried among Old Mennonites once before. But Franconia Mennonite Conference minister Heinrich Bertholet discontinued his *Die Evangelische Botschafter* after just one issue in 1836.[22] Now, nearly three decades later, the time was right to try again. Funk was encouraged by some influential and relatively progressive leaders, including the brothers John and Daniel Brenneman. "Like yourself I have for several years past felt the necessity of some means of correspondence with our brethren generally. . . . It is all right and natural that those who 'love one another with a pure heart fervently' will want to know of each other's estate," Daniel wrote Funk.[23] Also providing encouragement was Funk's friend Father John McMullen, who in 1865 would start his own magazine to serve American Catholics.[24]

The inaugural issues of the *Herald of Truth*, the first English-language Old Mennonite periodical, and its German sibling, *Herold der Wahrheit*, came out in January 1864. They were soon a success, posting a circulation of more than one thousand by the end of the year.[25] "The hearty support we have received from the brethren and our friends in general, has far exceeded our most sanguine expectations," Funk reported.[26] He sold his share of the lumber business in 1866 in order to concentrate full-time on publishing. Even before Funk decided to start the two periodicals, John M. Brenneman had suggested Funk leave Chicago, "a Dangerous place . . . and live a little more retired, & away from the noise & Bustle of this tempting world."[27] As his publishing ministry grew, Funk was again counseled to move to a Mennonite community, which would keep his work firmly in the embrace of the church. Brenneman proposed that Funk establish his office "wherein a church is organized, and to have a committee appointed of 3 or 5 faithful Brethren, to examine and approve of the reading matter before it goes to press."[28] Funk was beginning to recognize the importance of the religious community as a place of discernment and accountability. While still living in Chicago, he met a Mennonite in traditional plain garb who commented that Funk, dressed in contemporary urban fashion, did not look like a Mennonite. The encounter impressed upon Funk that while superficial expressions of faith may be deceiving, outward appearances could indeed reflect inner convictions.[29] When he finally decided to move, northern Indiana was a natural choice for a new home and base of operations. But at least one person, from Saint Louis, advised Funk to stay in Chicago: "I think it would be better for you to remain some distance from your church members lest they become too well acquainted with your progressiveness and thereby [you would] lose influence."[30]

Goshen was geographically well situated for Funk to serve his targeted audience, located between the Mennonites of Yellow Creek just a few miles to the west of town and the Amish Mennonite settlements of Clinton Township and LaGrange County on the east side. But Funk instead chose to locate in Elkhart, northwest of Goshen and a couple of miles south of the Michigan state line, even though there was only one known Mennonite and no congregation in the immediate vicinity. It was a business decision: Elkhart had better railroad service.[31] That was important for distributing his publications and receiving the supplies necessary for their production. Through the 1860s, Elkhart, a junction for several rail lines, became a significant center, with growing facilities for the maintenance of cars, locomotives, and track as well as for organizing cars into trains. Goshen only had a spur from Elkhart.[32] The city setting had another benefit as well. It served as a buffer, allowing for some space, geographic and otherwise, between the urbanized

Funk and the country church communities. That allowed him a large degree of freedom to implement a program of innovation in a church wary of change.

Pursuit of Peace

When Funk moved to Elkhart in April 1867, conflict between progressive and tradition-minded Mennonites had been churning for several years. John M. Brenneman told Funk:

> A great wound has been struck there, which still is in a festering condition. I was fully convinced the two last times I was their [*sic*] that there is fault on both sides, and each party seems to be jealous of the other. There was a goodeal [*sic*] of complaint brought to me against their Bishop [Wisler], and I thought some of it was groundless. That he is the man he should be in every respect, I will not affirm. But who is there without fault? . . . I think that if the ministers in Elkhart would manifest a little more love, [honor] & respect toward their Bishop, things would work better then [*sic*] what they do. They seem to me to be a little too independent, and work a little too much behind the Bishop's back. . . . The members too, show too much partiality. They have their Paul, Appollos and their Cephas.[33]

Brenneman urged Funk to "undertake nothing of importance, without the advice of the Bishop, try to gain his favor & esteem, so that he can have confidence in you." When people come to Funk to complain about Wisler, he continued, encourage them to pray for the bishop and "tell them what a heavy Burden is resting on him, and that they should have patience."[34]

In the wake of the departure of Joseph Rohrer and his spirited preaching came another challenge to Wisler and his tradition-minded supporters. This time it came from a progressive faction with Daniel Brenneman at the forefront. Opposition to the bishop reached new heights less than three months after Funk's arrival. In response, on June 28, 1867, Wisler voluntarily relinquished his duties until the congregation should vote him back.[35] Stepping down would allow the situation to settle down. And when the congregation would return Wisler to his office, as he no doubt expected, he would have a mandate and the definitive support of the members, since they would have restored him to maintain the traditional ways. A vote of church members to call Wisler back was scheduled for Saturday, August 17, and Wisler asked Isaac Hoffer, an Ohio bishop with similar conservative convictions, to come conduct the balloting.

That's when Wisler's potentially shrewd political maneuver went awry. To his and Hoffer's chagrin, 127 church members voted to suspend Wisler's ministry, while 119 voted for him to resume. Another five members voted that Wisler, Brenneman, and Joseph Holdeman, a deacon who was pressuring Wisler from an even more conservative position, all remain silent. Rather than resolving the situation, it was now more complicated than ever. The day after the vote, after leading the Yellow Creek worship service, Hoffer ignored the action of the congregation and restored Wisler and, more incredulously, suspended Brenneman, whose status had not been in question (the five votes notwithstanding). The church was in an uproar. Was Hoffer's action legitimate? Was Wisler really back in? Was Brenneman really out?

It took an investigating committee of sixteen ministers from four states and Ontario to sort through the chaos in October. According to the charges they heard against Wisler, he opposed evening meetings, English-language services, and audible prayers. He lacked love in dealing with the ministers and violated Matthew 18 in a dispute with his son-in-law.[36] And, of course, he went against the wishes of the congregation by returning to his role as bishop, as he did after Hoffer's actions. Funk was particularly harsh in his testimony before the committee, despite repeated admonitions from John M. Brenneman to remain neutral and work for peace. Funk called Wisler "selfish," "imprudent," "harsh and abusive," and "destitute of that love which is required of every true Christian and especially of a Bishop towards his flock." Furthermore, Funk charged him with teaching unsound doctrine, such as claiming that Jesus never said he was the Son of God, that Christ never sang, and that Scripture prohibits evening meetings.[37] In the end, however, the committee found Wisler guilty on only two points: failing to adequately counsel a church member (whom the bishop considered too much linked with Rohrer) in a spiritual matter and failing to discipline "certain persons." Wisler was called to repent and ask forgiveness, but his reinstatment was invalidated. Daniel Brenneman was admonished for assuming bishop responsibilities by baptizing new converts and for conducting evening services. In addition, the committee criticized Hoffer for "a serious mistake" in reinstating Wisler and disciplining Brenneman.[38] The committee found all sides culpable and held them all accountable, and its findings seemed to indicate a resolution was at hand. "Peace has been restored again," Greitja Jacobs Symensma, one of the Dutch immigrant church members, recorded in her diary.[39]

But it was only an illusion. One member of the investigating committee even repudiated the group's decision before leaving Elkhart County. George L. Weaver, a conservative Pennsylvania bishop who actually made the announcement that Wisler must repent before he could be reinstated, admitted that on the first day of the investigation he agreed with his fellow committee members to discipline the bishop.[40] He then spent that night at the home of a Wisler supporter and heard the traditionalists' side. The next morning, Weaver contended, he tried to change his position but the committee would not allow it "for the sake of peace."[41] After the committee's decision, Wisler claimed he had been treated unfairly and wanted to be restored to what he considered to be his rightful position. Furthermore, he called on the church to reject the progressivism embodied by Brenneman and Funk. A split seemed imminent when, in the spring of 1869, supporters called Wisler to be their bishop and started holding separate worship services in the Yellow Creek meetinghouse on alternate Sundays when the rest of the congregation did not meet.[42] Wisler's group numbered seventy or eighty, leaving Yellow Creek with at least three hundred members.[43] Several attempts, both internal and by visiting church leaders, to mediate the conflict were fruitless. Then in August 1870, after a separation of nearly a year and a half, John M. Brenneman was finally able to achieve reconciliation. Wisler and two allied ministers confessed and the church restored him as bishop. Once again Symensma was able to write in her diary, "Aug. 5, at the jellocreek peace was made between the Wisler and Brenneman."[44]

Once again, however, it was a short-lived peace. In the spring of 1871, Wisler was accused of attempting to thwart the budding Sunday school movement, which the conference three years earlier had declared permissible "when properly conducted."[45] But such approval did nothing to sway Wisler and other traditionalists throughout the church.[46] Imported from England, Sunday schools started appearing in North America in the late eighteenth century, during the Second Great Awakening. A few Mennonite congregations in Ontario and Pennsylvania had adopted them by the 1840s. But most Sunday schools were ecumenical, using a uniform curriculum produced by a national nondenominational Sunday school organization, and thus seen by Mennonites and Amish Mennonites as undermining church identity and loyalty as well as nonresistant and nonconformist beliefs. Members were also concerned that the schools would compel them to join with other denominations in the ministry, a clear violation of Anabaptist separatism. Furthermore, Mennonites opposed the movement's nationalistic tenor, complete with its militaristic and political connotations. The goal of the movement was to create not simply good Christians but good Christian citizens who would be politically active and contribute to God's realm in accordance with evangelical teachings. That generated Mennonite and Amish Mennonite concerns of a Sunday school–inspired theocracy.

Second Yellow Creek meetinghouse, built in 1861. Used by both the Yellow Creek congregation and the splinter Wisler group until the former built its own meetinghouse across the road in 1912. MCUSAA–Goshen.

Wisler's intransigence on Sunday schools unleashed another round of conflict, and a committee of six ordained men, including Daniel Brenneman's brothers John M. and George, who was also a bishop in Ohio, and the interloper Hoffer, was assembled for yet another investigation into conference affairs. The committee chided several leaders, including Daniel Brenneman, but the harshest measure was removing Wisler from office because "a bishop is to be blameless," although the committee allowed him to remain a minister.[47] Wisler and his supporters couldn't abide by the decision. Observed one, "The way people hear and see, they wanted to get Wisler out of the way so that they can carry out their matters."[48] On January 6, 1872, Wisler was expelled from Indiana-Michigan Mennonite Conference, culminating a saga that had been ongoing for at least six years. Out of some four or five hundred members, about one hundred went with the ousted bishop to form the Wisler Mennonite Church.[49]

Several attempts at reconciliation were made in the following decade but were unsuccessful, although some individuals would later rejoin Indiana-Michigan. (The only sizable group of Wisler members to later transfer back to Indiana-Michigan was at Brutus, Michigan, when several dozen left the local congregation to join Maple River Mennonite Church in the early 1920s.[50]) Meanwhile, Wisler quickly found support among Ohio Mennonite Conference conservatives, who joined their Indiana brothers and sisters in the spring of 1872 to inaugurate the Old Order Mennonite movement.[51]

Limits of Progressivism

With the exit of Wisler and his supporters came the ascendancy of the progressives, who drew heavily on the innovations the deposed bishop had so vigorously opposed. While Wisler saw them as undesirable ends, the progressives saw them as means to greater faithfulness. They did not set out to change core beliefs but rather to strengthen them with new methods. The same month as Wisler's departure, Funk and Daniel Brenneman were invited to undertake another landmark initiative, traveling to Masontown in southwestern Pennsylvania to conduct the first Old Mennonite revival meetings. But Funk's major focus upon moving to Indiana was promoting Sunday schools in the conference. With his considerable Chicago Sunday school experience, he was well qualified to spearhead the movement. Although many in the church were still suspicious of him, it was also apparent that Funk was not quite of the same mold as the evangelicals with whom he had associated. He was establishing his churchly credentials. He gave up a lucrative lumber business, which probably would have made him a millionaire, as it did for his brother-in-law Beidler and former partner McMullen.[52] Funk exchanged his fine worldly clothes for simpler Mennonite attire, and he curtailed his political involvements. And he left Chicago's fast-paced life. At the same time that Funk was promoting Sunday schools in the *Herald of Truth* and *Herold der Wahrheit*, he was also publishing articles preaching nonconformity, nonresistance, and community— the opposite of the nationalism, militarism, and individualism that the church saw in the broader Sunday school movement—and he was soon producing the first Mennonite Sunday school curricula. Shortly after arriving in Elkhart, he invited local Mennonites to an afternoon Sunday school.[53] Attendance was good, but Funk was dismayed that no one present could recite the Ten Commandments. Among them was a bishop observing the exercises, who told Funk afterward that if called on, he, like the students, would have also had to remain silent.[54]

While the post-Wisler climate allowed for new approaches and ideas, change was still a painful process. For some church members, such as Brenneman, it did not happen fast enough. For others, change needed to be made slowly. Funk, although of a similar progressive spirit as Brenneman, felt that innovations had their limits and must be made carefully. For example, despite his earlier trip to Masontown, Funk backed away from supporting revival meetings. He didn't start the *Herald of Truth* until he had sufficient backing, such as from the Brenneman brothers. Funk understood that dramatic changes in the church, such as forcing revival meetings, could have devastating effects.

But decelerating in deference to prevailing opinions could have the same consequences. In 1873, Daniel Brenneman and John Krupp, a like-minded minister at Pleasant Hill Mennonite Church near Burr Oak, Michigan, traveled to Ontario, having heard of spiritual revival spreading there among the Mennonites under minister Solomon Eby, a zealous proponent of powerful personal religious experience. Krupp was especially excited by what he saw and heard on the trip and returned home an unabashed advocate. Brenneman, obviously intrigued, wanted to

Daniel Brenneman. MCUSAA–Goshen.

investigate further and went back to Ontario later that year. There he learned that the local bishop had refused to baptize a number of new believers unless they gave up their demonstrative prayer meetings, which they would not do. Church polity held that visiting ministers and bishops could not conduct baptisms without permission of the local bishop. Nevertheless, Brenneman agreed to baptize the converts, citing the legitimacy of their faith, no matter how they came to it.[55]

When Brenneman returned to Elkhart County, he learned that Krupp had been expelled for his acceptance of prayer and revival meetings and for allowing women "to testify," or speak publicly in those meetings. Brenneman expressed his support for Krupp, telling a conference ministers' meeting, "Brethren, to be honest before God, if our people do nothing worse than go get together to sing and pray and read God's Word, thus seeking to edify each: that this should give us occasion or authority to expel them for church fellowship, I cannot see it that way."[56] Brenneman maintained his relationship with Krupp after his discipline, visiting him in Michigan, and led prayer meetings with another minister in Elkhart County. That generated anxiety among his fellow ministers. "We fear Daniel will so far allow himself to be misled as to leave the church," Funk recorded in his diary. "May God grant us grace to be faithful and remain true to doctrines of our Faith." Funk even attended a Brenneman-Krupp revival meeting to better understand his friend's actions. But Funk lamented that "much ado was made, loud crying and weeping—howling that could be heard a long distance—half a mile. S. Sherk said, there comes the Lord! Catch Him quick—folly, when the Lord comes he will come in judgment."[57] Even Brenneman's brother was upset. "If Daniel cannot be convinced of his error, and won back, he must be expelled, according to my judgement," Ohio bishop

John M. Brenneman wrote Funk. "Their [sic] must be order kept in the Church, or she cannot stand."[58]

Repeated attempts to bring Daniel Brenneman back to the path of more conventional Mennonitism failed, and the situation came to a head in early 1874. A ministers' meeting was held April 25 at the Yellow Creek meetinghouse, where Brenneman was charged with supporting the excommunicated Krupp, promoting practices considered "unscriptural" and "never sanctioned by the church," and "causing dissension and offense in the church." It was an intense, emotion-laden meeting, and when it was over, Brenneman was expelled from the conference. Upon learning of the decision, he fainted, the only time he was known to do so.[59] Leaving with Brenneman were more than fifty Mennonites, plus about another thirty people described as "too much Mennonites to be Evangelicals and too much Evangelicals to be Mennonites," and who with Eby organized the Reforming Mennonite Society, eventually known as the Mennonite Brethren in Christ.[60] Combined with the Wisler split, Indiana Mennonite Conference lost about a third of its membership in two years.

Brenneman's ouster ruptured not only the church but also a personal relationship. He and Funk were friends united in their love for the church, deep concern for its welfare, and commitment to restoring its vitality and faithfulness. They were coworkers in a holy endeavor.[61] But there were also keen differences between the two ministers. Funk wanted to uphold and strengthen the tenets of the church by the best means possible, such as churchwide periodicals and Sunday schools. Such instruments, he believed, were crucial for propagating the distinctives of the faith, such as nonconformity and nonresistance. Yet underlying that notion was his belief in the community of believers, of which he was a part, as the place for discernment and accountability. Funk patiently sought the middle ground between rigid traditionalism and unfettered newness. In contrast, Brenneman was more aggressive, even impudent, and directly challenged prevailing beliefs. That led to accusations of pride, of putting himself above the collective values of the church. For example, Brenneman willingly ignored the church's ban on four-part singing because he thought it "absurd and unreasonable . . . to refrain from using the strong bass voice which God had given me, to good advantage in rendering our singing more attractive and edifying."[62] Separated by the schism, Brenneman and Funk eventually reconciled, and Funk helped officiate his friend's funeral in 1919.

Funk's cautious progressivism proved prescient. Brenneman's departure could not stop change, but it did make it more manageable. He was ahead of his time, and after his expulsion it wasn't long until others took his place in advancing new ideas, albeit in more subtle and patient fashion. Over the next three decades, Mennonites and Amish Mennonites across the continent would accept much of what Brenneman called for, including evangelistic meetings and the use of English to worship God.

Influence and Immigrants

At the eye of this hurricane of change and resistance were Elkhart County and Funk, with his Mennonite Publishing Company (MPC). Until the late nineteenth century, there was little to formally link Mennonites and Amish Mennonites as they spread across the continent. They were only organized into regional fellowships, such as the two Indiana conferences; broader denominational structures had not yet emerged. One of the few practical things to keep the scattered church members connected was reading MPC periodicals and books.

The *Herald of Truth* and *Herold der Wahrheit* were Funk's flagships, but after relocating to Elkhart he added eight more periodicals, including children's and youth materials. He also printed books such as the *Martyrs Mirror* and *The Complete Works of Menno Simons*, plus prayer books, catechisms, the first Mennonite Sunday school lessons, doctrinal and theological works, hymnals, and history books. By 1900, the MPC catalog had more than one hundred titles in English and German.[63] Because of the power and prominence of the printed words coming from the MPC, Elkhart became the crossroads for the broader Old Mennonite fellowship and beyond. Church leaders and other travelers made sure to visit Funk and his downtown Elkhart business, and correspondence and orders poured in from coast to coast and around the world.

To carry out his company's work, Funk brought to northern Indiana some of the best and brightest men in the church, young workers with vision and energy. Hired for publishing work, they inevitably made their greatest contributions in other facets of church life and

Employees outside Mennonite Publishing Company, Elkhart, Indiana, 1888. MCUSAA–Goshen.

further enhanced Elkhart's, and the conference's, standing. Among the recruits was Virginia minister and *Herald of Truth* contributor John S. Coffman, whom Funk brought to Elkhart in 1879. While he moved to Indiana to be an MPC editor and writer, Coffman soon became widely known and loved as a preacher. He was so much in demand across the church that one year he spent only eighty-nine days at work in the MPC office.[64] Like Daniel Brenneman, Coffman held a deep concern for those outside the church and was willing to use new methods to gather them in. "When we see what others are doing and see the success which follows their efforts, we are sorely grieved at the apathy of our own members on the subject of evangelizing," Coffman believed.[65] But he was able to do what Brenneman couldn't: introduce revival meetings as a method of witness and nurture, albeit in a more subdued form that was more consistent with conventional Anabaptist sensibilities. His first meetings came in 1881 at the invitation of Bowne Mennonite Church in Kent County, Michigan. Coffman had earlier made several shorter visits to Bowne with encouraging results, and the time seemed right for a more concerted effort to bring people to Christ. Starting on Saturday, June 4, with a message on "Eating and Drinking Worthily and Unworthily," based on 1 Corinthians 10, Coffman preached eleven times over six days. He also met privately with unbaptized individuals who were considering joining the church. Coffman then spent two more weeks in shorter engagements across southern Michigan. It was a productive trip. "I feel God has blessed my journey. To his holy name be praise forever," Coffman recorded in his diary on June 24, the day he returned home.[66]

Another Funk recruit was Menno S. Steiner, an Ohio schoolteacher who came to Elkhart in 1889. But his MPC tenure was short, because in 1893 he went to Chicago as the first Old Mennonite mission worker. Funk also hired Maryland native George L. Bender, who would become the first executive of the Old Mennonite mission agency. One employee Funk did not invite was John Horsch, who left his native Germany for the United States in 1887 to escape both military conscription and his father, who expected his frail, bookish son to become a farmer. Horsch journeyed to Elkhart because he had been a reader of *Herold der Wahrheit* in his homeland, and found work helping produce MPC's German-language materials.[67] He eventually relocated to Scottdale, Pennsylvania, where he became a prolific writer and historian and outspoken champion of conservative Mennonitism.

Funk's churchwide influence was especially evident in the Russian Mennonite immigration of the 1870s, when the world literally came to his door. Starting in the late eighteenth century, much-traveled European Mennonites and Hutterites found sanctuary to live, work, and worship with practically total autonomy in Russia.[68] But in the 1860s, they began coming under state pressure to acculturate, including demands to teach Russian in their schools and pay state and local taxes, and losing their treasured exemptions to military service (although an alternative service program would eventually be implemented). Coupled with these developments was a stifling lack of land available in their growing communities.[69] So Mennonites and Hutterites started exploring emigrating elsewhere. Funk became a critical link because his *Herold der Wahrheit* was read by the German-speaking Mennonites in Russia. As early as 1870, Funk was suggesting the United States as a potential new home for these brothers and sisters in the faith, and in the following years printed frequent updates on their situation for the benefit of his North American readers.[70] In the summer of 1872, four young Russian Mennonites arrived in Elkhart unannounced and spent three days in the Funk home. The quartet was not an "authorized deputation" but came "on their own account simply for the purpose of becoming acquainted with the American people, their country, their privileges, their institutions and their religion," Funk reported in the *Herald of Truth*.[71] He accompanied the group to Minnesota, Dakota Territory, and Manitoba to explore potential sites for relocation, and then gave extensive coverage to the trip in his periodicals. He would do the same the next year when official Russian Mennonite and Hutterite delegations would arrive.

As the push for immigration grew stronger, Funk devoted most of the February 1873 issues of the *Herald of Truth* and *Herold der Wahrheit* to the Russian Mennonites, with articles on the opportunities awaiting them in North America. Twenty thousand copies of the German-language periodical were sent to Russia to encourage their immigration.[72] "Come unto us and we will try to do you good; you shall share with us the blessings of the land, and dwell in safety under the protection of our heavenly father," Funk urged.[73] He started publishing appeals for his readers to provide financial assistance for the Russians' migration and proposed the creation of a churchwide organization to oversee such work. In response, Indiana Mennonite Conference in October 1873 organized the first committee to accept and distribute funds for the Russian migration. Thanks to publicity in the *Herald of Truth* and *Herold der Wahrheit*, contributions and loan offers soon started coming from across the Amish Mennonite and Mennonite churches. Later that year the Indiana committee merged with a similar body formed by members of the General Conference Mennonite Church, creating the Mennonite Board of Guardians, a pioneer inter-Mennonite mutual aid organization. Pennsylvania and Ontario Mennonites also formed aid committees, which cooperated with the Board of Guardians.

Northern Indiana became an important station on the Russians' journey to their new homes on the Great Plains. Between 1873 and 1884, some twelve thousand Mennonite and Hutterite men, women, and children landed in the United States and Canada, many of them passing through Elkhart on the way west. They sometimes stayed for weeks in vacant houses or railcars rented by Funk. Among the newcomers were twenty-four Krimmer Mennonite Brethren families who arrived on Sunday, July 19, 1874.[74] They arrived at a heartrending time. At one o'clock that morning, the Funks' eight-week-old daughter, Grace Anna, died after five days of illness. Her father had spent much of that time at her side and was exhausted. But just hours after Grace Anna's death, Funk learned that the Krimmer Mennonite Brethren immigrants had arrived on the morning train. He was able to rouse himself, find lodging for the Russians, and persuade a grocer to open his store and sell them food and supplies. The group remained in Elkhart for nearly a month before settling in Kansas.[75]

The vast majority of immigrants found new homes on the prairies from Kansas to Manitoba, although a few settled elsewhere, including in Michigan. The largest such group, about ten families, went to Okemos, near Lansing, where they were served by Mennonite and Amish Mennonite ministers from Elkhart and LaGrange Counties as well as from the Bowne congregation, seventy miles west of Okemos. But the Russians never formally affiliated with their brethren in Indiana and Michigan, and the group died out as a worshiping body around the turn of the twentieth century.[76] In 1877, three Russian Mennonite families moved to Petoskey in northern Michigan, having found their original destination of Kansas not to their liking, although two of the families returned there the next spring.[77]

Several other immigrants settled in Elkhart and LaGrange Counties, two of whom would go on to hold leadership positions in Indiana-Michigan Amish Mennonite congregations.[78] Brothers Andrew and David Jantz—their last name would soon become Yontz—arrived in the United States with their family in 1874 at ages twelve and one, respectively. They initially settled near Belleville, Pennsylvania, where local Amish Mennonites had financially supported their move. Andrew later moved to Wayne County, Ohio, to work, then, having married, to his wife's home community of Topeka, Indiana. There he joined Maple Grove Amish Mennonite Church and was ordained a minister in 1903. Meanwhile, David and most of the rest of the family left Pennsylvania for southeastern Dakota Territory, where they had relatives. But he eventually joined his brother in Indiana and became a deacon at Clinton Frame Amish Mennonite Church east of Goshen.

The Scope of Innovation

The organizational ability demonstrated by Funk and others in facilitating the Russian Mennonite and Hutterite migrations was frequently replicated in the following decades. At the forefront of many of these initiatives was Prairie Street Mennonite Church, the Elkhart congregation founded after Funk started his publishing enterprise and brought Mennonites into the city. The nearest conference congregation was Olive Mennonite Church, nearly nine miles southwest of Funk's downtown business, so the small contingent of church members in Elkhart desired a closer place of worship—especially in winter.[79] After periodically meeting in homes, the Elkhart Mennonites in 1870 acquired property on the city's southern edge for a church building, which was constructed the next year. Funk was the first minister. Other than Germantown (Pa.) Mennonite Church, it was the first urban congregation for the Old Mennonites, who previously had been exclusively rural and usually worshiped in homogenous, family-centric enclaves. Prairie Street's founding members came from the families of Funk and his brother and early business partner, Abraham, plus John Snyder, an ordained minister who had been living north of Elkhart for fourteen years since moving from Snider County, Pennsylvania. As Mennonite activity in the city grew, so did the congregation and its diversity, which had sixty members by 1890. Among them was Russian Mennonite Brethren immigrant John F. Harms.[80] In 1880, two years after arriving in the United States and settling at Mountain Lake, Minnesota, Harms accepted an invitation from Funk to edit his new *Die Mennonitische Rundschau*, a German-language periodical for the immigrant communities on the Great Plains.[81] Harms also assisted in the production of *Herold der Wahrheit*. In 1884 he and his family moved to Kansas, where Harms became the founding editor of the first Mennonite Brethren periodical (which was initially printed by the Mennonite Publishing Company).[82]

Under Funk's leadership, and with freedoms resulting from the congregation's urban setting apart from the more tradition-minded rural church community, a creative, progressive spirit flourished at Prairie Street. The congregation began implementing wide-ranging and far-reaching programs, including children's and young people's meetings. The congregation also started holding services every Sunday rather than meeting every other week, as was customary. Two Prairie Street–born initiatives in particular would soon involve Amish Mennonites and Mennonites across the continent and profoundly shape the broader church.

In 1882, Funk and others at Prairie Street created the first Old Mennonite mission organization. In another sign of the evangelical influence on Funk, the congregation had been taking quarterly offerings for mission work.[83] In 1881, the Indiana Mennonite Conference suggested that its members take collections to help ministers defray the expenses of visiting struggling, underserved congregations and scattered members. Prairie Street put the conference measure into practice the next year by starting the Mennonite Evangelizing Committee. In its first year, it made only one disbursement: twenty-five dollars to the widely traveled preacher John S. Coffman. But in the following years the committee helped finance trips in all directions, from northern Michigan to Tennessee and from Pennsylvania to California. Even though under Prairie Street auspices, it soon became a de facto conference program, including members of other local congregations on its management committee and receiving contributions from Amish Mennonite and Mennonite individuals, Sunday schools, and congregations in Indiana and Michigan. But the Mennonite Evangelizing Committee would not remain localized for long. Aided by Funk's promotion in his periodicals and striking a chord in the broader Mennonite and Amish Mennonite church, the committee was soon receiving support from across the United States and Ontario. In 1891, the committee received an endorsement from the Western Amish Mennonite Conference.[84] As

George Lambert in India, 1897. MCUSAA–Goshen.

With his colorful, even flamboyant nature, George Lambert proved to be quite a contrast to the more staid Indiana-Michigan Mennonite Conference.[1] He had been a Mennonite Brethren in Christ (MBIC) minister, serving congregations in Kent County, Michigan, and Elkhart County, Indiana, until he withdrew from the denomination in 1897. He would eventually join Prairie Street Mennonite Church in Elkhart. Even though Lambert was not yet a member of the conference, he called an 1897 meeting of Indiana-Michigan leaders to consider responding to the needs in famine-ravaged India. The meeting, held at the Mennonite Publishing Company office in Elkhart, resulted in the creation of the Home and Foreign Relief Commission (which would eventually become Mennonite Board of Missions).[2]

Despite his high profile and significant contributions, Lambert's time in Indiana-Michigan would be short. He became dogged by accusations of improper relations with women, tobacco use, shady business deals, and conducting marriages of non–Old Mennonite Church members (one of them his own daughter).[3] Lambert, who was involved in real estate, was finally excommunicated in December 1911 when he was sued over a property dispute.[4] He immediately warned the disciplining bishops—Jacob K. Bixler, David Burkholder, and D. A. Yoder—to expect "proceedings of a heavy suit of justice."[5] In February 1912, Lambert filed a lawsuit in Elkhart Superior Court seeking $10,000 from the three men for slander. (Curiously, the bishops avoided church censure for being named defendants in a lawsuit, the same transgression that precipitated Lambert's expulsion.)

The case never came to trial. Two and half years later Lambert withdrew his suit because, according to his attorney, he "does not desire to be detained any longer in his work; not that he has no cause of action."[6] Lambert briefly rejoined the MBIC before transferring to the Evangelical Association.[7] But his funeral was held in an Elkhart MBIC church in 1928.[8]

---

1. Robert S. Kreider, email to author, May 10, 2006.
2. Minute book, Home and Foreign Relief Commission collection (VIII-1-1), box 1, MCUSAA–Goshen.
3. See J. E. Hartzler collection (HM 1-62), box 1, folders 5–8; and box 24, folder 20, MCUSAA–Goshen.
4. Undated, untitled document, John F. Funk collection (HM 1-1-6), box 65, folder 4, MCUSAA–Goshen.
5. Geo. Lambert to David Burkholder, Jacob Bixler, and David Yoder, December 26, 1911, J. E. Hartzler collection (HM 1-62), box 1, folder 6, MCUSAA–Goshen.
6. "$10,000 Slander Suit Dismissed," undated clipping from unidentified newspaper, J. E. Hartzler collection (HM 1-62), box 24, folder 20, MCUSAA–Goshen.
7. J. C. Wenger, *The Mennonites in Indiana and Michigan* (Scottdale, PA: Herald Press, 1961), 298. Through a series of denominational mergers, the Evangelical Association became part of the United Methodist Church.
8. Kreider email.

a result of this growing interest, Prairie Street's Mennonite Evangelizing Committee was reconstituted in 1892 as the Mennonite Evangelizing Board of America to serve all Old Mennonite area conferences. The board the next year selected its first mission worker, sending former Mennonite Publishing Company employee M. S. Steiner to Chicago.

The start of domestic ministry was naturally followed by overseas work. In 1897, in response to a well-publicized famine in India, the board, by now known as the Mennonite Evangelizing and Benevolent Board, formed the Home and Foreign Relief Commission to raise funds and distribute aid in the British colony. One of the commission's founders, George Lambert, a former minister in Daniel Brenneman's Mennonite Brethren in Christ, went to India to oversee the work. After he returned to the United States, he wrote the 1898 book *India, the Horror-Stricken Empire*, which helped stir church members to meet India's spiritual as well as physical needs. At a special meeting at Prairie Street Mennonite Church in November 1898, physician William D. and Alice Thut Page, Elkhart County residents who had earlier been mission workers in Chicago, and widower and minister J. A. Ressler of Scottdale, Pennsylvania, were selected as the first Old Mennonite foreign missionaries. Funk led the commissioning.[85] The program continued to grow, and in 1915 the organization, renamed Mennonite Board of Missions and Charities (MBM) after a merger with an Ohio organization, appointed George L. Bender as its first full-time administrator and erected its headquarters in Elkhart. Bender had left the Mennonite Publishing Company after six years to work for the post office and teach. Before being hired by MBM, he had also been the longtime volunteer treasurer of the mission board and its earlier incarnations. With his appointment, Bender became the first of many salaried Mennonite denominational executives in Elkhart County. His new office, just four blocks from Prairie Street Mennonite Church, was a three-story brick building that included meeting space and accommodations for missionaries in transit, as well as living facilities for Bender and his family.

At the same time, the Elkhart Institute of Science, Industry, and the Arts was taking the church's first tentative steps in higher education. Prairie Street member Henry A. Mumaw started the school in 1894, challenging North American Mennonites and Amish Mennonites' long-held suspicions of higher education. There had been a couple of short-lived attempts earlier by more progressive Mennonites: Abraham Hunsicker's Freeland Seminary and the Wadsworth (Ohio) Institute, operated by the General Conference Mennonite Church from 1868 to 1878. For many Old Mennonites, such enterprises were filled with worldly influences to undermine young people's faith and commitment to the church. Scholarship, critics feared, filled students' heads with questions and doubts about unassailable biblical truths and the collective wisdom of God's people. Nevertheless, by the late nineteenth century, more and more of the church's young people were going to college, particularly to colleges affiliated with other Christian denominations, since there obviously were no Mennonite options. That made concerns of losing members a self-fulfilling prophecy.[86] One who left for college—and subsequently left the church—was Ben Boller, son of Catherine and deacon George Boller of Maple Grove Amish Mennonite Church at Topeka, Indiana. Ben went to Hillsdale College, a Freewill Baptist school in southern Michigan, and then to Yale Divinity School before becoming a Congregational minister.[87]

From the beginning, Mennonite and Amish Mennonite school supporters considered seeking official church sponsorship for the Elkhart Institute but realized that the broader constituency was not quite ready for such a step. So Mumaw began the school as a private venture in 1894. A homeopathic physician by profession, his vision was of a business school. By the time he had arrived in Elkhart, he had already started and sold several such schools in Ohio and Indiana.[88] After one year of operation, the Elkhart Institute was incorporated with an all-Mennonite board and Mumaw as its president. The school soon started to strengthen its church connections. More Bible classes were added to the curriculum, and in 1896 it relocated from downtown Elkhart to a new building across the street from the Prairie Street meetinghouse. Although started by Mennonites, the Elkhart Institute also drew significant Amish Mennonite support. Jonas S. Hartzler left his ministerial assignment at Maple Grove to join the faculty in 1895, and the Indiana-Michigan Amish Mennonite Conference officially endorsed the school in 1899. The institute remained on Prairie Street for seven years until continued growth prompted the need for larger facilities. Enticed by an attractive offer from the city of Goshen, the school relocated to the city's south side in 1903 and was renamed Goshen College.

Prairie Street was not the only place in the conference developing new expressions of church life. Once Coffman successfully made revival meetings palatable, a number of other Indiana-Michigan leaders embarked on this now-acceptable way of building the church, often with fantastic results. Amish Mennonite bishops D. J. Johns of the Clinton Frame congregation near Goshen and Jonathan P. Smucker from Nappanee conducted a three-year series of meetings at Oak Grove Amish Mennonite Church in Ohio, resulting in the baptism of 112 new members during that span.[89] Revival meetings became so popular and were considered so important that the 1915 Indiana-Michigan Mennonite Conference assembly included a session on "Conditions Tending to a Successful Revival Meeting." The use of English also increased, with more preaching being done in the language. In 1887 the Mennonite conference declared its support for an English-language hymnal, and the Amish Mennonites did likewise eight years later. Sunday schools became commonplace by 1880, with hardly a congregation not having one. Clinton Frame hosted the first Old Mennonite Sunday school convention in 1892.

In 1905 the Indiana-Michigan Amish Mennonite Conference approved its first constitution and bylaws, while that same year a committee was appointed to draft a constitution for the Mennonite conference. That institutional impetus, however, didn't remain localized. In the 1850s, several Virginia Mennonite ministers earnestly worked for but ultimately failed to develop interest in a "general conference": a regular *Diener-Versammlung*-type gathering as a forum for churchwide discernment.[90] But it was an idea that eventually gained favor across the church, including in both Indiana-Michigan conferences. As early as 1866, the Indiana Mennonites expressed their support for a regular assembly of all Old Mennonite area conferences, and the Amish Mennonites in 1895 appointed D. J. Johns as a representative to a series of meetings to explore the possibilities of a general conference. At an 1897 planning session, twelve of the seventy participants were from the two Indiana-Michigan conferences. Johns was appointed to the committee that organized the first Mennonite Church General Conference, which was held in 1898 at Holdeman Mennonite Church, Wakarusa, Indiana, where he was selected as the first assistant moderator. J. S. Hartzler was one of two secretaries, and Jacob Shank, a minister at Olive Mennonite Church north of Wakarusa, was named treasurer; Funk gave the conference sermon from Ephesians 4:1-7.[91] The two Indiana-Michigan conferences' participation made them, in effect, charter members of the Mennonite Church.

The developments of the late nineteenth century had other effects as well. Women had long contributed to the cause of the church, but their efforts had been behind the scenes and uncredited. But the implementation of formal mission and education work gave them new opportunities for recognition, respect, and legitimacy as missionaries and as Elkhart Institute instructors. Elsie Drange and Eva Harder, serving with MBM in India, spoke at the 1908 Indiana-Michigan Mennonite Conference annual gathering, an interesting occurrence given the prevailing belief against women teaching men. At home, Prairie Street Mennonite Church was again on the cutting edge, beginning the first sewing circle in the conference in 1900.[92] Sixty women attended the inaugural meeting—so many that they ran out of chairs and some women had to stand. Most of the group's work went to benefit the mission in Chicago.[93] Two years before the meeting at Prairie Street, the women of Clinton Frame Amish Mennonite Church were invited to a local Lutheran "ladies aid." "We were very much impressed with what we saw and heard," reported one Clinton Frame participant. "They had Scripture reading and prayer and were a busy, social bunch."[94] But the congregation's sewing circle wasn't organized until 1907. The new organization's constitution was written in consultation with Clinton Frame bishop D. J. Johns, which meant the women's efforts were officially approved by the male leadership.[95] Another new avenue opened with the development of Sunday schools, allowing women to serve as teachers, superintendents, committee members, and even presenters at Sunday school conventions. Both conferences also considered the ordination of deaconesses, although no plan ever materialized.[96]

With the arrival of John F. Funk from Illinois, Daniel Brenneman from Ohio, John S. Coffman from Virginia, George L. Bender from Maryland, and others from elsewhere, the region was firmly established as the Mennonite and Amish Mennonite epicenter. The subsequent advent of mission organizations, publishing, higher education, Sunday schools, and revival meetings generated a fresh vitality in the Mennonite Church. They also produced new tensions. Both would dramatically change Indiana-Michigan.

3
Coming Together, Coming Apart

On a June day in 1916, trustee Noah Long took a ladder, brush, and paint to Clinton Frame Amish Mennonite Church east of Goshen, Indiana. With a few strokes, he had eliminated the third word in the congregation's name posted above the entrance to the meetinghouse.[1] Clinton Frame was one the oldest Amish Mennonite congregations in the state as well as one of the most prominent, blessed with an impressive parade of leaders through the years who served not the congregation but the entire Indiana-Michigan fellowship and beyond. But their Amish Mennonite identity was about to formally cease. On June 8, 1916, delegates to the Amish Mennonite conference's annual meeting approved uniting with their Mennonite counterparts, who would take similar action at their assembly in the fall. The name of the new body would be an old one: Indiana-Michigan Mennonite Conference. Shortly afterward, Long made the change strikingly apparent on the sign for the newly renamed Clinton Frame Mennonite Church. It was literally a sign of the times—and the times were most certainly changing.

For many church members, the word *Amish* was simply an adjective. Amish Mennonites were still considered Mennonite, just a different type, one created by a schism among Swiss-German adherents more than two centuries earlier. Now that split was being mended, at least on a small scale, by the union of the Indiana-Michigan Amish Mennonite and Mennonite conferences, rendering the Amish descriptor unnecessary. "We are once again made one in Christ Jesus," exulted Mennonite conference secretary J. S. Hartzler, himself of Amish Mennonite background, in the minutes after the Mennonite conference's approval of the merger in October 1916.[2] Across North America, the bonds between Amish Mennonites and Mennonites had been strengthening

John S. Coffman. MCUSAA–Goshen.

as they joined together in the new general conference, missions, publishing, education, and more. The *Gospel Herald*, the official Mennonite Church periodical and successor to John F. Funk's *Herald of Truth*, in 1917 noted the church-wide trend of the "gradual obliteration of the old line that used to separate the Mennonites from the Amish. We rejoice in our present unity, and pray for the time to come when the name 'Mennonite' may stand for the same things where ever the name is spoken."[3] They all were believed to now be the same kind of Mennonite.

But what kind was that? It wasn't a new question. Since the start of the Anabaptist movement in the sixteenth century, church members had discussed, debated, and argued the beliefs that should define the faith. In the 1850s, Amish Mennonites and Mennonites in Indiana and Michigan who were open to innovation and those wanting to preserve traditional understandings started going their separate ways, resulting in the birth of the Old Order groups. The Indiana-Michigan Mennonites also disconnected from the more progressive Daniel Brenneman–led faction, which wanted too much change too quickly.

By the advent of the twentieth century, however, the issue in the two conferences was not whether to change but what to change and by how much. New ideas were increasingly clashing with long-held and fiercely guarded beliefs and practice. What enhanced faithfulness and what threatened it? In a provocative 1896 address titled "The Spirit of Progress" and delivered to the Elkhart Institute students and staff, school board chair and noted evangelist John S. Coffman proclaimed that "true progress depends on improvement that does more than bring conveniences to man, does more than develop man's intellect; it is a grace that *makes man* better."[4] Such progress was, in short, centered in self-giving love, not selfishness, and engaged with, not fully detached from, the world. Coffman went on to applaud recent non-Mennonite activism such as a petition against military instruction in public schools and an international peace conference. Education is an essential part of the church's work, he said, so people can be "firmly established in the truths of Christianity."[5] Yet he also underscored the traditional necessity of withstanding the pressures of the world. "Let us never say there is no danger!" Coffman stated. "Only the true spirit of progress given, and directed, and kept by the power of God will form a pavilion round about us in which we can dwell in safety from the encroachments of popular opinion and worldly aspirations that will come dashing against us with the fury of a sweeping cyclone."[6]

While Coffman was articulating a proactive, positive faith of service to others, others in the Indiana-Michigan constituency continued to emphasize aspects of traditional, defensive separation that they felt were disappearing. In his conference sermon at the 1898 Amish Mennonite assembly, J. H. McGowen, longtime minister of West Market Street Amish Mennonite Church in Nappanee, Indiana, urged the church to take great care to maintain the boundaries between itself and the world. "Nonresistance, nonconformity, nonswearing of oaths, the ban, the holy kiss, the prayer covering and a number of other subjects which I have not time to discuss at present should be taught from the pulpit with more zeal and earnestness than they are in many cases, for we are living in dangerous times," he preached.[7]

Appearance was the most visible indicator of nonconformity, the first line of protection against the world's ways. It was the outward expression of a church member's loyalties. If simplicity in attire were modified, other standards and prohibitions would no doubt be more vulnerable. The focus was usually on women, such as the styles of their prayer coverings and dresses but also hairstyles and jewelry. But the men were also starting to receive attention. Indiana-Michigan Mennonite Conference said in 1891 that it was unjust for women to be held to "plain" standards while the men had fashion freedom.[8] In 1897, the conference specified that men's "standing collars with tipped-down corners, fancy neckties, jewelry, and other things of this nature" were "inconsistent with the Gospel of Christ."[9] The next year the Mennonites considered the question, "Is it becoming for brethren to wear the full beard in winter (except the mustache) and in the summer shave smooth?" No, the assembly ruled, and went on record opposing any changes to facial-hair styles.[10]

Such issues were especially acute at Clinton Frame, where hats and bustles on women and long mustaches on men had started to become popular. Even the congregation's bishop, D. J. Johns, wore a tie and "lay-down" collar.[11] Other Amish Mennonite leaders began pushing Clinton Frame to become less worldly, and in 1889 the congregation voted to tighten its discipline regarding attire as well as to eliminate open communion. Those who dissented would be expelled.[12] Tensions between the two factions churned for three years, and by the spring of 1892 two separate worshiping bodies using the same meetinghouse had emerged, with the progressives meeting on Sunday afternoons. But whose building actually was it? It was a new structure, built in 1888, and both sides claimed at least partial ownership. The progressives had been able to continue to have access to the church thanks to the building's janitor, who was a member of the faction. That changed one evening in June 1892. A conservative trustee replaced the lock, with another holding the lantern and a third, a progressive, standing by and fruitlessly arguing with his colleagues.[13] Locked out, the progressive group found a new home, eventually organizing themselves as Silver Street Mennonite Church east of Goshen and joining the Amish-originated Central Conference of Mennonites.[14] Johns wanted to repay the departing church members their share of the four-year-old Clinton Frame building. In an amazing example of love and grace, he gave them $1,000—his entire savings. Clinton Frame eventually raised the money to reimburse their bishop.[15]

Funk's Fall

Disputes over attire also ostensibly caused the downfall of John F. Funk. In 1902, the influential innovator was relieved of his bishopric at Prairie Street Mennonite Church in Elkhart after trying to enforce the conference's regulation dress on the Elkhart Institute. But his discipline was actually the result of a years-long accumulation of factors indicative of the forces making inroads in the church—many of which, ironically, could be directly attributed to Funk. The formation of organized church structures and institutions as vehicles for ministry could become conduits for power plays when differing understandings of faithfulness clashed.

The situation, which started in the mid-1890s, was often called the "Elkhart problems." It was a simple moniker for a tangled mess of associations resulting from the inbred leadership of the Mennonite organizations based in the city. When troubles afflicted one, all were inevitably affected. In addition to leading the Mennonite Publishing Company (MPC) and being ordained Prairie Street's bishop in 1892, Funk was also the first president of Prairie Street's Mennonite Evangelizing Commit-

George L. Bender. MCUSAA–Goshen.

tee. After it became the churchwide Mennonite Evangelizing Board, he helped organize the Home and Foreign Relief Commission under the board's auspices in 1897 to respond to needs in India.[16] Evangelist Coffman had been the Mennonite Evangelizing Committee's secretary and was president of the Elkhart Institute board, often raising money for the school when out preaching across the church. George L. Bender was treasurer of the Mennonite Evangelizing Board and the Elkhart Institute board and was a Home and Foreign Relief Commission founder. A. B. Kolb, who was married to Funk's daughter Phoebe, was president of the evangelizing board and an institute board member. All of them were at one time MPC employees, brought to Elkhart by Funk, and all were members of Prairie Street Mennonite Church.

Compounding the internal Elkhart stresses were challenges from elsewhere in the church that Funk considered attempts to undermine his work. He was sensitive to criticism and thought powerful elements in the church were constantly trying to start a rival publishing ministry. While Funk's perceptions sound almost conspiratorial in nature, competing movements were undeniably at work. One was the Mennonite Book and Tract Society, formed in 1892 in Ohio, with prominent supporters from Missouri, Pennsylvania, and Virginia as well as Indiana. In fact, Elkhart County and MPC provided the initial leadership. The first president was MPC's business manager, J. S. Lehman, while Bender was treasurer and Coffman was tract editor. M. S. Steiner, another MPC employee, was secretary. Rounding out the officers was vice president David Burkholder, minister at North Main Street Mennonite Church in Nappanee. Despite those connections, however, relations between the two publishers quickly became rocky as the society directly competed with Funk's work.[17] The tensions helped severely damage Funk's relationships with many of his MPC associates. A notable exception was Lehman, a Funk ally who was accused of trying to take over the society.[18] Bender, meanwhile, blamed Lehman for his ouster from the relief commission and claimed that MPC refused to print his monthly Mennonite Evangelizing Board report.[19] At the same time, opposition to Funk and his publishing enterprise was stirring, particularly among more conservative Mennonites in the East.

Because of the proliferation of institutions locally, Elkhart had become the de facto center of the Mennonite Church. It also meant that the Elkhart problems didn't remain localized. The roads bringing in various influences also took them out. Influential bishop Aaron Loucks of Scottdale, Pennsylvania, bemoaned in 1898 that such a distressing "condition of affairs exist [sic] at headquarters. Were it at Scottdale or Masontown [Pa.] or some other individual church it would not matter so much even if the whole thing went to pieces. That would be the end of it, but to have a schism grow out of things at E[lkhart], would be bad."[20]

The problems were part of the growing pains of an infant denomination. But an equally important factor was Funk's leadership style. His phenomenal record as a creator of church institutions was born out of his status as a Mennonite outsider, geographically if not politically. Chicago and even Elkhart in the 1860s and '70s were on the church's frontier, away from the constraints of established Mennonitism as found in the older communities of Ohio, Pennsylvania, and Virginia. In the Midwest, Funk not only absorbed and formulated new ideas but also had great space to implement them, and he took full advantage of it with his vision and ambition. He didn't have to be very flexible or diplomatic because those traits are necessary only when dealing with others—and Funk was practically working alone and in relative isolation. But that had changed by the 1890s with the growing reception of his institutions and with his ordination as bishop. Funk was officially sanctioned as a church leader, which required skills of tact and

diplomacy. That could be quite
confining for an individual accus-
tomed to operating heavily on his
own initiative. After decades of
working to establish a new order
in the untidy church, Funk saw
his new responsibility as maintaining it. "I have firmly stood for
this church and the word of God,
and also for the rules and order of
the church," he defiantly asserted
in the midst of the Elkhart problems, thus positioning his foes
as acting antithetically to church
standards.[21] The personal attri-

Henry A. Mumaw. MCUSAA–Goshen.

butes that made him successful on the edges of the church made him
an uncompromising and authoritarian insider to the new Mennonite
establishment that he started.

It was the Elkhart Institute specifically that led to the events that
caused Funk's demise as a church leader. Within a few years of opening in 1894, the school was drawing students from as far away as New
Hampshire and Texas as well as from more traditional Mennonite and
Amish Mennonite locations in Illinois, Ohio, and Pennsylvania. These
young women and men brought with them different understandings of
belief and practice, such as what was appropriate to wear. As the spiritual leader of the congregation attended by most students and employees, Funk strongly and repeatedly pushed school officials to more diligently enforce conference regulations. He soon became a harsh critic of
the institute, describing it as infused with "a spirit of arrogance, self-
righteousness, self-conceit, a spirit of contention, a disrespect for their
elders or superiors, become proud, vain, boastful and even abusive, irrev-
erent busybodies, heady and in many ways lead an inconsistent life."[22]

The Elkhart Institute changed course in 1896, when Coffman was
elected board president over incumbent and founder Henry A. Mumaw.
The winsome Coffman had been authorized the previous year to raise
money for the school during his many evangelistic trips. His efforts
were vital for not only generating financial support but also expanding

Elkhart Institute Class of 1901. MCUSAA–Goshen.

and strengthening the school's connections beyond Indiana. When the institute was incorporated in 1895, most of its stakeholders were Mennonites and Amish Mennonites.[23] Mumaw, however, had a more business-minded approach. He hadn't repudiated the Elkhart Institute's church identity but seemed willing to downplay it for the sake of success, at least in the short term.[24] Having lost control of the school he had started and unhappy with its direction, Mumaw withdrew and began a competitor, the Elkhart Normal and Business College, in 1898. Funk's conflict with the institute prompted him to align himself with Mumaw, which put Funk and Coffman on opposite sides. He dropped Coffman from the *Herald of Truth* masthead without explanation in 1897.

Tensions reached the breaking point in the fall of 1900 when some Elkhart Institute faculty members, students, and supporters left Prairie Street Mennonite Church and began holding their own worship services. The defectors were "the harvest of a seed sown by J. S. Coffman," accused Funk. "They wanted to have the school run the church and do just as they pleased and when I began to preach the truth as the Gospel gives it they could not stand it."[25] In January 1901, the nascent congregation invited bishop Daniel Kauffman from Missouri, a rising conservative leader and the first Mennonite Church General Conference moderator, to lead revival meetings. At their conclusion, ten converts asked for baptism. Not surprisingly, resident bishop Funk refused, so Kauffman conducted the baptisms himself. It was, at the very least, an irregular development. He defended his action by claiming that the newly baptized believers should be regarded not as part of either Prairie Street or a breakaway congregation but "as if they had been baptized into Mennonite Zion Church, Morgan Co., Mo., where my church home is."[26] Funk was justifiably irate at Kauffman for blatantly usurping authority.

Kauffman and the late Coffman, who had died of stomach cancer the previous year, were not the only ones to incur Funk's anger. After doing so much to bring together the disparate Mennonite and Amish Mennonite groups in North America, Funk now sought to drive wedges between them. Science Ridge Mennonite Church at Sterling, Illinois—the home congregation of Elkhart Institute principal Noah Byers and where Funk had made his first attempt to participate in the Lord's Supper four decades earlier—had appealed to Indiana-Michigan Amish Mennonite Conference to help find a place of worship for the group that broke away from Prairie Street. Funk called for an apology from both Science Ridge and Illinois Mennonite Conference, of which the congregation was a member, for "sowing discord" by meddling in Indiana-Michigan affairs.[27] Locally, the new Elkhart congregation was supported by Amish Mennonite bishops D. J. Johns of Clinton Frame and Jonathan Kurtz of Maple Grove, and one of its ministers was J. S. Hartzler, an institute teacher and former preacher at Maple Grove.[28] Furthermore, the Amish Mennonite students were considered particularly problematic because they came "from various states and conference districts, where the customs and church regulations were sometimes quite different . . . and some of which we did not approve," according to A. C. Kolb, the institute board's first secretary.[29] That propelled Funk to see them and the rest of the Amish Mennonite fellowship as opponents who should no longer be permitted to take communion with Mennonites because of "differences in housekeeping and differences of views."[30]

Another Funk target was the Mennonite Church General Conference, a cause he had earlier promoted with gusto. At the first conference session, in 1898 at Wakarusa, a committee was appointed to evaluate organizations that wanted to be endorsed as "church institutions" and "worthy of the support and encouragement of our people in general."[31] Committee members were Johns, Kauffman, and Daniel H. Bender, George L. Bender's brother from Tub in southwestern Pennsylvania. They issued a general invitation to all entities that wanted to be considered for denominational approval. The Elkhart Institute was among those that responded and was investigated. The committee's report was positive, highlighting the school's "good moral standards," strong student interest in the Bible and church work, and the "sisters" wearing the required prayer covering during daily chapel services. The report also noted that some students need "to make some improvement" in "worldly conformity," but the committee downplayed it because the students were no different from many other people in the church.[32] Delegates at the 1900 general conference endorsed the Elkhart Institute as well as the Mennonite Book and Tract Society and four other organizations as "church institutions."

Conspicuously absent was the Mennonite Publishing Company, the oldest and most recognized Old Mennonite institution in North America. Funk refused to submit his business to official scrutiny because he saw only two potential results, both negative.[33] The general conference could approve the MPC, which, in his estimation, would make the company directly accountable to the general conference, which could then be parlayed into a takeover of the company. The second possibility was that the MPC would receive a bad report—not an implausible scenario in Funk's mind—and thus undermine his and his company's service to the church. Funk also argued that through actions such as endorsing institutions, the general conference was overstepping its original purpose as an advisory body and becoming legislative.

In the fall of 1900, Funk started a campaign for Indiana-Michigan Mennonite Conference to withdraw from participation in the general conference. Although the real reasons were more self-serving and less idealistic, Funk couched the proposal's purpose as promoting unity. The older and more conservative Mennonite area conferences, such as Lancaster, Franconia, and Virginia, were extremely cool to the idea of a general conference. Until they decided to join it, Funk argued, Indiana-Michigan should step back "in order to preserve union and harmony between this conference and our eastern conferences."[34] It was a plan drenched in irony, since relations between the comparatively progressive Funk and Mennonites in Pennsylvania and Virginia were frequently strained. His proposal concluded by revealing his true goal: "until this shall be accomplished, we protest against the general conference taking any action that shall affect the church or members of the church in this district or any institution located in this district."[35] Funk wanted to protect his publishing company from general conference interference. He tested the proposal with others in Indiana-Michigan and received a mixed response. Amos Cripe, minister at Shore Mennonite Church in LaGrange County, supported the measure, calling the general conference

> one of those things . . . that cause misunderstanding, strife and contension [*sic*], and will eventually cause the good old time tried principles and doctrines of the Mennonite church to be a thing of the past. I feel that we can make no improvement on the doctrines, practices and rules of our church, as practiced by the old fathers of the church, that will stand the test as well as that that has been in use for hundreds of years by our Mennonite people.[36]

But Yellow Creek minister Noah Metzler pointedly told Funk that "if the Lord willing I expect to support and encourage the General Conference with my presence. I cannot see that it is the Conference which causes trouble but such work which was done by you in your home church."[37] Funk's proposal was never formally presented to Indiana-Michigan Mennonite Conference.

Funk had long asserted that, despite the churchwide ramifications, the Elkhart problems were fundamentally a local matter and should be handled by the local congregation and its bishop. But by late 1900, Funk could no longer withstand the growing pressure for outside intervention. After the withdrawal of the Elkhart Institute group from Prairie Street, twelve bishops from across the church developed a plan for addressing the situation. Funk agreed, and it was approved at the Indiana-Michigan Mennonite Conference annual session in October 1901. Five men were named to an investigating committee: George R.

Brunk from Kansas, Ira J. Buckwalter from Ohio, Lewis J. Heatwole from Virginia, and Pennsylvanians Isaac Eby and Henry D. Heller. They considered some thirty accusations against Funk, including marrying a non-Mennonite couple, calling the Elkhart Institute "Satan's synagogue," ordering the lock changed on the Prairie Street church door, overseeing the deteriorating financial condition of his Mennonite Publishing Company, and creating a "partnership with the ungodly."[38]

At a special Indiana-Michigan Mennonite Conference meeting at Prairie Street Mennonite Church on January 31, 1902, the investigating committee presented its final report, condensing its findings into seven wide-ranging charges against Funk: holding unfair counsel meetings, making deceptive and erroneous statements, exhibiting "self-will in Church government," violating conference rules, using "hard and unbecoming" language, being "uncharitable and impatient" in his ministry, and refusing to allow other ministers in good standing into the Prairie Street pulpit.[39] "We unanimously agreed from the testimonies received that Bishop John F. Funk has not been altogether faithful in his duties as bishop," the committee concluded. It called on him to publicly confess and then recommended that he be suspended from his office for one year. The reason for the suspension was not punishment, the committee contended, but to allow time so that Funk, "by his conduct toward his ministers, deacons, and members, may so gain their confidence that they would be prompted to again accept him as their acting bishop." During this time, he would retain all rights and privileges of the position but simply not carry its duties. After a year, Funk could be reinstated by a two-thirds majority vote of the congregations under oversight.

While he received the harshest terms from the investigating committee, Funk also received vindication.[40] Among the committee's other decisions was that the Elkhart Institute splinter group violated church order by calling a congregational meeting without the bishop's permission and by withdrawing from Prairie Street. Daniel Kauffman was instructed to publicly confess for having baptized participants in the group. Its ministers, J. S. Hartzler and Samuel Yoder, were also reprimanded. Prairie Street deacon Daniel Coffman, a brother to J. S. Coffman, was told to confess for sidestepping the bishop by issuing letters of membership transfer after Funk had denied them. Finally, the committee even ruled that the young people of the institute needed to adhere to church regulations about attire, which was the central issue leading to Funk's censure.

Despite those rulings, Funk responded to the committee's findings in what had become a typical defensive and self-righteous manner. "If the envy of my brethren, the envy of some of my fellow bishops has consigned me to prison for a year, I am faring well yet as compared with Paul . . . & I rejoice that I am accounted worthy to suffer for Christ's sake," he recorded in his diary.[41] His sentence didn't end after one year, however, as he was never returned to his bishop responsibilities. But Funk, who would live to age ninety-four, would remain active and become a sort of grand old man of Indiana-Michigan Mennonite Conference. A year after his discipline, he gave the closing prayer at the 1903 conference assembly. Funk served as secretary in 1907 and would hold periodic committee appointments. He preached the conference sermon in 1911, lamenting, "Church discipline is another thing that is fading away like the dew before the morning sun."[42] At the 1920 conference assembly, eighty-five-year-old Funk read Scripture and led in prayer.

The loss of his bishopric was the beginning of the end of Funk's highly visible and influential tenure on the churchwide scene. By the 1890s, some church members twenty to thirty years younger than Funk were rising to leadership.[43] They adopted the modern instruments introduced by Funk but for more conservative causes. Among them was a publishing ministry, owned by the church rather than privately, to promote orthodoxy and unity through print materials. In 1905, after more than a decade of discussion and discernment, forty-one-year-old bishop Aaron Loucks led the creation of the Gospel Witness Company in his hometown of Scottdale in southwestern Pennsylvania, to produce a periodical to compete with Funk. The first issue of *Gospel Witness*, edited by Daniel Kauffman, came off the press in April 1905. Although privately held, its founders' goal was to eventually turn the company over to the Mennonite Church, which it did in 1907, and was rechristened as the Mennonite Publication Board. It quickly purchased the Mennonite Book and Tract Society, which included many of the same men involved with the new publication board. The Indiana-Michigan Mennonite and Amish Mennonite conferences had both expressed support for an official denominational publishing house, and they were among the nine area conferences with representatives on an exploration committee.

Meanwhile, the MPC was in serious trouble. It had to declare bankruptcy in 1904, and its physical plant was extensively damaged by fire in 1907. The next year, Funk was finally forced to sell his company's periodicals to the Mennonite Publication Board. It offered $8,000, well below the MPC's original asking price of $20,500. The company then presented a compromise price of $14,250. But the new board held firm to its $8,000 offer, and the MPC had to capitulate.[44] The last issue of the *Herald of Truth* was dated April 9, 1908. It then merged with the *Gospel Witness* to create the *Gospel Herald*, which became the longtime official magazine of the Mennonite Church, with Kauffman as its first editor.[45] Minus its periodicals, the MPC would continue to function, but in a very limited and financially strapped condition, until its corporate charter expired in 1925.

Funk was also left in personal poverty. A farm he owned with his son-in-law, A. B. Kolb, produced fruits and vegetables that fed their families through the winter. But by spring, all that was usually left to eat was potatoes, a diet that sustained the Funks and Kolbs until their gardens started producing again. Buildings never again received a fresh coat of paint, and Funk's wardrobe was largely composed of secondhand clothes. When he died in 1930, at the age of ninety-five, he was buried in a vest and coat given to him by friend and former coworker George Lambert because he could no longer fit into them. Earlier, Kolb had given his father-in-law his straight coat when he left the Mennonite Church. The reason for the Kolb family's departure was the Mennonite Publication Board's apparent failure to uphold its commitment to Funk. When he sold his periodicals to the board, Funk's compensation was to include a lifetime pension. But the board stopped payment after a year, claiming Funk had found other sources of income, which voided the agreement.[46] Phoebe and A. B.'s twin sons, Jacob Clemens Kolb and John Funk Kolb, eventually joined the Episcopal Church and became priests.

Missions Movement

The Elkhart problems were huge and consumed much time and energy. But they were not indicative of the condition of the rest of the two

Indiana-Michigan conferences, which had been infused with a spirit of optimism and vitality. Organizations such as Mennonite Board of Missions, Goshen College, Sunday schools, and sewing circles dramatically increased religious relevance and generated energy. Amish Mennonites and Mennonites had unprecedented opportunities to practically apply their faith. One of them was the Indiana-Michigan Mennonite Mission Board. Among the Old Mennonites, the conference had been on the cutting edge with its creation of the Mennonite Evangelizing Committee in 1882. While the committee morphed into the churchwide Mennonite Board of Missions, by 1907 five area conferences had organized their own mission agencies to grow the church in their respective regions. The movement soon returned to Indiana-Michigan, and the Mennonite conference spent time at its 1908 assembly discussing the question of starting a local mission board.

Thanks in no small part to Goshen College, missions enjoyed a high profile in Indiana-Michigan. Noah Byers had made it a central component of the Elkhart Institute when he assumed leadership of the school in 1898. He was a graduate of Northwestern University in Evanston, Illinois, where he had been active in student evangelism organizations and even considered becoming a foreign missionary himself. Institute board chair John S. Coffman convinced Byers to become the school's administrator by describing it as a mission endeavor.[47] At the same time, India's physical and spiritual needs were unfolding, capturing imaginations and passions at the institute. Students committed themselves to supporting an orphan, the funds to be administered by missionaries J. A. Ressler and William and Alice Thut Page. In 1900, students Jacob Burkhard and Mary M. Yoder were married and sailed for India with the denominational mission board. In 1902, two more students, Bertha Zook and Irvin R. Detweiler, also wed and went to India. During a furlough in 1903, Ressler, a widower, married Bible instructor Lina Zook, a former worker at the Chicago Mennonite mission, and they spent the next five years in India. After the Elkhart Institute relocated to Goshen in 1903, the college's Young People's Christian Association financially supported the mission work in India, conducted weekly Bible studies on campus, and organized a Sunday school in East Goshen. In 1906, the college sponsored a series of meetings about missions and evangelistic work led by Detweiler and J. E. Hartzler, a LaGrange County native and popular evangelist.[48] In 1910, Goshen students assumed preaching responsibility at the struggling Barker Street Amish Mennonite Church, just across the border in southern Michigan.[49] Because of growing interest, Byers even proposed changing the name of Goshen's Bible department to Missionary Training School.[50]

With such a surge in interest and energy, the Indiana-Michigan Mennonite Conference approved the idea of a conference mission board in 1911. At its first regular meeting in May 1912, the new mission board's executive committee decided to establish a fund for ministers to visit needy areas and to work with the Indiana-Michigan Amish Mennonite Conference in exploring possible mission work on Goshen's north side (which was later deemed not feasible).[51] The Amish Mennonites were quite willing to work with their Mennonite brothers and sisters and in 1913 gave official approval to the Indiana-Michigan Mennonite Mission Board's new constitution. The Amish Mennonites had also become increasingly mission-minded, although they stressed congregational rather than conference initiatives. The conference in 1907 urged each congregation to organize a "Mission Study Class" and to annually hold two worship services on missions. Two years later the conference encouraged its members to take regular offerings for mission work. A conference evangelistic committee was created to assist congregations in holding revival meetings and Bible conferences.

The Indiana-Michigan Mennonite Mission Board appointed its first workers in 1913, four men to lead new or struggling congregations. William B. Weaver was sent to Barker Street, while Harvey N. Yoder went to Pleasant Valley Mennonite Church in DeKalb County, Indiana, where the fifty-year-old group was nearing extinction. William H. Haarer went to Midland, Michigan, and John M. Yoder was assigned to Homestead, Michigan, both new congregations.[52] The board's work would subsequently grow to include helping secure evangelists to visit congregations, providing church literature and songbooks, and even supporting international efforts.

The creation of the mission board produced another, albeit short-lived, benefit: it brought together a new generation of progressives and conservatives within the conference. All church members could embrace innovations such as the mission board, even if they did so for starkly differing reasons. Progressives saw God at work in society's advances.[53] "Better facilities of communication and travel have brought us nearer to the remote fields," observed Byers, the board's first president, in 1897, "and in the providence of God the national prejudices have been overcome and nearly every field has been entered by a few missionaries who have caught the true spirit of Christianity."[54] For likeminded believers, spreading the gospel reflected a broader understanding of what it meant to follow Jesus Christ, which included addressing humanity's physical as well as spiritual needs. The possibilities of a better world beckoned.

In contrast were the conservatives, for whom evangelism was more about personal conversion. They had a more negative view of the world than the progressives. Rather than getting better, the world was hopelessly deteriorating, so mission work was essential to save as many people as possible from the eternal condemnation resulting from the mire of decadence and immorality. "The tendency of many in the Church at present is toward the world," one rejected candidate for the home mission field was told. "For this reason, we believe that brethren standing for the conservative principles of the Church should be appointed to labor under the Board."[55] It was a position supported by the early Anabaptists' experiences of the world as inhospitable to Christ's true disciples. But the progressives could also draw from Anabaptism, which included an emphasis on the New Testament epistle of James and its linkage of faith and works, that a Christian's beliefs were evident in his or her actions.[56] The tensions between isolationism and worldly engagement would soon rip apart Mennonites and Amish Mennonites in Indiana and Michigan just as they were coming together.

From Cooperation to Union

The Indiana-Michigan Mennonite Mission Board was not the first apparatus to officially bring Amish Mennonites and Mennonites together in common ministry. By 1911, the two groups were already cooperating or had cooperated in a number of ways, including the various incarnations that would become Mennonite Board of Missions, Elkhart Institute/Goshen College, Mennonite Book and Tract Society, Mennonite Publication Board, and Mennonite Church General Conference. Furthermore, Indiana-Michigan Amish Mennonites and Mennonites had for decades participated in each other's annual assemblies. The idea of the two groups actually merging had arisen as early as 1865. Two years later, while preaching among the Amish Mennonites east of Goshen, Mennonite minister Daniel Brenneman, accompanied by R. J. Schmidt, bishop of the Dutch Mennonites in southern Elkhart County, and Ohio Mennonite minister J. P. King, met with the esteemed Amish Mennonite bishop Isaac Schmucker at his Topeka, Indiana, home. The idea of a "reunion" of Mennonites and Amish Mennonites was raised during their visit, Brenneman reported in the *Herald of Truth*. "No reason could be advocated why we, as brethren, whose views in point of faith and doctrine rest upon the same foundation, should stand apart from each other," he wrote. "We should much rather unite our efforts in promoting the grand interests of the Church of Christ." He added that "there are many who evidently earnestly long for it."[57]

But the idea didn't go any further at the time, as both groups soon had their own internal problems demanding attention. The Amish Mennonites had the churchwide *Diener-Versammlungen*, while troubles in the Indiana-Michigan Mennonite Conference led to the Wisler and Brenneman schisms. But the Amish Mennonites and Mennonites still found themselves joining efforts for the sake of the kingdom. Barker Street, the first congregation with members from both groups, was followed by more local unions. Prairie Street would also include Mennonites and Amish Mennonites as they were drawn to Elkhart by the Mennonite Publishing Company and Elkhart Institute. In LaGrange County since the late 1890s, Shore Mennonite Church had been conducting a Sunday school about five miles away in the tiny community of Emma in LaGrange County, Indiana. Shore members who lived in the area attended, as did local members of Forks Amish Mennonite Church, about eight miles away. By 1901, the Shore and Forks contingents had decided they wanted a closer place of worship and together started Emma Mennonite Church. Because it grew out of Shore's Sunday school, the new congregation was affiliated with the Indiana-Michigan Mennonite Conference. But its first minister was Amish Mennonite, as Forks native Oscar S. Hostetler, who had been the Sunday school superintendent, was called to fill Emma's pulpit.[58] The two groups also mixed in Middlebury when rural Amish Mennonites and Mennonites started moving to town. They first met together in homes for Sunday school in 1902 and the next year commenced worship services. The congregation, which would eventually be called First Mennonite Church, was officially established in 1904 as part of the Indiana-Michigan Amish Mennonite Conference.

That same year was the birth of the first dual-conference congregation, that is, a member of both Indiana-Michigan bodies. When the Elkhart Institute relocated to Goshen in 1903, there was no Amish Mennonite or Mennonite congregation in the city.[59] Worship accommodations needed to be found for students, faculty, administration, and staff, which included both Amish Mennonites and Mennonites. The idea of separate congregations was considered and dismissed, and in the fall of 1904, a single college-associated congregation was organized by Mennonite bishop David Burkholder and Amish Mennonite bishop D. J. Johns. It was functionally one congregation but with oversight by one bishop from each group.

In such an atmosphere of cooperation and collegiality, and as distinctions began to fade, it was inevitable that again should rise the matter of the two Indiana-Michigan groups joining together. The Mennonites, who held their annual assemblies in October and were subsequently known as the "Fall Conference," in 1911 called for the creation of a joint committee with the Amish Mennonites, nicknamed the "Spring Conference" because of their usual meeting time, to explore uniting the conferences. The approved resolution noted the two conferences' geographic proximity and nearly identical faith and practice. The resolution also included a very institution-centric reason for exploring a merger: "the present conditions are not conducive to the most effective church government."[60] The following spring, the Amish Mennonite conference endorsed merger exploration and appointed its representatives to the union committee.[61]

Its first meeting was February 13, 1913, at the Goshen home of J. S. Hartzler, a College Mennonite Church minister. He personified the new alignment because he was ordained in the Amish Mennonite conference but was an Indiana-Michigan Mennonite Conference representative on the committee. Mennonite bishop Jacob K. Bixler was named chair while Irvin R. Detweiler from the Amish Mennonite conference was selected secretary. The committee was ready in 1915 to present a new constitution and rules and disciplines for a merged conference. There had been virtually no difference between the Amish Mennonites' and Mennonites' rules and disciplines. The two constitutions, which described the conferences' organization and polity, were also quite similar.

A seemingly slight difference between the conferences was in regard to the executive committee. According to the Indiana-Michigan Mennonite Conference constitution, the committee, comprising all bishops plus the conference secretary, was in charge of conference work and was empowered to act between annual conference sessions.[62] The Amish Mennonite constitution didn't use the term "executive committee" but stated that the moderator, assistant moderator, secretary, and one bishop "shall constitute a committee having general supervision of the conference work and arrangements."[63] It was a vaguely worded description of responsibilities that, combined with Amish Mennonite congregationalism, lacked the strength and authority given to the Mennonite executive committee. The new constitution not only continued the power of the Mennonite executive committee but also expanded it—the committee was also given responsibility to examine all candidates for ordination and to reject those it deemed unqualified.[64] That was a radical departure from the old system in both conferences, in which congregations and their leaders called and installed deacons, ministers, and bishops. Another huge change was requiring the conference to discipline any congregation found to be in violation of church standards.[65] The conferences had previously disciplined only people, usually ministers, and not entire congregations. Unprecedented authority was now concentrated in a select few ordained individuals, with the laity excluded from conference business. The Amish Mennonites had explicitly encouraged lay attendance at conference assemblies "so that the church as a body may act in unison."[66] It was a codified reflection of

J. S. Hartzler. MCUSAA–Goshen.

The creation of the new Indiana-Michigan Mennonite Conference did more than unite two conferences in the United States. A third Mennonite Church conference was also involved. Pigeon Mennonite Church (also known as the Berne congregation) in the Thumb of eastern Michigan also joined, transferring from the Mennonite Conference of Ontario.[1] Canadians were among Michigan's settlers in the nineteenth century, and Ontario Mennonites joined Americans in establishing the Bowne, Caledonia, and Maple River congregations. They all eventually affiliated with the pre-merger Indiana-Michigan Mennonite Conference.

But all the Pigeon Mennonites came from Ontario, and so the Ontario conference took responsibility for their oversight, although ministers from Indiana and Michigan also periodically served them. The congregation was organized in 1894, and the first meetinghouse was built in 1897. Indiana-Michigan Mennonite Conference contributed one hundred dollars, which was a quarter of the cost of the lot and construction.[2]

By 1916, when the two Indiana-Michigan conferences were preparing to merge, the Mennonites were also in discussion with Ontario regarding Pigeon. At the 1916 Indiana-Michigan Mennonite Conference assembly, delegates approved that "in case the congregation is brought under the conference," Menno Esch, bishop of Fairview (Mich.) Amish Mennonite Church, would also have oversight of Pigeon.[3] In 1917, at the first annual assembly of the new, united conference, delegates heard that negotiations with the Ontario conference had been completed and Pigeon was now an Indiana-Michigan member.[4]

1. The towns of Pigeon and Berne were just a mile apart. The first meetinghouse was in Berne before the congregation relocated to Pigeon.
2. J. C. Wenger, *The Mennonites in Indiana and Michigan* (Scottdale, PA: Herald Press, 1961), 145.
3. Indiana-Michigan Mennonite Conference, *Minutes of the Indiana-Michigan Mennonite Conference, 1864–1929*, comp. Ira S. Johns, J. S. Hartzler, and Amos O. Hostetler (Scottdale, PA: Mennonite Publishing House, [1929?]), 138.
4. Ibid., 232.

the traditional Amish Mennonite decentralized, congregational polity. But that was eliminated in the new constitution, too.

But feelings of optimism and confidence prevailed. The ordained men of both conferences signed off on the proposed constitution and rules and discipline in 1915 and sent the document to the members of their congregations, who overwhelmingly approved it by similar margins: 728 to 71, or more than 90 percent, in the Amish Mennonite conference; and 1,319 to 155, or more than 88 percent, in the Mennonite conference. There was obviously little dissent, even on the part of the smaller Amish Mennonite conference, which had a higher approval rate and where three of the eight congregations were unanimous in their support of the merger. The 1916 assemblies were the last for each conference. Mennonite conference secretary J. S. Hartzler was especially joyous. He concluded the 1916 Mennonite conference minutes: "There was a general rejoicing at the thought that hereafter we would not be known as Spring and Fall conferences, but that after centuries of separation, we are again made one in Christ Jesus. Warnings were also given that Satan does not favor such a union and that we need to be watchful that this which is source of our joy does not become a weapon in the adversary's hand to do us injury."[67] It was a noble sentiment, but one that would not be realized, as much pain and damage would soon be suffered in the new Indiana-Michigan Mennonite Conference.

4
Threats from Without and Within

Noah W. King of rural Kokomo, Indiana, was a basketball fan, one of the legions of Hoosiers who followed the exploits of various teams and their players. James A. Naismith had invented the game in 1891 in Springfield, Massachusetts, and Indiana quickly embraced it as nowhere else in the country. Naismith himself called the state "the center of the sport" when he was in Indianapolis in 1925 to present the awards at the state boys' high school basketball tournament.[1] Among the recipients was the squad from Kokomo, which lost to Frankfort in the championship game.

King was also a deacon at Howard-Miami Mennonite Church, a congregational leader in a denomination that proclaimed nonconformity to the world. For some members, that meant popular pastimes such as basketball were out of bounds. Indiana-Michigan Mennonite Conference hadn't specifically addressed the matter, but surely it was like baseball and theatrical shows, which its predecessor conferences had earlier determined to be incompatible with their faith. Basketball had been created by a Presbyterian theological school graduate for the YMCA, an ecumenical Christian organization making inroads in Indiana but was off-limits to conference members. King was accommodating worldly influences considered dangerous to the church, even if they were Christian in origin.

In 1926, as Kokomo High School was again enjoying a successful season, Niles Slabaugh, Howard-Miami's tradition-minded minister, was asked by a fellow Mennonite if King attended basketball games, as was rumored. "I said yes, and [the questioner] was astonished that we allowed it but I can't help it," Slabaugh lamented, feeling helpless and fearing for the future of his congregation.[2] He was writing to conference secretary Ira S. Johns about the possibility of Howard-Miami hosting either Indiana-Michigan's annual assembly or its Sunday school convention. That part of the letter was relatively short. But since he was sending the letter anyway, Slabaugh wrote, he would add a postscript. It far exceeded the length of main body of the letter as he complained that "liberalism is growing wonderfully fast here." Some Howard-Miami members, in addition to attending basketball games, were also going to movies, while women in the congregation had started sporting more fashionable hats instead of the usual plain bonnets.[3]

The merger of the Indiana-Michigan Mennonite and Amish Mennonite conferences was heralded as an advancement of God's kingdom, a glorious example of unity in faith and mission. But it also coincided with an explosion ignited by political, cultural, and religious dynamics, both internal and external. The ensuing firestorm would quickly engulf the young fellowship and burn many members.

War and Peace Collide

The first threat came only months after the conferences' merger was finalized. The nations of Europe had been mired in war for nearly three years when, in April 1917, the United States formally entered the conflict against Germany and its allies. Military involvement initially generated significant public opposition, but that quickly changed into a crusade to make the world "safe for democracy," in the words of president Woodrow Wilson, who had reversed course from his earlier proclamations of peace and neutrality. Wilson signed the Espionage Act in June 1917, which made speaking or writing against the war a crime punishable by imprisonment or even death. Thousands of war opponents were jailed, and organizations were denied use of the U.S. mail for antiwar periodicals. Also in 1917 was the creation of the federal Committee on Public Information to disseminate propaganda and curry popular support for the war. Among its efforts were sponsoring seventy-five thousand speakers nationwide and encouraging Americans to spy on their neighbors. Civilian organizations such as the American Defense Society, American Protective League, and National Security League, some of them funded by the federal government, fueled the frenzy through vigilantism.[4] They applied extreme pressure on Americans to demonstrate wholehearted allegiance to the United States.

As a people who not only opposed military service but also professed loyalty to God above any worldly fidelities, the new Indiana-Michigan Mennonite Conference, like most of the rest of the Mennonite Church, was clearly at odds with the culture around it. The most immediate issue was how the church should respond to the prospects of conscription of its young men. On May 18, 1917, Congress passed the Selective Service Act, authorizing a national draft with no military exemption for conscientious objectors. Members of peace churches or organizations were eventually allowed to serve in noncombatant roles, a provision rejected by many Mennonites because such positions were still considered part of the military machine. Three weeks after the act was approved, Indiana-Michigan delegates met at Clinton Frame Mennonite Church east of Goshen for their first assembly as a united conference. They approved a resolution reaffirming their long-held position on nonresistance and requested from the federal government exemptions from all forms of military service, including noncombatant. The conference executive committee also appointed a committee to monitor the war situation and its potential impact on the conference. On July 21, the executive committee decided to hold a meeting just three days later for young men and their ministers to share information about conscription as well as testimonies to encourage nonresistance. Despite little advance notice, Clinton Frame was packed with participants from six Mennonite groups.[5] To appeal to an authority greater than the White House or Congress, the evening of August 22 was designated as a time of prayer in all Indiana-Michigan churches.[6]

It didn't take long for such actions to attract unwanted attention. Mennonites, Amish, and Brethren were "somewhat of a handicap to our progress" in mobilizing support for the American cause, the chair of the LaGrange County Council of Defense had reported in a June 29, 1917, letter to state officials.[7] Barely a month later, his frustration had noticeably increased. He claimed the peace churches were "embarrassing to the work we have to do" and "causing much dissatisfaction in the county."[8] Indiana-Michigan Mennonites would soon be part of an action that would not just make them an irritation but put them squarely in the public's and government's crosshairs.

1917 Mennonite Church General Conference at Yellow Creek Mennonite Church. MCUSAA–Goshen.

The 1917 biennial Mennonite Church General Conference assembly was scheduled to be held in Virginia, but an outbreak of polio there prompted it to be quickly relocated to Elkhart County, where it convened at Yellow Creek Mennonite Church on August 29 and 30. The war was an obvious priority on the agenda, and on the first day the delegates adopted a resolution that draftees "meekly inform [authorities] that under no circumstances can they consent to service, either combatant or non-combatant, under the military arm of the government."[9] The general conference considered positions such as a medic to be part of the military system and thus as contributing to the war effort. The resolution was signed by 183 Mennonite Church bishops, ministers, and deacons, including 52 from Indiana and Michigan. Also signing it were 15 members of other Mennonite groups, such as the Defenseless Mennonite Church and Mennonite Brethren in Christ, which each had sizable numbers of adherents in the area. The Yellow Creek statement was not only a comprehensive peace statement; it was an inter-Mennonite one, albeit in a limited scope.[10] The resolution was rushed to Elkhart, where it was immediately printed by James Bell, who had purchased John F. Funk's printing operation, and was back at Yellow Creek yet that evening.[11] The delegates also appointed a committee to guide the denomination's response to the war. Aaron Loucks from

Scottdale, Pennsylvania, was named chair, while general conference secretary J. S. Hartzler, a minister at the Goshen College congregation, would serve as the committee's secretary.

The general conference's action helped reinforce Mennonite non-resistance, but it also generated a severe federal response. Edwin Wertz, the U.S. attorney for Ohio's Northern District, tried to indict the Yellow Creek signatories for violating the Espionage Act of 1917.[12] Meanwhile, a U.S. Army intelligence officer, citing the number of German-sounding names on the published statement, called it "a very insidious piece of pro-German propaganda."[13] U.S. Justice Department investigators, looking for evidence of sedition, confiscated Hartzler's general conference secretary's book, and rumors swirled of church members being taken into custody.[14] While itinerating in churches after a visit with government officials in Washington, Hartzler spoke to a large crowd at Fairview (Mich.) Mennonite Church. He reiterated the church's intent not to undermine the government but to seek mutually acceptable ways for conscientious objectors to remain true to their religious beliefs. Unknown to Hartzler, two officials from the Justice Department were in attendance to arrest him. But after hearing him speak, they departed without incident, assured by his speech that he was not a threat.[15]

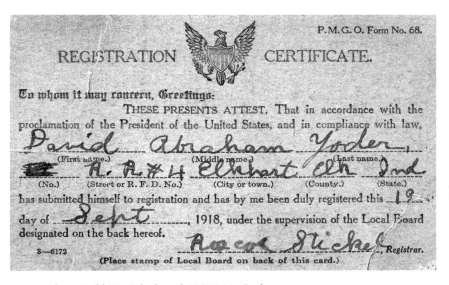

D. A. Yoder's World War I draft card. MCUSAA–Goshen.

While the Yellow Creek investigation died with no further action taken, the status of conscientious objector draftees remained unclear. A significant number of conscripted young men from Indiana-Michigan maintained their nonresistance and followed the church's teaching by refusing to wear uniforms and do most types of work.[16] That exasperated military officials who didn't know how or didn't want to deal with pacifists, despite several directives from Washington to treat them respectfully.[17] Once in camp, conscientious objectors were often pressured to conform. Methods of coercion included verbal abuse, beatings, mock executions, and imprisonment in the camp guardhouse. John H. Smeltzer from Holdeman Mennonite Church, Wakarusa, Indiana, was knocked unconscious, jabbed with a bayonet, strung up by one thumb with his feet barely touching the floor, dragged around the camp, and buried in his bed under seventeen wool blankets.[18] He was eventually sent to the military prison at Fort Leavenworth, Kansas. David Burkholder, also from Holdeman, was treated so badly in camp that he eventually acquiesced and accepted combatant service. Shipped to France, he was killed in combat on November 4, 1918, just a week before the armistice that ended the war.[19]

The ultimate legal punishment for conscientious objectors was court-martial, usually for disobeying orders and insubordination. On May 21, 1918, Allen B. Christophel, son of Yellow Creek bishop Jacob W. Christophel, was tried for refusing to rake ground in preparation for seeding grass at Camp Zachary Taylor in Kentucky. He maintained that it was a task he should not have been required to do. "The one thing I objected to is, because this work and all work in the military arm of the government has for its sole intent, one purpose, that of taking vengeance, and that of destroying life, which thing has been taught against by our church ever since it was founded in 1525," Christophel argued, citing Scripture passages including Matthew 10:16; Romans 12:19; and Galatians 5.[20] He was found guilty and sentenced to ten years at Fort Leavenworth, where he had plenty of company. By the spring of 1919, more than three hundred religious conscientious objectors were incarcerated there, including Smeltzer and thirteen others from Indiana-Michigan.[21] Despite the original stiff sentences, convicted conscientious objectors were released shortly after the war's conclusion.

Indiana-Michigan Mennonites were opposed not just to killing but also to what they considered a general environment of worldly corruption. Conscripted conscientious objector Payson Miller from Shipshewana was disgusted with the amount of swearing, smoking, and drinking by his fellow draftees on the train to Camp Taylor. "I am convinced that there is a big difference between our boys and these fellows," he wrote a friend. "I also feel more sure that I do not want to be part of a system which turns out such men."[22] Hartzler argued that, in addition to the violence, profanity and tobacco use were reasons to oppose the war. He noted that the "tobacco trust" encouraged the sending of cigars, cigarettes, and snuff to soldiers as a show of support.[23]

As Indiana-Michigan draftees took the peace position with them when they entered the military system, conference leadership went to their camps to encourage them in their often hostile environments. Bishops D. D. Miller from Forks Mennonite Church, Shipshewana, and D. J. Johns from Clinton Frame Mennonite Church, Goshen, "are in a military camp about every Sunday," an Elkhart County Council of Defense official complained to his superiors at the state level. He proposed that Miller and Johns be barred from "entering these camps for the purpose of giving 'spiritual advice,'" which was obstructing the army's efforts to turn the draftees into fighting men.[24] The *Middlebury (Ind.) Independent* reported that two local boys had been wearing military uniforms in camp until they were visited by an Elkhart County minister.[25] Like the regulation attire of the conference, military uniforms, whether the wearers were armed or not, were key in demonstrating loyalty. So with the minister's counsel, the nonresistant beliefs of the would-be fighting men were strengthened and the uniforms came off, despite the risk of retribution, official or otherwise.

Not all conference conscripts, however, felt that high level of support and counsel. Charles Kauffman from Fairview Mennonite Church joined the regular army, albeit as a noncombatant, serving as a messenger during the war. He subsequently lost his congregational membership. When he returned home, he was fully restored after he confessed for acting against the will of the church. But in making his confession, Kauffman noted the lack of help he received from the congregation. "Many problems were left for me to solve alone," he said. "I did the best I could."[26]

Other young men willingly, even enthusiastically, joined the military. Rollin Hershberger, who came from but was not a member of Forks Mennonite Church, volunteered for the army and was killed in France on July 24, 1918. According to bishop D. D. Miller, the Hershberger family asked him if he was planning to attend Rollin's memorial service in Middlebury. Miller replied that he couldn't because of a previously planned trip to visit conscientious objectors at Camp Taylor. When he returned home, however, he learned that the family was circulating the story that the bishop had refused to do the service because Rollin had been a soldier.[27] The news spread quickly and stoked the ire of the patriotic public. Miller went to the media to defend himself. "I was not asked to preach the memorial service for Rollin Hershberger, and I have been falsely accused," he told the *Goshen Democrat*. "These attacks on me are unwarranted in every particular way."[28] Miller and the Hershbergers eventually resolved the matter and made peace between themselves.[29]

The War at Home

For members of Indiana-Michigan Mennonite Conference, the home front was not much friendlier than the army camps. Civilian Mennonites tried valiantly to assure the public that they were not traitors or subversives. In public statements, letters, and personal conversations, the conference and its members repeatedly declared their support of the United States and appreciation of the freedom of religious belief the country offered. The Yellow Creek statement advocated that "we refrain from uncharitable criticism in any form" and that conscientious objectors be careful not to do anything that might be considered treasonous.[30] In April 1918, Goshen College accepted a U.S. flag and flagpole donated by local citizens because, according to the *Goshen Daily News-Times*, "Much agitation has resulted in the south end due to the lack of the display of the national emblem over the buildings or on the grounds of Goshen College." When presented with the gift, college president Irvin R. Detweiler said Mennonites were loyal to their country—as far as their religious convictions allowed.[31]

But in that era of hyperpatriotic hysteria, Mennonite convictions were often easily equated with treachery. The Elkhart County Council of Defense kept local Mennonites and other war resisters under close scrutiny, at times interrogating individuals suspected of disloyalty. The council gathered allegedly incriminating information on Henry Weldy, minister at Olive Mennonite Church, Wakarusa, and then called him before the council in Goshen on July 19, 1918, where he was "thoroughly grilled and temporarily parolled [*sic*], subject to call before this Council at any future time," according to the minutes of the meeting.[32]

Weldy's offense was opposing the purchase of Liberty Bonds. The most important test of national loyalty apart from military service was to help finance the war effort, such as by buying government-issued Liberty Bonds and Thrift Stamps, which could later be redeemed for the purchase cost plus interest. Americans were also asked to support the Red Cross and YMCA, which provided canteens, entertainment, recreation, medical care, and other programs for soldiers and sailors. But many Indiana-Michigan members were loath to directly support the war financially, since that was contributing to the fighting as much as actually firing weapons in battle. In Elkhart County, the townships with heavy Mennonite populations consistently fell short of fundraising goals, prompting the county chair of one fundraising campaign to request state leaders in Indianapolis to send someone to make the stubborn nonresistant people "realize their duty."[33] Representatives from the Elkhart County Council of Defense attended the 1918 Indiana-Michigan Mennonite Conference annual assembly, held at Holdeman Mennonite Church, and asked the assembly for resolutions in favor of purchasing war bonds and supporting the Red Cross and YMCA. While the visitors were politely received, the conference took no action other than reaffirming the Mennonite Church's Yellow Creek statement from the previous summer.[34] Newspapers repeatedly blasted "slackers" in extraordinarily harsh, even inflammatory, terms. In the middle of the heavily Mennonite and Amish population of western Elkhart and eastern LaGrange Counties, the *Middlebury Independent* published an article headlined "Middlebury Should Be 100% Patriotic." In grandiose and overwrought style, it declared that conscientious objectors were "not fit to mingle with the vermin of the earth" and that they "will avail not, and there will be no other country in the universe to which they can flee in order to escape their galling chains."[35]

The Elkhart County school superintendent made the purchase of war bonds or financial support of the Red Cross and YMCA requirements to teach in the county. It was part of a new loyalty oath for all teachers, and Mennonites were especially targeted. According to the oath, teachers also had to declare their support for "the constitution and laws of the United States of America" (based on the assumption that the actions of religious conscientious objectors must be illegal) and that they would encourage their pupils to do the same. A third provision of the oath called for teachers "to render services to the United States [if] called upon to do so." Two Indiana-Michigan members refused to take the oath and were terminated, while a third resigned.[36]

Other methods used to try to bring conscientious objectors into line often strayed into unchecked vigilantism. In the Howard-Miami community, minister and basketball opponent Niles Slabaugh and his brother-in-law Joe Martin were forcibly taken from their homes by several men claiming to be police officers and were driven to Peru, the Miami County seat, because neither man had contributed to campaigns to finance the war. Slabaugh and Martin were subjected to several hours of interrogation and ridicule by seven hundred people in a Peru auditorium. At one point Slabaugh was taken down a dark alley, where his accosters "called me a damn S. of B. a dirty cur, said I was not even a human, threatened to take my life," he related afterward. Still he refused to contribute and was eventually let go with a warning not to remain in the county. Martin did agree to make a contribution.[37] Slabaugh didn't leave the county, however, and two weeks later, a dozen people grabbed him from his bed about midnight, hauled him twelve miles from home, shaved his head and face, and painted him yellow. "The manner in which the paint was used would cause one to believe it was the work of an artist and that it was a masterpiece, so skillfully was the job done," gleefully reported the *Peru Republican*.[38] Such artistry was also applied to a number of Mennonite meetinghouses and buildings owned by church members as well as to the people themselves. Such measures were sometimes accompanied by signs labeling Mennonites as lovers of the Kaiser and hoarders of foodstuffs that were supposed to go to feeding the soldiers repelling the tide of evil.

The most egregious vigilante attack was suffered by Fairview (Mich.) Mennonite Church, which lost its meetinghouse to arson. Some congregational members had been active in local Democratic politics in heavily Republican Oscoda County, and two ran for office in the spring of 1918. William F. McNeely, chair of the county division of the American Defense Society and an aspiring Republican politician, was incensed. He had a long record of making anti-Mennonite comments, and issued a blistering and exaggerated, if not libelous, broadside. "Shall we, in this bitterly crucial hour when the shaft of death is poised for a blow at our blood-bought Liberty, elect men to office in Comins Township who ... [have] the official o.k. of the Kaiser and weakens our cause in the war that means more to you than any other contest since the dawn of the first day?" McNeely rhetorically demanded.[39] But his missive was not enough. On April 4, 1918, two nights after the election (which the Mennonite candidates lost), McNeely and John H. Speck, the local American Defense Society secretary and a suspect in an earlier arson attempt on a Mennonite-owned store, set fire to the fourteen-year-old Fairview church building.[40] Also involved in the plot, although not in the actual arson, were the sheriff, which explains why there was no initial investigation of the incident, and the local newspaper editor, who actually wrote the article on the fire before it happened.[41]

Having paid the price for its beliefs, the congregation, which was meeting in a new building by December, was willing to let the matter rest. That was naturally fine with the local civil authorities, who were intent on maintaining their impunity. McNeely even wanted to extend the intimidation to preventing Fairview's reconstruction efforts.[42] But a group of county residents petitioned for a grand jury, which circuit judge Albert W. Widdis convened in April 1920.[43] Two days of proceedings revealed the scope of the conspiracy, including the arsonists' hope for a westerly wind so the flames would also ignite a nearby store owned by a Fairview member.[44] Local Republicans sprang into action and got Michigan attorney general and future governor Alex Groesbeck, also a Republican, to rule that the case was without merit. That was immediately followed by a crusade to disbar Widdis, a native Canadian and a Democrat who had earlier sought political office on the Socialist ticket. He survived the attack but was unable to further pursue the arson investigation during the two years he spent defending himself. The grand jury expired and so did the case. A group of Mennonites and non-Mennonites later hired a lawyer in Bay City, about eighty-five miles south of Fairview, to revive the case. Members of the group set out one day to meet with their lawyer, but their car broke down and they never arrived. They decided that was indicative of God's will to let the matter rest.[45]

But that didn't mean that justice of a different sort wasn't achieved. McNeely and Speck would become bitter enemies, but each man would eventually enjoy cordial relations with the Fairview Mennonites. They would even make financial contributions to the congregation.[46] One of the arsonists, while on his deathbed, summoned a Fairview minister, accepted Jesus Christ, and was baptized.

In the face of such intense pressure and persecution, some Indiana-Michigan Mennonites not surprisingly found methods of accommodation, although often reluctantly. Some succumbed and bought bonds and contributed to the YMCA and Red Cross, which war supporters trumpeted. "The Mennonite ladies shipped a box of Red Cross supplies containing over 100 pieces Tuesday of this week. Included in the shipment were knit wool sweaters, caps, bed gowns, etc.," reported the *Middlebury Independent*.[47] Northern Indiana Mennonites were able to find one alternative to war bonds. Church leaders, bankers, and those overseeing the sale of war bonds agreed that Mennonites could invest in bank certificates of deposits, the money from which the banks would use to buy bonds. That technicality spared the Mennonites from directly purchasing war bonds while still allowing counties to reach their quotas.[48] One Goshen newspaper applauded the plan because "it shows that [the Mennonites] are now disposed to do their full part."[49] Some individuals participated in other ways. W. W. Oesch, pastor of the Barker Street congregation, just across the state line in Michigan, was a member of the Elkhart County Council of Defense's Committee on Food Conservation and Production, while Goshen College agriculture professor C. B. Blosser started a campaign to encourage farmers to erect silos in order to better preserve livestock feed as part of the nationwide wartime rationing efforts.

There was one positive result from the public pressure on Mennonites to financially support the war effort. Rather than give money to the YMCA and Red Cross, many church members began making contributions to Mennonite Board of Missions (MBM) to aid those most affected by the war, even though MBM had no such programs. So in December 1917, it founded the Mennonite Relief Commission for War Sufferers, which by April 1919 had received more than $463,000.[50]

The organization started sending Mennonite volunteers to France in late 1918 for postwar reconstruction projects and the next year began working with refugees in the Middle East.

The Internal Conflict

During World War I, Indiana-Michigan Mennonite Conference was united in its defense against repeated assaults from the U.S. military, government, and the public in general. But at the same time, the conference was experiencing internal conflicts, which intensified after the war ended in November 1918. The conference's all-consuming focus on war-related concerns had only obscured competing forces already at work within Indiana-Michigan and postponed their devastating effects. Many people in the church worried that they would not just cross the boundaries between church and world but completely obliterate them.

Nineteenth-century visionaries such as John F. Funk and John S. Coffman had borrowed from mainstream Protestantism to create institutions such as publications, schools, and mission agencies with the goal of fostering greater faithfulness and revitalizing the church. But it wasn't long before there were rumblings of discord in the church over the very definition of that faithfulness. Would these relatively new institutions uphold traditional Mennonite beliefs limiting engagement

Two Goshen College students in dorm room, 1916. MCUSAA–Goshen.

with the world? Or would new ways of understanding undermine non-conformity, nonresistance, and even the Bible itself? These were theological questions, and they put Goshen College, until 1909 the only Mennonite Church postsecondary school, in the middle of controversy. While a Goshen student in the 1910s, Orie Miller, who would go on to become a builder of twentieth-century church institutions to rival Funk in the nineteenth century, learned from Bible professor J. E. Hartzler that Shadrach, Meshach, and Abednego's experience in the fiery furnace, as found in the Old Testament book of Daniel, probably didn't happen but was a parable. Miller then found in the college library a book on the subject, which he passed along to his father, influential LaGrange County bishop D. D. Miller. D. D. became quite disturbed about his son's education and went to campus, where they spent an unproductive evening discussing the matter.[51]

Professor Hartzler, like Funk and Coffman, also borrowed heavily from broader Christianity. He had impressive credentials, at least by worldly standards, and was one of the most educated members of the Mennonite Church. After graduating from Goshen College in 1910 and before returning to teach, he studied at McCormick Theological Seminary in Chicago and Union Theological Seminary in New York; the latter especially was considered a center of liberal Christian scholarship. But Hartzler also had good standing in the church as a popular evangelistic speaker. None other than conservative champion Daniel Kauffman trusted Hartzler. The two men knew each other from Missouri, where both grew up, and Coffman was instrumental in each of their ministerial careers. Kauffman asked Hartzler to author the "Plan of Salvation" section in *Bible Doctrine*, which Kauffman edited. The book, first published in 1914, would become a standard resource on church orthodoxy, although a revised edition came out fourteen years later without any contribution from Hartzler. By then Hartzler had found it impossible to balance both ends of the theological spectrum.

Hartzler was named Goshen College's president in 1913, succeeding Northwestern University–educated Noah Byers. Initially the principal of the Elkhart Institute, Byers led the school through its move to Goshen and its development into a quality college. But he also drew the ire of conservatives—he once had to confess his sin of helping judge an educational exhibit at the county fair—and in 1913 left for a more hospitable environment at Bluffton (Ohio) College, affiliated with the General Conference Mennonite Church.[52] In his inaugural address, Hartzler declared the continuation of an optimistic, progressive approach to higher education and the belief in active Mennonite participation in world affairs as expressions of the faith. "Myriads of unrevealed truths are still waiting to present themselves to the world," Hartzler said. "The future is pregnant with unborn truths and accomplishments."[53] That was, according to conservatives, hardly consistent with a faith that saw the world not as an arena for God's people and God's

J. E. Hartzler at Bethel College. MCUSAA–North Newton.

work but as an enemy of righteousness. But the new president was unfazed, as he saw himself as boldly carrying on Coffman's "Spirit of Progress" and Noah Byers's agenda. "The inability of the present generation to accept the religion of the past does not mean that we are less religious, sincere, or right," Hartzler said.[54]

His inauguration speech was published in the *Goshen College Record*, the school's student periodical, and quickly produced a response from prominent conservative John Horsch, the former Mennonite Publishing Company employee now writing and editing for the Mennonite Publishing House in Scottdale, Pennsylvania. He fired off a letter to Hartzler, criticizing the new president's liberal drift from what Horsch considered solid biblical fundamentals. "I believe religion must be founded on an unchanging body of dogma," he wrote. Responded Hartzler: "Christianity never changes; [C]hristianity never disintegrates; the Gospel of Christ is always the same. But men do change their interpretations of the Gospel and change their methods of application of the same." He then took another shot at Horsch and other critics, writing that "no individual person or generation can form a system of creeds or dogma which will meet the religious demands and needs of men for all time to come."[55]

With such views and eagerness to express them, the forthright and even imprudent Hartzler was a favorite target of conservatives, who derided him and other like-minded Amish Mennonites and Mennonites as modernists.[56] Earlier conflicts between progressives and traditionalists had essentially been over the means to the same end. John F. Funk's Sunday schools and periodicals, for example, were meant not to change church positions on nonresistance and nonconformity but to be instruments to uphold them. But now Mennonite orthodoxy was perceived to be threatened by a menace labeled modernism, which had been growing in the wider Christian church for several decades. Religious faith itself was considered in peril. In modernism, according to its opponents, the pursuit of intellectual knowledge as a path to truth trumped the often-mysterious lessons from Scripture. As a result, Christian modernists denied Jesus Christ's divinity and the Bible as the literal word of God, both impossibilities by pure scientific standards, while upholding evolution and salvation through works.[57] By such a definition, there were virtually no Mennonite Church modernists in the early twentieth century.[58] The primacy of Scripture, Christ's redemption of humankind through his crucifixion and resurrection, and other core tenets remained firmly in place. But conservatives feared a slippery theological slope. If Shadrach, Meshach, and Abednego hadn't been actual human beings, might the creation accounts and virgin birth also be reduced to myths? Mennonite progressives did share some common understandings with Protestant modernists, particularly that God is revealed through worldly progress.[59] For Hartzler, higher education, as the key to progress, was not in tension with faith but very much consistent with it. Subsequently, he and others of similar outlook were tainted by full-blown modernism.

Many Mennonites found their rebuttal to modernism in a broader Christian movement that would be called fundamentalism, and Horsch would be its staunchest and most articulate Mennonite advocate.[60] "The modern apostasy . . . disowns the fundamentals of the faith," Horsch would write in *Modern Religious Liberalism*, which was first published in 1920 and would become a popular and acclaimed book, even among non-Mennonite readers.[61] Some aspects of fundamentalism were hardly new to Amish Mennonites and Mennonites. They were certainly theologically orthodox. Even the movement's name was connected with church members. *Foundation*, an etymological cousin to *fundamental*, had long been used in Indiana-Michigan and broader Mennonite and Amish Mennonite circles.[62] The 1919 Indiana-Michigan annual assembly approved a resolution about "the present spirit of religious unrest and dissatisfaction" having led to conditions where "fundamentals are apt to be sacrificed for cooperation" and urged "allegiance anew to the faith for which our Church has always stood."[63]

At the heart of fundamentalism was the belief that culture was increasingly and irreversibly turning from God to immorality, in contrast with the more positive views held by progressives.[64] Such negativity resonated with traditional Mennonite beliefs, which put Romans 12:2 ("Do not be conformed to this world, but be transformed by the renewing of your minds, so that you may discern what is the will of God—what is good and acceptable and perfect") theologically and culturally central. When Dwight L. Moody, a former associate of John F. Funk in Chicago and one of fundamentalism's grandfathers, said, "A line should be drawn between the church and the world, and every Christian should get both feet out of the world," he was, to many Mennonites, echoing centuries of Anabaptist life and thought.[65] In fact, some thought of themselves as more fundamentalist than the non-Mennonite adherents. "The Mennonite Church is firmly committed to the Fundamentalist faith," Daniel Kauffman asserted, "including some unpopular tenets of faith which so many so-called Fundamentalists reject," such as nonresistance and regulation attire—two precepts considered particularly crucial in defining Mennonitism.[66]

But more was at stake than just theological faithfulness. It went hand in hand with fears of the loss of Mennonite cultural identity. The German language had long been a major characteristic of American Mennonite and Amish Mennonite separation from the world, but it was rapidly being replaced by English at the turn of the century.[67] That meant it was even more important for the church to maintain other distinctives. More boundary markers were needed, and the emerging fundamentalist movement helped provide them. Mennonites had never described the Bible as inerrant or infallible, and in fact, the earliest Anabaptist confessions of faith hadn't even included articles on the Bible.[68] It was simply assumed that it was ultimately accurate and authoritative. So it was a logical extension of belief to use fundamentalism's buzzword of *inerrancy* to describe Scripture. Fundamentalism also emphasized a common sense, rather than intellectual, approach to faith. That was consistent with conservative Mennonites' fears that higher education could undermine faith, with Goshen College serving as the most visible and contentious example.

Another attribute of fundamentalism that found favor with at least some church members was its militancy.[69] It was a pronounced shift from *Gelassenheit*, the traditional Anabaptist emphases of humility, self-denial, and willingness to suffer. But a new generation was rising to prominence with new notions. At the first annual assembly of the new Indiana-Michigan Mennonite Conference in 1917, just ten of the twenty-three ordained men in attendance had been born before John F. Funk arrived in Elkhart in 1867, and sixteen had entered the ministry after 1900. They were comfortable with a church defined by structures and institutions and were willing to start others should the existing ones be found lacking. Dissatisfaction with Funk's Mennonite Publishing Company led to the emergence of the Mennonite Book and Tract Society and the Gospel Witness Company. Goshen College's progressivism helped fuel the creation of competing, more conservative schools in Hesston, Kansas, and Harrisonburg, Virginia. Such developments institutionalized not only the expression of faith but also alternative expressions of it. Furthermore, institutions narrowed and elevated authority and gave it broader powers. The president of a churchwide agency or the chair of a conference executive committee could wield influence more profoundly than a local bishop ever could. When coupled with a righteous cause, authority could easily become authoritarian and emasculate traditional communal Mennonite discernment processes.[70]

These forces combined to create a level of strident activism previously unknown in the Mennonite Church. *Gospel Herald* editor Daniel Kauffman called it "aggresso-conservatism." "The truly conservative are truly aggressive," he told the 1915 Mennonite Board of Missions annual meeting. "I strongly advocate conservatism and aggression. Conservatism is not a synonym of deadness, nor is aggressiveness a synonym of worldliness."[71] Three years later, at the Indiana-Michigan annual assembly, Kauffman called for such combativeness when he preached on the apostle Paul's exhortation to "fight the good fight of the faith" as found in 1 Timothy 6:12. "The text shows a Christian warfare," Kauffman said. "This warfare must be by people who are born again. . . . We must know the Sword of the Spirit."[72]

Fundamentalism also introduced Mennonites to something else new: dispensational premillennialism, the belief that time, both past and future, is divided into dispensations, or eras. According to its proponents, the world was in the second to last dispensation, which would conclude with Jesus Christ's second coming and his thousand-year reign. Mennonites were much less agreed on that point, even among those who adhered to the other tenets of fundamentalism. Kauffman cautioned against dispensationalism, while longtime Indiana-Michigan secretary Ira S. Johns, a self-described pessimist, prominently displayed a timeline of dispensations in his dining room.[73]

The coalescence of fundamentalism's influence with the new Mennonite organizational apparatus to implement and enforce orthodoxy allowed for the emergence of Jacob K. Bixler as Indiana-Michigan's unsurpassed aggresso-conservative and most powerful individual. He was ordained in 1904 as a minister at Holdeman Mennonite Church, Wakarusa, became bishop three years later, and moved to Elkhart and Prairie Street Mennonite Church in 1914. He was named assistant secretary of the old Indiana-Michigan Mennonite Conference in 1906, and over the next thirty-five years, Bixler would become a fixture on the conference executive committee. He would serve as moderator of the old and merged conferences for thirteen years plus another seven years in other committee positions. In addition, Bixler was secretary of the Indiana-Michigan Mennonite Mission Board from its inception in 1911 until 1925, and for a time he served as bishop over the mission stations. As such, he was known as the "pope of Michigan," where most mission work was done.[74] He was passionate about evangelism, and was known to weep while baptizing new believers.[75] After preaching a sermon at Clinton Frame Mennonite Church calling for more missionaries, Bixler invited himself to Sunday dinner at the home of Clyde X. and Rosetta Kauffman and told them that God wanted them to go to Brutus, Michigan.[76] The Kauffmans went in 1921 and had great success reviving a dying congregation, thanks in part to an influx of unhappy members of a local Wisler Mennonite fellowship.

Bixler's approach with the Kauffmans was indicative of his under-standing of authority. In his conference sermon at the 1917 Indiana-Michigan assembly, Bixler spoke from Revelation, noting the messages to the seven churches. "This message was sent by angels, and that doubtless means bishops," he said.[77]

Two Opponents

J. E. Hartzler's Goshen College tumultuous presidency came to an end in 1918. During his five years in office, relations deteriorated between the school and an increasingly conservative church leadership, particularly the Mennonite Board of Education (MBE), a denominational organiza-tion established in 1905 to keep the progressive school in the bosom of the church. At the same time, Goshen was flailing amid a grow-ing financial crisis, which finally forced Hartzler's resignation. MBE officially depicted him as a well-meaning administrator who was inept in fiscal matters. Privately, Hartzler's departure was met with gladness among conservatives. Some even suggested that Goshen's money prob-lems were divine retribution for siding with the ways of the world and against the church.[78]

But while Goshen College and MBE were rid of Hartzler, Indiana-Michigan was not, as Hartzler and the conference continued battling even after the deposed president left the state. After resigning, Hartzler immediately accepted a faculty position at Bethel College, a General Conference Mennonite Church school in Newton, Kansas. Despite his employment with another Mennonite denomination, Hartzler sought to participate in the nearest Mennonite Church congregation, Penn-sylvania Mennonite Church, located between Newton and Hesston.[79] He intended his Kansas sojourn to not last long enough to warrant transferring his congregational membership from Indiana, but he did want to partake in the Lord's Supper while in the area. The Pennsylva-nia bishop, Tilman Erb, said he would welcome the embattled Hartzler if he was in good standing in the congregation where he was member, Prairie Street Mennonite Church. (Hartzler had been a Prairie Street minister even while teaching at Goshen, but relinquished the position when he became the school's president. He then wanted to transfer his membership to College Mennonite Church but, he claimed, Prairie Street requested that he not do so.[80]) Prairie Street bishop Bixler ruled that Hartzler was, in fact, not in good standing, even though he had never denied Hartzler communion, a common indicator of a member considered at variance with the church. After more than a year and a half of wrangling between Hartzler and the two bishops, Prairie Street minister William B. Weaver, another member of Indiana-Michigan's progressive faction, issued a letter in

J. K. Bixler. MCUSAA–Goshen.

July 1920, declaring Hartzler in "full standing" in the congregation. But Erb continued to deny him communion when Bixler argued the letter was sent without Prairie Street's consent.[81]

Hartzler continued to spar with Bixler and Erb until he moved to Bluffton, Ohio, in 1921 to become the first president of the inter-Mennonite Witmarsum Theological Seminary, affiliated with Bluffton College. Bluffton was organized in 1899 primarily by the Middle District of the General Conference Mennonite Church (GCMC) but with substantial support from the GCMC Eastern District Conference and the Central Conference of Mennonites. Like Goshen College, Bluffton was in conservatives' crosshairs, even within the General Conference Mennonite Church. For Indiana-Michigan, the school was even more sacrilegious because it had become the new home for a number of apostates from Goshen, including former president Noah Byers and historian C. Henry Smith. The fact that Witmarsum's board included two representatives from the Mennonite Church, as well as from five other Mennonite denominations, did nothing to mitigate criticism.[82] Hartzler, who had advocated for a Mennonite seminary for many years, didn't improve his standing in Indiana-Michigan with his new post. With Weaver's letter from the previous summer, Hartzler was able to join Chapel Mennonite Church, an Ohio Mennonite Conference congregation at New Stark, about a dozen miles southeast of Bluffton. But now, since he intended to stay at Witmarsum long-term, Hartzler wanted his Indiana-Michigan Conference ministerial credentials, called a "conference letter," also transferred.

But he was stonewalled until the fall of 1922, when the Indiana-Michigan executive committee finally sent a letter acknowledging his credentials. But the committee expressed its disapproval of him serving as president "of an institution which is not one with us in faith and practice" and of his speaking at a 1919 inter-Mennonite convention, which was not attended by anyone from the Mennonite Church.[83] "However, it is the wish and prayer of this committee" that Hartzler become a "loyal" and "earnest worker" in Ohio Conference, the letter stated.[84] Indiana-Michigan leadership was ready to let him go but still wanted him to adhere to expected standards.

That, however, did not conclude Hartzler's saga. He had started preaching at the Chapel congregation, and Ohio had approved accepting him upon receipt of his letter from Indiana-Michigan. When the letter finally arrived, Hartzler presented it to the conference and waited. But like Indiana-Michigan, Ohio leaders dragged their feet for nearly three years.[85] They finally made a decision in June 1925: the conference could not accept Hartzler as long as he was affiliated with Witmarsum.[86] But the matter soon became moot. Ohio was also going through its own internal turmoil of progressives versus conservatives, and Chapel would withdraw from the conference and join the General Conference Mennonite Church in 1927.

Hartzler was not the only one struggling with the conference's increasingly doctrinaire environment. William B. Weaver left Prairie Street and Indiana-Michigan in 1920 for the Central Conference of Mennonites. "All this commotion on account of hoods, strings [on prayer coverings] and Premillinialism," he wrote Hartzler in Kansas.[87] Wilbur Miller, son of well-regarded Forks Mennonite Church bishop D. D. Miller, was ordained a minister at Forks in June 1921 but a year later had still not been recognized by the conference.[88] The reason, according to one progressive observer, was that Miller wore a necktie.[89] For an emerging network of Indiana-Michigan progressives who were feeling persecuted, prospects did not look promising. "I believe we'll have a split before it's over with," Weaver forecasted in the spring of 1921. "I wish the progressives could get together somehow and organize and saw wood."[90] The political and doctrinal wrangling about Indiana-Michigan's leadership left rank-and-file conference members in a state of constant uncertainty. "One does wonder who is in the wrong," mused Mary Schantz Zook of Maple Grove Mennonite Church, Topeka, Indiana.[91] But she was suspicious of bishop Bixler's motives, stating, "If he is not sincere time will tell sooner or later."[92]

The conference turmoil, particularly over the propriety of women's headwear, was personally challenging for the Zook family. In the spring of 1921, Mary's daughter Vesta and Vinora Weaver from Forks Mennonite Church became the first women to serve with Mennonite Central Committee (MCC). The organization had been created the previous year at Prairie Street Mennonite Church by several North American Mennonite groups to respond to Mennonites starving in Russia after the upheaval of the Russian Revolution and a catastrophic famine. Weaver and Zook were single and teaching at Goshen College when LaGrange County native Orie O. Miller asked them to go to Constantinople. He and fellow Goshen alumnus Arthur Slagle were based in the city and needed assistance with the great number of refugees arriving from Russia.[93] Back in northern Indiana, Mary Zook was concerned about what the two women were wearing on their heads. "Well, we both bought ourselves hats and they have rims," Vesta admitted when she wrote home several weeks after arriving in Turkey, "but as hot as it is over here we must have something like it to shade our eyes. These are silk but we thot [*sic*] later on we should get straw. They are very plain."[94]

What Zook did not report at the time to her family was that on the voyage from New York to the Middle East, she and Weaver ceremoniously threw their customary bonnets overboard, giving them a watery grave in the Atlantic Ocean.[95] Once in Turkey, Weaver noted that the local Muslim women were beginning to show their previously veiled faces in public. She considered it an act of liberation similar to Mennonite women discarding their bonnets.[96] Vesta, meanwhile, was emboldened and mailed home photos of herself and Weaver in their un-Mennonite hats. Her mother affirmatively responded, "I heard a preacher say sometimes the bible is a good place to hide something also is a good sign you don't read your bible much. I know I don't read in the big bible. That is why I put those pictures in. Send all of the pictures you have. We will be glad for them."[97]

When Vesta was preparing to return home after more than a year in Constantinople, Mary advised her daughter not to wear her hat when she arrived, "not that *we* are opposed to it, but for what it might cause later," given Indiana-Michigan's official stance on attire; anything but a bonnet would court controversy.[98] Women's hats were in style, so to Indiana-Michigan stalwarts, wearing them was a sign of worldly acquiescence.[99] For the Zooks, however, accepting change did not have to mean compromising their faith. Nevertheless, it was important to be prudent. "We did not tell or let anyone read that you have a Victrola but was glad to hear that you have one," Mary had earlier written Vesta.[100] A record player was yet one more item deemed to be incongruous with the Mennonite faith.

The turning point in Indiana-Michigan's struggle between conservatives and progressives was soon at hand. Bixler's power in the conference was unsurpassed, but his heavy-handed, authoritarian methods were ruffling some conference members. In the spring of 1922, a petition against Bixler was signed by 149 people from seven congregations. The organizers, members of the progressive network, claimed the signatories also included conservatives.[101] Their charges against Bixler included "self-willed administration of the bishop's office," "untruthfulness," interfering in congregations not under his charge, using his office to advocate against church institutions and individuals, and "his manner of conducting excommunications."[102] The conference was forced to act.

According to its constitution, Indiana-Michigan Mennonite Conference "shall always be open to hear and consider" appeals from members, and matters needing arbitration were to be handled by a committee elected by the conference. Yet to the consternation of the petitioners, who were already worried about cronyism and the concentration of power in a few individuals, the conference executive committee kept the Bixler petition to itself, directing Indiana-Michigan's bishops to appoint the investigating committee. The executive committee of the old Mennonite conference had similarly acted unilaterally before when dealing with a dispute at Bowne, Michigan, but then it confessed its error to the conference in 1915 and asked that an arbitration committee be appointed. Now, however, despite precedent and the constitution's instructions, the executive committee was no longer just supervisor and coordinator of Indiana-Michigan affairs but final arbiter of faithfulness as well.

The investigating committee consisted of five members from outside Indiana-Michigan. Progressives were comfortable with at least two of the choices, but the committee's mandate drew howls of protest. While the original petition focused solely on Bixler and his conduct, the executive committee used the allegations as an opportunity to probe the entire conference. The executive committee expanded the investigation to also include "all the conditions which have in any way tended to bring about the present unrest," including Hartzler's conference letter, which was still unresolved. Then the executive committee empowered the investigators to "adjust everything that gave rise to the present unrest."[103] The petitioners felt targeted as a result of their own appeal. And in the end they were.

From Bluffton, Hartzler was trying to make his own contribution to the investigation and bring down Bixler. Hartzler set out to substantiate a rumor that his nemesis suffered from syphilis and was thus "physically unfit" for his office, even querying a nurse at the Elkhart hospital where Bixler had recently received medical attention. Hartzler admitted that it normally would be inappropriate to ask her to divulge patient information but claimed it was justified in this case because Bixler "is a man without conscience." The nurse shared Hartzler's disdain for the bishop but could not provide any proof of infection.[104] In an exchange with Barker Street pastor W. W. Oesch regarding the fervent Bixler, Hartzler claimed scientific studies showed that "85% of the religious fanatics" have a venereal disease.[105]

The investigating committee came to Elkhart County and spent ten days interviewing individuals and exploring the situation before presenting its findings at a special session of the conference on August 26.[106] The committee's report shockingly indicted those in Indiana-Michigan with "a tendency to question and disregard church authority" and called the bishop "a man of strong conviction, firm in position, manifesting an intense zeal for the faith and in support of the doctrines of the World and the Church, and orthodox in his teaching." Bixler was mildly chided for occasional questionable judgment, but the committee attributed it to his ardor, which made it largely excusable. The only definite action taken against him was relieving him as Prairie Street bishop, not because "the charges against him have been sustained" or because "his integrity of character or qualifications as a bishop are questioned" but because of the "strained circumstances" in the congregation caused by rebellious members. On the charge that Bixler misused his office to advocate against Goshen College and others, the investigating committee stated, "In so doing he at times overstepped the bounds of wisdom and propriety under the circumstances as a result of his intense zeal for soundness and orthodoxy. We could find no evidence that this was done with malignant intent on his part, but as a means to safeguard the church and her young people." Bixler had hastily excommunicated Prairie Street members "in an instance or two," the committee admitted, but he was trying to rein in a congregation that had drifted in part because of "the lenient methods" of previous ministers. The investigating committee then cemented the authority of the executive committee, calling on it to bring Indiana-Michigan congregations "into harmonious relations with the doctrines of the church and the regulations of conference." Anyone challenging the investigating committee's decisions was to be censured.

It was the reverse of the John Funk case two decades earlier, when the bishop was stripped of his duties while those who opposed him received relatively mild punishments. There was now officially little room for dissent, and notice was served that Indiana-Michigan leadership would seek to dramatically purge and purify conference ranks. Members now needed to unquestionably submit to the conference's authority. "We all knew the rules of the Church before we joined. Is it wise for us to unite and then insist that she change her practices?" Prairie Street minister J. S. Hartzler rhetorically asked Violet Bender, daughter of longtime mission board administrator George L. Bender and who was refusing to wear the conference-mandated bonnet. For Hartzler, tradition was evidence of values long discerned and upheld by the church; it could not be changed simply in response to trends or whims.[107] Bender, however, saw issues such as attire as secondary concerns. "I am a Mennonite in principles, and I believe I always will be," she told Hartzler. "And I hope I also made it clear to you that our only difference, so far as I could see, was merely one of *method* in applying the principles which we both consider very important."[108] Progressives accused conservatives of codifying tradition, elevating it to the same level as Scripture. Progressives further complained that wearing the right clothes had become a sort of litmus test, superseding all other issues. "Dress, like charity, covers a multitude of sins," charged one critic. "If you are right there you will be dealt with leniently on most anything. Some have said that dress has become more important with us than sound morals."[109]

Goshen College and the Final Campaign

With the Bixler decision and conservatism's triumph, 1923 would become a year of carnage in Indiana-Michigan Mennonite Conference. On a churchwide scale, the most prominent casualty was Goshen College. The school had been under increasing scrutiny as it became an established and respected institute of higher education. That was at the heart of the tensions over the school. Goshen and its supporters emphasized scholastic integrity, presenting and considering a variety of perspectives as a way of discovering truth. But for conservative critics in Indiana-Michigan and beyond, the truth was already known, as revealed in the Bible. Goshen's purpose, they argued, was to teach those beliefs to the church's young people so they would not depart from them. The school was supposed to keep the faith traditional. Pedagogy was pitted against orthodoxy, scholarship against church authority.[110] The question was who would decide which approach would prevail.

Conservatives were bolstered by the dangers of modernism, which was gaining traction in broader Christianity and had already affected some European Mennonites, particularly the Dutch.[111] Now it seemed prepared to assault the last vestiges of pure faith—which, according to the church's conservatives, were found among America's Old Mennonites. Among the defenders was Horsch, one of the few church members with the scholastic ability and inclination to grapple with modernism. In a booklet titled *Is the Mennonite Church of America Free from Modernism?*, he lambasted Goshen for resisting antimodernism efforts and for being unwilling to adhere to a Mennonitism "defined by the Conferences and Boards of the Church."[112] Indeed, some modernist elements could be found in the college's classrooms. History professor C. Henry Smith, considered the first American Mennonite to earn a doctorate and remain in the church, taught that the world was advancing, spiritually as well as temporally. President and would-be missionary Noah Byers introduced a course on comparative religion, which could be interpreted as legitimizing other faiths and subverting the need to make converts to Christianity. Literature professor S. F. Gingerich was fascinated by the pantheism and mysticism found in Romanticism.[113] And some faculty members held differing views of Christ's atonement.[114]

Overall, however, the college was not racing toward heresy.[115] Not supporting antimodernism was not the same as actually being modernist. Rather, Goshen was anti-antimodernist, loath to submit to conservatives' doctrinaire demands. Despite Horsch's academic arguments, the issues were not theological but cultural: photographs of immodestly dressed students (at least by the church's criteria), intercollegiate athletics, debate tournaments, musical instruments, questionable theatrical and musical productions, dress violations, inappropriate library books and textbooks, and other worldly indiscretions.[116] For some church members, modernism was an easy and provocative peg upon which to hang their criticism.

In 1918, an MBE-appointed committee secured unanimous agreement from the Goshen faculty on a resolution that they would "subscribe to and pledge themselves to loyally support . . . the decision of standards suggested by the General Conference, local conference and representative bodies of the church."[117] Indiana-Michigan conservatives rejoiced that the school would now adhere to the positions of the church, although technically the resolution only described conference actions as "suggested," which led some faculty members to consider it nonbinding.[118] Within two years, attire was again a point of contention, as were larger concerns about school officials' apparent willingness to thumb their noses at conference authority. A special conference meeting was called. The 1920 annual Indiana-Michigan assembly, held at Olive Mennonite Church north of Wakarusa, Indiana, concluded at 3 p.m. on Thursday, June 3. All ordained men then adjourned to the nearby home of Olive deacon Irvin Long to meet with the Goshen faculty regarding instructors not wearing conference-dictated clothing.[119] The meeting only underscored the differences between school and conference. Dean C. B. Blosser said he was not convinced of the necessity of regulation attire and further argued that MBE did not require it. J. C. Meyer, who had just completed his first year teaching at the college, claimed that as a member of Oak Grove Amish Mennonite Church at Smithville, Ohio, he was not under Indiana-Michigan's jurisdiction. Vocal conservative B. B. King from the Fort Wayne mission placed the blame for the situation on MBE, and the following year the conference approved a motion urging the board to enforce church standards at Goshen.[120] The Bixler investigating committee blamed the college's doctrinal laxness and lack of "loyal submission" to the church as one reason for the troubles in the conference.[121]

In the wake of Hartzler's departure in 1918, dissension and instability had become the norm, as four men served as college president over the next five years. The last one was the Mennonite Church's preeminent church leader, Daniel Kauffman, but even he could not resolve Goshen's problems. In March 1923, students called on Kauffman and several MBE members to resign.[122] Emblematic of the conflict was a gathering of young men four years earlier, not on campus but in postwar France.[123] When fighting ceased in November 1918, Quakers, through their American Friends Service Committee (AFSC), immediately began an ambitious relief and reconstruction program across Europe. It caught the attention of a number of Mennonites. Most of them were progressive Goshen alumni who wanted to join their fellow pacifists in healing the wounds of war. An AFSC unit was created just for Mennonites, which started work building and rebuilding houses at Clermont-en-Argonne, which had been ravaged by the Battle of Verdon in 1916. The unit was led by former Goshen student and future instructor J. C. Meyer.

The Mennonite volunteers were critical of the Mennonite Church and the small cadre of men who controlled it, including Kauffman. While the points of contention varied, the underlying issue was, once again, separation from the world. In the wake of the war, the AFSC workers, many of whom had been conscripts persecuted during the war, saw a tremendous opportunity to apply their convictions and provide a witness to the God of peace. The conservatives in charge, however, were reluctant to allow a less insular expression of faithfulness. In June 1919, the Mennonite AFSC workers in France gathered at Clermont to discuss their concerns and hopes for their church. It resulted in the creation of a short-lived organization, the Young People's Conference, which naturally was met with great suspicion by conservatives, who cited the "Church rebels" as evidence of Goshen's waywardness.[124] In 1921, an Indiana-Michigan committee told the MBE annual meeting that "the first and fundamental work of the church is to evangelize the world rather than to reform the world. . . . Our young people should be led to foster a deep loyalty to the Church and her distinctive standards rather than affiliation with distinctly social reform organizations."[125]

By early 1923, it was becoming apparent that the long-brewing conflict would not be settled in any mutually acceptable way, leaving Goshen's future in jeopardy. On April 4, 1923, the Mennonite Board of Education approved shutting down the college for the 1923–24 academic year, citing "existing conditions brought on by dissatisfaction between the different elements in the church generally, found especially prominent within the conference district . . . where Goshen College is located."[126] The closure provided time for reorganization, and a dramatically different Goshen College reopened its doors in September 1924. The faculty was revamped, with all members vetted for their adherence to orthodoxy; only three instructors on the new faculty had taught at Goshen before its closure. Enrollment numbered just 70 students, compared with 125 during the 1922–23 school year and 210 in 1921–22.[127]

The action to close the college was met with great approval by conservatives and with sad resignation by church moderates. Current and recent students, however, were markedly upset. J. H. Eigsti of Goshen said young people had lost confidence in church leadership and asked, "Which of the two elements, conservative or progressive, is responsible for advancement in missionary activities & service to mankind?"[128] Elva May Schrock of Nappanee turned prevailing religious nomenclature against those who closed the school: "Through the College God has led many of us into having a larger life, into a fuller appreciation of the *fundamentals* of Christianity as embodied in the Mennonite faith, and has given to many of us the call to definite life service."[129]

Caught in the maelstrom was College Mennonite Church, which met in the Goshen College chapel and included many of the suspect faculty, administration, and students. The Indiana-Michigan executive committee flexed its constitutional muscle when, on February 21, 1923, it asked College members to vote yes or no on their allegiance to conference ordinances. Of more than four hundred congregants, only fourteen participated—and some of them voted no. As a result, communion was observed on March 25 with just twelve people.[130] Five days later, the executive committee decided to ask all Indiana-Michigan members if they accepted the conference's authority. If they did not, they would be denied communion.[131]

The executive committee then focused on the ministers, bringing to the 1923 annual assembly a resolution calling for stricter adherence to existing rules on attire and life insurance.[132] It also included requiring all members of the ministry to enforce existing positions "and other regulations of Conference" or be silenced. The resolution passed with fifty-three of the sixty delegates voting for it. The executive committee and bishops soon started interviewing suspect ministers and deacons. Irvin R. Detweiler, former college president and minister of the College congregation, told the committee, "I am willing to try to apply the rulings of conference in as far it will not destroy or demoralize the congregation." That local emphasis was echoed by Barker Street minister Oesch: "I am willing to try to apply recent decisions as best we can under conditions, reserving freedom of judgment and action when the integrity of the congregation is at stake."[133] Barker Street, still under the auspices of the Indiana-Michigan mission board, had been at the center of the petition against Bixler, who was bishop of the mission congregations. Among the complaints was that he tried to prevent Barker Street from calling the notorious J. E. Hartzler as a guest speaker, claiming that it was the responsibility of the mission board, since the congregation was officially a mission station. "I insisted that they could hardly assume that right without getting consent of the congregation to do so," Oesch told a friend.[134]

With their tradition of congregational discernment, conference congregations of Amish Mennonite background, such as West Market Street in Nappanee, Indiana, or with sizable Amish Mennonite membership, such as College, suffered the most. On September 4, the executive committee silenced five ministers: Oesch and Detweiler, plus Raymond L. Hartzler of Maple Grove, Ezra S. Mullet of North Main Street, and S. S. Yoder of Middlebury. Another minister, Wilbur W. Miller at Forks, lost his pastorate the next year. He had been arguing with his bishop—and father—D. D. Miller about life insurance. D. D., in an obviously difficult situation, asked the conference to step in. The Indiana-Michigan executive committee removed the younger Miller, an action later ratified by the congregation. (He proceeded to leave the ministry and the Mennonite faith and became a successful school administrator and a Presbyterian.[135]) In the fall of 1924, when Goshen College reopened, members of the campus congregation had to sign a statement pledging their loyalty to the conference. Only sixty-nine people, roughly a third of the congregation, did so.[136]

The purges of 1923–24 were unprecedented for two reasons. First, discipline had long been the responsibility of the local bishops and ministers, who were expected to uphold conference standards but had relatively wide latitude to do so. Now power was located in a centralized Indiana-Michigan executive committee, which began a conference-wide campaign to impose orthodoxy. The second reason was the scope of that campaign. The Wisler and Brenneman schisms of half a century earlier, while dramatic and traumatic, had been largely localized, limited to a couple of leaders and their followers in the Yellow Creek community. This time, however, the problems were widespread.

In Nappanee, West Market Street and North Main Street experienced a wholesale reorganization in composition as they swapped members. West Market Street withdrew from the conference in 1923 and called ex–North Main Street pastor Mullet to be its minister. He was accompanied by about thirty-five members of his former congregation. West Market Street would join the General Conference Mennonite Church, becoming the second member of that denomination in Indiana (after First Mennonite Church at Berne).[137] At the same time, about fifty people from West Market Street transferred to North Main Street in order to remain with Indiana-Michigan. Barker Street also withdrew from the conference upon the executive committee's action against Oesch, eventually moving several miles north to Mottville, Michigan, and joining the Central Conference of Mennonites.

On the east side of Elkhart County, S. S. Yoder and about one hundred members left First Mennonite Church in Middlebury to form Pleasant Oaks Mennonite Church, which would join the Central Conference in 1926. Among those transferring to the new congregation were Rebecca Hostetler and Treva Schrock, wife and granddaughter, respectively, of First pastor A. J. Hostetler. (Schrock, then a teenager, was living with her grandparents.[138]) Nevertheless, the family remained together; A. J. died in 1925. Yoder later repented and returned to First Mennonite Church in 1941. Across the line in LaGrange County, Raymond L. Hartzler led a split from Maple Grove in 1924. The new group

For nearly forty years, Indiana-Michigan Mennonite Conference was akin to a circus in one aspect: they both met under a large tent. But instead of featuring elephants, clowns, and trapeze artists, the conference's tent was for fellowship, worship, and church business. By making Indiana-Michigan visible in a very tangible way, the tent essentially became the conference symbol.

Because few buildings were large enough, conference delegates in 1920 appointed a committee to work with Indiana-Michigan's Sunday school committee to purchase a tent for their events. The first one, to be used for the 1921 annual assembly, was not what was ordered and was thus returned.[1] After being replaced, the tent was regularly used for the annual assembly as well as for other conference functions. It was also available to congregations for evangelistic meetings and to other area conferences. Even the Mennonite Church used it for its general conference sessions. Rental fees went into a fund for tent repair and eventual replacement.

The tent was in poor condition by the late 1940s, and a new one, measuring seventy feet by one hundred feet, was purchased in 1949 for $2,444.[2] Rental rates for the new tent were set at $40 plus $4 a day for Indiana-Michigan congregations, $50 plus $5 a day for nonmembers.[3] The old tent was rendered unusable in 1950 when it caught fire while being used for evangelistic meetings in Saginaw, Michigan.[4]

With the growing availability of large indoor spaces, such as new church buildings and Bethany Christian High School just south of Goshen, Indiana, the conference had ceased using the tent for its annual assemblies by the late 1950s, although it was still being rented out four or five times a year. Meanwhile the era of tent meetings was coming to a close. In 1964, Indiana-Michigan authorized the sale of the tent to Camp Amigo, the new conference-affiliated retreat center near Sturgis, Michigan.[5] Indiana-Michigan's big top had come down permanently.

---

1. Indiana-Michigan Mennonite Conference, *Minutes of the Indiana-Michigan Mennonite Conference, 1864–1929*, comp. Ira S. Johns, J. S. Hartzler, and Amos O. Hostetler (Scottdale, PA: Mennonite Publishing House, [1929?]), 256.
2. "Report of the Annual Sessions of the Indiana-Michigan Mennonite Conference, May 31, June 1, 1950," 35.
3. Indiana-Michigan Mennonite Conference Executive Committee minutes, October 13, 1949, Indiana-Michigan Mennonite Conference collection (II-5-2), box 1, folder 2, MCUSAA–Goshen.
4. Indiana-Michigan Mennonite Conference Executive Committee minutes, July 19, 1950, Indiana-Michigan Mennonite Conference collection (II-5-2), box 1, folder 3, MCUSAA–Goshen.
5. "Report of the Annual Sessions of the Indiana-Michigan Mennonite Conference, July 30–August 2, 1964," 5.

invoked its heritage by calling itself Maple Grove Amish Mennonite Church and affiliated with the Central Conference in 1927.[139] The congregation was short lived, as two years later it joined nearby Topeka Mennonite Church, another Central Conference congregation. Hartzler would go on to be one of the conference's outstanding leaders.

Detweiler was the only member of the disciplined group not pastoring an Indiana-Michigan congregation at the time. A former missionary to India, he had become president of Goshen College in 1919 but was ousted in 1922 amid the school's turmoil. He then returned to the pulpit of the College congregation, a position he had held before assuming the presidency. But in the summer of 1922, Detweiler, followed by a number of other College members, departed for Eighth Street Mennonite Church, a Central Conference congregation just up the street from campus. The Bixler investigating committee had drafted an action specifically aimed at Detweiler, declaring that ministers serving congregations "outside our church" should be considered "no longer in standing or in position to do work in the church."[140] Detweiler's affiliation with the conference and with the Mennonite Church had come to an end, as had that of many others.[141]

Overall, during the 1920s, Indiana-Michigan expelled an average of fifty-one members a year for "backsliding."[142] With dissenters out of the conference or otherwise silenced, the aggresso-conservatives ushered in a dramatically different era for Indiana-Michigan Conference, one that made boundary maintenance a priority.

5

Expanding the Boundaries

With a new Ford motorcar and a trailer full of camping equipment and supplies, Clarence A. and Maggie Shank and Edwin J. and Mary Yoder were ready for a trip to Michigan's Upper Peninsula. Their destination may have only been their neighboring state to the north, but the Shanks, from Wakarusa, Indiana, and the Yoders, from Topeka, Indiana, were leaving traditional Mennonite notions of belief and community for a new frontier of faithfulness. By 1934, when the quartet headed north, the Upper Peninsula had been dubbed the "Playground of America," annually drawing thousands of tourists to its forested lands and miles of Great Lakes coastline. The Shanks had vacationed there ten years earlier, spending several weeks near Engadine on account of Clarence's health. They discovered that among the bountiful trees, rivers, and lakes were scattered small, struggling churches, both Protestant and Catholic, which were usually served by circuit riders who would make periodic stops to preach to handfuls of believers.

The Shanks, having worshiped in a moribund Methodist congregation during their respite, returned to Indiana impressed with the potential for a Mennonite witness in the Upper Peninsula. That idea finally resulted in action after Clarence Shank became vice president of the Indiana-Michigan Mennonite Mission Board in 1933, which authorized Shank and Yoder, the board's president, to investigate the possibilities of establishing a Mennonite presence in the region.[1]

So at 3 a.m. on Sunday, July 29, 1934, the Shanks and Yoders set out from Indiana to expand the conference's boundaries, arriving in time to worship with the Mennonite congregation at White Cloud, Michigan. The two couples crossed the Straits of Mackinac by ferry two days later, landing on the Upper Peninsula. They had already traveled nearly four hundred miles, but their real sojourn was just beginning. Over the next ten days the Shanks and Yoders canvassed the entire peninsula, from Sault Ste. Marie in the east to the Wisconsin border three hundred miles to the west, stopping at each of the fifteen Upper Peninsula county seats.

But it was on a side trip to Germfask that the Shanks and Yoders found the greatest potential. The village was home to the only person in the entire Upper Peninsula with whom they had any acquaintance, even if it was only by name: Violet Livermore. At the age of two, she had contracted a disease (possibly polio) that left her limbs under-developed.[2] Now twenty-four, she used a wheelchair and lived with her parents. The family had previously lived at White Cloud, where she had been introduced by local Mennonites to *Words of Cheer*, the popular children's magazine from Mennonite Publishing House.[3] Through it the Livermores eventually made contact with Indiana-Michigan Menno-nite Conference, prompting the Shanks and Yoders' visit to Germfask. "How eager they were to hear the truths about which they had read," Yoder reported in the *Rural Evangel*, the mission board's periodical. "It was during this visit that the invalid daughter gave her heart to the Lord and confessed Him as her personal Savior. How it did encourage us on our way to know that seed which had reached this place where so little Gospel seed was being sown to root and 'produced fruit.'"[4] With that connection, Germfask became the inaugural site for conference mission work. Bible schools and evangelistic meetings were held there during the next two summers, and the first Upper Peninsula Mennonite congregation was organized in 1938.

The impulse to form new congregations and expand the church was not new. It had long been an integral part of Indiana-Michigan church life, starting in the mid-1800s when ordained men would travel great distances to minister to Mennonite settlers living in isolated com-munities without congregations or ministerial leadership, both within Indiana and Michigan and in other states. More formal conference connections had developed by the close of the nineteenth century, fol-lowed by the founding of the Indiana-Michigan Mennonite Mission Board in 1911. Despite that record of outreach, the Upper Peninsula initiative was groundbreaking. Previously, new mission congregations had largely been the result not of evangelism but of "colonization":

First Bible school at Germfask, Stauffer School, 1935. MCUSAA–Goshen.

Mennonites moving to new areas to establish a presence that local residents could join, drawn by the daily living of Mennonite discipleship.[5] But colonies rarely added members from outside the ethnic and cultural fold, making the new congregations like the overall conference—largely homogenous in composition.[6] By the 1930s, the strategy had faded away.

While colonization proved to be an ineffective strategy, an emphasis on rural missions remained paramount. The traditional, agriculture-based communities of farmers and small business owners were considered safe and secure bastions of Mennonitism, keeping church members geographically and spiritually away from urban temptations. Vices such as alcohol, dancing, and movies, as well as the fickle whims of fashion and other worldly trends, were deemed much too alluring and much too accessible in the comparatively fast-paced and brightly lit cities. Even employment in such settings had its dangers, such as the possibility of working on Sunday and having to join a labor union with its potential use of violence and coercion.[7] Ira S. Johns, the conference's longtime secretary, called city settings "deteriorating to religious life, especially to our simple, nonconformed faith."[8] It was believed better to remain in the country and in the church's geographic embrace where there were fewer distractions from godly living, working, and worshiping. That was most evident in the name of the Indiana-Michigan

Mennonite Mission Board's periodical. The *Rural Evangel* was begun in 1919 to give the board the ability to directly, regularly, and efficiently promote its work. Board president Yoder declared:

> The rural communities are sorely neglected religiously. And too as everywhere so many that are teachers do not hold out a whole, evangelical message. The rural people as a rule are not attending the city and village churches. The people of the rural sections and smaller towns are unusually open-hearted and eager to hear and read. There is a cordiality and friendliness that the stranger feels among them that you do not find in the more densely populated parts of our country. This is a great advantage in doing personal work among them. There is a hungering for the Truth of God's Word in the hearts of many when you approach the subject of Spiritual things.[9]

City and Country

Within the borders of the conference were two notable exceptions to the emphasis on rural missions, although they were only tangentially connected to Indiana-Michigan. About 1854, a group of Mennonites moved from Columbiana and Holmes Counties in Ohio and settled around Gar Creek, a dozen miles across the state line in Allen County in northeastern Indiana. Given their origins and location, they remained affiliated with Ohio Mennonite Conference. In 1884, John Federspiel, a Catholic, was baptized at Gar Creek and shortly afterward moved with his wife, Tilda, to the nearby city of Fort Wayne, where they began advocating for a Mennonite congregation. Finally in 1902, Eli Stoffer, who had baptized Federspiel, took the idea to Ohio Conference, even though the location was not in Ohio and Stoffer was not an Ohio minister. (He pastored Pleasant Valley Mennonite Church in DeKalb County, Indiana). Ohio approved starting a mission in Fort Wayne and appointed M. S. Steiner to lead the project. He was the former employee of John F. Funk who went to Chicago in 1893 to begin the first Mennonite urban mission. He and his bride, Clara, then opened a mission in Canton, Ohio, the next year. In 1897, Steiner was among a group selected by the Mennonite Evangelizing and Benevolent Board to oversee an orphanage and old people's home in Ohio. By the end of the

While the strict, conservative ethos of the 1920s and 1930s kept women behind the ministerial scenes, they still made vital contributions to the cause of the church. They were especially needed on the edges of Indiana-Michigan Mennonite Conference, where conditions were often starkly different from those in more established environs, and the opportunities for ministry more apparent.

In Detroit, for example, Clara Jennings Raber was able to serve in ways that would have been more difficult, if not impossible, for her husband, Frank, who was the minister of the city Mennonite mission congregation.[1] He recognized that Clara would be more effective in some cases, such as ministering to victims of sexual abuse, including those abused by other clergy. One woman in the Detroit congregation died of venereal disease contracted from her husband, who had been jailed several times for sex crimes. Clara assisted young Mennonite and Amish women with out-of-wedlock pregnancies who were sent to the city by their families until they delivered. She also attended many births to support the mother.

In the tiny community of Brethren, Michigan, where Claude Culp was minister of Pleasantview Mennonite Church, his wife, Emma Habig Culp, helped make funeral arrangements, whether or not the deceased had been part of the congregation. In this way she was a pastor to the entire community. Emma and Claude also frequently sang duets at funerals.[2]

Death and dying also provided Mabel Weaver the chance to put her religious beliefs into action. The wife of Norman Weaver, pastor of Maple Grove Mennonite at Gulliver, Michigan, Mabel would daily visit a woman with cancer in the community to pray with her and bathe her. She would also take the woman's laundry home to wash.[3] Even though women couldn't be ordained, they were still ministers.

1. Clara S. Jennings Raber, *Special Handling: An Autobiography* (privately published, 1994), chap. 4.
2. Mary Swartley, "She Has Done What She Could" (paper presented to Michiana Anabaptist Historians, October 26, 2002), 7.
3. Rosella Prater, *Mennonite Stirrings in America's Playland* (Naubinway, MI: privately published 1987), 34.

century, the Ohioans had, under Steiner's leadership, become a separate organization, the Mennonite Board of Charitable Homes and Missions. But the distinctions between and responsibilities of the two mission agencies were vague. Although the Fort Wayne work started under the auspices of Steiner and the Ohio board, Federspiel was appointed the first Sunday school superintendent by the Indiana-based Mennonite Evangelizing and Benevolent Board. Even the Fort Wayne workers were unsure of their lines of accountability.[10]

The two mission organizations eliminated that ambiguity when they merged in 1906 to create Mennonite Board of Missions (MBM). Before long Ohio had no direct links to the Fort Wayne work, as Indiana-Michigan bishops assumed oversight of the mission. The conference financially supported it and appointed a representative to its board, and Indiana-Michigan members served short- and long-term assignments in the city. But the Fort Wayne mission remained an MBM mission until 1953, when it became a full-fledged Indiana-Michigan member named First Mennonite Church. The mission had an amazing record of bringing people to faith and then sending them out to do Mennonite city mission work elsewhere. Among them were Geneva and Maurice O'Connell. Geneva was converted at an evangelistic service in Fort Wayne and joined the mission. Maurice was initially only a marginal participant in the congregation until he had his own conversion experience. He quit smoking, made restitution for earlier petty thefts, and became active in church work. Maurice was appointed superintendent of the Lima, Ohio, Mennonite mission and would eventually become a bishop and evangelist.[11]

Although successful, Fort Wayne highlighted the perils of city work. The mission's first location was above a saloon, a rented second-floor room that served as a lodge and dance hall during the week. Many times the room had to be cleaned from the previous night's activities before Sunday worship could be held, and saloon patrons were known to disrupt services.[12] But urban areas continued to beckon. Two decades after work started in Fort Wayne, seeds were planted for another city congregation when Mennonites started moving to Detroit for its employment opportunities, many of them in the booming automotive industry.[13] By 1926, bishop Peter Ropp had also relocated to the city, arriving from Imlay City, Michigan, where he had been serving

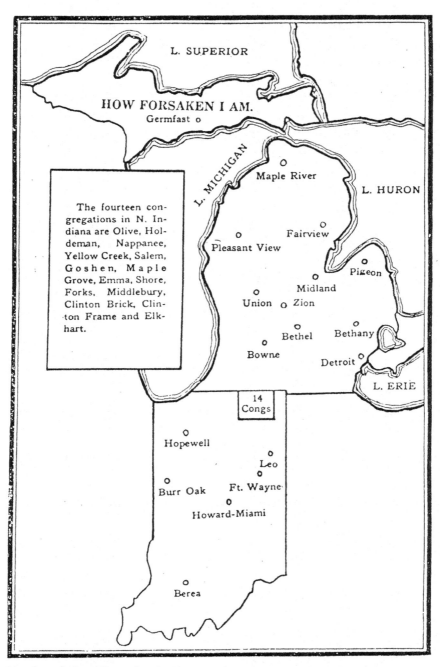

The fourteen congregations in N. Indiana are Olive, Holdeman, Nappanee, Yellow Creek, Salem, Goshen, Maple Grove, Emma, Shore, Forks, Middlebury, Clinton Brick, Clinton Frame and Elkhart.

Map from the Rural Evangel *with "How Forsaken I Am" across Upper Peninsula.*
MHL–Goshen.

under the Indiana-Michigan mission board. In Detroit he set out to organize the resettled Mennonites into a congregation, acting independently of the mission board although with its blessing. The board offered its assistance in compiling a list of Mennonites in the city and also in finding a meeting place for the fledgling group of worshipers. The work came under conference mission board auspices in 1927 when Ropp was called back to Imlay City and new leadership needed to be found for Detroit. Working with MBM, the conference board called C. C. King, a lay worker at MBM's mission in Canton, Ohio, and paid the rent and provided furnishings for his Detroit home. King believed the Christian message transcended earthly geography and population density. "The Gospel of Christ fits into any place, the doctrines of the Mennonite Church are based on the Gospel, and consequently will fit into Detroit," King asserted.[14] But the board's country ministers felt increasingly ill-suited to oversee urban missions and soon entered into negotiations to transfer the work to MBM, which was finalized in 1930.

Five years after divesting itself of the Detroit work, the Indiana-Michigan mission board threw itself into promoting missions in the Upper Peninsula. After the Shanks and Yoders returned to Indiana with a favorable report, the *Rural Evangel* stated, "It is the plan of the Board to keep this field before the readers of the *Evangel*."[15] With regular features and periodic maps with "How Forsaken I Am" emblazoned over the region, the magazine depicted an exotic, distant land, filled with natural wonders, inhabited by few people, and economically and spiritually impoverished— and quite different from most of Indiana-Michigan Mennonite Conference. While MBM was sending workers to India and Argentina, the Upper Peninsula became Indiana-Michigan's foreign country. Articles in the *Rural Evangel* described the region's geography, soil, crops, climate, and other characteristics as if the Upper Peninsula was an overseas mission field. Commercial lumbering had started on the forest-covered peninsula in the 1840s and reached its peak between 1860 and 1890. By the turn of the century, copper and iron mining had become the Upper Peninsula's major employers. But copper was already in decline when the Great Depression hit, which left the iron industry in dire condition. That combined with the dying lumber industry and the overused, underproducing farmland to make the region's economic status painfully low.[16] One bright spot was the emergence of the Upper Peninsula as a tourist destination. Clarence Shank declared it "a strange land when viewed as a whole."[17]

The region's residents were a hard-living mix of Finnish, Swedish, Italian, French, Native American, and other ethnic groups. They embodied an individualistic, pioneering ethos that in many ways clashed with the nonresistant, family- and community-minded, and primarily Germanic members of Indiana-Michigan. In crossing the Straits of Mackinac from lower Michigan, the conference was for the first time intentionally trying to move beyond its ethnic and cultural boundaries. There was no prior Mennonite presence in the Upper Peninsula, although it had several residents with Mennonite connections. Two Ontario families of Mennonite background had homesteaded in the Germfask area in the late nineteenth century. One was the family of Jerrod Stauffer, a first cousin to noted Goshen College professor and church leader Harold Stauffer Bender. A disaffected Mennonite from Iowa was also reported to be living at Manistique on the western end of the peninsula.[18]

After several years of searching for full-time workers for the Upper Peninsula, the mission board finally found newlyweds Chester and Eva Osborne of Kokomo, Indiana. The couple had married in 1936 and agreed to go into service if called. The invitation to go north came four months after their wedding, and the Osbornes moved to Germfask in the summer of 1937, initially living in part of a house owned by Norman Stauffer, son of Jerrod Stauffer.[19] But the Osbornes almost didn't go. Chester confessed to the board that, in addition to lacking biblical knowledge, "I am a very poor singer and Eva has never led congregational singing."[20] After all, how could Mennonite evangelism be accomplished without a capella singing? Even if the music might have been substandard, by October the Osbornes were holding regular worship services at Stauffer School, across the road from the Stauffer house. Germfask Mennonite Church was officially organized the next spring with nine charter members.

The Osbornes didn't limit their work to Germfask but energetically sought to reach out to new areas. In the summer of 1939, a Bible school was held in a school building at Sandtown, seventeen miles east of Germfask, which was soon followed by regular Sunday school and worship services. Later that summer the Osbornes began holding worship services at a lumber camp near Alger Mills, twenty-five miles to the north. In addition to being employed in order to financially support the family, Chester, with Eva's active assistance, maintained an ambitious ministerial schedule: Sunday school and worship at Germfask on Sunday mornings, Sunday school and worship at Sandtown in the afternoons, then back to Germfask for evening services. Worship and Sunday school were held Wednesday evenings at Alger Mills and prayer meeting on Thursday evenings at Germfask. Visitation was squeezed into a couple of other evenings during the week.[21] The work at Alger Mills continued even after the lumber camp broke up, as several families remained in the area. Chester Osborne reported in the *Rural Evangel*: "We were so touched by their spiritual starvation and the attempts of Satan to choke out the new life born in them last spring that we are again spending our Sunday afternoons by driving the fifty miles to minister to the spiritual needs of these, as well as a few others who are still there. How long we shall continue is up to the Lord, as well as the opening of other needy regions. We go forward as He leads, and try to stand still until He does prompt."[22]

The Osbornes' dedication and success were impressive, but assuming responsibility for the entire Upper Peninsula was a heavy burden to carry. They finally received help in 1940 when the Clarence and Wavia Troyer family arrived from Topeka, Indiana, to fulfill a commitment to God. Three years earlier their oldest son, two-year-old Calvin, was deathly ill with pneumonia, prompting Clarence and Wavia to pray that if he would survive, they would go into service wherever called. Calvin lived, and his parents let the conference mission board know of their willingness to serve. They were appointed to work in the Upper Peninsula, where Clarence and Wavia would live and minister for the rest of their lives.[23]

The board had originally assigned the Troyers to Baraga, near Marquette on the peninsula's northwest coast. The Osbornes had conducted Bible school there in 1939, but after World War II erupted, Mennonites were considered German sympathizers and were not welcome.[24] So the Troyers instead moved to Sandtown, where they took over the Osbornes' work, which became Wildwood Mennonite Church. In 1942 the Troyers led the creation of a congregation in Naubinway, about fifteen miles to the southeast. That same year, Germfask started Maple

Grove Mennonite Church at Gulliver, twenty miles to the southwest. Filled with evangelistic vigor, the Mennonite presence in the Upper Peninsula was spreading. Services were being held in eleven locations across the region within fifteen years of the Osbornes' arrival.

With its emphasis on rural outreach and its tradition of unsalaried ministers, Indiana-Michigan was well suited for mission work in the Upper Peninsula. The conference continued to shy away from the professional pastorate, or full-time, salaried ministers. Subsequently, those in congregational ministry needed to have other sources of income. That was also the expectation of the conference's church planters. Although they received nominal support from the mission board, they had to find work in other vocations to make ends meet. In many cases in mostly rural Indiana-Michigan, ministers' occupations were often in agriculture, which offered great flexibility while also sustaining the minister and his family. Attempts at farming were made in the Upper Peninsula, but with mixed results. Instead, most of the early ministers found employment in forestry, fishing, and carpentry. Naubinway minister Ora Wyse operated a laundry, while Joe Swartz of Rexton Mennonite Church, about fifteen miles east of Wildwood, drove a school bus.[25]

Ora Wyse (right), son Larry, and wife, Esther, in family laundry, Naubinway, Michigan. MCUSAA–Goshen.

Such work demonstrated to their neighbors that the Mennonites were not simply passing through but were full-fledged, permanent residents of their communities. Thus they were able to provide what the circuit rider preachers could not, such as Sunday schools, Bible studies, and visitation in addition to regular worship services. The Mennonites—a group many in the Upper Peninsula had never before even heard of—were also able to practice daily discipleship that went beyond Sunday mornings or Wednesday evenings. The minister often had the only car in the community, so when it wasn't packed full of children going to Sunday school, it was often the community's de facto taxi during the rest of the week. Wyse made so many emergency trips taking people to the doctor that he had a siren installed on his station wagon.[26] One family was drawn to the Mennonites after hearing that after a coworker of the husband fell off his barn and broke his back, men from the Brutus and Petoskey congregations in northern Michigan came to finish fixing the barn, plus harvest the injured man's crop and cut wood for the winter.[27]

But those same characteristics of love and service could also work against Mennonite church planting. The newcomers' clean living, while garnering respect in their communities, was often seen as too high a standard for many Upper Peninsula residents to attain. In addition, beliefs such as nonresistance and regulation attire were often puzzling barriers that kept people from joining. Some longtime and regular churchgoers never did join, particularly women who refused to wear the prayer covering. Meanwhile, other congregations accused the Mennonites of raiding their flocks for members. For that reason, the Grand Marais Methodists denied the Mennonites use of their building for Bible school.[28]

Compared with their neighbors, the Mennonite church planters were usually better off economically. They received some financial support from the Indiana-Michigan mission board, and friends, family, and congregations down south would provide money, clothing, and foodstuffs. Workers warned their children not to flaunt their material advantages. Chester Osborne even made his children go barefoot at Bible school so as not to differentiate them from the local residents.[29] The Wildwood Mennonite Church initially did not take offerings, since circuit riders were known not to return if the collection plates weren't full enough. Wildwood's attempt to avoid that gold-digging reputation piqued local residents' curiosity about these newcomers who didn't ask for money.[30]

Nevertheless, the Mennonites were not immune to the challenges of Upper Peninsula life. Like the rest of the area's residents, they often lived in houses without electricity and indoor plumbing. Groceries sometimes had to be purchased on credit—an embarrassment to usually self-sufficient Mennonites. Farther south, financial difficulties could keep someone from the ministry because it suggested some sort of irresponsibility and thus moral shortcoming. Gardens, hunting, and fishing were crucial for feeding families. One minister survived one winter almost entirely on suckerfish he had caught and pickled the previous summer.[31]

Home and Away

While the Upper Peninsula was the most exotic conference mission field, it was not the only location receiving attention. The addition of Germfask in 1939 made for eight stations under the Indiana-Michigan mission board, geographically ranging from northern Michigan to southern Indiana; by 1943 the board had started more than twenty plants.[32] But it wasn't alone in such efforts, as individual congregations were also reaching out. Seventeen of the conference's thirty-two congregations were doing some sort of outreach in 1936.[33] In Elkhart, Prairie Street Mennonite Church planted two congregations. Belmont Mennonite Church was started in an underserved part of the city in 1929. The second congregation began when members Effie and Paul Wittrig were enjoying a drive through the country east of Elkhart and saw an abandoned church building. Further investigation revealed that no religious services were being held in the entire township. So Prairie Street renovated the old meetinghouse and started holding services, resulting in the formation of Pleasant View Mennonite Church in 1936.[34] At Vestaburg, Michigan, tiny Zion Mennonite Church, with just sixteen members, conducted a summer Bible school in 1938 that drew an astonishing 107 pupils. "We feel that we are too small a group to start a mission Sunday school . . . but we can do some good this way, and our people want to do all they can for the Master," the congregation's correspondent reported in the *Rural Evangel*.[35] That year some two thousand children were enrolled in summer Bible schools conducted by congregations across Indiana-Michigan.[36] Another congregation not limited by its small size was Bethel Mennonite Church at Ashley, Michigan, which was sending used Sunday school materials to be used in the Philippines.[37]

Goshen College, often derided for being at odds with the church, was also instrumental in expanding Indiana-Michigan. In 1929 a student organization, the Christian Workers Band, started distributing literature in the East Goshen and North Goshen neighborhoods, leading to the start of a Sunday school in East Goshen the following year. After beginning with only 14 children, attendance soon exploded to 112, some coming from North Goshen. So a Sunday school was started in that part of the city, too, and by 1931 attendance at both sites was more than 300.[38] The North Goshen work turned into a congregation in 1936, although it generated some opposition. When the church building was being erected, a neighbor across the street came over and cursed the builders. Surprisingly, he also attended the meetings in the church and eventually joined the congregation.[39] East Goshen Mennonite Church was formed in 1947, four years after Goshen students started work in southwest Elkhart that became Locust Grove Mennonite Church.

The *Rural Evangel* was pivotal in the development of a missions-oriented culture in the conference. While the Indiana-Michigan executive committee and annual delegate assembly relied almost exclusively on the bishops, ministers, and deacons to take information back to their congregations, the mission board proved adept at marketing, going straight to the lay membership with its clear message that home missions was not just an enterprise for ordained men. The *Rural Evangel* repeatedly highlighted ways that members not ordained could also help fulfill God's call to make disciples of all nations. In addition to making themselves available for full-time mission work, they could serve on congregational mission committees, teach Sunday school classes, distribute tracts, and help construct meetinghouses for new congregations.

At the same time that Indiana-Michigan members were being encouraged to witness within the borders of the conference, others heeded calls to spread the gospel message elsewhere. In 1930, MBM appointed three new city mission superintendents, two of whom were Indiana-Michigan natives. Warren Long from North Main Street Mennonite Church in Nappanee, Indiana, was chosen for the Mennonite mission in Peoria, Illinois, and Perry Heller went from Fort Wayne to Los Angeles. The third appointee was Missouri native and Goshen College graduate Frank Raber, who was assigned to lead the Detroit mission. All three would go on to long ministerial careers.

Indiana-Michigan Mennonites were also going overseas to serve. One was Genevieve Yoder from Topeka, Indiana, the daughter of Maple Grove Mennonite Church bishop and Upper Peninsula missions explorer Edwin J. Yoder. She felt called to foreign mission work, and at Goshen College majored in Bible, was secretary of her Bible study group and of the Christian Workers Band, and was a member of the Peace Society.[40] Yoder also met fellow student John A. Friesen, the son of P. A. and Magdalena Hiebert Friesen, longtime MBM workers in India.[41] John was intent on returning as a missionary in his own right, and he found a partner in Yoder. They married in 1939 and later that year began more than four decades with MBM in India. (A third generation of Friesens would also serve in the country.) Another Indiana-Michigan missionary was Jonathan G. Yoder from Goshen. He attended Goshen College, then went on to earn his medical degree. After three years in private practice at North Lima, Ohio, Yoder and his wife, Fyrne, went to India with MBM in 1937.[42] That year another Indiana-Michigan couple went to proclaim the gospel to foreign peoples but never left the country. Amsa and Nona Kauffman left LaGrange County, Indiana, to be the first permanent MBM missionaries in South Texas, working with Mexican immigrants. The Kauffmans decided to enter the mission field after Amsa was kept out of the lot at Forks Mennonite Church because he had attended Goshen.[43] T. K. Hershey, an MBM worker in Argentina on furlough, had started work in South Texas in 1936 but returned to South America when the Kauffmans arrived. They founded Calvary Mennonite Church in Mathis in 1944, then moved back to Indiana two years later when Amsa was called to pastor Clinton Brick Mennonite Church east of Goshen.

Shoring Up the Center

Despite the early support it had from across the theological spectrum, Indiana-Michigan Mennonite Mission Board soon became an instrument not just for winning converts for Christ and the Mennonite Church but for instilling in them an exclusively conservative understanding of the Mennonite faith. Already in 1912, just a year after the board's formation, it was asking mission candidates, "What is your attitude toward the more liberal churches?"[44] The 1914 appointment of Jacob K. Bixler as bishop of the mission stations ensured that beliefs considered doctrinally unsound would be carefully and earnestly screened out. The mission board made available conservative, even fundamentalist tracts such as "The Atonement," "A Vision of the Second Coming of Christ," and "Three College Ship-Wrecks" and distributed free copies of *1,000 Questions and Answers on Points of Christian Doctrine* by *Gospel Herald* editor Daniel Kauffman. From his home and office in Scottdale, Pennsylvania, the former Goshen College president had emerged as the era's greatest and most influential articulator of Mennonite conservatism, starting with his *Manual of Bible Doctrines* in 1898 and over the next three decades followed with books such as *The Conservative Viewpoint* (1918), *The Mennonite Church and Current Issues* (1923), and *Doctrines of the Bible* (1928).

For conservatives, the conference's spiritual well-being was always in peril, on the edge of succumbing to the real and perceived worldly influences that had already infected the rest of Christianity. "We have been compromising too much," asserted Ira S. Johns in 1935, a self-indictment since he and his conservative brethren had been ruling Indiana-Michigan for a dozen years.[45] Johns's father, Amish Mennonite bishop D. J. Johns, was relatively progressive, particularly in his support of Elkhart Institute, but Ira aligned himself with the fundamentalists. He was Indiana-Michigan conference secretary for twenty-nine years, and throughout the 1930s he was one of only seven people to serve on the five-member conference executive committee. Three of the seven also served on the Indiana-Michigan Mennonite Mission Board, further concentrating power in the conference. Prairie Street Mennonite Church minister J. S. Hartzler was not on either the conference or mission board executive committees, but he held the important position of editing the *Rural Evangel*. In his sermon at the 1931 Indiana-Michigan annual session, he spoke on the unassailable nature of church authority. "I am not preaching salvation through conference regulation," Hartzler said, "but I am saying that when decisions are made for the good of the church, the keeping of them is just as obligatory as they were at the Jerusalem Conference."[46]

Dissent was granted very little latitude. The Indiana-Michigan executive committee took a heavy-handed approach to keeping order and maintaining boundaries. Among its actions were disciplining Yellow Creek Mennonite Church's bishop, minister, and deacon for voting in the 1928 presidential election, silencing church planter C. L. Ressler of North Webster, Indiana, because of "business relations of such a nature and to such an extent that his influence as a minister has been lost and since he has failed to give satisfaction to his creditors," and forcing James Bucher, who wanted to become an evangelist in California, to instead remain as minister at Berea Mennonite Church in Daviess County in southern Indiana.[47] Conference delegate action made tobacco use a test of membership and reiterated opposition to granges and labor unions, singing groups in church, flirting (presumably by both boys and girls), and cut hair for women. The hair requirements also affected some men. Before becoming superintendent of the mission in Los Angeles, Perry Heller ran a barbershop around the corner from the Fort Wayne mission and drew the church's criticism for cutting women's hair in fashionable styles.[48] Conference delegates, facing yet another "impending crisis on dress," called for stricter discipline in 1931, and seven years later endorsed a plan for the general conference's General Problems Committee to investigate institutions and conferences "departing from the established standards of the Mennonite Church."[49] Salem Mennonite Church of New Paris, Indiana, one

Clinton Frame sewing circle, 1918. MCUSAA–Goshen.

of the more conservative congregations in the conference, did its part to uphold those principles by loaning $25 to the "bonnet maker of the Salem congregation" to purchase supplies so that women's heads would remain covered in the proper way.[50]

After their pre–World War I advances, women's place in the conference was pushed back to the margins, even while their service increased, when Indiana-Michigan came under conservative control. Sewing circles were dotting the Mennonite Church landscape from Pennsylvania to Kansas by 1910. In Indiana-Michigan during the next decade, at least ten congregations started sewing circles, leading to the creation of the conference-wide "Indiana-Michigan Branch, Women's Work of the Mennonite Church" in 1917.[51] That growth in the conference was a reflection of denominational trends. At the 1915 Mennonite Church General Conference sessions at Wauseon, Ohio, several hundred women attended a meeting on sewing circles and mission work. Sabina Landis was selected chair and Mamie Hartzler as secretary (spouses of Indiana-Michigan ministers A. S. Landis and J. E. Hartzler, respectively). Another meeting was held the next year, when a permanent churchwide women's organization was formed. Its first president was Mary Burkhard, a member of College Mennonite Church who brought international missions experience to the position. She and her husband, Jacob, had gone to India in 1900 with the Mennonite Evangelizing and Benevolent Board. Jacob died there in 1906, and Mary stayed until 1915. Despite the excellent credentials of its leadership and its popularity among female members, the new ministry drew opposition because of fears it could draw resources and attention away from other, male-directed efforts.[52] Others in the church, however, saw sewing circles as leading to more significant work and influence.[53]

In 1916, the pre-merger Mennonite bishops recommended that two "sisters" be appointed to a conference committee on attire, a logical move as such regulations affected women more than men.[54] Eleven years later, however, women could not even publicly speak about their own work. Sewing circles were the topic of presentations at the 1927, 1934, and 1935 Indiana-Michigan annual assemblies. But all three were led by men. To do otherwise, according to bishop J. K. Bixler, would be "heresy" because women were to be silent when the whole church was assembled; they could only teach children and other women.

"Every serious-minded Christian woman who has given any thought to this subject will not press herself into any doubtful service and no unconscientious or untaught brother should be permitted to urge our sisters to perform any service not in full harmony with God's Word," Bixler opined in the *Gospel Herald*.[55]

After Hartzler became *Rural Evangel* editor in 1930, the periodical broadened its scope beyond evangelism and religion to include issues of culture and politics. Popular targets were socialism, modernism, liberalism, fascism, and atheism because "Christians are allowing themselves to be seduced by them. . . . There is no room for Christ in their program. Man is supreme," according to one editorial.[56] As the Great Depression produced great domestic social and financial instability and Josef Stalin ruthlessly ruled the Soviet Union, one *Rural Evangel* article asserted that Communist influences were making the United States' economic woes even worse: "Many of the unemployed are making a noble effort to gain a livelihood, but it is also true that many of those who make the loudest howl about unemployment would not hold a job if you got one for them even with good pay. They are not interested in good government and honest living."[57] The author of another article wrote, "We wonder if our church privileges, unmolested, are fully appreciated. Our country, apparently drifting fast towards communism, may at some future time take these privileges away."[58] But while shoring up the faith's defenses, the *Rural Evangel* was also on the cutting edge in its attack on another "ism," pronouncing racism's hostility toward people of different skin color incompatible with Christian faith. "Enmity and spiritual death are closely related, but when spiritual life comes in that enmity is slain," stated one editorial.[59] The magazine later reprinted a piece by Virginia Mennonite fundamentalist George R. Brunk I, who harshly condemned white immigrants' treatment of Native Americans. He wrote, "What a bloody story is that of Christians (?) settling America and trampling down the Savior's doctrine of Non-resistance. . . . What wonder that the Indian did not take kindly to the religion of the Pale Faces!"[60]

The Great Depression

While largely withstanding the world's cultural and religious gales that many saw as threatening to throw the church off course,

Indiana-Michigan was also buffeted by the era's economic woes. After the prosperity of the 1920s, much of the country was battered by the Great Depression in tandem with repeated crop failures in the 1930s. To be sure, not all church members were hit with the same degree of severity. In Elkhart County, which did not suffer through the drought, the Yellow Creek Mennonite Church trustees in 1931 were considering investing some of their funds and brought the matter to a congregational meeting, where they were advised that "safety, rather than a high rate of interest should receive first consideration."[61] That same year, however, Zion Mennonite Church in Vestaburg, Michigan, saw its Sunday morning offerings drop to $114.80 from a high of $216.54 the year before.[62] Worship attendance at various locations suffered because people couldn't afford to drive to church. The *Rural Evangel* reported in the fall of 1933 that contributions for mission work had fallen by half and sanctimoniously asked, "Have we decreased our own expenses in proportion to the decrease of our offerings? . . . There is no juggling of the books in heaven."[63] Yet it was some of the mission board's workers who most acutely felt the depression's effects. Because of crop failure, Claude C. Culp, ministering at Brethren, Michigan, was forced to buy feed for his livestock in addition to having to make repairs to his car. "Then the last years [sic] tax is not paid yet, and I have not been able to get enough money to buy [the] 1934 car license," he told the mission board in appealing for financial assistance.[64] *Rural Evangel* editor and Prairie Street minister Hartzler also eventually had to ask for help, admitting, "I do not have anything in sight to pay my taxes."[65]

By 1931, Indiana-Michigan congregations had become so overwhelmed in assisting impoverished members that they appealed to the conference for help. A conference committee was formed in 1932 to solicit relief funds as needs arose. But after that initial flurry, there were few requests for aid throughout the rest of the decade. One person needed help paying rent, another to buy a cow, and two more to buy coal. Congregations didn't receive many pleas, either. Leo (Ind.) Mennonite Church's Poor Fund paid out $180.00 in 1936, but $118.50 was to one person for medical bills. The annual amounts Leo otherwise distributed during the 1930s ranged from $9.15 in 1933 to $42.64 in 1932.[66] Indiana-Michigan members did make use of president Franklin D. Roosevelt's alphabet soup of New Deal welfare programs, even though participation was officially discouraged by the conference. Reflecting the faith's long-held separation from the world, Indiana-Michigan's delegates declared that the church needed to take care of its own in times of need "since the accepting of government help is a step in shirking our responsibility or neglecting a Christian opportunity."[67] At Fairview (Mich.) Mennonite Church, the Civilian Conservation Corps was deemed especially problematic because it was under the military. But congregational members did serve in other federal programs.[68]

But the suffering of the 1930s also produced opportunities for Christian witness. With their time-honored emphasis on frugality coupled with adequate growing conditions for crops and produce, northern Indiana Mennonites were able and willing to alleviate the needs of others less well off. Salem Mennonite Church collected bulk food for distribution among the urban needy in the city of Elkhart.[69] One woman was drawn to the Detroit Mennonite mission because it shared with her fruit and vegetables sent by rural church members.[70] The assistance was not just food. Germfask workers Chester and Eva Osborne spent their first Christmas Eve in the community distributing boxes of donated clothes and Christian calendars.[71]

Yet at the same time they were feeding the hungry and clothing the naked, church leaders were trying to distance themselves from such work. They wanted to make it clear that the salvation message was preeminent and that they had no social gospel inclinations. The social gospel cause developed in the late nineteenth century in response to the physical needs of those people left behind by the dramatic increase in American urbanization and industrialization. The movement not only provided assistance but also sought to reform the elements of society that caused those needs in the first place. As a result, the social gospel agenda was often associated with socialism, the labor movement, and other causes considered liberal.[72] It didn't help that some Mennonites whose adherence to nonconformity and nonresistance was considered suspect—particularly the General Conference Mennonite Church and the Central Conference of Mennonites—embraced some of the same understandings found in the social gospel movement. (Ironically, those Mennonites did so not out of liberal or modernist convictions but because they saw such efforts as in line with traditional understandings of community and discipleship.[73]) D. D. Troyer, bishop of the Indiana-Michigan mission stations, made the conference's position clear: "In some localities the [mission] Board helps to keep soul and body together by stretching a hand of helpfulness which I think is right, but above all the needs of the Soul should be supplied."[74] Indeed, evangelism was presented as an antidote to the physical plight caused by the Great Depression. The *Rural Evangel* callously said distributing literature available from the board's tract program "would do much more good" than the advertisements that regularly came from local grocers: "Why not help those tender-hearted ones to get more light and a deeper insight into things spiritually when it can be done without cost, and at the same time will bring much more joy than to be idle and brooding over conditions."[75]

Bouncing Back

In the wake of the turmoil and uncertainty of the first years after the conservatives' hard-line discipline, Indiana-Michigan membership fell from 4,052 in 1923 to 3,444 in 1924.[76] But that number quickly began to rebound. An early reason was the resumption of classes at Goshen College. In the first two years after reopening, the College congregation gained 129 members by letter of transfer as students and faculty returned to campus. Conference membership reached 4,256 in 1930 and climbed to 5,821 ten years later. Much of the growth during the 1930s was due to a streak of large numbers of baptismal classes across the conference, an average of 206 candidates per year during the 1930s, including 271 during the 1931–32 business year. Indiana-Michigan's church-planting emphasis was still in its infancy, so nearly all new members were received into existing congregations, not new ones. Between 1925 and 1940, Prairie Street Mennonite Church grew from 214 to 351 members; North Main Street Mennonite Church in Nappanee, Indiana, went from 217 to 305; College Mennonite Church jumped from 108 to 226; Leo Mennonite Church increased from 138 to 230; and Hopewell Mennonite Church in Kouts, Indiana, nearly tripled, going from 60 members to 173. Even Maple Grove Mennonite Church at Topeka, Indiana, which lost more than 100 members between 1924 and 1925, was back up to 180 fifteen years later. Some congregations, such as Howard-Miami near Kokomo, Indiana, and Fairview in Michigan, attracted new members from local Old Order Amish districts wrangling over issues such as automobiles and electricity.[77] Those gains easily offset the losses incurred because of the conference's stricter discipline, which contributed to the dismissal of an average of fifty-three "backsliders" per year between 1923 and 1939.[78]

Despite the calmness and growth, however, there were still those who challenged the status quo, even if they had to do it more delicately and surreptitiously than before. Goshen College was no longer a hotbed of progressivism, but it was still a home to a few people who were able to adeptly balance their commitment to the church with their own beliefs that were in tension with official positions. One of those individuals was rising denominational star Harold S. Bender, son of long-time mission board administrator George L. Bender. When Goshen reopened in 1924, Harold joined the faculty as a history professor. That was a huge surprise to him, since he thought he was going to teach Bible and theology, which is what he was studying in graduate school. Goshen president Sanford C. Yoder told him to be patient. Bender would have to start in the history department because his theological credentials were suspect. When the college resumed classes after its yearlong hiatus, the Indiana-Michigan executive committee was granted the power to vet all prospective faculty candidates and had already rejected several of them, Yoder informed Bender.[79] The young instructor's record offered good reason for caution. Bender was a graduate of the progressive preclosure Goshen and had been critical of conservative attempts to control the school. He had also been chair of the Young People's Conference, which had been soundly denigrated for its activism and quickly collapsed. Yet he had also taught at Hesston College, a Mennonite school in Kansas with a more acceptable conservative reputation. And his father-in-law was the prominent fundamentalist John Horsch. As an indicator of his willingness to work within the new church environment, Bender and his wife, Elizabeth, very reluctantly agreed to pledge their "loyalty" to the principles of the Mennonite Church and Indiana-Michigan Mennonite Conference.[80] But Harold also frequently wore a necktie under his straight coat as a sign of protest.[81]

Bender was not alone in his subtle defiance of expectations at Goshen. He joined with Guy F. Hershberger, another history professor, and Edward Yoder, professor of Greek and Latin, to form a "kind of reading circle," according to Yoder, by subscribing to *Christian Century* and *Christendom*, "two periodicals which are not considered orthodox and Biblical" by the conservative leadership.[82] The three colleagues formed a nucleus that, through their academic scholarship and broader church work, deftly fostered new understandings and critical examinations of Mennonitism in a climate resistant to change. They were editors of *Mennonite Quarterly Review*, a daring experiment to link scholarship with faith, something conservatives doubted was possible. All three also wrote prolifically on nonresistance, helping turn it from a provincial withdrawal from the world's problems to active, engaged, yet faithful discipleship. In a prophetic 1932 *Gospel Herald* article titled "In Time of Peace Prepare for War," Bender introduced "alternative service," a nonresistant option to joining the military, to a constituency scarred from its World War I experiences.[83] He was active in inter-Mennonite activities, such as Mennonite Central Committee and Mennonite World Conference, the latter of which was not even officially supported by the ecumenically fearful Mennonite Church. Hershberger fleshed out Bender's alternative service idea and began examining the practical application of nonresistant values to the arenas of labor and business. Yoder was skilled at biblical interpretation and became a leading peace proponent. While at Goshen he also worked for the Mennonite Church's Peace Problems Committee, including writing a regular section for the *Gospel Herald* on "Peace Principles from a Scriptural Viewpoint."

Yoder, a conference newcomer, found the Indiana-Michigan atmosphere particularly distressing. After five years as an instructor and administrator at Hesston College, the Iowa native joined the Goshen faculty in 1933. The next year, he attended several sessions of the conference annual delegate assembly in order to assess for himself the state of affairs in Indiana-Michigan. While in Kansas, he had heard about conference leadership's "high-handed, sometimes radical and reactionary ways of working," but it still hit him hard when he observed it firsthand.[84] Yoder wrote in his diary: "It is somewhat of a rude shock to listen in on the naïve and uncritical discussions which they have, uncritical I mean in the sense of a blind, literalistic, often ignorant, and always dogmatic approach to the Bible and to the consideration of religious subjects. . . . Blanket phrases and statements take the place of analysis and straight thinking with many. The ideal, the goal to be reached, and the program for reaching it are apparently fixed and set-tled in the minds of many of these zealous brethren."[85]

Despite its reorganization and a more moderate environment, Goshen College remained a source of aggravation for the conference. Several faculty members, including a former fundamentalist, were ousted in the 1930s because of their liberality.[86] Russian Mennonite immigrant Gustav Enss was teaching at the General Conference Men-nonite Church's Bethel College in Newton, Kansas, when, in 1916, he accused the school of harboring modernism. That helped produce over the next several years a culling of faculty members with suspect pro-gressive beliefs. Enss himself left Bethel in 1918, eventually moving to more conservative Hesston College, then to Goshen in 1928. He began taking graduate-level theology courses and embraced the work of Karl Barth, a neo-orthodox theologian. Neo-orthodoxy, born in Europe after World War I, was a reaction to the liberal theology denounced by conservatives, but it also downplayed doctrinal heritage, which was considered by Mennonite Church leadership to be in opposition to tra-ditional practices such as the prayer covering and footwashing. Enss had two articles on Barthian theology published in *Mennonite Quar-terly Review* in 1932, which were met with conservative protests. Enss was gone two years later, despite Bender's support.

Meanwhile, students from more progressive parts of the church, such as Illinois and Iowa, chafed under attempts to enforce Indiana-Michigan standards on campus. Students were expected to attend chapel five days a week in the administration building on campus—in the same room that was also the home of College Mennonite Church, where students were supposed to be on Sunday mornings. It was the only Indiana-Michigan congregation in the city until 1936, when North Goshen Mennonite Church was organized. Desiring a change of scenery, some students would venture out for worship at Eighth Street Mennonite Church, a congregation in the Central Conference of Men-nonites that was located nine blocks directly north of the college's front gate. Eighth Street was also home for many refugees from Indiana-Michigan purges of alleged unorthodoxy. But not all Goshen students would make it to the church. On one occasion, a group of first-year students was about a block away when Bender, having been alerted to the pedestrians and their probable destination, came along in his car and asked, "Do you want a ride?" Nothing more needed to be said as the students climbed in and went to worship back on campus.[87] It was not an isolated incident but one experienced by others as well.

A five-member investigating committee, appointed by moderator Bixler, reported in 1932 on the school's effects on conference life. Goshen has accomplished "some good," the committee admitted. "However, acknowledging the fact that the tendency in all higher education is worldward," the report continued, "it behooves us as a Church and Conference to spare no efforts that will help us hold our ground against the drift." After all, the committee stated, Goshen's purpose was "safeguarding the young people of our church," and thus the conference had "a right to expect 'oneness of mind' between school and church." The committee recommended that the denomination's Mennonite Board of Education be reorganized to allow the conference to have more direct control of the college.[88] While the plan ultimately failed at the denominational level, Indiana-Michigan did create a long-standing School Problems Committee to continue monitoring Goshen. It raised concerns about the college's athletic activities, debate tournaments, musical programs, attire, and use of non-Mennonite speakers for college events. As Goshen pursued accreditation in the early 1940s, the committee urged the college to "be very careful not to sacrifice Bible principles by compromising with requests from the [accrediting] association or otherwise that are dangerous to the safety of the Faith the Mennonite Church has held to."[89] The open-minded, academically unfettered progressivism desired by Edward Yoder and others was still being rejected.

But changes were in the air, literally as well as figuratively. Starting in the 1920s, the radio had become a fixture for many Americans, offering news, entertainment, and sporting events for millions to enjoy. But its reception was not so good everywhere. Mennonites had long tried to erect barriers against undermining influences from the outside. Now came a contraption that, left unchecked, would bring those influences straight into church members' homes practically undetectably. Indiana-Michigan never took explicit action against radio use, but there was little doubt what leadership thought of it, repeatedly citing it as evidence of the need for constant vigilance against worldliness. The soap operas were bawdy, the comedies frivolous, the westerns violent, the music ribald, and the commercials materialistic. While acknowledging some potential benefits of radio, the *Rural Evangel* posited that it was "more a curse than a blessing."[90] Yet, one survey discovered, radio was growing in popularity in Indiana-Michigan at a rate that surprised even conference leaders.[91] Church members tuned in to the news, weather, and market reports, plus Christian programs such as those from Moody Bible Institute in Chicago and gospel singer Edward MacHugh, while eschewing jazz, swing, "barn dance programs," and "Amos & Andy." Said one survey respondent, "The radio programs must be sifted the same as magazines and papers."[92] Church members were proving themselves capable of reconciling with the world's influences without losing their distinctive faith. Boundaries and crossroads were not always incompatible.

6
The End of Isolationism

In early 1945, World War II was in its final months, and yet it was still challenging nonresistant Mennonites. With clouds of crisis on the horizon five years earlier, the church had helped create Civilian Public Service (CPS), which allowed conscripted conscientious objectors to military participation to perform alternative service.[1] Now those men were returning home from their assignments, where they had served for no or little compensation, and they needed financial assistance for peacetime pursuits such as farming, business, or college. The Mennonite Church (MC) began exploring how to best meet those needs, and the solution was mutual aid, a longtime Anabaptist practice of the church providing assistance to its own members, rather than relying on help from beyond the faith community.[2]

So five men gathered in Goshen, Indiana, on March 16, 1945, to continue planning for a new mutual aid ministry. One came from eastern Pennsylvania and another from south central Kansas, while the other three were Goshen residents. All of them were among the most talented and influential Old Mennonite church members, holding positions of the highest responsibility and serving on many boards and committees that often took them across North America and around the world—all in addition to their regular jobs. Through their writing and teaching, Goshen College professors Harold S. Bender and Guy F. Hershberger had become highly visible leaders of a new generation that, as in the late nineteenth century, would revitalize the church. C. L. Graber was the college's business manager and a former minister of College Mennonite Church who had served in a number of MC and Mennonite Central Committee (MCC) capacities during World War II. Orie O. Miller, now living in Akron, Pennsylvania, was a northern

163

Indiana native, the son of respected bishop D. D. Miller of Forks Mennonite Church in LaGrange County. While overseeing a successful shoe company, Orie was distinguishing himself churchwide as the MCC executive secretary.[3] The only meeting participant without any Indiana-Michigan ties was Kansas bishop and former denominational moderator Harry A. Diener.

The quintet was unwilling to let mealtime stop them from conducting business. So while seated around the dinner table, they picked Graber to be executive secretary of the organization.[4] It would be christened Mennonite Mutual Aid (MMA) and provide loans as well as financial and vocational counseling to ex-CPS workers.[5] Because Graber lived in Goshen, MMA's office naturally was also placed in the city, in a couple of rented rooms in a college-owned house. Thus MMA became the third MC churchwide agency to be headquartered in Elkhart County and Indiana-Michigan Mennonite Conference. Mennonite Board of Missions (MBM) emerged from an Indiana-Michigan initiative and remained in Elkhart after becoming the denominational mission agency in the early twentieth century. Mennonite Board of Education (MBE), with D. A. Yoder, bishop at Olive Mennonite Church near Wakarusa, Indiana, as its longtime president, was essentially based in the county. (It would have no staff or office until the 1960s, when it located to the Goshen campus). That left Mennonite Publication Board (MPB) and its publishing house in Scottdale, Pennsylvania, as the only MC program agency not situated in northern Indiana.

It made sense for MMA to be in Goshen, since it practically was an Indiana-Michigan creation. The Goshen College trio was directly responsible for the proposal that became MMA, which was presented to the Mennonite Church General Conference in 1943 by three denominational committees: the Bender-chaired Peace Problems Committee; the Committee on Industrial Relations, with Hershberger as its staff person; and the Stewardship Committee, of which Graber was secretary. The three men and Miller had been promoting the idea of a churchwide mutual aid program since the 1930s. In doing so, they were continuing in the spirit of John F. Funk, who in 1882 persuaded the Indiana-Michigan Mennonite Conference to authorize the creation of the Mennonite Aid Plan to cover members' property damage. It was one of the earliest such organizations among North American Mennonites, and within three years it had attracted members from as far away as Minnesota.[6] Some sixty years later, the concept of mutual aid had new significance.

The new agency wasn't the only manifestation of the war's effects on the church. In fact, there was hardly a dimension of Mennonite religious and social life that was unaffected. As the war redrew borders globally, so too did it help challenge many of the boundaries that Indiana-Michigan and the rest of the Mennonite Church had used to separate themselves from the rest of the world. Many long-held beliefs and practices were no longer tacitly accepted. Rather, countless young men—and some women—had their perspectives profoundly altered by their CPS alternative service in the United States or by doing international relief work with MCC. They encountered other Christians, particularly Mennonites of other affiliations, and situations that would have otherwise been unfathomable. As a result, workers started considering new ideas and asking difficult questions as they sought to remain faithful but relevant in a dramatically changing environment. World War II took the United States out of an isolationist stance in world relations, and the same was true for U.S. Mennonites. Many alternative service workers returned from their assignments feeling called to a more activist faith that pushed the boundaries of belief and practice. They would proceed to infuse the church with a vitality reminiscent of the late nineteenth century, when church members found fresh ways to apply their understandings of Mennonite distinctives.

In conjunction with that trend was a shift in denominational power. The Funk era of the 1870s, 1880s, and 1890s gave way in the early twentieth century to nearly four decades of strictly enforced doctrinal correctness. One way that was exerted was through the two denominational program boards conceived specifically to counter Indiana's churchwide impact. MBE was created in 1905 to rein in Goshen College's progressivism, while MPB was born three years later after Funk was forced to sell to his Pennsylvania-based competitor. Scottdale, Pennsylvania, subsequently became the official intellectual center of the Mennonite Church, producing denomination-approved periodicals, curricula, hymnals, and books to promote and disseminate orthodoxy. Meanwhile, new schools opened in Hesston, Kansas, in 1909 and Harrisonburg, Virginia, in 1917, providing conservatives with educational alternatives considered safer than Goshen.[7] Of the fifteen men who were Mennonite Church General Conference moderators or who gave the conference sermons between 1923 and 1943, or both, eleven served on MBE, MPB, or both during that span. A twelfth, 1923 moderator J. A. Ressler, was an editor at Mennonite Publishing House for twenty-five years.[8]

But the creation of MMA helped reestablish northern Indiana's influence. Like Funk's publishing enterprise, MBM, MMA, and Goshen College brought talented, committed individuals into their employ and to Indiana-Michigan Mennonite Conference. Barely two decades after being shut down, the college was resurging with strong hints of the academic freedom of preclosure Goshen, thanks to outstanding faculty members such as Bender, Hershberger, and J. C. Wenger, who taught theology in Goshen's new seminary program.[9] Established in 1946 under the name Goshen Biblical Seminary, its purpose was to train ministers for the Mennonite Church, many of whom had their start in Indiana-Michigan congregations. Meanwhile, MBM was about to be infused with a new vitality under the leadership of J. D. Graber, who arrived in 1944. With all the comings and goings, the conference was again a major crossroads of the Mennonite Church.

War Response

After being caught unprepared during the First World War, U.S. Mennonites—with Goshen College as a driving force—had strengthened their beliefs on peace and nonresistance by the time World War II erupted. As early as 1932, Bender, who helped start a Goshen College peace organization in the 1920s, raised the idea of alternative service. Writing in th *Gospel Herald*, the official MC periodical, he stressed that conscientious objectors to war "must be prepared to offer some alternative service for the common good and which will lay as heavy burdens of sacrifice and loyalty upon them as their fellow countrymen bear."[10] At a conference on peace and war held at Goshen College in 1935, Hershberger presented a paper outlining such a potential program should conscription be again enacted.[11] Both the draft and alternative service became reality in 1940 when the U.S. government enacted the Selective Service Act and also approved the creation of Civilian Public Service. By the time the Japanese attacked Pearl Harbor on December 7, 1941, Indiana-Michigan had already been holding draft workshops and approved a resolution reiterating its nonresistance and support for a federal alternative service program.[12] Meanwhile, the conference mission board's *Rural Evangel*, the de facto Indiana-Michigan periodical, encouraged the conference to remain steadfast even though its position might be unpopular. "As hysteria increases, we can expect an increasing number of Christian leaders . . . to be swayed [against nonresistance]," warned one writer.[13]

This time, however, the global conflagration did not produce the troubles for Mennonites that World War I did. Other than a few isolated incidents with local draft boards, Indiana-Michigan members were spared the yellow paint, public denunciations, and other tactics of intimidation and coercion used a quarter century earlier.[14] While their young men were away performing work of "national importance," which was CPS's mandate, conference members at home endured the same challenges as the rest of the civilian population. For example, gasoline rationing prevented members of Hopewell Mennonite Church at Kouts and Burr Oak Mennonite Church at Rensselaer from traveling to rural Kokomo for their annual joint Thanksgiving service with Howard-Miami Mennonite Church.[15]

A major exception to the relative domestic tranquility was Michigan's Upper Peninsula, which the conference had recently identified as a mission field ripe for harvest. The region's rough-and-tumble miners, lumber workers, fishermen, and hardscrabble farmers didn't take too kindly to the nonviolent newcomers. After being accosted on the streets of Manistique for his lack of support for the war effort, Wildwood Mennonite Church minister Clarence Troyer took all his business from the city to Newberry in the other direction.[16] Manistique town officials also called the Federal Bureau of Investigation to look into Germfask Mennonite Church. A nurse who cared for a local cancer patient regularly worshiped with the Mennonites, since Sunday mornings were her only time off and the meetinghouse was conveniently located. She was once questioned by two FBI agents, but nothing came of the investigation.[17]

The fledgling Mennonite fellowship in the region was also tainted, ironically, by a local CPS camp. Most camps were created for religious conscientious objectors and operated by denominational organizations. (Mennonite Central Committee administered camps for U.S. Mennonite,

Amish, and Hutterite groups.) But CPS Camp No. 135 near Germfask was one of several operated by the U.S. Selective Service System for conscientious objectors who didn't want to participate in the religiously based camps, usually because their opposition to war was for political or philosophical reasons. Some—not all—of the men believed that not only the war but the entire draft and alternative service system was wrong. As a result, they saw themselves as incarcerated at Germfask and providing slave labor. One inductee even arrived at camp wearing a wooden ball attached to his leg with a log chain.[18] *Time* magazine described the campers as malcontents who refused to work, destroyed property, and were a menace in the towns where they caroused.[19] It was easy for the local population, unfamiliar with Mennonites and their nonresistant ways, to lump them with the camp's secular troublemakers. On one occasion, Germfask pastor Chester Osborne and his wife, Eva, hosted the wife and small daughter of one of the campers, who had accompanied him to Germfask. The wife had worked as a maid and cook for a prominent family in town in return for room, board, and a small salary. But public pressure soon left the wife and daughter feeling threatened. So the Osbornes, who lived in the country, took them in for several weeks before they moved away permanently.[20] Such hospitality was perceived as supporting the camp's renegades.

In the summer of 1944, Osborne served three months as camp manager and also as a spiritual advisor, routinely visiting with the campers and holding worship services. During his short tenure, he inadvertently compounded the Mennonites' difficult relationships with their neighbors. Osborne was helping take camp inventory when he found a package marked "Storm Flag." Thinking it a weather warning flag for a harbor or other coastal location, he remarked, "I don't see how we will have any use for that" at the inland camp. But Osborne was mistaken. It was the U.S. flag, made of material to withstand wind and precipitation, and his comment was interpreted as disparaging the Stars and Stripes.[21]

Osborne's work at CPS Camp No. 135 was almost over before it began. He seriously considered resigning when he was told that the FBI wanted camp staff to gather information on some of the men in order to monitor them for anti-American activity. Osborne felt that participating in such surveillance violated the injunction of Romans 14 to grant forbearance and patience to all and worried that it would "eventually callous and harden me, and very likely cause me to lose those finer and deeper sensitive traits which I must retain if I am to continue to minister to the spiritual and moral needs of the family of humanity," he wrote in his resignation letter.[22] But he never submitted it and stayed on. (Two other members of the camp administrative staff also had to be talked out of quitting because of the FBI's expectations.[23])

CPS was a different experience for the rest of Indiana-Michigan. Sixty-three percent, or 277, of the conference men who were drafted chose alternative service.[24] While MCC operated the camps, the workers' home communities also provided support, including foodstuffs and financial assistance. Salem Mennonite Church of New Paris, Indiana, was the most generous, giving $180 a month to each of its members in CPS, plus $6 per month served at time of discharge. Forks Mennonite Church of Middlebury, Indiana and Hopewell Mennonite Church of Kouts, Indiana, gave their CPS men annual allowances of $120 each. In addition, the congregations also provided transportation to and from home during furloughs. But other congregations gave as little as $5 a month or even nothing.[25]

World War II started a chain reaction that proceeded to shake the Mennonite Church to its core. Veterans of wartime alternative service and international relief work had returned home with new ideas about serving God and church. For many of these young men and women, just leaving home changed them and, by extension, the church.[26] They had experiences that would have been inconceivable to many of their forebears, be it witnessing racism in Florida and Mississippi, assisting mental patients in deplorable conditions in New Jersey and Pennsylvania, or providing comfort to hungry refugees in France and Germany. CPS workers were also the recipients of a grand formal education. MCC developed an extensive program of courses to be offered in the CPS camps. In addition to business, trade, and Bible classes, the conscientious objectors studied Anabaptist-Mennonite history and theology, using a curriculum written by Harold S. Bender, Guy F. Hershberger, and other great minds in the church, including from the General Conference Mennonite Church and Mennonite Brethren. Some of the classes could even be taken for college credit.[27] So the CPS workers, who began their terms of service with an average of ten and a half years of schooling, exited not just with the lessons of experience but also with actual academic knowledge that prepared many of them for transforming the Mennonite Church.[28] In fact, their new level of education was often more than that of their bishops and ministers back home.

CPS, however, wasn't just for men. In the summer of 1943, Goshen College hosted a CPS training school to prepare conscientious objectors for relief and reconstruction assignments. Among the instructors was Edna Ramseyer, a home economics professor at Bluffton (Ohio) College and a member of the General Conference Mennonite Church who had spent 1940 in France with the American Friends Service Committee working with refugees of the Spanish Civil War. At the Goshen school, Ramseyer taught nutrition to the male students but also discussed with women present, such as CPS workers' wives, how they might become involved in alternative service. The result was the formation of COGs, or CO Girls, who advocated female participation in CPS. A COG chapter with about fifteen women was soon started at Ypsilanti (Mich.) State Hospital, a mental hospital where a Mennonite CPS unit was already in operation. Overall, some three hundred young women worked with male conscientious objectors in eight psychiatric institutions.[29]

Meanwhile, 164 Indiana-Michigan men, when drafted, enlisted instead of entering alternative service. Forty-nine chose noncombatant status, while 115 went into unrestricted active duty, 2 of whom were killed in action. Those figures were on par with percentages across the Mennonite Church.[30] Nevertheless, they were too high for conference leaders, who scheduled a discussion on "The Apparent Breakdown in the Practice of Non-Resistance" at Indiana-Michigan's 1944 delegate assembly. Increasing acculturation, allowing for non-Mennonite and thus non-nonresistant influences to enter and affect Mennonite communities, was a significant factor for conference males who chose to join the military. Fifty-eight percent were factory workers or day laborers—men who had regular and significant interactions outside the traditional bounds of Mennonite community.[31] But weakening nonresistance was also a legacy of the fundamentalist forces that had been so prevalent in the conference.[32] Dispensationalism, with its concepts of cataclysmic battles ushering in the kingdom of God, justified and even encouraged violence as a way for good to repel evil. Furthermore, fundamentalism was highly individualistic, downplaying community and social action and instead focusing heavily on personal salvation. That emphasis on saving souls helped spur Indiana-Michigan's church-planting efforts of the 1920s and 1930s. But nearly half the men from conference congregations started after World War I—largely those born out of fundamentalist-influenced conservatism—joined the military, compared with a third of the men from the older congregations.[33]

How congregations dealt with their members in the military varied even more than how they dealt with their members in CPS. Most considered the soldiers to not be in good standing but kept their names on the membership rolls. Seven congregations immediately excommunicated their military members upon induction. When the soldiers, sailors, and airmen returned from duty, some congregations required them to make formal public confession to be reinstated, while in others, the soldiers only had to privately meet with the pastor. Still other congregations required nothing.[34] In the end, just 17.8 percent of Indiana-Michigan men who joined the military returned to the conference. Only Virginia Mennonite Conference was worse, with 14.5 percent.[35] One reason was the lack of communication between Indiana-Michigan congregations and their members in the military. While the Mennonite Church's Peace Problems Committee had urged maintaining relationships in order to help lead the soldiers and sailors back into the nonresistant fold, the only contact some of them had with their home congregations were excommunication letters.[36]

Transition Time

While wartime circumstances took many of Indiana-Michigan's young adults out of their communities and dramatically broadened their horizons, life back home didn't remain static either, despite conference efforts. Indiana-Michigan in 1941 passed a resolution decrying the "present drift in the Mennonite Church in conforming to the world" and called for repentance.[37] A resolution the next year opposed playing in bands "because of the vain display in uniforms being worn, in the parades they march in [and] in playing at patriotic rallies, and other occasions which are contrary to the nonresistant and nonconformed principles as taught by the Word of God."[38] In 1943, the conference

admitted that its historic isolation was fading because of "intricate relationships with other people, . . . public education, . . . and the world-wide
trend toward totalitarian government" and urged "every possible effort
toward the new birth experience of every member" and "redemptive
discipline" to ensure the church's purity.[39] Future Goshen College faculty member Melvin Gingerich, at the time teaching at Bethel College,
the General Conference Mennonite Church school in Kansas, warned
against mass media—daily newspapers, radio, movies—and suggested
that high schools and 4-H clubs were also invaders, breaking through
the buffers that rural life had long provided Mennonites.[40]

But the church's diminished isolation wasn't all bad. In fact, some
of it was encouraged. "We could have no part in actual warfare, but
there is no limit to the part that we can have in restoring, in some measure, what war has destroyed," the *Rural Evangel* exhorted.[41] By the
time Germany and Japan surrendered in 1945, the walls that had been
erected to keep church and world apart were crumbling, allowing in
a host of faithful possibilities. As it had been in the contentious years
before World War I, Goshen College was again emerging as a base
for exploring new understandings of belief and witness in an antago-
nistic world. But it was different this time. Instead of challenging the
traditional external expressions, faculty members such as Bender and
Hershberger recast Mennonitism by focusing on its theological and historical cores.

Bender encapsulated that in his December 1943 address "The Anabaptist Vision" to the American Society of Church History, of which he
was president. The speech was published the next year, and for many it
would provide the definitive explanation of what Anabaptism was and
should be. Bender highlighted discipleship, voluntary church membership, and love and nonresistance as the three essential characteristics of
the faith.[42] Not once did he mention straight coats, prayer coverings,
or jewelry. Bender was moving the Mennonite Church to the essences
of the faith in order to advance God's realm on earth.[43] Hershberger's
seminal book *War, Peace, and Nonresistance* also came out in 1944
and would become a classic on Mennonite peace and discipleship.
Like Bender, Hershberger avoided progressive/conservative factionalism. Instead, he articulated a peace position that was neither traditional antiwar isolationism nor full-blown political and social activism.

Rather, nonresistance was an explicitly biblical, apolitical stance that nevertheless led to worldly involvements, not by demanding peace and justice, which could be coercive, but by doing it.[44]

At the same time, developments beyond Indiana-Michigan were also contributing to a new religious climate. The Mennonite Church had created the General Problems Committee in 1929 to be attentive to and work for solutions to issues considered to be threatening the prevailing notions of orthodoxy. While it did so aggressively, the committee didn't propose any actual penalties for noncompliance until World War II, when it declared that the denomination was yet again in crisis. "It is becoming increasingly evident that the Church cannot continue in its stand on [nonresistance and nonconformity] with our youth going into the army in large numbers and our people drifting into disunity on the practice of the doctrine of nonconformity," the committee reported to the 1943 general conference, meeting on the Goshen College campus. Chaired by Indiana-Michigan bishop D. A. Yoder, the committee's recommendations included calling for each area conference to pledge its fidelity to the Mennonite Church and its standards or be forced out of the denomination.[45] It was the doctrinaire Indiana-Michigan Mennonite Conference of the 1920s on a churchwide scale.

With the very real prospects of wholesale expulsions or defections looming, a special session of the general conference was held in Goshen in the summer of 1944 to deal with the General Problems Committee report. At the center of the matter was Illinois Mennonite Conference, which conservatives believed to be too liberal, with Indiana-Michigan leading the charge against its western neighbor.[46] The week before the Goshen meeting on the front page of the *Gospel Herald*, Sanford Shetler, an outspoken Pennsylvania conservative, had defined a liberal as "one who is not concerned for the historic values of the faith and who makes no scruples in altering or even discarding the faith or practice of the church."[47] Bitter dissension and even division seemed imminent. But more even-handed views prevailed in Goshen and set a new course for the Mennonite Church. It started with the assembly's opening session on Tuesday evening, August 15, when Goshen Biblical Seminary professor and College Mennonite Church minister John H. Mosemann (who was also the namesake son of a high-profile conservative Lancaster Mennonite Conference bishop) spoke on "Unity of the Spirit or Division." Subsequent sessions continued the theme of the "sin of factionalism," reported Paul Erb, Daniel Kauffman's more moderate successor as *Gospel Herald* editor.[48] The turning point came Thursday evening, August 17, when delegates began specifically addressing the General Problems Committee report. Discussion and debate were in full roil when Sanford C. Yoder rose to speak. He was supremely qualified to address the issue at hand, since he had often been caught in the cross fire between divergent views in the church. Yoder was president of Mennonite Board of Education when it closed Goshen College in 1923, then was named president for the reorganized school, a position he would hold until 1940. The reason for the current condition of the denomination, he told the assembly, was not because of disagreements over church standards or authority. Rather, it was because fellowship and love had broken down and had been replaced by distrust and ostracism.[49] Contentiousness gave way to a powerful session of prayer and confession by the delegates. The meeting finally concluded about midnight.[50] While the General Problems Committee report was overwhelmingly approved the next morning with slight changes, it was obvious that the authoritarianism inherent in it had given way to new, profound feelings of harmony. Erb concluded his *Gospel Herald* article by stating:

> There are no significant theological disputes among us. . . . Apparent differences in the application of our teachings and in their local administration, where most of our difficulties arise, are for the most part not essential differences, and can usually be understood by a consideration of the history of the various groups and localities which have joined themselves in this General Conference fellowship. . . . Mutual understanding and acquaintance will do much. This session of General Conference, we are persuaded, did much to further the purity and the unity of the church.[51]

In 1952, Goshen hosted another gathering that underscored the new era. Billed as a "prophecy" conference, it addressed topics such as dispensationalism, the second coming, and the New Testament book of Revelation. Among the speakers were noted fundamentalist-leaning church members such as John L. Stauffer, retired president of Eastern Mennonite College in Harrisonburg, Virginia, and revivalist George R. Brunk II, namesake son of the ardent conservative champion. But the program also included moderates such as Bender and Millard Lind, a Mennonite Publishing House writer and future Goshen Biblical Seminary professor. The conference had all the ingredients for a fiery stew of strife. Instead, it was devoid of the fighting that had been so common since the turn of the twentieth century. Paul Erb once again celebrated the calmness. The *Gospel Herald* editor described the conference as simply a discussion of issues "with love and understanding." He said, "This good news should go out to the church that we can come together and discuss a highly controversial subject and keep the temperature down. It was evident that we are capable of openness of mind."[52]

Urban Embrace

For Indiana-Michigan Mennonite Conference, theological and cultural changes coalesced in 1947 with the appointment of a six-member Community Life Committee "to carefully review the entire structure of our community life, home, social, and economic, and bring Biblical and wholesome recommendations to our next annual conference" because "present world tendencies and influences are making rapid inroads into the Home Life, in social life, and in the economic phases of effective Christian witness in our communities."[53] One of the committee's members was Guy F. Hershberger, the most qualified person in the conference, if not the entire denomination. He taught history, sociology, and ethics at Goshen College and was the driving force in the "Mennonite community" movement, a sweeping, churchwide attempt to preserve and practice nonconformity and nonresistance in a rapidly changing environment.[54] By the 1930s, increasing urbanization and industrialization were challenging the long-held, farm-based, insular notions of faith and life. The Mennonite community movement attempted to resist the changes by promoting rural, geographically defined communities of church members as the best places to live out the Mennonite faith. It was a concerted effort to promote Mennonite isolationism with explicit sociological, theological, and economic underpinnings. To that end, Hershberger initially advocated methods such as mutual aid organizations and specialized financial institutions to serve and support those communities. But after World War II, he shifted his attention to include citified realities, such as labor unions, race relations, and the role of higher education.

The work of the Community Life Committee would turn out to be a comprehensive examination of virtually every facet of individual and corporate faithfulness in Indiana-Michigan. The committee's 1948 report included recommendations on church, home, school, and social and economic life. Some of the recommendations were hardly surprising, such as encouraging more pastoral visitation and ministers becoming more familiar with the tenets of the faith. But the younger generation received special attention, as they were seen to be especially at risk in an atmosphere with more secular threats. The committee called for conference programs on parenting, a church-affiliated high school, and the formation of a permanent Indiana-Michigan Mennonite Youth Fellowship to replace the ad hoc system of congregational youth groups. The committee also proposed the formation of a standing Committee on Economic Relations to help the conference address matters related to labor unions, insurance, and vocational counseling.[55] All of the committee's recommendations were approved during the 1948 and 1949 annual sessions. Instead of taking the sort of defensive, protectionist approach that had characterized the conference's past attitudes toward newness, Indiana-Michigan was working to proactively respond to manage the changes it was experiencing.

Another development in 1948 indicated the sweeping changes occurring within Indiana-Michigan. As evident by its name, the *Rural Evangel* was begun in 1920 by the conference mission board to help create new Mennonite communities and congregations in the country. But the time had come to "recognize a definite responsibility to the foreign field, and to the urban areas within our borders. . . . There are a number of congregations which cannot be classified as rural," the magazine explained in announcing its new name, *Gospel Evangel*, which took effect with the first issue of 1948.[56] In the following decade, Indiana-Michigan would have eleven city congregations, the result of both its expanding evangelistic efforts and the increasing urbanization of the church membership.

But those efforts did not include reaching out to people of color, despite the fact that tens of thousands of African Americans from the South had for decades been moving north for work, such as to the Michigan cities that were home to the booming automobile business and later World War II–related manufacturing. Indiana-Michigan was

After Sunday morning worship at Ninth Street Mennonite Church, Saginaw, Michigan, 1949. LeRoy Bechler.

Attenders of Ninth Street Mennonite Church, Saginaw, Michigan, 1950. LeRoy Bechler.

not oblivious to the problems of race relations. In 1944, a year after devastating race riots in Detroit, the *Rural Evangel* editorialized, "Race prejudice is a disgrace to any nation and sin against both God and man. The yellow, the black, the red, the brown are the creation of God as well as the white race. They have souls as well as we."[57] Hershberger was a major proponent of multicultural outreach, helping spur Mennonites' African American awareness across the church.[58] Nevertheless, whites continued to receive Indiana-Michigan's undivided evangelistic attention. Between 1945 and 1950, twenty-eight congregations were started (not all of them survived), all but one of them in white communities.

That one exception was in Saginaw, Michigan. But its genesis was in Chicago and Holmes County, Ohio, and the influence of a minister and his wife who would never hold a position in Indiana-Michigan. James and Rowena Lark had joined Rocky Ridge Mennonite Church while living at Quakertown, Pennsylvania, in the 1930s. In 1945, at the invitation of Illinois Mennonite Conference's mission board, they moved to Chicago to lead a newly established African American congregation. James was ordained the next year, becoming the first African American Mennonite minister. Meanwhile, LeRoy Bechler, a white farm boy from Pigeon, Michigan, with no intercultural experience, was studying at Hesston (Kans.) College, where he felt led to mission work.[59] When a classmate shared that he was going to spend the summer of 1947 in voluntary service working under the Larks in Chicago, Bechler was intrigued and decided to accompany his friend. The experience set the direction for his life's work. Bechler spent six weeks teaching Bible school and doing visitation. He was also inspired by James Lark, a personable, creative leader who envisioned far-reaching ministries by and for African Americans. One of those was a camping program, Camp Ebenezer on the Holmes County farm of Tillie Yoder's parents.[60] Tillie had grown up in Indiana's Howard-Miami Amish community before moving to Ohio with her family. As a young adult, she also developed an interest in work among African Americans after teaching Bible school in Chicago under the Larks. The Larks and Yoders organized Camp Ebenezer in 1947; Bechler was its director in 1948. One day while walking across the grounds, he sensed God telling him to go to Saginaw, about sixty miles from his Pigeon home. Bechler's familiarity with the city had been limited to occasionally visiting family friends and back-to-school shopping with his parents.[61] Nevertheless, he felt God affirming his desire to serve in African American ministry.

Bechler, who was still studying at Hesston, convinced Mennonite Board of Missions to sponsor a voluntary service unit in Saginaw for the summer of 1949, which would be under his leadership and located in the city's predominantly African American First Ward. A group of Indiana-Michigan volunteers conducted a Bible school, which enrolled some five hundred children. Organizers had a tent that could serve only two hundred, so they had to rent the basement of a neighborhood church for additional space. The Bible school was followed by two weeks of revival meetings for the adults, which resulted in twenty-eight conversions.[62] That led to the founding later that year of a mission that would become Ninth Street Mennonite Church, the first African American congregation in Indiana-Michigan. Bechler was the founding pastor, serving until 1960. The mission initially met in a house purchased by a group of Mennonites from Midland, Michigan, including members of the Conservative Mennonite Conference. A church building was later erected, with Fairview Mennonite Church felling trees and sending the lumber plus volunteers to Saginaw.[63] The new mission quickly undertook further outreach, starting a community center, holding Bible schools around the city, and conducting a two-week summer camp on a farm near Pigeon.[64] In 1955, Ninth Street spawned another Saginaw Mennonite congregation, Grace Chapel. By 1957, Ninth Street had 56 adults and 130 children.[65]

Other Indiana-Michigan Mennonites were aware of the mission opportunities in more heavily populated settings. In 1951, the Murrel Brothers family moved from Albuquerque, New Mexico, where they had been involved with a fledgling Mennonite fellowship, back to their former home of Battle Creek, Michigan, and joined Bowne Mennonite Church, about forty-five miles to the north. That connection led the congregation to start holding services in Battle Creek in 1952 near the city's famous breakfast cereal factories. A meetinghouse for the new group, called Heath Street Mennonite Church, was erected two years later.[66] At the same time, Leo Mennonite Church of rural Grabill, Indiana, started holding summer Bible schools in a predominantly African American section of nearby Fort Wayne. The congregation took over an existing nondenominational mission in 1954 and turned it into

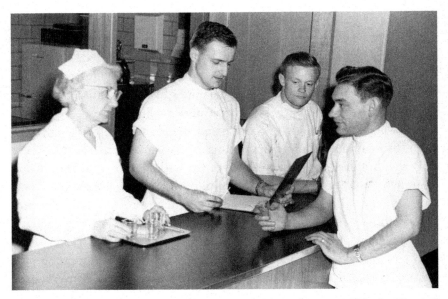

Three 1-W men in the Indianapolis unit on the job with a colleague at Methodist Hospital. MCUSAA–Goshen.

Fairhaven Mennonite Church.[67] In northern Indiana, Tobe Schmucker, a Goshen insurance agent and member of East Goshen Mennonite Church, was part of a local Christian businessmen's group that held street meetings in a seamy section of South Bend, Indiana. Schmucker was moved to start Hope Rescue Mission in that neighborhood in 1954, with MBM giving oversight and area Mennonites providing monetary and volunteer support.[68]

Mennonites were going to the cities for other reasons, as well. In Indianapolis in 1951, two Mennonites in medical school and one in dental school and their spouses began meeting together.[69] They were soon joined by conscientious objectors performing alternative service under the new 1-W program. Rather than creating Civilian Public Service–like camps, the 1-W program allowed conscientious objector draftees to find their own service assignments in existing government and non-profit, charitable organizations such as hospitals, schools, and laboratories. About half the participants from various Mennonite groups went to urban areas of more than fifty thousand people, such as Indianapolis, which naturally was a popular option for Indiana men.[70] In 1953, Cleo Mann arrived in the city from Pleasant View Mennonite Church near

Elkhart to serve as the 1-W unit minister. But the goal was not just to create a congregational home for Mennonites relocated from traditional rural communities. The city's population included many low-income people who had moved from Kentucky and Tennessee for employment. "And why should there not have been a Mennonite Church in Indianapolis long ago?" asked Mann.[71] A 1954 summer Bible school drew about one hundred children, more than half of them African American.

Meanwhile, Guy Hershberger was trying to familiarize the church with urban dynamics from another perspective.[72] In early 1949, he circulated a proposal from fellow Goshen faculty member and Kokomo native Elaine Sommers for a summer study and service unit to expose Mennonite college students to the economic and cultural realities of the city. While Hershberger was on sabbatical, Mennonite Central Committee took the idea and implemented it in Chicago for the summer of 1949. It drew seventeen students from Bethel, Bluffton, and Tabor Colleges as well as from Goshen.[73] Following his sabbatical, Hershberger returned to the urban unit idea. He proposed a joint effort of the Mennonite Church's Committee on Industrial Relations and MBM, and in 1951 twelve Mennonite Church students spent the summer in Detroit experiencing city life and learning about city challenges.

This new urban awareness coincided with a growing mentality that a person didn't have to leave home for an extended period of time to be a missionary. In 1944, J. D. Graber, a veteran India missionary and younger brother of MMA architect C. L. Graber, arrived in Elkhart as MBM's first full-time executive secretary, a position he would hold until retirement in 1967. He soon and successfully began preaching "A Mission Outpost for Every Congregation."[74] While it became a popular slogan across the Mennonite Church, it was hardly a new notion in Indiana-Michigan. In a 1922 article titled "How Can I Be a Missionary in My Home Community?" the *Rural Evangel* suggested, "Perhaps the best way to proceed is for the minister to have the congregation appoint a committee to investigate the situation."[75] In 1929, the magazine proposed that each congregation should organize a branch Sunday school every two years.[76] Another article the next year declared that it was the larger congregations' "serious duty" to deploy members "to organize Sunday schools, distributing Christian literature and holding church services of various kinds."[77] In 1944, the same year that Graber took over at MBM, Chester Osborne, the pioneer pastor of Michigan's Upper Peninsula, presented "A Program of Evangelism for Every Congregation" at the annual Indiana-Michigan delegate assembly.[78]

With a maturing ethos of Christian ministry and service inspired by the experiences of World War II, the conference began giving those matters greater consideration. Summer Bible schools, which required church members to serve just a few weeks rather than months or years, were seen as an important first step toward starting new congregations. Between 1943 and 1947, the numbers rocketed from eighteen schools to sixty-eight and from 2,040 students to 7,705.[79] The conference soon had a burgeoning summer volunteer program under the auspices of the Indiana-Michigan Mennonite Mission Board. Already in 1941 the mission board had purchased a house trailer for its workers.[80] Many of them were high school- and college-age students who led Bible schools, but workers also included adults who built mission churches. In 1952, seventy-six people spent part of the summer in eight locations.[81]

All these initiatives resulted in a mushrooming number of congregations in the conference. Seven were started between 1920 and 1940, and eleven more were planted during World War II. But that was just the prelude. In 1945, Indiana-Michigan had eleven congregations under the conference mission board, five under individual congregations or Goshen College student groups, and two under MBM. Fifteen years later, those numbers had jumped to twenty-four conference mission board congregations and twenty-two started and shepherded by individual congregations, plus three under MBM. Overall during that time, Indiana-Michigan grew from 6,021 members in thirty-nine congregations to 9,005 members in ninety-three congregations, from Grand Marais on the shores of Lake Superior in the north to Caney Creek in Kentucky, a distance of more than eight hundred miles. A congregation was even started at International Falls, Minnesota.

The congregational thrust created an expansive genealogy of church planting. Established congregations would start new congregations, which would start still more congregations. One of the most prolific church-planting families was that of Shore Mennonite Church, one of Indiana-Michigan's earliest congregations. Located near Shipshewana, in western LaGrange County, Indiana, it started Emma Mennonite Church, six miles away, in 1901. Emma in turn planted Plato

Mennonite Church in central LaGrange County in 1948. It blossomed and within six years had more than one hundred members and a Sunday school enrollment of 165. In 1956, Plato started Lake Bethel Mennonite Church in the eastern part of the county, thus creating a fourth generation in the Shore family. In addition to Emma, other congregations that could count themselves as Shore progeny were White Cloud at Union, Michigan; Marion at Shipshewana; Bean Blossom at Morgantown, Indiana; Locust Grove at Burr Oak, Michigan; and a Sunday school at Jetson, Kentucky. Bean Blossom planted Mount Pleasant Mennonite Church in Morgan County, Indiana, while Locust Grove started South Colon Mennonite Church in Saint Joseph County, Michigan. In northern Michigan, five-year-old Naubinway Mennonite Church, working with the Indiana-Michigan Mennonite Mission Board, began Rexton Mennonite Church in 1948. With assistance from Clinton Frame Mennonite Church, Petoskey (Mich.) Mennonite Church was organized in 1949, which eight years later established an outpost at nearby Stutsmanville, which became Stutsmanville Mennonite Church.

The conference was also unintentionally expanding well beyond its namesake states. In New Bremen, New York, First Mennonite Church was established in 1941 by former members of a local Conservative Mennonite Conference congregation that had been struggling with internal dissension over attire. Indiana-Michigan bishops D. A. Yoder and Sanford C. Yoder were among those called in from the outside to try to mediate the problem. The attempts failed, and the progressives started a new congregation. They requested bishop oversight from the two Yoders and from Simon Gingerich of Iowa-Nebraska Mennonite Conference, who had also helped try to resolve the dispute. The Yoder connections led First Mennonite Church to affiliate with Indiana-Michigan in the late 1950s.[82] About the same time, a new congregation was emerging in Blountstown in Florida's panhandle, the result of families relocating from Hopewell Mennonite Church at Kouts, Indiana. Hopewell bishop S. S. Miller provided initial oversight, and the new group soon united with Indiana-Michigan.[83] For both First Mennonite Church and the Blountstown congregation, called Oak Terrace Mennonite Church, there were no local Mennonite Church area conferences to join. They eventually transferred their memberships when conferences were formed in their regions.

Increasing Inter-Mennonite Relations

Since the late nineteenth century, Indiana-Michigan had considered the General Conference Mennonite Church (GCMC) as a more acculturated and liberal body, which had become a spiritual home for disaffected former conference members. But after World War II, the denomination started growing in stature and legitimacy in the eyes of the conference. That was evident in the tragedy suffered by the family of Melvin and Verna Gingerich. They were devoted to the Mennonite Church in their native Iowa, but Melvin nevertheless took a position teaching history at Bethel College, the GCMC-affiliated school in North Newton, Kansas, in 1941, where the family was part of Bethel College Mennonite Church. That association would have been scandalous fifteen or twenty years earlier, as J. E. Hartzler learned. But now it didn't keep Melvin from being named archivist of the Mennonite Church (MC) archives, located on the Goshen College campus, in 1947. Several months after the Gingerich family moved to Indiana, thirteen-year-old son Loren was delivering newspapers on his bicycle in Goshen when he was struck by a car and died six hours later.

While the Gingeriches' GCMC sojourn was rare in the Mennonite Church, even more exceptional was Loren's funeral, which was conducted by both GCMC and MC officials. Held in the Goshen College chapel, the service was officiated by Sanford C. Yoder, bishop of the College congregation and former president of the school; Ernest E. Miller, the current president and a College Mennonite Church minister; and Lester Hostetler, Bethel College Mennonite Church's lead pastor. Even more remarkable was the fact that Hostetler was an MC refugee who earlier would have been persona non grata. He had left Ohio Mennonite Conference during its own progressive-conservative tumult of the 1920s, leading a breakaway congregation that joined the General Conference Mennonite Church. Barely twenty years later he was sharing ministerial duties with two prominent leaders in the Mennonite Church.

Relations with the General Conference Mennonite Church were warming in other ways. The new Indianapolis congregation featured MC and GCMC members in 1-W assignments and university students worshiping together. Its impact on Indiana-Michigan was initially limited, however, since service workers and students inevitably left once

The Gingerich family just a couple of days before Loren's death (from left): Loren, Owen, Melvin, and Verna. MCUSAA–Goshen.

they were finished with their responsibilities while new people arrived. The constant turnover in congregational participants made it difficult to establish the types of connections important to breaking down walls in the conference. Furthermore, Indianapolis was on the conference's geographic and cultural fringes.

The redefinitions of acceptable fellowship applied not just locally but globally, as Goshen helped host the fourth assembly of Mennonite World Conference (MWC) in 1948.[84] Even during the heady inter-Mennonite era of CPS, conservative MC members urged the denomination to keep its distance from other Mennonite bodies. While MCC had administered the CPS camps, for Mennonites of all stripes plus Amish and Hutterites, the MC Peace Problems Committee in 1944 started a unit just for its own denomination's conscientious objectors.[85] In 1947, Mennonite Church General Conference delegates voted against participation in the next MWC gathering, which was scheduled to be held in North America after having always been in

Europe. Formal interaction with the Europeans, long considered liberal, "unbelieving Mennonites," was simply unacceptable.[86] The only Old Mennonites who had ever attended an MWC assembly were Harold S. Bender and Orie O. Miller and his family, all of whom went to the 1936 event at Amsterdam in the Netherlands. Miller was MCC's executive secretary and had professional reasons to attend. Bender's involvement was the result of being in the right place at the right time. He was finishing his doctorate at the University of Heidelberg in Germany in 1935 and had formed a pleasant relationship with Christian Neff, the preeminent German Mennonite leader who had initiated the first MWC gathering in 1925 to celebrate Anabaptism's four hundredth anniversary. Neff invited Bender to join him at a planning meeting for the next conference. Despite his unofficial status, Bender actively participated in the proceedings and was given responsibility for finding North American speakers.[87]

Eleven years later, Bender and Miller again unofficially acted on behalf of the Mennonite Church. As a result of its international relief and refugee efforts during World War II, MCC had emerged as an ambassador for international Mennonitism and so assumed responsibility for convening the first postwar MWC assembly. After the MC delegates rejected participation in 1947, Bender and Miller stepped in as de facto denominational representatives by virtue of their membership on the MCC executive committee. Conversations continued between MCC's MWC planning committee and MC officials, and in January 1948 they successfully negotiated an agreement that would allow the Mennonite Church to participate. Among the terms were assurances that "a Christ-centered evangelical attitude and position" would be primary, nothing would be done to embarrass other groups, and "controversial points" would be avoided.[88]

The 1948 conference met in two locations, first in Goshen, then moving to south central Kansas. Some 2,700 people from ten countries filled the Goshen High School auditorium for worship, presentations, and business meetings, turning Indiana-Michigan into a global crossroads. Sanford C. Yoder gave words of welcome, Indiana-Michigan moderator Paul Mininger spoke on nonconformity, and Bender, Hershberger, and Goshen Biblical Seminary professor John H. Mosemann made presentations on peace topics. Bender was also the recording

Goshen college music professor Walter Yoder leading singing at 1948 Mennonite World Conference assembly. MCUSAA–Goshen.

secretary for the business sessions, and Goshen music professor Walter Yoder was the chorister. Indiana-Michigan and the rest of the Mennonite Church had crossed another line of separation, this time to embrace their sisters and brothers in the faith who were members of other Mennonite groups.

The matter of inter-Mennonite relations became unavoidable when it came to Indiana-Michigan's heartland of Elkhart County. In the wake of the tremendously fruitful experiences of CPS, students at Goshen Biblical Seminary (GBS) and at Mennonite Biblical Seminary (MBS), the GCMC seminary in Chicago, began calling for more cooperation between their schools. So a joint summer session of classes was held at Goshen in 1954. It was such a success that Erland Waltner, an MBS board member and future president of the seminary, suggested to GBS dean Bender that they should consider exploring a permanent working relationship.[89] The two men had struck up a friendship through their work with CPS, MCC, and MWC. As a result, Waltner could credibly tell his GCMC constituency that the Mennonite Church was not necessarily the stridently conservative, bishop-dominated autocracy depicted by stereotypes. And Bender could accurately report to MC members that the General Conference Mennonite Church wasn't simply a backsliding bastion of liberal worldliness.

Representatives of the two seminaries began conversation in late 1954. There was surprising openness on both sides to some sort of cooperative venture in graduate-level theological education. But its location was a major obstacle, as each school was unwilling to move to the site of the other. At the same time, MBS was in flux. Since its inception in 1945 as the successor to the Witmarsum seminary in Bluffton, Ohio, MBS had been associated with the Church of the Brethren's Bethany Biblical Seminary in Chicago. While relations between the two were good, both seminaries were coming to realize that, for a variety of reasons such as finances and facilities, the long-term viability of their ties and their location was in doubt.[90] That made for MBS the prospects of a new cooperative program even more appealing. As a compromise location, Waltner proposed Elkhart as the new home for MBS. Located about ten miles from the GBS campus, it was close enough to allow cooperative classes and programs but also far enough apart to allow each school to operate separately and maintain its own identity.[91] MBS relocated to fifty-five acres of former farmland on Elkhart's south side in 1958, and the gap between the schools, known jointly as Associated Mennonite Biblical Seminaries (AMBS), quickly began decreasing.[92] The Elkhart campus soon became home to a new joint research arm called the Institute of Mennonite Studies, and in 1964, Ross T. Bender was named dean of both seminaries. By 1969, GBS had moved from Goshen to the Elkhart campus, further reducing the distance between the two denominations, both literally and figuratively.

The arrival of MBS naturally brought a contingent of GCMC members, both seminary employees and students, who needed a place to worship. Despite the warming relations, it was not yet feasible for the newcomers to participate in Indiana-Michigan congregations. There were still too many differences to be bridged. So a new group, which would eventually be called Hively Avenue Mennonite Church, started meeting in an Elkhart grade school in the fall of 1958 and would join the General Conference Mennonite Church the next year. It was just the fifth GCMC or Central Conference of Mennonites congregation in Indiana and Michigan that did not have its roots in an Indiana-Michigan

THE PAID PASTORATE

T he pastorate in Indiana-Michigan Mennonite Conference had long been an unpaid occupation, usually requiring ministers to have other employment to support themselves and their families. That's why Goshen College in its early years offered agricultural courses. "The country preacher must be a farmer rather than a theologian," declared school president J. E. Hartzler in 1914.[1]

By the mid-twentieth century, however, it was becoming apparent that the viability of the traditional model was questionable. Congregations were being encouraged to provide some financial support to their ministers, yet that was often not enough. "I promised to place the ministry first in all my work & consideration but lack of support has prevented this," said one minister in a 1951 survey of ordained men in the conference.[2] He was devoting 15 percent of his time to the pastorate, for which he received $145 a year.

The highest-compensated Indiana-Michigan minister, according to the survey, received $1,500 a year working half-time for a ninety-member congregation. Four congregations paid between $550 and $900, five between $200 and $350, eight between $100 and $180, and nine between $5 and $90 a year. Twelve ministers received nothing, including a minister who devoted a quarter of his time to a congregation of 350 people.

One pastor estimated he spent two-thirds of his time in ministry, the most of any survey respondent. He received $900 a year from his 340-member congregation. The least amount of time was fifteen days a year by a minister annually paid $50 by his congregation of 345 members.

---

1. J. E. Hartzler to Daniel Kauffman, March 13, 1914, J. E. Hartzler collection (HM 1-62), box 22, folder 4, MCUSAA–Goshen.
2. Ministerial survey, Indiana-Michigan Mennonite Conference collection, (II-5-12), box 1, folder "Data 1947–56," MCUSAA–Goshen.

conflict. The first was First Mennonite Church in Berne.[93] The second was started in 1895 when a Stuckey Amish minister, D. D. Augsburger, settled in the Goodland area of northwestern Indiana and began Zion Mennonite Church.[94] In 1916, several members of the Central Conference moved from Illinois to Kouts, Indiana, which led to the formation of Kouts Mennonite Church two years later. The fourth congregation, and the only one to attract any Indiana-Michigan members, was Washington Center Mennonite Church at Ashley, Michigan. Central Conference members from Pekin, Illinois, moved to the area in 1924 and were joined by three families from Bethel Mennonite Church, the local Indiana-Michigan congregation. Washington Center, however, never had a minister and died out within a decade.[95] All other GCMC or Central Conference congregations within Indiana-Michigan were former Indiana-Michigan congregations, splinter congregations, or started by those congregations.

Institutional Development

When it arrived in 1958, MBS was the second new Mennonite school in Elkhart County in four years. Bethany Christian High School had opened its doors in September 1954 after more than a decade of periodic discussion in Indiana-Michigan. The idea of a conference-affiliated high school was first publicly expressed at the 1940 assembly by Ira S. Johns in his conference sermon. His criticisms of the church's willingness to compromise with the world, loss of nonconformity, and lack of discipline of errant members were just part of an overall theme. Also at that year's assembly were presentations on "Worldliness: The Fruit of Wrong Thinking" and "Steps Leading to Apostasy," an approved resolution that urged upholding traditional scriptural teachings, and the Indiana-Michigan School Problems Committee denouncement of the worldly attire of members of Goshen College's singing groups. "It seems quite evident to us that when all different classes of people sing in these College choruses at our churches it has its influence on breaking the conscience or convictions of our people on the doctrine of complete separation from the world," the committee declared.[96] A Mennonite high school would be another means of upholding that doctrine, and a Church High School Study Committee was appointed in 1945.

While the early motives were isolationist, some in Indiana-Michigan after World War II saw the need for a school for the opposite reason: engagement with the world. With the broadening of faith from simple separation to one of witness and service, it was critical to provide children and youth of the church a solid Mennonite foundation. Goshen education professor Silas Hertzler stated that Mennonite parochial education could "permeate and leaven the life of both the individual and the community."[97] Guy Hershberger's Community Life Study Committee acknowledged that public schools were doing "much good" but noted that their "emphasis must be largely secular, that extra-curricular activities frequently include undesirable features which help to break down Christian standards, and that the total impact of the life of the public high school makes it difficult for our people in our present militaristic world to maintain a firm stand for the principle of nonresistance." A church high school was deemed an important part of preparing young people to carry out Christ's command to go and make disciples of all nations.[98] At a special Indiana-Michigan delegate assembly in December 1950, a conference-affiliated high school was approved in principle. The Church High School Study Committee became the Church High School Committee, which was no longer charged with exploring the idea but directed to develop plans to implement it. Delegates gave their final approval in 1953, and, fourteen months later, Bethany Christian High School welcomed its first thirty-one students to its new campus in the village of Waterford Mills, just south of Goshen College.

Bethany was part of a larger trend across the church. Between 1942 and 1958, nine other Old Mennonite high schools were started in Arkansas, Florida, Iowa, Oregon, Pennsylvania, and Puerto Rico. But not everyone in Indiana-Michigan was behind the new school. Some members were quite satisfied with the public education offered in their communities, a position that some in the conference considered virtually indefensible. "Certain families are so thoroughly wrapped up in the activities and sports of their local high school that they look for any conceivable excuse to oppose a Christian school," criticized one supporter of a church school, although he also had to admit, "Some others are entirely honest in their convictions that the schools need a Christian

MBM general secretary and bishop J. D. Graber speaking to Bethany Christian students at the school, 1964. MCUSAA–Goshen.

witness, and the children need to experience what it means to live 'in' the world but not 'of' the world."[99]

Bethany was not a boarding school, which required students from a distance to find their own accommodations in local private homes. Bethany was originally conceived as serving only the immediate vicinity, not the entire conference, even though it was an official Indiana-Michigan project. A preliminary survey about a conference school didn't include congregations that were not local.[100] Nevertheless, the school drew from well beyond the immediate population center of Elkhart and LaGrange Counties. Two students from Michigan and one from Minnesota enrolled for Bethany's first year. For the next four years the school had an annual average of fourteen students from a distance, as far north as International Falls, Minnesota, and Michigan's Upper Peninsula and as far south as Odon and Montgomery in Daviess County, Indiana. Two students even came from Birmingham, Alabama. The Kokomo-area Mennonites were especially supportive, sending fifteen students between 1955 and 1963.

But the number of students from a distance didn't keep pace with the overall growth of the student body and of the conference, making them a decreasing percentage of the enrollment. Bethany started the

1955–56 school year with 120 students and reached 250 just four years later. When enrollment hit a record of 307 in the fall of 1965, only 7 students attended from Indiana-Michigan congregations more than about thirty miles from the school. Howard-Miami and Leo each sent 2 students, and 1 each came from First Mennonite Church in Fort Wayne, Indiana, Cedar Grove at Manistique, Michigan, and Calvary at Pinckney, Michigan. Another 9 students were not from Indiana-Michigan congregations: 5 from Latino Mennonite congregations in Chicago, 2 from local Conservative Mennonite Conference congregations, 1 from Ohio, and 1, an exchange student, from Kenya.

At the same time that Bethany was starting, some Indiana-Michigan members were recognizing a need for a conference camping program. As with schools, Mennonite camping boomed after World War II, with more than twenty programs starting during the 1950s. In 1952, twelve northern Michigan congregations began renting local camp facilities for their children.[101] Farther south, some Indiana-Michigan children were attending Mennonite Youth Village, a Mennonite Board of Missions–owned camp at White Pigeon, Michigan. It was intended to serve children from church plants, but it was becoming too small to accommodate the growing number of campers.[102] By 1955, the conference was renting the GCMC-affiliated Camp Friedenswald, near Cassopolis, Michigan.[103] The question of starting an Indiana-Michigan camp came before the delegates at the 1956 conference assembly and quickly turned contentious. Among the advocates were former CPS men who had found spiritual refreshment in the outdoors while building dams and doing forestry work. Camp opponents quoted 1 Timothy 4:8: "For bodily exercise profiteth little" (KJV). Conference moderator J. C. Wenger restored order by gently admonishing both sides. The assembly quieted and the motion to start a camp passed.[104]

A site was soon located on Perrin Lake near Sturgis in southern Michigan, and it was purchased by the end of the year. In August 1958, about twenty youth from College Mennonite Church in Goshen became the camp's first official campers, even though the property had yet to be developed. The group had to use tents and pit toilets, as well as campfires for cooking. Cabins, bathhouses, a kitchen, and other structures started going up that fall, and the camp was dedicated in August 1959.[105] But it still lacked a name. An invitation for conference members to submit suggestions produced nothing satisfactory. Finally in the following spring, *Gospel Evangel* announced that the new ministry would be called Camp Amigo: "The term, meaning friend, comes from the Spanish and is pronounced ah-me'-go."[106] Its selection was tinged with irony. A pacifist people who emphasized separation from the world and had historically avoided political involvement had borrowed the moniker from the recent goodwill tour of Latin America by World War II hero and president Dwight D. Eisenhower, dubbed Operation Amigo. It was yet another indicator of the evaporation of Mennonite isolation.

7

The Priesthood of All Believers

It was October 1957, and Russell Krabill, a member of the Indiana-Michigan Mennonite Conference executive committee, and conference moderator J. C. Wenger were driving home after a joint meeting of the executive committee and the conference mission board at East Goshen (Ind.) Mennonite Church. A graduate of Goshen Biblical Seminary (GBS), the forty-year-old Krabill, pastor of North Goshen Mennonite Church, was a dozen years into a distinguished lifelong ministerial career in Indiana-Michigan. Wenger, who was seven years older than his companion in the car, was highly respected across the Mennonite Church (MC), teaching theology at GBS, authoring several well-received books, and currently serving as MC moderator in addition to his Indiana-Michigan responsibilities. Both men were quite aware that their abilities as church leaders were soon going to be tested. At their meeting that evening, Krabill, Wenger, and their associates had heard how close communion, unaccompanied singing, attire regulations, and other longstanding and self-imposed boundary markers of their Mennonite faith were actually barriers to evangelism. In the car after the meeting, Wenger said to Krabill, "Russell, you know I believe that I am living to see some things I gave my life to lost. I believe my work now will be to help keep the Mennonite Church together in the future as she goes through a process of change."[1]

That process would produce changes of a far-reaching and unprecedented scale, with the likes of Wenger and Krabill representative of the new conference dynamics. They were joined on the five-member executive committee by Peter Wiebe, minister and bishop at Yellow Creek Mennonite Church, Goshen. All three had postsecondary education, were not Indiana-Michigan natives, and had extensive experience beyond the conference's boundaries. Wenger was born in Pennsylvania and studied at the University of Zurich in Switzerland and the University of Michigan as well as Goshen College. Wiebe came from the Russian-Mennonite Bergthal group in Manitoba to study at Goshen College and GBS, then began his ministry at Yellow Creek.[2] Krabill was an Iowan who also moved to Goshen for more education. The church's crisscrossing roads had brought all three into the conference. The other two executive committee members were Galen Johns and Tobe Schrock. The former was born and raised in Indiana-Michigan, the son of longtime Clinton Frame minister Ira S. Johns but who was much more progressive than his fundamentalist father. Schrock, born in Shipshewana, Indiana, and ministering at Bowne, Michigan, was the only real conservative on the committee.

In fact, some of Indiana-Michigan's strongest leaders came from elsewhere, an inevitable consequence of being at the crossroads of the church. J. D. Graber, bishop of Prairie Street Mennonite Church in Elkhart, was an Iowa native and longtime Mennonite Board of Missions worker in India before becoming the agency's chief executive. Goshen College president and North Goshen bishop Paul Mininger was born in Ohio and held degrees from Goshen and two Baptist seminaries plus a doctorate from the University of Pennsylvania. John H. Mosemann, bishop of College Mennonite Church, Goshen, was from Lancaster, Pennsylvania, and served in Tanzania with the Lancaster Conference mission board.

With such diversity of background and experiences, Indiana-Michigan emigrants could often understand cultural and religious changes that many people born and raised within the conference could not. That made them particularly able leaders as the conference wrestled with the external and internal forces affecting postwar Mennonites. One of those was the democratization of the church. With Civilian Public Service (CPS) as a primary catalyst, many young men—and a few women—were no longer content with just lay participation in their congregation. With new understandings of faith and vocation, they sought careers in pastoral ministry, missions, church-related education, and church administration as well as in secular service professions—pursuits that often required advanced schooling. As more Mennonites were going to college and, for the first time in sizable numbers, to graduate school, their perspectives were being even more profoundly broadened. In tandem with these developments was the rediscovery of the Reformation-era tenet of the "priesthood of all believers," which endowed all church members, not just those who had been ordained, with the responsibility to actively discern and then participate in the mission of the church.[3] The CPS generation was Mennonite democratization personified.

As with Mennonite alternative service workers, much of the impetus for change throughout American society was the result of World War II. The worldwide battle against Adolf Hitler, Benito Mussolini, Hideki Tojo, and their ilk had united many disparate American elements in a common political and military cause. Women stepped in to keep industry rolling when the men went off to battle. Among the troops were people of color, who, like whites, saw military service as a patriotic duty. After the war, however, members from such disenfranchised groups resisted being forced back to the margins of society and began concertedly pushing for equality.[4] African American civil rights gained a higher profile as a result of the U.S. Supreme Court's 1954 desegregation ruling in *Brown v. Board of Education of Topeka, Kansas*; the 1955–56 bus boycott in Montgomery, Alabama, led by Rosa Parks and Martin Luther King Jr.; and a series of nationwide sit-ins to protest racially segregated establishments. The campaign for gender equality was energized by those women who had ably served in wartime factories while also leading their households. But with the war's end and the return of war veterans to domestic employment, they now had to go back to cooking, cleaning, child-rearing, and other "women's work." That helped stir Betty Friedan to write her 1963 classic *The Feminine Mystique*, which was pivotal in the development of the women's

Harold S. Bender. MCUSAA–Goshen.

rights movement of the time. Young people were also involved in the democratization process, as teenagers feeling repressed found their voice in movies and rock 'n' roll music.

The effects of such forces for change in Indiana-Michigan were being monitored by leaders such as GBS dean Harold S. Bender. Much of postwar Mennonite change can be attributed to his "Anabaptist Vision" and its recasting of the faith. Bender's impact was largely at the churchwide level through his academic career and in various leadership positions with the Mennonite Church, Mennonite Central Committee (MCC), and Mennonite World Conference (MWC). But his mark on Indiana-Michigan was also indelible. Through the World War II years, the conference was a hierarchical organization, with the bishops and their authority at the top, followed by the ministers and then the deacons in their congregational settings. Mennonites who were not ordained had little say, at least officially, in church affairs. But that began to shift after the war, with Bender and other like-minded American Mennonite intellectuals arguing that the church was a community in which all participate in discernment and are mutually accountable to one another. That meant lay members were more than just subjects of the proclamations of bishops and ministers.[5] "All believers have a priestly office to perform for each other in that in Christ each can be a channel of God's grace to his fellow [believers] and indeed has a responsibility to be such," Bender wrote.[6] But it was just a theological sentiment unless it was practically applied. Bender called for just that in his conference sermon at the 1954 Indiana-Michigan annual assembly. He proposed: "If really all the members of the church are the body of Christ locally in the congregation, does this not mean that every member should share in the life and the work and the spiritual ministry of the congregation? . . . Should not this apply also to our conference work? . . . If the conference is to represent the whole body of Christ, why should we not also have lay delegates sharing in the work of the conference?"[7]

It was a clarion call, strong and clear, for a more democratic body of believers and a radical change from the authoritarian years of the 1920s and 1930s. And it was proposed by none other than the esteemed Bender, who had come to churchwide prominence as a layperson, one of the few recognized leaders in the denomination who was not ordained. Yet that didn't diminish his influence. His contributions to the church included, ironically, overseeing the education of future Mennonite Church ministers as GBS dean, even though he wasn't a minister. Bender's seminary position, coupled with the broad scope of his other church work, finally led Indiana-Michigan to take the unprecedented step of ordaining him in 1944, the same year his "Anabaptist Vision" address was published.[8] Previously the only people ordained were those in congregational ministry and missionaries, although many of them ended up in church-related administrative and educational positions. Indiana-Michigan leadership considered the possibility of ordaining someone in another role to be an issue of such magnitude that it declined to make a decision on Bender and chose instead to send it to the delegates, who approved it. Bender, who could only give the conference sermon because he was ordained, was obviously extremely well-qualified to champion the layperson's cause. In 1956, two years after his proposal, the Indiana-Michigan ministerial committee recommended adding lay delegates, saying they would bring broader perspectives to the assembly and also foster greater conference ownership among the rank-and-file members. The committee also cited the positive experiences of six other MC area conferences that were already using lay delegates. But more importantly, the committee recognized "that Christ gives spiritual discernment to every Spirit-indwelt and mature Christian, and not only to the ordained men."[9] Bender's counsel and the ministerial committee's recommendation were heeded by the conference, which welcomed lay members to the annual assembly delegate floor for the first time in 1957.

Bender unwittingly spurred further, more radical developments in the lay movement. The early 1950s found a number of his former Goshen College students in Europe serving with Mennonite Board of Missions (MBM) or MCC, pursuing graduate education at well-respected universities on the continent, or both. They were young men of keen intellect whose overseas experiences were combining with their academic pursuits to generate new insights about the nature of the church. Seven of the men gathered in Amsterdam in 1952 for a two-week retreat that launched the Concern movement. For nearly two decades it would provide critical analysis of Mennonitism and its mission in the world, primarily through a series of pamphlets also called *Concern*.[10] One of the retreat's foci was what participants saw as the hierarchal and excessive structure of the church, which they considered to be at odds with their belief in the centrality of the local body of Christians and its inherent egalitarian ethos. What the Concern participants wanted was the "priesthood of all believers" concept writ as large as possible. Yet Bender and other MC leaders back in the United States vociferously protested the group's critiques as unrealistic and undermining the denomination. They thought that leaving decision making to grassroots members would open the door to chaos. But the young Americans responded with equal force. John Howard Yoder, a brilliant 1948 Goshen alumnus serving with MCC in France and studying part-time at the University of Basel in Switzerland, brazenly told his former professor that he was more Benderian than Bender himself. "I have put together an interest in Anabaptism, which you gave me, an MCC experience to which you were instrumental in assigning me, and theological study to which you directed me, to come out with what is a more logical fruition of your own convictions than you yourself realize," Yoder wrote Bender.[11]

In 1954, Concern participant John W. Miller, having earned his doctorate from the University of Basel, joined the GBS faculty to teach Old Testament. He also continued the historical and theological explorations of church renewal the Concern group had started two years earlier. Miller and seminary colleague C. Norman Kraus authored a paper published in *Concern* that suggested a new understanding of church that was based on the past. Citing Matthew 18:20—"For where two or three are gathered in my name, I am there among them"—they argued for new understandings in stark contrast to the conventional:

> Christ's teachings here seem to suggest that there is no assembly of two or three traveling companions or the periodic gathering of geographically related neighbors, that is not at the same time filled with the possibilities of the 'church.' Not necessarily where the membership rolls are kept, not necessarily where the preacher stands Sunday by Sunday to present his twenty- or forty-minute discourse, at least not *only* here is the church, but *wherever* Christ is reigning in the midst of His gathered people.[12]

College Mennonite Church, where much of the GBS community attended, started forming small groups in 1955, but their primary purpose was fellowship, not discernment and accountability, as Miller and Kraus envisioned. But the two instructors continued to promote their concepts. That spring, their small group took the radical step of celebrating the Lord's Supper on its own without being led by a bishop or a bishop-designated minister, as was customary.[13] If all baptized members were indeed part of the priesthood of all believers, as the group determined, then all were empowered to administer the bread and the cup to one another.

Not everyone, however, saw it that way. Some College Mennonite Church members accused the small group of orchestrating a split and subverting the congregation and its leadership. Some wondered if, since the group's members had held its own communion service, they would also conduct their own baptisms and thus decide on their own who could be Mennonite, much less Christian.[14] Paul Mininger, president of Goshen College, which included the seminary, even considered such small-group activity a repudiation of the Mennonite Church.[15] (In their *Concern* article, Miller and Kraus expressly stated their belief that small groups should be part of existing congregations, not separate from them.[16]) As in the past with Sunday schools, higher education, and other matters, newness was still producing anxiety and fierce resistance. Criticism of the communion service grew so severe that all faculty and their spouses who made up the small group, except for Miller and his wife, Louise, soon pulled back. But the Millers and a handful of GBS students continued exploring ways of being the church and created Fellowship House, a new exercise in communal living in Goshen.[17]

Meanwhile, Miller's school administrators grew increasingly wary of their Old Testament instructor. In 1959, GBS placed him on a leave of absence and never brought him back.[18] In 1960, Miller and his wife, Louise, joined the rest of Fellowship House in relocating to Evanston, Illinois, to start Reba Place, the first Mennonite intentional community.[19] Not all Fellowship House members moved immediately, however. Virgil Vogt tried to work for renewal in a more traditional congregational setting as pastor of Leo (Ind.) Mennonite Church. But his positions on decision making, evangelism, nonresistance, money, and other issues were considered too radical, even socialist, and he resigned in 1962 and eventually joined the others at Reba Place.[20] GBS professor J. C. Wenger regretted Vogt's departure, particularly the loss of his views on economics and consumerism as the country continued to enjoy the postwar economic boom. "The Lord knows that Christians need to be critical of Americanism at many points including attitudes toward money. . . . I wish you could have stayed with us to help win this 'battle' with materialism," he wrote Vogt.[21]

Generation Gap

As it had long been in the Mennonite Church, the bishop system was at Indiana-Michigan's ecclesiological core. Bishops usually held the key leadership positions in the conference and so were responsible in determining the boundaries that separated the church from the world, and then held ultimate earthly authority for enforcing them.[22] By the 1950s, however, that system was being seriously challenged by the articulate, educated, and experienced leaders of the church's emerging congregationalism. It was a classic generation gap. On one hand were younger and sometimes brasher ministers, often with new perspectives gained from alternative service and higher education, who were trying to be both faithful and relevant in confusing times. On the other hand were their bishops, who for years diligently sought to uphold the church's time-honored standards, often amid times of great tumult. Many bishops were effective and well respected by their ministers and church members. But clashes between bishops and ministers, while not an uncommon occurrence in the past, were increasing in intensity. One Indiana-Michigan minister, who was five years old when his bishop was ordained, accused him, "Your way is not the way of the Spirit. This is a harsh thing for me to write my spiritual overseer, but . . . you haven't been overseeing, but rather dictating, if you will allow me to use that word."[23]

It was a trend that wasn't unique to Indiana-Michigan. South Central Mennonite Conference in 1954 became the first Mennonite Church area conference to abolish bishops, who usually served until retirement or death, and replace them with a system of overseers serving three-year terms.[24] By the mid-1960s, Indiana-Michigan's ministerial committee acknowledged that "the bishop situation in the [conference] is far from satisfactory" and started exploring alternatives such as overseers and organizing congregations into geographic clusters for discernment and counsel.[25]

Willard Handrich preaching at Grand Marais Mennonite Church, 1965. MCUSAA–Goshen.

The bishop system was particularly problematic in northern Michigan, the conference's land of paradox. It had been for years one of the two most conservative regions of the conference (along with southern Indiana), and its leaders sought to uphold the authority of conference, even if they personally disagreed with some of its positions and practices. At the same time, northern Michigan was Indiana-Michigan's greatest mission field, where some of the hallmarks of customary Mennonitism were considered barriers to growth. The requirements of attire—such as the prayer covering and no wedding rings—made people reluctant to join. Some ministers wanted to use musical instruments in worship, since their congregants were often less proficient singers than those in more traditional locales farther south. Another flashpoint was communion. Participation was an exclusive sacred ritual, reserved for church members who were deemed in good standing in the fellowship. Only a bishop could administer the bread and cup, and in doing so he could bypass a member he thought did not meet church standards, such as a woman whose sleeves were too short or who was wearing lipstick.

Thus communion could become a source of great struggle between a bishop and a minister who might be inclined to be more accepting.

Called "close communion," it wasn't used just to separate church members in good standing from those who weren't. Christians who weren't MC members also couldn't participate. The Indiana-Michigan executive committee said close communion represented a "oneness of faith and practice" that those who weren't Mennonite Church members couldn't share.[26] That ignited a conflict at Grand Marais Mennonite Church that would dramatically alter Indiana-Michigan's ecclesiology. The congregation was the only Protestant one with a resident minister in the tiny Michigan village of Grand Marais on the shore of Lake Superior. As a result, Grand Marais Mennonite Church became, in effect, a community church, albeit one adamantly Mennonite under minister Willard Handrich. Among the people he considered part of his flock was a woman who grew up in Grand Marais but had moved to Detroit, where she met her husband and joined a Baptist congregation. But the couple frequently returned to her hometown, where they maintained a cabin. When they were in Grand Marais, they attended and supported the town's Mennonite fellowship. The couple was present one Sunday in 1957 when communion was observed. Since they were not members, the officiating bishop, Clarence Troyer, excluded them. The woman spent the rest of the service outside the church crying, having been denied a place at the Lord's Supper in a congregation she identified as hers.[27]

Handrich had called for open communion at least a decade earlier.[28] Now he began earnestly promoting it because of his distress that one of his congregants, although not technically a church member, had been so grievously marginalized. Handrich even suspended communion services for a time due to the disagreement between him and Troyer. "The fence we have put up seems to hold people out better than it holds people in," Handrich wrote the Indiana-Michigan executive committee. "If Christ came for His church tonight I would expect these people to go with me and there is the crux of my burden." He even called his nonmember congregants "Christians with standards above many who receive communion regularly in our established churches."[29]

A native of Fairview, Michigan, Handrich was part of the Civilian Public Service generation, which was so instrumental in reshaping the church after World War II. His last assignment had been smoke jumping in Montana—parachuting from airplanes to fight wildfires. He was on the line when the war ended, and didn't learn of the news until three days later.[30] Like so many other religious conscientious objectors, Handrich's CPS experiences fostered in him a desire to actively serve the church. When he returned home, Willard and his wife, Mary, let Menno Esch, their bishop at Fairview Mennonite Church, know that they were available for service; Indiana-Michigan called them to Grand Marais in 1948. The Handriches initially couldn't find a place there to live, so they commuted weekly from Fairview, where Willard was still employed at a feed mill, to Grand Marais, a distance of 170 miles one way.[31] Willard and his brother Bruce, another CPS veteran and pastor of nearby Germfask Mennonite Church, soon developed reputations as mavericks among the Upper Peninsula's more conservative church leadership as they tried to make the Mennonite faith germane to a local population for whom the cultural distinctives often overshadowed the religious ones.

The Grand Marais communion impasse wasn't resolved until 1961, when conference leaders from Indiana went to the Upper Peninsula to investigate. What they found was a vibrant little congregation trying to serve a community in "unique circumstances." [32] Handrich was granted permission to officiate communion services himself to whomever he felt appropriate, despite Indiana-Michigan's official position. "These deviations are to be tolerated at present in the expectation that many who are now happy attendants and supporters will affiliate eventually with the church," the investigators ruled. They also cited his "basic commitment to the Mennonite Church," comfortable that Handrich, a staunch believer in nonresistance, was not leading his flock down the wide road to apostasy. By excusing Troyer from communion responsibilities at Grand Marais, the decision also released the bishop from the no-win situation of having to choose between conference requirements and a minister with the best of intentions and a heart for mission.

The decision, an acceptable compromise to everyone involved, was not meant to apply to the entire conference but was only an exception to Indiana-Michigan practice. Nevertheless, five years after C. Norman Kraus and John W. Miller's small group generated opposition with its communion celebration, Handrich and Grand Marais struck a blow to traditional conference polity. A congregation and its minister had been granted powers that had previously belonged to the bishops and could officially discern on their own how to best proclaim Christ in word and deed in their distinctive context. More broadly, the Grand Marais decision heralded the impending demise of the bishop system. The next year Bruce Handrich was rebuffed in his attempt to institute open communion at Germfask.[33] But soon after that, Pigeon (Mich.) Mennonite Church asked that a member of the conference executive committee be appointed as its bishop rather than a local ordained man. "We would prefer to have the bishop serve as a counselor to the pastor and the church council, rather than coming to be in charge of baptism, communion and receiving and granting of church letters," congregational leadership wrote. The request was approved.[34]

The new direction received mixed reviews. "I believe the trend is good to put more of the responsibility back on the local congregation rather than conference making most of the decisions. The church needs to be extremely local," said Fairview minister Virgil Hershberger, echoing the Concern movement in a 1968 survey of Indiana-Michigan ministers.[35] Hershberger was just twenty-four years old, having returned to his home congregation with a bachelor's degree in Bible from Goshen College. In contrast was David J. Graber of Berea Mennonite Church at Loogootee in southern Indiana. Fifty-seven years old and with a seventh-grade education, Graber believed the trend toward congregational freedom was undermining faithfulness. "Many of our churches are departing from [official conference standards] and nothing is done about it as far as I know," he lamented in his response to the survey.[36]

As the rise of the ministers changed the bishops, so were the ministers changed by the rise of the laity. More and more lay members were becoming involved in leadership and discernment in unprecedented ways. By the early 1960s, congregations had begun implementing boards of lay elders to assist their ministers, a move the Indiana-Michigan ministerial committee officially recommended in 1964, seven years after lay delegates were first allowed at the annual assembly.[37] A pastor's responsibility, conference secretary Galen Johns counseled one minister, was to "work closely with the brethren in your congregation who are leaders, whether it is a Board of Elders, Church Council, or whatever you have there. You are called to provide leadership as a pastor, as a man of the Word, but not to be the decisionmaker [*sic*] for the con-gregation."[38] That trend even trickled down to the church's younger participants, as an influx of new college- and seminary-trained teachers at Bethany Christian High School eschewed teaching that indoctrinated their students in favor of a student-centered, inquiry-based approach to education.[39] So at all levels new voices and ideas were being heard and duly considered, despite the potential pitfalls. The conference didn't approve of everything that was happening, but it was preferable to the downsides of "authoritarian rule," as Johns described it.[40]

Change Rebuffed

The rapidity of postwar developments did not mean the complete elimi-nation of the lines separating Indiana-Michigan and the world. Sig-nificant parts of the conference still emphasized their traditional under-standings of Mennonitism, which required change to be managed as carefully as possible. One such change was acceptance of the radio. Indiana-Michigan had originally frowned upon it, but as it became more and more commonplace, conference leaders recognized that the radio could be a valuable tool in the work of the church. The *Rural Evangel* editorialized in 1947, "It's not too serious a matter that we as a church have more or less waited in this area—especially during the experimental years of the radio. But the radio is now an estab-lished institution and we can no longer ignore it. . . . We have carried the message in many different ways up to this point. . . . But we must use *every* possible means in spreading the Good News to a perishing generation."[41]

On September 7, 1947, the Mennonite mission in Fort Wayne began broadcasting a weekly program on a local radio station, with the message usually given by pastor Allen Ebersole.[42] The Detroit mis-sion started its own radio ministry two years later. At the same time, the conference warned of the dangers of television, the latest innova-tion in communication and entertainment. While not explicitly bar-ring it, Indiana-Michigan delegates discouraged television's use because of its "contribution to the lusts of the flesh and [because it is] infil-trated with evils which have tendency to break down the spiritual life of the child of God."[43] It was almost identical to the criticisms of radio three decades earlier. Indiana-Michigan was even more forthright in delineating the church from the world when the Mennonite Board of Education explored the possibility of starting a nursing school at the hospital in Elkhart. The conference executive committee felt that "contractual obligations" could place the church "in situations which would make the maintenance of our position as a church difficult or impossible." It also suggested that if a dormitory was needed, it should be placed on the Goshen College campus "so that the church environment and control be safeguarded."[44] Not surprisingly, the idea was eventually scrapped, and the college started offering its own nursing courses in 1950.

Another long-held position that remained unchanged was divorce and remarriage, but it had to withstand a rigorous attempt to update it. It certainly was not a new issue. The pre-merger Mennonite conference spoke to it during assembly sessions six times between 1867 and 1907, while the Amish Mennonites addressed it twice. Even as late as 1960, more Indiana-Michigan ordained men believed divorce and remarriage were grounds for immediate excommunication than were combatant military service or violent crime.[45] But it had already become apparent that change was coming. In 1946, delegates bemoaned "the laxness . . . in the marriage and divorce laws of the land."[46] Yet three years later, conference leaders considered making only "the aggressive party in a lawsuit for divorce" subject to church censure. Those being sued could remain members in good standing if they were to challenge the divorce "as unbiblical and attempt in a humble manner to show reason why a divorce should not be granted."[47] The proposed change was never implemented. Indiana-Michigan was not alone in grappling with the problem. In 1953, the Mennonite Church General Conference accepted the call of the General Problems Committee for "standing firm against divorce and remarriage" in light of an increasing devaluation of marriage and "a sex craze that may compare with that of the people of Sodom and Gomorrah."[48]

But other, high-profile voices were challenging the church's official stance. At South Central Mennonite Conference's 1954 annual assembly, featured speaker J. C. Wenger urged flexibility, grace, and even common sense in dealing with divorce and remarriage. The conventional position was that a divorced person married to another person was committing adultery. Correcting the transgression, however, was often problematic. "We are forced to at least reconsider a stand which has nothing to offer such remarried people except to tell them to cease living together as husband and wife," Wenger said.[49] While he addressed the pertinent biblical passages on divorce and marriage, he also noted what wasn't in the Bible: "Would not God have put in His Word some such statement as the following: 'Anyone who lives in a second marriage with a former companion still living cannot be saved unless he breaks up the second marriage'?"[50]

The issue was especially acute in home mission settings, where often one or even both spouses in a marriage had been previously divorced. The conference's hard line could make it impossible for converts to join the church, even if they were willing to remove their wedding rings and wear different clothing. Longtime Upper Peninsula bishop Clarence Troyer outlined the intricacies: "A & B were married and divorced. B married C and they were divorced. C married D and they applied for church membership. D had never been married before. There [*sic*] pastor instructed them that B & C in the eyes of God were not married, therefore C & D could be received. It is no use to try and explain what kind of predicament I was in."[51]

Sometimes divorce was literally a matter of life and death as women fled abusive marriages. In other cases, no one knew where the ex-spouse was, which made it impossible to seek reconciliation between the partners, as the church mandated. At Saginaw, Michigan, Ninth Street Mennonite Church's first baptismal class included a divorced woman. But any problems were avoided thanks to a timely injury—or perhaps a shrewd maneuver by a bishop in a difficult situation. Tobe Schrock, a leading Indiana-Michigan conservative, was supposed to conduct the baptisms but had to back out shortly before the service because of a "sore shoulder." Schrock suggested a local Conservative Mennonite Church colleague, Emmanuel Swartzendruber of the Pigeon River congregation, as a substitute. Swartzendruber was also a conservative bishop but strongly mission-minded, and agreed to replace Schrock. Thus Schrock was able to maintain the church's standards on divorce while not hindering the work at Saginaw.[52] (That a member of another Mennonite body could and would conduct the baptisms illustrates the theological and cultural similarities of the Indiana-Michigan and Conservative Mennonite Conference congregations in Michigan.)

Given the complexities around any divorce, Wenger suggested that the church consider each case individually and not enforce some "elaborate code" that might rarely be applicable. "This means a certain amount of freedom must be given to individual bishops and congregations to deal with individual cases on their own merits in the light of God's Word and the leading of the Holy Spirit," he told his South Central audience.[53] Doing so would not undermine the teachings of the faith. "Rather, we are magnifying His grace by offering salvation and church membership to those who are called of the Spirit to repentance and faith after having grievously sinned," Wenger said.[54] Afterward, his presentation was published in booklet form and widely distributed.

In 1952, Indiana-Michigan named a five-member committee to study marriage, divorce, and remarriage and then prepare recommendations for the conference. It was a landmark development. Reflecting the embryonic less-authoritarian climate, the committee didn't just easily invoke the usual biblical and traditional precepts. "If we should continue to take into Church membership mainly children of Mennonite parents, and if those within the Church whose homes break up and end in divorce were simply excommunicated, the problem would seldom arise," the committee noted with collective tongue in cheek.[55] Rather, it set out to actually explore the many facets of marriage and divorce, soliciting input from beyond Indiana-Michigan Mennonite Conference, writing papers to circulate among themselves, and honestly seeking to discern if there was something different the church could do. The committee members were certainly not united in their views, but their differences didn't translate into contentiousness and divisiveness, as had happened so often in the past. After more than two years of work, a direction was becoming apparent, one that committee chair Anson Horner, bishop at Howard-Miami Mennonite Church near Kokomo, Indiana, did not agree with. But he was not going to prevent the committee's report from going to the conference delegates. All he asked was that it be accompanied by a disclaimer that it didn't represent all the members' positions.[56] Horner's request was honored.

Although Wenger was not on the committee, its report mirrored his South Central speech in sentiment and often in actual wording. The delegates tabled the report in 1955 and appointed another committee to try again. It consisted of the members of the previous committee plus three men who counterbalanced any concerns of liberality. Ivan Weaver, bishop of Petoskey (Mich.) Mennonite Church; Norman Weaver, bishop of the Maple Grove congregation in Michigan's Upper Peninsula; and Wayne J. Wenger, minister at Caney Creek, Kentucky. Also added was Harold S. Bender.[57] The two Weavers and Wenger represented strong conservative convictions, and Bender, a moderate on many other issues, staunchly held the line on divorce and remarriage.[58]

Nevertheless, the new committee, like its predecessor, still developed a proposal that was too permissive for most delegates.[59] The committee presented three resolutions at the 1956 annual assembly. The first two affirmed customary understandings of courtship and marriage and declared that "nothing should be done in handling such problems which will in any way militate against the basic Scripture teaching." They were easily approved. Not so with the third resolution. It sought to allow for local determination, giving congregations permission to handle cases as they see "best in the light of Scripture requirements," should they feel it "necessary to consider other possible solutions beyond separation." But it wasn't blanket permission. A congregation could only do so if its bishop and two consulting bishops agreed. The final resolution was defeated.

Even regulations on attire remained intact, despite years of criticism from some parts of the conference. Indiana-Michigan had long required ordained men to wear the plain coat and no necktie, but a 1958 proposal called for ministers to only be "encouraged" to wear the traditional apparel, even as much of the laity had abandoned it. The proposal received a majority of votes at that year's delegate assembly—82 to 62—but fell short of the 75 percent needed for adoption. Meanwhile the prayer covering for women received a boost in 1953 when the conference published "The Prayer Veiling: An Expository Study of 1 Corinthians 11:2-16," a treatise by GBS instructor Paul M. Miller. It soon became popular across the Mennonite Church for its articulation of the custom.

Yet also being articulated was growing awareness that attire could not automatically be equated with faithfulness. In 1954, South Central Conference secretary M. M. Troyer wrote Galen Johns, his Indiana-Michigan counterpart, in support of John Landis, a Kansan and Mennonite Church layperson being considered for the pastorate at Bethel

Mennonite Church at Ashley, Michigan. "He dresses very modest, wearing a black tie and a conventional coat," Troyer said. "As far as I know him he is deeply spiritual and in some respects his line of separation from questionable conduct is superior to many Mennonite ministers who wear the plain coat."[60] Charles W. Haarer put a practical spin on the matter by raising concerns such as location, time, and money as factors in nonconformity. He was pastor of Bean Blossom Mennonite Church near Morgantown, Indiana, where he had difficulty finding acceptable plain coats. Haarer had two tailor-made in Indianapolis, requiring several hundred-mile round-trips for fittings—and they still didn't fit to his satisfaction. "On top of that, the suits cost me $30 more than a ready made suit of equal quality," Haarer wrote the Indiana-Michigan executive committee. So he tried mail-order plain coats but also found those lacking. "Is that simplicity? Is it actually wrong to go to a store and purchase a modest suit at a modest price?" Haarer asked, while also assuring the committee that he wanted "to abide by the principle of modesty as taught in the scriptures." The executive committee was sympathetic but said, "We wish it were possible to pass from a dependence on this rule to a real spiritual fortification against worldliness in dress."[61]

As the legacy of the 1920s-era doctrinaire understandings of faith and polity was fading, the old guard had not given up. The executive committee's explanation to Haarer was a vestige of the authoritarianism of years past, with its assumption that the people couldn't be trusted and thus needed their leaders to enforce correct belief and conduct. A year after College Mennonite Church bishop Sanford C. Yoder's conference sermon emphasized unity of spirit and not unity dictated by rules and regulations, Tobe Schrock, bishop from Bowne, Michigan, preached the opposite position at the 1952 assembly. He stressed the importance of the conference to maintain biblical standards in the face of threats to faithfulness.[62] Aging fundamentalist Ira S. Johns from Clinton Frame Mennonite Church continued to financially support Goshen College's historical nemesis, Eastern Mennonite College, and tried to get his grandchildren to attend the Harrisonburg, Virginia, school. "It certainly is a hard task to be pastor of a church and be located within five miles of Goshen College," he lamented.[63] Meanwhile, D. A. Yoder of Olive Mennonite Church, Wakarusa, was

D. A. and Frances Yoder. MCUSAA–Goshen.

distressed at the increasing visibility of women in the church: "Ministers taking their wives along and giving them a prominent place in the [worship] services. . . . Women being elected as delegates to Sunday School Conferences, women elected as choristers in churches. . . . Instructors in Church classes where men and women are in classes."[64] But he admitted that his generation of conservatives had fewer people to pass their torches to. "Unless some of you younger men express yourselves biblically we will soon be where the Brethren are," Yoder told J. C. Wenger.[65]

Yoder would become a casualty of the transformations occurring in the church.[66] By the late 1940s, he had the second-longest tenure in Indiana-Michigan congregational ministry and was the longest-serving bishop.[67] Yoder was ordained as minister in 1907 at Holdeman Mennonite Church at Wakarusa and the next year assumed the pulpit at Olive, where he would serve for the next forty-two years. He became bishop in 1914 and would oversee several other congregations during his career. He also served on the Mennonite Board of Education for four decades, half of them as president. Olive flourished under Yoder and Clarence Shank, who had been ordained minister in 1917. Attendance was just 31 in 1905 but had skyrocketed to 250 in 1940. But by that time, the bishop's more traditional, authoritarian leadership style was starting to fuel tensions between Yoder and Shank as well as between Yoder and deacons M. C. Weaver and Andrew Miller. The situation came to a head in May 1949 when Weaver announced his resignation. The congregation submitted a petition asking the Indiana-Michigan executive committee to intervene, and an investigating committee was appointed. It concluded its task by relieving both Shank and Yoder of their Olive responsibilities; the two men were allowed to minister in other congregations and could be reinstated by the congregation after one year. But like John F. Funk nearly half a century earlier, they never were. Shank declined to seek reinstatement, and Olive voted down recalling Yoder as bishop. His loss of office plainly heralded the end of an era.

Some of the changes in the conference were being resisted not just by the older conservatives but also occasionally by the contemporary, ostensibly more progressive generation of church members. J. C. Wenger, who spoke for a new approach to divorce and remarriage, wrote *Glimpses of Mennonite History and Doctrine*, in which he underscored the "restrictions" of the faith—such as not joining the military, not swearing oaths, not joining secret societies, and not wearing worldly attire—and defended them against charges of "neo-legalism." "The obedience of love is never legalism; it is loveless conformity to a code which is legalism," he wrote.[68] Wenger was harkening back to the era when the faith was defined more by what Mennonites were not allowed to do rather than what they did do. Meanwhile, Harold S. Bender, the proponent of lay participation at conference delegate assemblies, was one of the harshest critics of Fellowship House and its successor, Reba Place. One of his concerns, interestingly, was that the group was too rigid in its discipline, including the loss of individual choice to group discernment.[69] Yet Wenger, Bender, and other conference leaders had demonstrated flexibility and willingness to engage difficult issues and consider alternative perspectives, characteristics that were largely absent several decades earlier.

Wenger, as Indiana-Michigan moderator and secretary, was a particularly able leader, politically adept at bridging the expanding gap between conservatives and progressives. He called into question the church's broad application of 2 Corinthians 6:14 (NIV)—"Do not be yoked together with unbelievers"—which was often used to prohibit church members from participating in non-Mennonite organizations.

J. C. Wenger teaching, 1957. MCUSAA–Goshen.

There were exceptions, such as academic societies, claimed theology professor Wenger, who was a member of the Indiana Philosophical Association.[70] "This membership makes it appropriate for me to attend their meetings and get the stimulation of good discussion," he said. At the same time, Wenger acknowledged the validity of the argument that many organizations, such as labor unions and political groups, used tactics not compatible with Mennonite nonresistance to exert influence. He said he would withdraw from the philosophical association should it become a "pressure group." The traditional position still had validity, but nuances were now recognized and acknowledged.

While inclined toward traditional Mennonite understandings, Wenger prized church unity and tried to be sensitive to the sentiments throughout Indiana-Michigan, including those that he might have disagreed with. He was loath to use the sort of heavy-handedness that had been applied by previous generations. Rather, Wenger had confidence in the collective beliefs of the membership. Delivering the 1958 conference sermon, he pleaded that the conference be Christ-centered rather than problem-centered.[71] It was, at least at first blush, a repudiation of the older, conservative generation and its myriad of "problems" committees—such as General Problems, Labor Problems, and School Problems—that were often employed to address concerns at both the Indiana-Michigan and denominational levels. But then Wenger could also complain about new trends in Mennonite funerals and vow, "I hope to use my influence for conservatism all my days."[72] He was a member of the conference committee that in 1955 came out with guidelines for wedding ceremonies, including limited decorations and prohibitions on photographs, confetti, and wedding veils.[73] Yet three years later Wenger counseled fellow bishop J. D. Graber to permit the wedding veil. "My own sentiments are all for simplicity at weddings, not to follow the fashions of society. However there come times when the wise leader needs to open a valve to prevent worse trouble," Wenger wrote, noting that several Indiana-Michigan congregations had already allowed use of the veil.[74]

Another Indiana-Michigan change was women's increasing status. A 1951 issue of the *Gospel Evangel* included two articles noting the central role of women in outreach. One "sister" had expressed a desire for a Sunday school in eastern LaGrange County, which resulted in the formation of Plato Mennonite Church in 1948.[75] The church plant at Caney Creek, Kentucky, was growing because women were responding to the call of salvation.[76] Four years later, the *Gospel Evangel* published an article on "The Challenge of Being a Pastor's Wife" by Delilah Miller Yoder of Midland, Michigan, although in print she was identified only as Mrs. Clarence Yoder.[77] Conference delegates even considered allowing women representatives to the Christian Workers Conference, an Indiana-Michigan lay organization, but the ordained men ultimately rejected the idea.[78] Single church members were also not ignored. Twenty-four young adults attended a carry-in supper at Yellow Creek Mennonite Church to inaugurate what was believed to be the first organization for unmarried people in the Mennonite Church.[79]

Michigan Conference

As with deliberations on divorce and remarriage and the ministerial plain coat, there was another change that was considered but ultimately didn't happen, one that would have dramatically altered the very composition of the Indiana-Michigan Conference. In 1950, after percolating in a number of minds for some time, the Michigan ministers proposed a conference separate from their Indiana brethren, an idea supported by two-thirds of the ordained men in the state.[80] The primary reason given was geographic. The Upper Peninsula congregations were obviously on the edge of the conference. But even Michigan's stalwart Mennonite congregations were far afield. The one closest to northern Indiana—and the second largest in Michigan—was Locust Grove Mennonite Church near Sturgis, just a dozen miles from the state line and LaGrange County, Indiana. No other congregation was closer to Indiana than 120 miles. The state's largest congregation was Fairview Mennonite Church, about 300 miles away. With their own conference, proponents contended, more Michigan church members would be able to attend annual delegate assemblies.[81] Since the 1916 merger of the Amish Mennonite and Mennonite conferences, Indiana-Michigan held its annual assembly in Michigan only three times prior to 1950: at Bowne in 1929, at Pigeon in 1937, and at Fairview in 1947. (The Michigan congregations weren't the only ones slighted. During that same time period, delegates gathered outside of Elkhart or LaGrange Counties only four other times, twice each at Leo Mennonite Church and Howard-Miami Mennonite Church.)

The distance between the two states was evident in ways other than geography. Northerners often complained of being marginalized by Hoosier conference members, who seemingly always knew best. For example, when the Indiana-Michigan Mennonite Mission Board built the first Mennonite meetinghouse in the Upper Peninsula, at Germfask, it was modeled on typical church buildings farther south. So the new building had a basement, which was impractical because of the local water table. The church also had a high ceiling, which was more expensive to build and more difficult to heat.[82] In addition, between 1916 and 1950, no conference moderators came from the state and only four Michigan men presented the annual conference sermon.

But the greatest chasm was belief. Advocates of the new conference asserted that the proposed separation was not driven by "conscious difference from the Indiana-Michigan Conference in doctrine or practice, or any deliberate antipathy . . . or reactionary spirit."[83] But not everyone believed that. "If, as alleged, the questions were purely geographical, and those others which have been publicly discussed, I could go along with the movement with enthusiasm," said Ezra Beachy, pastor of Calvary Mennonite Church at Pinckney, Michigan. "I have been unable to convince myself that such is the case."[84] He noted that the supporters of the separate conference were more conservative on higher education and attire, so granting a new fellowship would be akin to "a schism rather than as normal growth and development," he argued. "It is my conviction that both [Michigan conservatives and Indiana progressives] need the modifying influence of the other. . . . It is quite certain that differences will increase rather than diminish, and that once separated the two groups will tend to get farther apart as time goes on."[85]

Many of the congregations in Michigan had been under the Indiana-Michigan Mennonite Mission Board and J. K. Bixler, who, as the passionately conservative bishop of the mission congregations, could ensure their adherence to prevailing notions of orthodoxy. Largely isolated from the cultural and religious developments centered in the more heavily populated and more diverse Elkhart County, those congregations were able to keep their conservative convictions through the years. Pastor Ralph Birkey of Wayside Mennonite Church at Brimley once sent home a group from Indiana that traveled north to lead Bible school because the young women had cut hair. Victor Miller at Seney Mennonite Church in the Upper Peninsula acted more proactively: he warned potential groups that if the women had cut hair, they shouldn't come.[86] (That belief was also found at the other geographical end of the conference. After a group of girls from North Goshen Mennonite Church helped with summer Bible school at a church plant at Caney Creek, Kentucky, its pastor complained to their home congregation that one girl's bangs "were an embarrassment somewhat to this phase of the Bible teaching program here."[87]) Given their similar beliefs, Michigan church members enjoyed cordial relations with their Conservative Mennonite Conference neighbors. Both groups supported the Michigan Mennonite Bible School, a six-week program held every winter at Fairview Mennonite Church, and Indiana-Michigan and Conservative ordained men participated in the same ministers' group for fellowship and discernment. One minister, Joe Swartz, even came directly from the Conservative Mennonite Conference to lead Rexton Mennonite Church.

The Michigan ministers brought their proposal to divide the conference to Indiana-Michigan leadership in the spring of 1951. Their concerns were taken seriously, and an exploratory committee was appointed at that year's annual delegate assembly, with members coming from both states as well as from the mission board. The next step was for each congregation in Michigan to decide whether to join the new fellowship. Those voting affirmatively would be charter members of the new conference, while those remaining would stay with their Indiana sisters and brothers, although they would be free to switch membership at any time. Only ten of the twenty-five Michigan congregations voted in favor of joining the new conference, although the backers did account for 60 percent of the membership in the state, as Fairview and Locust Grove, the largest congregations in the state, voted affirmatively.[88] The lack of support was troubling. The proposal was tabled at the 1952 Indiana-Michigan annual assembly with a resolution encouraging the Michigan Mennonites to work at developing more unity.[89]

Another obstacle was the success of Indiana-Michigan's church-planting program in the state. Separation would mean new work would be nearly impossible, since all costs to sustain existing mission congregations would have to be borne entirely by the Michigan members, who would have to more than double their financial contributions or scale back the work.[90] A related issue was the connections that many of the Michigan church plants, particularly in the Upper Peninsula, had with Indiana congregations, which had started a number of the congregations and initially sent the first ministers and, later, volunteer groups to lead Bible schools and build meetinghouses. Those ties could be greatly weakened should a new Michigan conference be formed.

But proponents kept trying to curry support, despite indications that their efforts would be futile. A 1955 poll of Michigan ministers showed 82 percent of Michigan's ordained men favored a new conference, but that didn't translate into support among the laity.[91] A survey two years later revealed only 55 percent of Michigan church members and seventeen of thirty-one congregations favored separation.[92] A final attempt came at the 1958 annual assembly. But the submitted proposal had been signed by only twenty people: all three Michigan bishops, nine ministers, two deacons, and six laypeople. Once again it was tabled, this time with instructions for the Indiana-Michigan executive committee to interview the petitioners. By the next morning, the committee members had spoken to eighteen of the twenty signatories, all of whom agreed to drop their proposal for the time being. "We find considerable sentiment that if and when the matter of a separate Michigan Conference is taken up, a fresh approach should be made," the committee told the assembly. For the sake of procedure, the executive committee then recommended voting down the current proposal because it was "no longer relevant." The motion was taken off the table and defeated.[93] The idea was never resurrected, and Indiana-Michigan Mennonite Conference remained intact.

O n January 24, 1900, the Elkhart Institute began a four-week "Short Bible Course," the first winter Bible school in the Mennonite Church.[1] Its purpose was to provide education on religious topics for people who couldn't attend college. Since most church members were farm-based, they had fewer responsibilities in winter and could take time for school in short stretches. Ministers were particularly targeted. J. S. Hartzler, one of the instructors, thought that only one in twenty preachers was able to make an outline for a sermon.[2] The school offered various Bible classes as well as classes on Anabaptist history, Sunday school work, and church doctrine.

Winter Bible schools were soon being held across the Mennonite Church in the United States and Canada. One of the most successful was the Michigan Mennonite Bible School at Fairview. Several Michigan ministers, both Indiana-Michigan Mennonite Conference and Conservative Mennonite Conference, had attended a school at Johnstown, Pennsylvania, in the 1940s, and returned impressed and decided to conduct their own winter Bible school. The first one was held in January and February 1946 at Fairview Mennonite Church, the only facility large enough to host it. Fifty young people and six ministers were enrolled.[3]

Many students, as well as most instructors, came from Michigan and Indiana. But pupils also came from as far away as Delaware and Kansas for courses such as "Biblical Basis for Missions," "Christian Nurture of the Child," and "Methods of Bible Study." They also came for the social opportunities, and the coed school soon developed a reputation as a place to find a spouse.[4]

The Michigan Mennonite Bible School reached its highest enrollment in 1951, with 152 young people and fourteen ministers. Students usually stayed in private homes, but such high attendance had school organizers considering building a dormitory. Those levels, however, couldn't be sustained. The size of the student body started to decline, and in 1966, only twenty-four people, all but six of them local, attended.[5] It was the last year for the Bible school.

Goshen College had shuttered its program twelve years earlier. Other winter Bible schools in Indiana-Michigan were held at Bowne and Midland in Michigan and at the Leo, Howard-Miami, Berea, and Shore Mennonite congregations in Indiana.[6]

1. Paul M. Lederach and Harold S. Bender, "Winter Bible Schools," *Mennonite Encyclopedia*, vol. 4 (Scottdale, PA: Mennonite Publishing House, 1959).
2. "Biography," J. S. Hartzler collection (HM 1-3-3), box 3, folder 3, MCUSAA–Goshen.
3. Ora Troyer, *Fairview Mennonite Church* (Fairview, MI: privately published, 1990), 178.
4. Esther Shaum and Lois Miller interviews by author, both June 22, 2006, Engadine, MI, recordings in author's possession.
5. Troyer, *Fairview Mennonite Church*, 179–80.
6. Lederach and Bender, "Winter Bible Schools."

8

A New Look

The first preacher ordained in what would become Indiana-Michigan Mennonite Conference was Amish Mennonite Jonas Hochstetler, in the spring of 1844.[1] He had moved from Pennsylvania to Elkhart County, Indiana, in the fall of 1841, several months after the first Amish Mennonites arrived in the area. Two and a half years later, Hochstetler was chosen by lot to provide spiritual leadership to the growing community. In the years and decades that followed, hundreds of men were given official sanction to serve as deacons, ministers, and bishops to foster faithfulness and uphold righteousness. Ordination was a sacred act but also a common part of conference life, since new leaders were always needed to succeed those who had died, retired, moved away, or, on occasion, been disciplined. It was part of the ebb and flow of routine conference life. But the ceremony on February 17, 1980, was hardly routine. For the first time ever, Indiana-Michigan credentialed a woman for the ministry, licensing Wilma Bailey as assistant pastor at Grace Chapel in Saginaw, Michigan.[2]

Like so many of Indiana-Michigan's pioneers, Bailey's journey started in the East. An African American, she was born in New Jersey and raised in New York City, where she started attending Friendship Community Church, a Mennonite Church congregation in the Bronx. As a teenager interested in things religious, she studied Judaism and Catholicism, and at summer camp she preferred the Bible courses to the recreation times that interested most other kids. After graduating from college, Bailey was a community worker in Omaha, Nebraska, for a year before returning to New York, where at Friendship she taught Sunday school, directed the summer children's program, worked in its daycare center, and became the first woman to chair the church council.[3]

Wilma Baily preaching at Grace Chapel, Saginaw. MCUSAA–Goshen.

Bailey arrived in Saginaw from Goshen Biblical Seminary, where she had earned her master of divinity degree in 1979. While there, school officials recognized her gifts and began touting her for future service. "She is quiet, mature, gifted intellectually, and led by the Holy Spirit in her life so far," Leland Harder, the seminary's director of field education, told a group of pastors. "I regret to report, however, that the Spirit is thwarted occasionally by the fact that our students wanting placement happen to be women, or happen to be black."[4]

The roads that brought Bailey to Indiana-Michigan still had barriers. With her licensing, she and Grace Chapel embodied momentous change in a fellowship that had long been the purview of white, rural, Germanic congregations under the leadership of white, rural, Germanic ordained men. Starting in the 1950s, Indiana-Michigan, like the rest of the Mennonite Church and American society in general, was confronted with sweeping upheaval that challenged many conventional understandings, assumptions, and practices—and they were all being challenged at the same time. Earlier attempts at secular democratization, to provide equality to marginalized people, were maturing into full-blown social and political movements and countermovements.[5] Women's and civil rights, the Vietnam War, and other concerns had become legislative as well as religious, moral, and ethical issues demanding direct engagement with governmental institutions at all levels.[6] After all, it was the law that dictated where African Americans could sit and it was the president who controlled U.S. military involvement in Southeast Asia.

For some church members, witnessing to the state and challenging governmental authority were expressions of their Mennonite peace convictions, which led them from the faith's longtime sectarian quietism to a more activist faith.[7] The passive, docile connotations of Anabaptist nonresistance, derived from Jesus Christ's teaching to "not resist" evil and sometimes translated as "defenselessness," were slowly dissipating.[8] In 1960, Goshen College alumnus and future Goshen religion professor J. R. Burkholder urged Mennonites "to give serious consideration to radical protest, direct action if you will, as a necessary part of its evangelistic and prophetic peace witness."[9] For church members of that mind-set, there was little fundamental difference between marching in Washington, D.C., to oppose militaristic policies and starting mental health centers to care for individuals with psychological and emotional problems, as happened after the Civilian Public Service experiences of World War II. Both were efforts to bring justice to unjust situations. That willingness to engage the world, combined with the recent empowerment of Indiana-Michigan congregations to do their own discernment, paved the way for the acceptance of divorced and remarried individuals, the removal of women's prayer coverings, the conducting of their own communion services, the adoption of new forms of worship, and other divergences from long-held beliefs and practices. The increasing de-emphasis of strong, centralized conference authority that kept change in check was well underway.

But that made the more tradition-minded Indiana-Michigan members profoundly fearful for the future. It was becoming increasingly apparent to them that, without an ultimate arbiter and disciplinarian to maintain separation, the very foundations of the faith were rapidly eroding and Mennonite distinctives were disappearing in the face of acculturation. The certainties provided by belief in God and Christ as articulated by the church's leaders were being replaced by a constant state of flux, leading one Indiana-Michigan minister to cry, "When will the changes in the church stop?"[10] They wouldn't. The Mennonite

Church General Conference tried to prepare denominational members for that in 1963, declaring that in the "midst of some of the most swift-moving and astonishing changes in history," the church "is to be the instigators of change for good, and need, therefore, to discern the up-to-date leading of the Spirit."[11]

A major reason for the conservatives' differences with their more progressive brothers and sisters was their attitudes toward the culture around them.[12] It was an issue that had been a factor in almost every previous conflict since the first Amish Mennonites and Mennonites settled in the region. Conservatives, such as those who would form the Old Order groups and, later, the fundamentalists, saw the culture of the world as threatening the life to which God called them. Such a life was meant to be anticultural, or directly opposed to the prevailing culture, and kept as distant as possible in order to avoid temporal infections. Since the world was always introducing new challenges for the church, it was a stance that had to be continually renegotiated. Progressives, meanwhile, willingly accommodated many outside influences and subsequently became acculturated to varying degrees; some even became so "worldly" that they discarded the peace position.

By the 1960s, however, a new approach had emerged. A counter-cultural kind of Mennonitism began actively seeking to provide an alternative to the ways of the world that didn't require automatically accepting them or rejecting them wholesale. It was not quite the same as the era's stereotype of counterculture—long-haired, free-loving, drug-using hippies—but there were definite similarities. A countercultural Mennonitism may not have meant ingesting psychedelic pharmaceuticals or dancing in San Francisco with flowers in one's hair (although some church members no doubt did). But countercultural Mennonites did see themselves as part of the world, even if not "worldly," and engaged it and its problems using select worldly methods, such as participating in nonviolent demonstrations, holding conferences and seminars, and creating organizations and coalitions. Like the hippies, their goal was an improved world that differed from the current mainstream one, albeit one based on their understandings of Mennonite religiosity.

One of the most visible indicators of that change was the new paid position of conference minister, created in 1968. The first person in that job, which was originally half-time, was Galen Johns. He was the

Galen Johns. MCUSAA–Goshen.

pastor of Bonneyville Mennonite Church, Bristol, Indiana, and also worked part-time at Bethany Christian High School in public relations and teaching Bible. He was also carrying on a family tradition. Galen's grandfather was bishop Daniel J. Johns, who was elected assistant secretary of the 1896 Indiana-Michigan Amish Mennonite Conference assembly and of the 1899 Mennonite conference assembly. (He was also twelve times moderator or assistant moderator of the Amish Mennonite conference and twice for the merged conference.) But it was Galen's father, Ira, who solidified the Johnses' hold on the secretary's office. Ira was a substitute secretary for the 1912 Indiana-Michigan Amish Mennonite Conference assembly, then was elected to the post for the conference's final four years. But that was only the beginning. After an eight-year hiatus, Ira was elected secretary of the merged conference for the 1924 annual assembly, then reelected every year until 1947. Galen became the family's third generation to serve as secretary, beginning in 1953. He transitioned from volunteer into paid executive and continued serving until 1970, when he left the conference for a pastorate in Ontario. By then D. J, Ira, and Galen had a combined forty-nine years of Indiana-Michigan secretarial service. Shortly after Galen became secretary, Niles Slabaugh, the venerable conservative bishop of

Howard-Miami Mennonite Church, Kokomo, Indiana, wrote him, "I always thought so much of your father & grandpa as disciplinarians and hope you will be like them."[13] Slabaugh would be sorely disappointed, as the youngest Johns would be key in the development of Indiana-Michigan's congregationalism.

Johns's new job as conference minister was just one part of a tremendously turbulent year. In broader society, 1968 included the assassinations of Martin Luther King Jr. and Robert F. Kennedy, the riots at the Democratic National Convention in Chicago, the deteriorating war in Vietnam, the protest of racial segregation by Olympians Tommie Smith and John Carlos, the growing impact of rock music, and more. In Indiana-Michigan, delegates to the annual assembly heard a report on conference reorganization, including rearranging and reconstituting existing commissions and committees, clarifying responsibilities, and streamlining financial operations. Most significant, however, was a plan to codify the continuing shift from centralized authority and the pursuit of uniformity to greater latitude for members to express their faith. The report plainly stated that "the congregation is the functioning group in the life and the church" and that the conference's organization "should be molded to serve the congregation."[14] During the following year, culminating with the adoption of a new constitution, Indiana-Michigan would officially turn 180 degrees from its pre–World War II position.

Congregational Challenges to Convention

College Mennonite Church in Goshen, Indiana, was often at the forefront of change in the conference. The congregation included much of Goshen College's intelligentsia as well as other Mennonites, also frequently well educated, who moved to the city from elsewhere in the country for employment or retirement. That combination of education and diversity often tested prevailing Mennonite norms in the conference. Indiana-Michigan had long been firmly opposed to accepting members who had been divorced and remarried. But it had usually been an issue confined to the conference's geographic and cultural fringes, such as church plants that attracted individuals who might not have been Christian and certainly not Mennonite. But in 1969, it came to the heart of Indiana-Michigan when a distinguished church leader wanted to marry a divorced woman.[15] Christian L. Graber's resume included pastor, Goshen College business manager, and the first executive of Mennonite Mutual Aid and later of Mennonite Disaster Service. He and his wife, Mina, were living in Goshen and members of the College congregation when she died of cancer in 1968. The next year he became engaged to Phebe King Erb, a family friend who also lived in Goshen and was active in the same congregation. She and her husband had divorced some twenty years earlier while living in Colorado when he, also a Mennonite, became associated with radical politics and left her. Even though she was not responsible for the dissolution of her marriage, Erb wasn't able to join College Mennonite Church. She bemoaned that she could be forgiven for murder but not for divorce.[16]

Because Graber wanted to marry a divorcee, his membership became an issue. As befitting a congregation associated with an academic institution, College took the opportunity to start a study on divorce and remarriage in the summer of 1969. Not wanting to wait until the discernment process was completed—whenever that might be—Graber withdrew his membership, thus making him free to marry Erb. The church's prohibitions applied to members, not nonmember attenders. Graber and Erb were wed in September 1969 and continued to participate in College Mennonite Church as they had before.

In the meantime, another case arose when Harold Hartzler, a divorced member of the congregation, became engaged to Rachel Nafziger, who had not been previously married. By early 1972, College finally finished its study, concluding with a statement reaffirming belief in the permanence of marriage but declaring that when divorce and potential remarriage did occur, the congregation "must act in a way that is according to biblical understandings in helping people deal with their situation." In other words, membership was now possible. In April 1972, the congregation, by a vote of 124 to 7, approved Hartzler retaining his membership and granting membership to Nafziger, who was attending but hadn't joined College.[17] C. L. and Phebe Graber became members two months later.

During this same time, College Mennonite Church also tackled the long-standing question of the prayer covering, which had ensnared a male Goshen College professor. In 1961, Marlin Jeschke joined the faculty as a Bible and religion professor, with the expectation that he would join the Mennonite Church.[18] He was a member of the Krimmer

Mennonite Brethren, and Charmaine, his wife, was Baptist. But joining an Indiana-Michigan congregation wasn't theologically problematic for them, except for the requirement for Charmaine to wear a prayer covering. She refused to do so, with her husband's support. So the Jeschkes attended but didn't join the College congregation. But not having Mennonite Church membership caused the school to deny Marlin tenure.[19] The Jeschkes' situation was just one challenge to the covering in the congregation. About the same time, four women wanted to be baptized and join College but also refused to wear the covering.[20] In 1967, the congregation initiated a study of 1 Corinthians 11, the passage usually cited in support of wearing the covering. Because Marlin was on sabbatical, the Jeschkes were away from Goshen during the 1968–69 academic year. When they returned, they learned that the congregation had decided to only encourage, not require, women to wear prayer coverings. A 1968 survey found that 71 percent of the congregation did not think that not wearing the covering was a sign of spiritual decline, and 56 percent opposed disciplining women who didn't wear the covering.[21] Bare heads soon became the norm for women worshiping at College Mennonite Church. The four baptismal candidates joined the congregation, as did Charmaine and Marlin, who later received tenure. With the covering falling out of favor across Indiana-Michigan, the conference executive committee in 1973 recommended that pastors' wives still wear them and that pastors still encourage women members to wear them.[22] But they were now optional.

So was the straight coat for ordained men. In 1959, one year after Indiana-Michigan delegates voted down a measure to no longer require the coat, a conference committee again recommended encouraging ministers to wear "conservative, modest clothing," not necessarily the traditional coat. The committee said, "We believe that a man worthy of the calling to the Christian ministry should have the ability to discern what is consistent with our concept of Christian discipleship."[23] Nevertheless, as in 1958, the coat requirement survived votes in 1960 and 1964, despite a majority of delegates opposing it both times, as they fell short of the two-thirds vote necessary for adoption. It finally passed in 1965, receiving an overwhelming 101 affirmative votes against just 12 dissenting.[24]

Opposition to wedding rings also began to dissipate, although it would remain an issue in some Indiana-Michigan congregations well into the 1970s. In 1961, First Mennonite Church in Fort Wayne approved allowing wedding rings with a 71 percent vote of the members. It was recognition of the church's changing contexts. "When the motive for wearing the wedding band is that of conformity of display, we are in danger," stated congregational leadership. "However, in our urban culture, a symbol of marriage may clarify the morality of a young wife or an expectant mother who needs to move about in public."[25] Meanwhile, Ruth Rudy, wife of Carl Rudy, pastor of the new Mennonite congregation in South Bend, was causing a stir because she wore a ring and no prayer covering.[26]

In 1962, Bethany Christian High School was courting a candidate to be its new principal, R. C. Laurie Mitton, a teacher and administrator at the Mennonite school at Belleville, Pennsylvania. He was found to be well qualified for the job, except that he and his wife refused to remove their wedding rings. Mitton pointedly asked Bethany officials, "Is it a wise course that you are pursuing in letting the ring or any other minor issue stand in the way of your Christian High School program? Are you really putting first things first or are minor issues taking precedence in your decision making?"[27] He went on to explain his and his wife's decision: "The rings hold a special significance to both Norma and I and to our families. To say the least, our families are not sympathetic to the Mennonite cause. It seems needless to us to place an additional unnecessary barrier between ourselves and our families. . . . We have prayed, searched the Scriptures and found peace. Do not take our peace from us for the sake of an unnecessary standard."[28]

J. C. Wenger, the Indiana-Michigan moderator and a Bethany board member, could only offer political considerations as a defense of the ring requirement, asking Mitton to put himself in the school board's position. "I am sure that there is no more wrong in wearing a mustache than a beard," Wenger wrote. "Yet our people have had a conscience against the mustache for so long (because of its military flavor centuries ago) that it would be most imprudent to hire a teacher who wears a mustache."[29] Mitton was not hired.

The evolution of acceptable attire as well as the presence of women in leadership literally gave the church a different look. So too did the growing popularity of organizing congregations into lay-led small groups for greater spiritual intimacy and accountability. In 1966,

Southside Fellowship was started in Elkhart, primarily by members from Belmont Mennonite Church, for an even greater small-group experience and also to explore new ways of worship and evangelism.[30] Campus Church was started the next year at Goshen College, a worship service for students who considered more traditional worship to be outdated, impersonal, and irrelevant.[31] Campus Church never joined Indiana-Michigan and died out after a few years, but it spawned a series of house churches that, along with a College Mennonite Church small group, formed Assembly Mennonite Church in 1974.[32] At about the same time, a group started the Fellowship of Hope intentional community in Elkhart. Members all lived within three blocks of one another, shared two meals together a week, had a common treasury, and employed joint decision making.[33]

New congregations were also started as a result of educational and professional trends. In the 1960s, increasing numbers of Mennonites were leaving their traditional, rural enclaves to pursue graduate studies at large universities in urban settings. Once in the academic-oriented diaspora, the students often found themselves coming together for fellowship, Bible study, and eventually worship. The first such group in Indiana-Michigan was related to the University of Michigan.[34] Called Ann Arbor Mennonite Fellowship, it joined the conference in 1966, twelve years after it began meeting. Over the next twenty years it would be followed by four more congregations in university cities: East Lansing, Michigan; Valparaiso, Indiana; and Bloomington, Indiana, plus a second congregation in Ann Arbor.

Such congregations brought new dynamics to Indiana-Michigan. Of the fifty-six adults who were part of the Ann Arbor Mennonite Fellowship in 1967, for example, eighteen were graduate students in fields such as anthropology, economics, linguistics, psychology, and social work. The membership list also included an instructor in the university's School of Education. For most students, putting their education to work would take them to locations outside traditional Mennonite enclaves. Their studies also made them better educated than many church leaders. According to a 1968 conference survey, less than 25 percent of active Indiana-Michigan ministers had seminary degrees, and about 40 percent had no education beyond high school.[35] Furthermore, the Ann Arbor congregation was hardly homogenous in its

Mennonites in Paoli gather in 1975. MCUSAA–Goshen.

religious composition, drawing participants with Mennonite Church backgrounds but also General Conference Mennonite Church, Brethren in Christ, Baptist, and Evangelical United Brethren members.[36] That diversity led Ann Arbor to affiliate with the General Conference Mennonite Church in 1967, one year after joining Indiana-Michigan, becoming the first conference congregation to simultaneously be a member of both denominations.

Paoli (Ind.) Mennonite Fellowship was another new type of conference congregation.[37] In the early 1970s, several students in medical school in Indianapolis who attended the city's First Mennonite Church started considering how to best apply both their faith and their vocational training. After several years of discernment, the group, assisted by members of the congregation, chose Paoli as a place to live, serve, and worship. Located in economically depressed southern Indiana, it was in particular need of medical services. In 1974, the first Mennonites bound for Paoli were commissioned by First Mennonite Church and moved south to start offering healthcare. They initially tried to fit into local congregations, but feeling that their attempts were unsuccessful, the group started Paoli Mennonite Fellowship in the fall. In following years, the original group was joined by other medical professionals as well as Mennonites of other occupations. The congregation also drew local residents.

Even though Indiana-Michigan continued to expand and grow, the great postwar church-planting explosion had subsided by the mid-1960s. Thirty-three congregations joined the conference ranks between 1960 and 1980, and only about two-thirds of them were conventional church plants. The rest were one of two types: organic, such as those in Ann Arbor and Paoli, where there had been no intention of starting a congregation, or groups that left existing congregations, either because of internal conflict or as intentional spin-offs. Overall, Indiana-Michigan's membership rose from 9,399 in 1960 to 12,191 twenty years later.[38]

A Woman's Place

As Indiana-Michigan Mennonite Conference increasingly recognized the diversity in its midst, it was soon forced to face the contentious issue of the role of women in the church. With its public demonstrations, campaigns, political involvements, and outspoken leaders, the strategies of the feminist movement in the 1960s and 1970s were considered by many to be inconsistent with Mennonite nonresistance. As a result, progress in the conference was slower and more subtle. Goshen College education professor Mary Royer was invited to speak on "Effective Teaching" at the 1964 delegate assembly. She would have been the first woman to address the assembly, but she had to decline because she would be away on her sabbatical. In 1968, the Women's Missionary and Service Auxiliary of Indiana-Michigan, which usually met separately but in conjunction with the annual delegate assembly, had charge of a public session during the assembly. The leader was "Mrs. Don McCammon" (Dorothy), a former missionary to Japan. The featured speaker, however, was male: Walter Drudge, a psychologist from Oaklawn, the Mennonite-affiliated mental healthcare center in Elkhart, and a member of College Mennonite Church. Men also were involved in the planned responses to his presentations, as three married couples—no woman was unaccompanied by a man—spoke after Drudge. The worship litany that closed the session was led by Loretta and Richard Yoder, who were the worship leaders for the entire assembly. It wasn't

Peace and Service Commission, 1975: Daniel Slabaugh and Evelyn Kreider (seated); Beth Berry and Earl Sears (standing); Lee A. Lowery (not pictured). MCUSAA–Goshen.

until 1972 that a woman by herself addressed the entire assembly, when Doris Reynolds Schrock of Yellow Creek Mennonite Church, Goshen, spoke on "The Gospel Bearer Experiences God's Grace."

Schrock's presentation was only one sign of women's growing stature in Indiana-Michigan Mennonite Conference. By then they were serving as conference delegates, and four women were among the members selected to represent Indiana-Michigan at the 1973 Mennonite Church assembly. In 1971, two members of Belmont Mennonite Church, Elkhart, were appointed to conference positions: Beth Hostetler Berry, an education instructor at Goshen College, to the Peace and Service Commission, and Doris Liechty Lehman, president of the denominational Women's Missionary and Service Commission, to the nominating committee. The next year, Carrie Yoder Diener, an elementary school teacher and member of Prairie Street Mennonite Church in Elkhart, joined the Bethany Christian High School board.

As opportunities increased for women to serve, the next issues to arise were pastoral ministry and credentialing. Just as with the prayer covering and divorce and remarriage a few years earlier, College Mennonite Church was again at the vanguard. In 1975, new lead pastor

Arnold Roth invited congregational member Rachel Fisher to join the College pastoral team. She had been working for the Mennonite Board of Congregational Ministries at its Elkhart office, where her administrative skills were readily apparent. Fisher had no desire to preach but excelled as a worship leader and in doing visitation.[39] In 1977, Art Smoker, another member of the College pastoral team, was going through the Indiana-Michigan ordination process when congregational member Dorothy Yoder Nyce asked, why not Rachel too?[40] Four years earlier, Illinois Mennonite Conference had ordained Kokomo, Indiana, native Emma Sommers Richards to serve at Lombard (Ill.) Mennonite Church, the first woman credentialed for pastoral ministry in the Mennonite Church. But neither College nor Indiana-Michigan was yet ready to take that step. The conference had initiated a study process in 1976, and the congregation did likewise the next year. In 1981, College decided not to make credentials dependent on the conference. Rather than wait for Indiana-Michigan to ordain Fisher—who by then had been joined by another woman on the ministry team, Nancy Kauffmann—College would simply "commission" all its pastors.[41]

Later in 1981 and after five years of work, the conference finally completed its study of women in leadership. It had started in northern Michigan, with Alma Coffman of Petoskey Mennonite Church, a nurse who felt called to ministry. In 1973, she applied for scholarship money from Indiana-Michigan to help pay for her studies at Associated Mennonite Biblical Seminaries (AMBS) but was denied because of her gender.[42] A woman cannot be a minister, the conference ruled, thus Coffman was not eligible for financial support to help her become one. Undaunted, she continued her studies, graduated in 1976, and soon accepted an invitation to become pastor of Ottawa Mennonite Church in Ontario.

Meanwhile, her Petoskey pastor, Homer Yutzy, was troubled that a gifted candidate for the ministry was deprived of the possibility of fully using her gifts in Indiana-Michigan. "This member has been treated first as a woman, then as a Christian and has been denied many things on the basis that she is a woman," he complained. "These are things that would have been readily granted to a man of her character and Christian commitment." It was time, he argued, for Indiana-Michigan to examine the issue and definitively decide whether women could be ministers. "If the answer is no, so be it, but let us not continue to ignore this or evade it. It will not go away," Yutzy said.[43] He noted a dilemma regarding transferring her congregational membership to Ottawa: "Can we give her a good church letter and recommend her to this congregation? Or should we register a concern for Alma that she is not fully obeying the Word in that she, a woman, wants to serve as a pastor of a Mennonite congregation? Or should we just praise God that she is going someplace outside our conference and congregation, give her a good letter (which means we agree with her and sanction what she is doing) and send her on her way?"[44]

Dean Brubaker, secretary of the Church Life Commission (CLC), the Indiana-Michigan body responsible for ministerial matters in the conference, responded to Yutzy. He said Coffman was not transferring as a minister but simply as a member of one congregation to another, missing Yutzy's question as to whether Coffman was a member in good standing if she was engaged in something that the conference disapproved of. Brubaker then added, "As [the CLC] read and re-read your letter, it seemed that perhaps you were trying to send us a message!"[45]

Yutzy certainly was. But his attempts with the CLC were fruitless, so he took his concerns directly to the delegates. At Indiana-Michigan's annual meeting in July 1976, he asked the conference to study the issue of women in leadership. The delegates approved the motion. The first step, however, gave short shrift to the side favoring women in leadership. The study committee was all male: Harold Bauman, Howard Charles, and J. C. Wenger, all AMBS professors. No women were appointed to examine women's roles in Indiana-Michigan. Delegates objected to their absence in 1978, and so three were added to the committee: Joyce Rutt Eby, a schoolteacher and member of Belmont Mennonite Church; Mary Baer Martin, a nurse from Olive Mennonite Church, Wakarusa; and Doris Reynolds Schrock, the first woman presenter at an assembly. As the process continued, conservatives began to feel slighted. Presentations at several assemblies were accused of being one-sided, and a number of congregations considered study resources sent to them by the conference to be skewed and refused to use them.[46] "I feel it is biased, slanted and falsely [interpreted]," said Tom Schwartz, pastor of Heath Street Mennonite Church at Battle Creek, Michigan. "I feel it is a shame and a disgrace coming from a biblical conference as ours."[47]

After being tabled at the 1980 assembly, the study committee's recommendation to allow the ordination of women was approved in 1981 with a 63 percent vote. More precisely, the action did not bar women from the ministry or other leadership positions but gave each congregation the responsibility of deciding how to use women's gifts in its particular context.[48]

But by then other conference actions had unmistakably signaled the new course. Two years earlier, the CLC had approved Wilma Bailey's licensure, all the while claiming that it was not a precedent nor should it influence the study process in progress.[49] Critics didn't believe it. "It looks like you [conference leadership] can do whatever you please. It doesn't really matter what some of us think," Roy K. Yoder, pastor at Pleasant View Mennonite Church of Goshen, told the CLC.[50] Indiana-Michigan's second woman in ministry, after Bailey, was Charlotte Holsopple Glick in the summer of 1980, when she and her husband, Del Glick, were installed as copastors of Waterford Mennonite Church, Goshen. Charlotte had been a schoolteacher who decided to join her husband in studies at AMBS, leading to their positions at Waterford. In 1983, the CLC accepted the credentials of Evelyn Childs to become minister at Peace Community Church in Detroit. She had been ordained in 1974 in a Missionary Baptist congregation, but she was later drawn to the Mennonite faith because of its stances on service, peace, and missions. Childs served as Peace's interim pastor after its minister resigned in mid-1985.[51]

The CLC also approved providing scholarship money for female seminarians, and conference minister John S. Steiner kept in touch with AMBS students, both men and women, about their future plans.[52] Overall, the percentage of women enrolled at AMBS jumped from 14.6 percent during 1971–72 to 34.4 percent ten years later. (Nationwide, the female enrollment at all seminaries more than tripled between 1972 and 1980.[53])

Peace and Race

The old understandings of separation were no longer adequate for the church, in part because they defined Mennonite belief and practice by negatives, such as not going to war, not using musical instruments, and not wearing contemporary fashions. It was a "glass half empty" approach that didn't address the issues raised by a growing social awareness. By the 1960s "new nonconformities," in the words of conference minister John H. Mosemann, were needed to guide the church in the face of the country's increasing affluence, the possibility of nuclear war, civil rights, relations with the government, and other challenges to American Mennonite consciences.[54] New understandings were calling for new, more proactive approaches to faithfulness in a broken and fallen world.

That shift was several decades in the making. In 1950, representatives from the Mennonite Church and sixteen other North American Mennonite groups meeting at Winona Lake, Indiana, approved a landmark peace statement that suggested a more activist ethos.[55] The statement mentioned *love* seventeen times, compared with only two mentions for the more traditional word *nonresistance*. Love was, by definition, an outward action and could be used as a verb—"Love your neighbor"—while nonresistance was a noun and nonresistant an adjective, and both more passive. The Winona Lake statement, drafted by a committee chaired by Harold S. Bender, also highlighted the necessity of witness to the state, again drawing the church out of its historic isolationism. The Mennonite Church adopted the statement in 1951. Similar themes were found ten years later when the denomination approved a statement on "Christian Responsibility to the State."

Driving the trend toward greater interaction with the world were young, well-educated church members such as participants in the Concern movement and future Goshen College president J. Lawrence Burkholder.[56] The Pennsylvania native and Goshen graduate was a relief administrator for Mennonite Board of Missions during World War II. After the war, he was seconded by Mennonite Central Committee to the interdenominational relief and development agency Church World Service in China, where he flew airplanes over the Himalayas to deliver supplies to refugees who were fleeing China when the Communists took control of the country. The experiences exposed him to the complexities of living out Christ's commands to alleviate human injustice and suffering. To meet those needs, Burkholder advocated active participation in the world, as messy as it might be, which was in tension with the church's generally accepted limits on social involvements at the time. His Princeton Theological Seminary doctoral dissertation, on "The Problem of Social Responsibility from the Perspective of the Mennonite Church" and completed in 1958 while a Goshen faculty member, impressed his Princeton professors but was roundly criticized in Mennonite circles, particularly by Guy F. Hershberger.[57] Burkholder left Goshen for Harvard Divinity School in 1961 but returned to campus ten years later to become president. By then, his position on world involvement had become less suspect.

While the definition of peace was expanding to more explicitly include the pursuit of justice, Indiana-Michigan was unsure of the best ways to address the issues such a definition raised. Writing congressional representatives and petitioning government were acceptable to most members, while demonstrations and civil disobedience were strongly opposed.[58] But that didn't stop those who were inclined to activism. Ann Arbor Mennonite Fellowship pastor Daniel Slabaugh, chair of the conference's new Peace and Social Concerns Commission, went to Washington, D.C., in 1968 to participate in an anti–Vietnam War rally "even though I have been told by other Mennonites that a good Mennonite shouldn't get involved with this," he said. Slabaugh further decried the many church members who opposed activism because they "proudly consider themselves 'Anti-Communist (spelled militant) Evangelicals.'" One Peace and Social Justice Commission member, feeling stymied, resigned to work on projects more directly related to social justice issues without feeling encumbered by the church.[59]

Their frustration and impatience overshadowed the support that already existed in the conference for a more activist Mennonitism. As on campuses across the country, activism could be found at Goshen College. Religion professor J. R. Burkholder had been involved with demonstrations since working with the interfaith Fellowship of Reconciliation (FOR) in the 1950s. In 1964, he led seventeen students in picketing a hotel in South Bend, Indiana, where segregationist and presidential candidate George Wallace was staying. Also that year, the college hosted Jean Lasserre, a French FOR official, which prompted an anonymous party to send a flier to a number of area Mennonite ministers denouncing Goshen and accusing FOR of being a Communist front.[60] Five Goshen students went to Alabama in 1965 to join a civil rights march from Selma to Montgomery. The next year, the college hosted a two-day conference with representatives from the left-wing

Students for a Democratic Society, an event that strikingly illustrated the emergence of a countercultural Mennonite ethic.[61]

A constant looming concern was the possibility of a sit-in, takeover, or some other disruptive demonstration as was happening across the country. Etril Leinbach, pastor of Valparaiso (Ind.) Mennonite Church near Chicago, wrote the Indiana-Michigan office that his congregation "is much concerned about what our actions should be if 'angry Negro Militans' [sic] should come in some Sunday morning and demand time to speak and demand money. . . . Could it be that Conference could give some guidance? There are many of our congregations that could be involved since we are close to angry Negro communities."[62] But no worship service in Indiana-Michigan was commandeered until Sunday, April 5, 1970. That morning six young adults, all Goshen College alumni, took over morning worship at College Mennonite Church. Congregational leaders had caught wind of the plan several days earlier and so were prepared should something happen. When the ministers entered the sanctuary for the service, they discovered the activists already occupying the platform at the front. Lead pastor John H. Mosemann went up to greet the group and asked if the service could go on as usual until sharing time, when they could present their concerns. The group declined, so Mosemann went to the pulpit, made a few announcements, and delivered a prepared statement about the situation encouraging the congregation to listen and be courteous. He then shook hands with everyone on the platform and sat down in a pew.[63] Each of the young people then addressed the congregation, speaking about the Vietnam War, racism, and gender equality.[64] Several speakers said they chose College for their demonstration not because they considered it closed-minded but because they suspected the congregation, one of the most liberal in Indiana-Michigan, would be more receptive to hearing the group's concerns.[65] Some of the demonstrators attended Sunday school classes after the worship service.[66]

The Vietnam conflict generated some of the most intense clashes among Americans. As young men burned their draft cards or fled to Canada to avoid conscription, a 1968 Indiana-Michigan survey showed that 87 percent of conference members disagreed or strongly disagreed with refusing to register for the draft.[67] But the church's position would begin to moderate the next year. In 1969, Doug Baker,

Devon Leu, and Jon Lind, all former Goshen College students still living in the area, undertook a radical expression of the peace position. The three men successfully appealed to the 1969 Mennonite Church General Conference to officially endorse nonregistration, even though it was illegal, as an appropriate demonstration of Christian pacifism.[68] That same year Jim Hochstedler from Parkview Mennonite Church in Kokomo (Ind.) took refuge in Canada after refusing to register. He later returned to the United States but remained underground until he was arrested in 1971. While Hochstedler awaited trial, Indiana-Michigan prayed for him during that year's annual assembly. He was later sentenced to probation and two years of alternative service.[69]

While the activists who took over the College Mennonite Church worship service highlighted racism as an issue facing the church and society, Indiana-Michigan was already somewhat cognizant of the inequalities, particularly between whites and African Americans. By the 1950s, Indiana-Michigan Mennonites were working with African Americans in Fort Wayne, Indianapolis, and Saginaw, Michigan. Grace Chapel pastor Melvin Leidig, a white man who left his job in Midland, Michigan, to minister in Saginaw's First Ward, was at the fore of race discussions as president of the Saginaw Area Religious Council on Human Relations. In 1963, Goshen College entered into exchange programs with two historically black schools in the South, with Howard Zehr going to Morehouse College, Martin Luther King Jr.'s alma mater in Atlanta, and Eli Hochstedler (brother of future draft resister Jim) going to Tougaloo (Miss.) College. While there, Hochstedler was arrested for trying to integrate the city auditorium by seeing a show with an African American friend.[70]

At the same time that white Indiana-Michigan members were going to the cities to meet African Americans, people of color were traveling to the conference's rural heartland. Bethany Christian High School welcomed its first Latina students in 1955, Esther and Theresa Ventura, daughters of early members of the Chicago Mennonite Mexican mission. Bethany's first African American student, Georgia Thompson, also from Chicago, arrived two years later. Starting in the late 1960s, students enrolled through a Mennonite Board of Missions program to bring youth from minority groups to Mennonite high schools. During summers, rural Indiana-Michigan families would host children from

Fairhaven pastors Martin Brandenberger (left) and Art Cash (right) and spouses Loraine Brandenberger and Nancy Cash, circa 1960. MCUSAA–Goshen.

urban areas for a week or two via the Fresh Air program, a nonprofit unaffiliated with the Mennonite church.

But not all of the interactions were positive, and some were blatantly racist. A young African American woman from Saginaw's Ninth Street Mennonite Church who was studying at Goshen College wrote her pastor, LeRoy Bechler, "Some of the white fellows said that the colored boys were here just for the white girls and that we are from Africa."[71] She continued, "The problem of race is almost torture. I've never run up against race relations nearly as much as I have in college compared to my high school experiences. It hits you right in the face, but I know that it doesn't have to be a torture if our hope and self dedication is in the Lord."[72]

Fifteen years later, Lee Lowery, the African American pastor of Ninth Street, told an Indiana-Michigan conference on race relations, "For too long the church has been a taillight, instead of a headlight, in this problem."[73]

One of Indiana-Michigan's greatest successes in racial diversity was in Fort Wayne. In 1954, Leo (Ind.) Mennonite Church began conducting Bible school in an African American section of nearby Fort Wayne. A congregation soon developed, named Fairhaven Mennonite Church and attended by white students from a local Bible college and members from Leo as well as local African Americans. Art Cash joined Fairhaven's pastoral staff in 1959 and was ordained the next year, becoming the first African American minister in Indiana-Michigan Mennonite Conference. A native of Texas, Cash had served congregations in Washington, D.C., and Atlanta before joining the Mennonite Church. He was one of a number of people of color who were drawn to the faith in the 1950s and 1960s because of its peace emphasis, which they saw as especially applicable to the civil rights movement.[74] Cash was working in Saginaw when called to Fort Wayne.[75] Twenty years later, Fairhaven was still maintaining its racial diversity. Conference minister Galen Johns reported in 1979 that Fairhaven has "an unusual mixture of Black and White persons. I know of no congregation that seems to ignore the color as much as they."[76]

Elsewhere, however, relations with black Mennonites were more complicated, particularly in Saginaw, where the requisite prayer covering was met with stout resistance. In 1963, Marvin Sweigart, who two years earlier had succeeded LeRoy Bechler as pastor of Ninth Street Mennonite Church, was being considered for ordination. When Sweigart and his wife, Miriam, met with the Indiana-Michigan examining committee, its members were shocked to see she was bareheaded. The Sweigarts had decided that the traditional prayer covering was unsuitable for an urban, African American congregation.[77] In Ninth Street's early years, the covering was regarded as like a Catholic nun's headdress and had been a respected and accepted practice (although the plain coat was considered a hindrance).[78] But by the early 1960s, that position had changed. Ninth Street adopted a statement in 1964 affirming belief in male headship but claiming the importance of freedom to worship based on "the leading of the Holy Spirit through the background experiences of our group" and asked for "consideration for us, and for all other peoples whose ethnic and cultural heritage differs from the Swiss-German and associated traditions."[79] For conference leadership, however, it was not a cultural conflict but rather an issue of keeping important historical practices of biblical faithfulness.[80]

The conference decided to take the stopgap measure of relicensing, rather than ordaining, Sweigart for another year to allow time to resolve the issue. But it wasn't resolved, and by the fall of 1965, Grace Chapel, the other Indiana-Michigan congregation in Saginaw, was also questioning the covering. New conference moderator Russell

Krabill recommended ordaining Sweigart because he was "satisfactory in every other area." Krabill, a history buff, was looking both ahead and behind. The issue of the prayer covering was gaining traction in the church and would soon require a concerted response. At the same time, he invoked the casualties of authoritarianism through the years. "In the past history of the Mennonite Church too many good men have been lost because the leaders were not willing to make concessions on similar questions," he maintained.[81] Sweigart was subsequently ordained.

Indiana-Michigan's racial diversity further increased when the conference started outreach efforts among Mexicans in the mid-1960s. Tens of thousands were coming to the Midwest as migrant workers, first agricultural and later industrial, under a U.S.-Mexico government program to alleviate American labor shortages.[82] Unlike African Americans, who were located in urban areas, many of the Mexican workers took jobs in the small cities and rural communities that were home to most Indiana-Michigan members. There was also another notable difference. The migrants' needs were immediate and relatively easy to address—housing, English-language instruction, worship. Issues facing African Americans were more systemic and complex given the legacy of centuries of white American racism and discrimination. So because of geographic proximity and the nature of their needs, Mennonites responded better to the Mexican newcomers. Burr Oak Mennonite Church at Rensselaer, Indiana, was already working with migrants by 1965.[83] In 1971, the Indiana-Michigan Peace and Social Concerns Commission appealed to Goshen-area congregations to make their facilities available for emergency housing for a growing number of migrant families and asked conference members to help pay the costs of three migrant students studying at Goshen College.[84]

One workplace that hired Mexican migrants was Pine Manor, a Mennonite-owned poultry processing plant south of Goshen. The president was Annas Miller, a respected member of College Mennonite Church and a longtime Bethany Christian High School board member. In addition to giving seasonal employment, he also provided housing for the workers in a converted chicken coop on the property. In 1969, a forty-six-year-old Mexican employee in a Pine Manor residence died from a self-inflicted gunshot. What exactly happened was never determined. One theory was that he was cleaning the gun when went it

Iglesia del Buen Pastor, Goshen. MCUSAA–Goshen.

accidently went off. But some people thought the worker committed suicide because he was despondent over his living conditions.[85]

Regardless, the incident brought attention to the migrants' circumstances, with local Mennonites holding contrasting views. Supporters of Miller, including some of his Latino employees, contended that the coop-turned-apartments, while hardly luxurious, was adequate.[86] At the same time, Goshen College students joined with several other organizations in a short-lived boycott of Pine Manor. Four days after the shooting came the creation of an advocacy group affiliated with Indiana-Michigan. Called the Spanish American Committee, its founders were Goshen congregations Berkey Avenue, College, East Goshen, and North Goshen, plus Goshen students. The committee spoke out early about the Pine Manor incident but refused to join the boycott, much to the consternation of boycott leaders.[87] The situation smoldered until 1971, when Elkhart-based Mennonite Board of Missions (MBM) agreed to build new accommodations at Pine Manor.

The tragedy also spurred some local Mennonites to provide for the migrants' spiritual needs in addition to their physical ones. Kathryn Troyer, who with her husband, George, had served in Puerto Rico with MBM, started holding women's Bible studies for the Latina employees

Templo Hermosa, Kalamazoo, circa 1985. MCUSAA–Goshen.

at Pine Manor.[88] Local congregations Waterford Mennonite Church and East Goshen Mennonite Church were soon providing support. The Bible studies were held Sunday afternoons at Bethany Christian High School and began attracting men as well as women. In 1970, a vacant Methodist church building in New Paris, south of Goshen, was rented for $30 a month for regular worship services. The pastor for the first three months was Amzie Yoder, a missionary to Honduras living in Goshen at the time, followed by Teofilo Ponce, who grew up in Mexico and came to faith at the Chicago Mennonite Mexican mission. The New Paris group, christened Iglesia Menonita del Buen Pastor, joined Indiana-Michigan in December 1970, becoming the first Latino congregation in the conference. It was soon drawing as many as one hundred people each Sunday and running out of space, so in 1974, the congregation moved into a former Lutheran church building in Goshen.

Ponce and his wife, Mary, would become vigorous church planters among Latinos in the Indiana-Michigan region. They started the second Latino congregation in the conference after distributing tracts in migrant camps near Marion, Indiana; Iglesia Menonita Emanuel was established in the small town of Sweetser in 1977 and moved into nearby Marion in 1980.[89] Two years later, the Ponces started holding services in Kalamazoo,

Michigan, first in homes and later in a Methodist church. That resulted in the creation of Templo Menonita de la Hermosa in 1984 with nine charter members.[90] Another congregation, Iglesia Anabautista Emanuel, began several years later in South Bend, Indiana. Unfortunately, all three congregations would have short life spans.

Other Newness

The charismatic movement came to Indiana-Michigan about 1960 when members of Bean Blossom Mennonite Church at Morgantown, Indiana, began telling of speaking in tongues and being slain in the Spirit. They had been introduced to the writings of Gerald Derstine about his experiences when a fiery spiritual revival consumed the little Mennonite Church congregation he was pastoring in Minnesota during the winter of 1954–55. Derstine was silenced by the area conference in 1956 when his Pentecostalism was ruled incompatible with Mennonite belief and practice. Nevertheless, he received support and encouragement from some Mennonites as he started his own independent ministry.[91] None of this was a welcome development for Bean Blossom pastor Charles Haarer. "If you have any advice to offer in combating this doctrine, feel free to give it," he solicited Indiana-Michigan moderator J. C. Wenger.[92] Charismatic expressions would pop up sporadically over the next several years: at North Main Street Mennonite Church in Nappanee, Indiana; at Hopewell Mennonite Church in Kouts, Indiana; and at a church plant in Jetson, Kentucky.

In February 1968, Roy Koch, pastor of South Union Mennonite Church at West Liberty, Ohio, and a future conference minister for Indiana-Michigan, heralded the movement's impending popularity in the Mennonite Church. In a letter to the denominational magazine, *Gospel Herald*, he wrote, "I wonder if Mennonites should perhaps study this phenomenon anew and with more openness."[93] Unlike Haarer at Bean Blossom, pastor Harold L. Mast of Howard-Miami Mennonite Church was gratified to hear of it. "I have had for more than a year now the use of an unknown language as a part of my growing relationship with the Lord," he wrote Koch. "One of the problems that I had to deal with is the fear of being rejected by persons in the Mennonite brotherhood. So you can see how much it meant to me to see your comments."[94] In the late 1960s and early 1970s, Goshen-area

When Teofilo Ponce in 1970 assumed pastoral leadership of the new Hispanic congregation Iglesia Menonita del Buen Pastor in Elkhart County, Indiana, he completed an Indiana-Michigan Mennonite Conference circle of ministry. He was born in Texas and spent his early years in Mexico before moving to Chicago, where he was baptized at Lawndale Mennonite Church.[1] It was the first Hispanic Mennonite congregation in the United States and the direct result of an Indiana-Michigan initiative.

In 1892, the Mennonite Evangelizing Committee, organized ten years earlier by John F. Funk and Prairie Street Mennonite Church, became the church-wide Mennonite Evangelizing Board of America. The next year it sent out its first worker, Menno S. Steiner, previously a staff member at Funk's Mennonite Publishing Company in Elkhart.[2] That was the start of the Chicago Home Mission. It began holding Spanish-language worship services in 1932, led by J. W. Shank, a Mennonite Board of Missions worker on furlough from the Argentine mission field. He was succeeded by David Castillo, the first Hispanic minister in the Mennonite Church and who would do coursework at Goshen College. After several moves and name changes in the subsequent decades, the congregation purchased a former Baptist church on Chicago's Lawndale Avenue and took the Lawndale name in 1964.[3]

Ponce, who had lived in Indiana since 1961 and was a charter member of Iglesia del Buen Pastor, brought the fruits of an Elkhart County–born venture back to northern Indiana. After two stints at Iglesia del Buen Pastor in the 1970s, Ponce went on to lead Hispanic Indiana-Michigan congregations at Marion, Indiana, and Kalamazoo, Michigan.

---

1. "Teofilo Ponce Family," *Gospel Evangel*, January–February 1971, 15.
2. See chap. 2.
3. Rafael Falcon, *The Hispanic Mennonite Church in North America, 1932–1982*, trans. Ronald Collins (Scottdale, PA: Herald Press, 1986), 34.

1972 Festival of the Holy Spirit at Goshen College. MCUSAA–Goshen.

Mennonites and others, especially students at Goshen College and Bethany Christian High School, were drawn to Zion Chapel, a new charismatic group led by Goshen alumnus and Goshen High School teacher Vic Hildebrand.[95] At the college, a charismatic worship group started holding weekly gatherings that attracted as many as one hundred people. In 1972 and 1973, Goshen College hosted a "Festival of the Holy Spirit" attended by several thousand people.[96] Several northern Indiana Mennonite congregations in 1977 sought to organize monthly interdenominational charismatic worship services.[97] Their emotional and individually expressive nature resonated with people wanting something different from the more staid and conventional Mennonite forms of corporate worship.

Indiana-Michigan struggled to know how to respond to the charismatic movement and its supporters, who often felt misunderstood and accused of deviating from orthodoxy. Dean Brubaker, the conservative pastor of Locust Grove Mennonite Church at Sturgis, Michigan, reflected the sentiment of others in Indiana-Michigan when he declared that the charismatic movement was "not faithful to our theology and our tradition." He called for more efforts to bring together all sides for constructive conversation and suggested that the next annual assembly include "something of an old fashioned Bible Conference" with "serious" Bible study to bolster traditional understandings.[98] But Koch, as conference minister, extolled the movement for "bringing genuine spiritual renewal and conversion to thousands upon thousands in many denominations. Praise the Lord!"[99] The *Gospel Evangel* later editorialized: "Thank God that there is life in the church, that old bones can live again. Let us offer only thanks to God for the Spirit's working among us. Let no groans arise because we fear into what that working may lead. Surely God does not send the Holy Spirit to confuse, but rather to comfort."[100]

Despite attempts to foster unity and tolerance, some members still found Indiana-Michigan stifling and unwelcoming. Two supporters of the charismatic movement withdrew from Roselawn Mennonite Church in Elkhart in 1977 to start a new congregation south of Middlebury, prompting concerns that they would raid not just Indiana-Michigan but also other Mennonite groups and the Old Order Amish for members.[101] In 1983, the conference helped the Pentecostal-leaning Community Bible Chapel of Ironwood, Michigan, transfer from Indiana-Michigan to the Assemblies of God.[102] The charismatic movement would remain an unresolved issue for the conference well into the 1980s.

Other changes were much less contentious, such as a pioneer program in criminal justice. Prison reform had become another social justice issue in the early 1970s, and Indiana-Michigan supported two northern Indiana agencies: House of Simon, a halfway house for prisoners started by Abe Peters, a former pastor of Topeka (Ind.) Mennonite Church in LaGrange County, a General Conference Mennonite Church (GCMC) congregation; and the Steering Committee on Corrections, which also included local GCMC and Conservative Mennonite Conference congregations. After the House of Simon was destroyed by fire, the two organizations merged in 1979 to form the Committee on Corrections, which became an Indiana-Michigan ministry the next year. The new agency focused its attention on the emerging field of victim-offender reconciliation. Already in the mid-1970s, a group of Elkhart-area Mennonites, including Elkhart's chief probation officer and Mennonite Board of Missions staff, had been discussing the need for alternatives to the usual measures meted out by the judicial system. They received a big boost when Mark Yantzi came to study at AMBS in 1976. As a probation officer in Ontario, he had helped launch the world's first victim-offender reconciliation program (VORP) in 1974. As the name implies, the program brings together the perpetrator of a lesser crime and the victim who, through a mediator, try to determine a solution focused on justice for both parties instead of just punishing the offender. With Yantzi and the Ontario program offering inspiration and AMBS students providing assistance, the first VORP in the United States, and the second in the world, was born in Elkhart in January 1978 under the auspices of the Elkhart Probation Department.[103]

Under its first staff person, a probation department intern, VORP showed promise as an alternative to the usual judicial and prison systems.[104] That potential was realized under Howard Zehr, who was director until 1982. He had arrived in Elkhart in 1978 to direct the House of Simon and then was put in charge of the new Committee on Corrections. The namesake son of a former Prairie Street minister and Mennonite Church executive secretary, Zehr graduated from Bethany Christian High School and attended Goshen College before going to the historically black Morehouse College as an exchange student in 1963, graduating from there in 1965. He moved to Elkhart from another historically African American school, Talladega College in Alabama, where he was on the history faculty and codirector of a research program called the Social Science and the Law Project. Zehr would later go on to become an internationally renowned expert on criminal justice.

Another Elkhart ministry was a downtown coffeehouse, called Partly Dave. During the 1950s and 1960s, coffeehouses were founded nationwide as venues for disenchanted young adults to socialize and as forums to explore contemporary issues. Partly Dave opened its doors in September 1966 and was technically an interdenominational ministry, although much of its support came from local Mennonites. The name came from a character in a short story by rock musician John Lennon.[105] Partly Dave took Indiana-Michigan into the ecclesiological unknown in 1973 when conference member J. Robert Charles sought credentialing as manager of the coffeehouse. But there were no guidelines and few precedents for officially recognizing someone not in congregational ministry.[106] It was the same problem surrounding Harold S. Bender's ordination thirty years earlier, and it was still just as murky. But Partly Dave soon closed, rendering Charles's request moot. The issue, however, was not. At the same time the Church Life Commission was dealing with Charles and Partly Dave, a request came to ordain conference youth minister Sherm Kauffman, another person in ministry but not based in any specific congregation. He was eventually licensed but not ordained.[107]

Indiana-Michigan created the Peace and Social Concerns Commission in 1965 and was soon tackling issues that had often fallen outside the sphere of typical nonresistance, such as alcohol and drug abuse, poverty, the environment, and abortion. The commission also promoted the Overground Railroad. It was akin to the Underground Railroad that helped slaves escape the antebellum South. The 1980s incarnation was an informal network of congregations with a range of denominational affiliations, including Mennonite, that were willing to be "stations" for Latin Americans fleeing persecution in their home countries, which were beset by Cold War–related political and military instability as the United States tried to purge the Americas of Communist influences. At the same time, the United States had set restrictive immigration policies, denying many refugees entrance into the country, even though the United States directly contributed to the conditions that created the situation in the first place. Once in the country, the refugees could continue north to Canada and asylum with the help of the Overground Railroad, which covertly provided shelter, food, and other assistance along the way. The Peace and Social Concerns Commission even made a $500 no-interest loan to Reba Place in Chicago for its refugee bail fund.[108] Refugee assistance had earlier been a form of ministry, as at least ten Indiana-Michigan congregations in the 1970s and 1980s sponsored immigration for Southeast Asians displaced by the chaos after the Vietnam War. By 1980, LaGrange County, Indiana, congregations Plato and Shore joined efforts with local Methodists to sponsor twenty refugees.[109]

VORP, Partly Dave, and the Peace and Social Concerns Commission were indicative of Indiana-Michigan's heightened social awareness. Not that it had been absent before. In the late nineteenth century, conference members had sent material assistance to the Mennonite missions in Chicago and Fort Wayne, and church-planting efforts often included meeting physical as well as spiritual needs. But the spiritual was usually emphasized over the physical.[110] With World War II and

Civilian Public Service, however, came new approaches to feeding the hungry, clothing the naked, and attending to the sick that did not have to include overt evangelism.[111] One of the most successful was mental healthcare. The experiences of Mennonite conscientious objectors serving in psychiatric hospitals during the war directly led Mennonite Central Committee in 1947 to implement a plan to establish and oversee church-affiliated mental health facilities as expressions of Christian love and compassion. Three centers—one each in Maryland, Kansas, and California—were in operation in 1957 when the decision was made to start a fourth in Elkhart.[112] Called Oaklawn Psychiatric Center, it was an inter-Mennonite venture, with Indiana-Michigan an active participant. In preparation for the center's launch, the Indiana-Michigan Mennonite Mission Board sponsored several mental health conferences in the area, and the conference committed to raising $25,000 for the project.[113] Oaklawn began providing services in 1963.

Meanwhile, interest was growing in another inter-Mennonite idea, this one to provide care for older adults. It originated at Eighth Street Mennonite Church, the General Conference Mennonite Church congregation in Goshen, which in the late 1950s was pondering the needs of elderly people and how the church could best respond to them. The conversations soon drew in Indiana-Michigan members who shared Eighth Street's concerns. Also among the participants was Mennonite Board of Missions, which was already sponsoring several retirement and nursing homes, including one at Sturgis, Michigan. In 1962, organizers and supporters decided to establish such a facility in Elkhart County, which, for legal reasons, would be affiliated with MBM. Later that year MBM appointed the project's first board of directors, with ten of its members from Eighth Street and four from local Indiana-Michigan congregations. One of the directors was Eighth Street's A. E. Kreider, a former Goshen College instructor and College Mennonite Church pastor who had left Indiana-Michigan during the turbulent 1920s but was now cooperating with the conference in ministry. It was yet another indication of change in the church as it moved beyond old antagonisms. The name Greencroft was chosen for the new retirement community, which was built just east of the Goshen College campus. The first residents moved in on August 29, 1967.[114] In 1975,

Greencroft and MBM completed renovations on the nine-story former Hotel Elkhart in the city's downtown, converting it to apartments and denominational offices.

In 1966, the conference executive committee accepted an invitation to attend Central District Conference's annual delegate assembly. It was hosted by Comins Mennonite Church near Fairview, Michigan, but held in the larger Fairview Mennonite Church. That was yet another sign of progress, as Comins had split from Fairview in the 1920s over matters of dress and discipline and joined the Central Conference of Mennonites.[115] Indiana-Michigan soon returned the hospitality, inviting to its annual sessions representatives not only from Central District Conference but also from the Brethren in Christ and the Conservative Mennonite Conference. Meanwhile the Indiana-Michigan Peace and Social Concerns Commission and its Central District counterpart were working together, and discussions were held about the possibility of joint church planting. At the 1977 Indiana-Michigan annual assembly, Ken Bauman, pastor of First Mennonite Church in Berne, Indiana, a conservative GCMC congregation that had long emphasized missions and evangelism, brought the Saturday evening message on "The Church: A Missionary Community." The General Conference Mennonite Church had become an acceptable source of instruction for Indiana-Michigan Conference.[116]

In the face of these rapidly diminishing boundaries from the world, union membership remained a line of separation for Indiana-Michigan Mennonites. Conference officials continued to advocate for members who were feeling pressured to join unions, which had grown in power and importance in the workplace, particularly in heavily industrialized Michigan. When J. B. Shenk, chair of the conference's Committee on Social Concerns, sent a letter on behalf of a church member to the International Union of Operating Engineers for Michigan, he received a condescending response from a union official. While trotting out the usual arguments about the union's role in improving workers' standards of living, the official noted that union members were not only community leaders but also generous supporters of their churches. "I am sure the Lord is not against these principles," he wrote. "Therefore, we feel that Brother David E. Kuhns should cherish his membership in this Union as religiously as his Church membership."[117] In the Upper

Peninsula, James Troyer, a school guidance counselor and pastor of Maple Grove Mennonite Church at Manistique, was fighting attempts to force him to join the educators' union, which then tried to have him fired.[118] Troyer eventually prevailed, invoking the work of Guy F. Hershberger, who had been a pioneer in negotiating union exemptions for Mennonite employees.[119] Mimicking agreements brokered by Hershberger, Troyer, instead of paying union dues, made contributions to charitable causes, first to a camp for children with disabilities and later to a local education foundation. His reasons for refusing to join the union, in addition to the church's traditional stance on the use of force and coercion, included his opposition to alcohol at union functions, which was paid for by union dues. For Troyer, the issue was more than just his personal decision to abstain. Alcoholism was a problem in the economically depressed Upper Peninsula, and he strongly believed that the community's educators were contributing—or at least not trying to mitigate—further abuse.[120]

Palm Sunday Tornadoes

As the Mennonites of Indiana-Michigan wrestled with the impact of the human world on their attempts to maintain faithfulness and vice versa, they were also not immune to the vagaries of the natural world. The most catastrophic came on Palm Sunday, April 11, 1965, as a devastating storm system roared through the Midwest, unleashing thirty-seven tornadoes in six states. The worst was in northern Indiana, where multiple twisters killed sixty-seven people in Elkhart and LaGrange Counties, including nine people from Shore Mennonite Church of Shipshewana, four from Forks Mennonite Church of Middlebury, and one each from Sunnyside Mennonite Church, Elkhart, and Olive Mennonite Church, Wakarusa. The storms caused millions of dollars of damage, including destroying the Sunnyside and Shore meetinghouses. The two congregations just missed suffering greater casualties. At Sunnyside, several families had already gathered at the church for evening services when it was decided to cancel due to the weather.[121] The building was hit just after the last person left. The Shore tornado roared through only twenty minutes before services were scheduled to start at the church.[122]

Sunnyside Mennonite Church, Elkhart, destroyed by Palm Sunday tornado, 1965.
MCUSAA–Goshen.

A mass funeral for eight fatalities from Shore (the ninth died from her injuries the morning of the service) drew an estimated one thousand people to the local school gymnasium. Shore minister O. H. Hooley, who lost his house in the storm, couldn't bring himself to give the sermon. Instead, he read from Revelation 21, while Plato Mennonite Church minister Dean Brubaker preached from Job. Paul Mishler, chair of the Shipshewana town board and a Shore member, read a telegram of condolence from president Lyndon B. Johnson.[123]

While survivors mourned, Mennonite Disaster Service swung into action and stayed for four months.[124] The agency estimated that on April 17, only six days after the storms, five thousand volunteers were working with MDS in northern Indiana. A group from Benton Mennonite Church south of Goshen helped clean the Shore cemetery's headstones, all but six of which had been toppled. Maps of the cemetery were found at Bronson, Michigan, some thirty miles to the northeast.

In addition to cleaning and repairing damaged building sites, volunteers removed debris from fields in preparation for the upcoming planting season.[125] The storm also left Indiana-Michigan's Mennonite Aid Association appealing for help. It had a balance of only $230,000 before the tornadoes, and within a month of the tragedy, losses that the association was responsible to cover were estimated to top $600,000.[126] But members of the mutual aid plan acted quickly, as 87 percent of them responded to an emergency assessment by the association to raise the money necessary to meet its claims.[127]

Divergent Paths

Like the changes of the late nineteenth century, the post–World War II developments had an energizing effect on Indiana-Michigan Mennonite Conference as new forms of church, new ministries, and new concepts of faithfulness took shape. And in the 1960s, as in earlier eras, those changes generated profound tensions between conference members who accepted the newness and those who desperately wanted to maintain the old ways as much as possible. The latter could be found throughout Indiana-Michigan but especially at the northern and southern ends of the conference. That was one of the findings of Alta Mae and Paul Erb. Paul, the former *Gospel Herald* editor who had recently stepped down from his position as the first general secretary of the Mennonite Church, and Alta Mae, his wife, were hired by Indiana-Michigan to spend 1965 visiting member congregations, speaking on a range of topics, and assessing the state of the conference. Because of their opposition to women in leadership, some members of Wildwood Mennonite Church near Engadine, Michigan, stayed away when Alta Mae spoke to the congregation. The Erbs later found Berea Mennonite Church at Loogootee, Indiana, to be "the most conservative area of the conference" and said that "some are worried about the influence of the rest of the conference on their people."[128]

That was clearly a critical reference to northern Indiana. In the opinion of conservatives, many of the congregations in Elkhart County and, to a lesser extent, LaGrange County, plus institutions such as Goshen College and AMBS, seemed more than willing to acquiesce to the trendy ways of the world. Elkhart County was also the home of Indiana-Michigan's administrative office (which was, at different times, in Elkhart and Goshen). Rather than enforce long-established standards in the face of change, as Indiana-Michigan leaders did in the 1920s, in the 1960s they were trying to manage change in an increasingly diverse fellowship. Congregations, rather than the conference, were quickly becoming the place for discernment and discipline. As more and more congregations started to relax their standards, conservative bishops and ministers did their best to remain steadfast. In Michigan's Upper Peninsula, Ora Wyse, minister of Naubinway Mennonite Church, declared that he would refuse to grant letters of membership transfer to women who cut their hair or to anyone who thought cut hair was appropriate.[129] When a Goshen College group went to sing at Locust Grove Mennonite Church near Sturgis, Michigan, pastor Dean Brubaker asked the women to wear coverings, which they did.[130] In Kentucky, relations between Orlo Fisher, pastor of Talcum Mennonite Church, and the young people of the Mennonite Board of Missions voluntary service unit associated with the congregation became so bad that MBM relocated the unit to nearby Hazard in 1972.[131] Even conservatives were at odds with each other. In Daviess County in southern Indiana, tensions arose between the pastors of neighboring Bethel and Providence congregations because one of them wore a necktie.[132]

In 1969, twenty Indiana-Michigan ordained men attended a meeting at Bowne Mennonite Church in Michigan to discuss concerns such as the proliferation of jewelry, cut hair, "worldly wedding practices," and social activism. It was a landmark attempt to organize Indiana-Michigan's tradition-minded segments and hold the conference accountable for the drift they perceived. While they had been critical for years, they had never before united for advocacy. In a letter to Indiana-Michigan leadership, participants at the Bowne gathering issued no threats but asked, "Is there any indication that we expect to change this trend or do we by [the conference's] disregard intend to continue these trends? If so, what scriptural reasons can be given to support them?"[133]

By the late 1970s, conservative members had been withdrawing from Indiana-Michigan in significant numbers for two decades. Shortly after writing a 1959 treatise against neckties, Wayne Wenger, who was leading a church plant at Hardshell, Kentucky, left for the Conservative Mennonite Conference. In 1961, five members of Salem Mennonite Church at New Paris, Indiana, withdrew to form a splinter faction, decrying television, higher education, competitive athletics, and more. The previous year, one of the departing members had written a critique of the church that was reminiscent of an earlier time. "Modernism, rationalism and secularism are demanding their homage, and exacting their toll among us," he wrote.[134] Seney Mennonite Church in the Upper Peninsula left in 1965, the first withdrawal of an entire Indiana-Michigan congregation since Barker Street forty-two years earlier.

Some conservatives remained active in Indiana-Michigan, such as Dean Brubaker, who served as CLC secretary, was the conference representative to the Mennonite Board of Education, and presented at conference assemblies. Others, however, felt marginalized and limited their participation. With a stinging explanation, Paul Horst, pastor of Soo Hill Mennonite Church at Escanaba in the Upper Peninsula, declined to serve as a discussion leader at the 1966 delegate assembly. "I know very well I do not go along with [the conference's] trend of thinking so why should I stand up and lead a group of discussion," he said. "It appears that the liberal men in our conference have pretty well taken over and I do not plan to go along with this trend."[135] Rich Valley Mennonite Church, the result of a 1963 conservative split from Howard-Miami Mennonite Church, kept denominational programs at arm's length until it finally withdrew from Indiana-Michigan in 1972.[136] The congregation was quite adamant about resisting change, criticizing the conference for straying from the Indiana-Michigan handbook of 1956, even though it had been replaced by the constitution adopted by the conference in 1969.[137] The older document included regulation attire, general submission to "earthly authorities," temperance, the holy kiss, and prohibitions on divorce and remarriage, "mixing of sexes at bathing beaches," and card playing.[138] But those standards had been eliminated in the 1969 constitution. Following Rich Valley's departure were Michigan congregations Bowne in 1973 and White Cloud in 1974.

Within two months of the 1981 decision to permit the ordination of women, three more congregations also decided they couldn't remain in the conference. Salem Mennonite Church at New Paris and its two daughter congregations, Toto Mennonite Church at North Judson and Milford (Ind.) Chapel, withdrew in August and September of that year. Salem had been an Indiana-Michigan stalwart, rooted in the original nineteenth-century settlement of Mennonites in southern Elkhart

County, and its longtime minster and bishop Ray F. Yoder had been a leading force during the conference's conservative heyday. The congregation continued the traditional method of baptism in streams, the use of the lot for selecting ministerial leadership, and having no salaried ministers.[139] Other Indiana-Michigan congregations were building new meetinghouses or extensively renovating existing ones in the 1950s and 1960s, but Salem didn't even have a telephone in its church building until 1971. In order to further limit corrupting influences, the congregation in the mid-1970s discontinued receiving the *Gospel Evangel* and voted to no longer participate in the local Mennonite Central Committee relief sale.[140]

The exodus of conservative congregations was cause for some soul-searching by Indiana-Michigan's mainstream members. Even though they had their own disagreements with one another, they wanted to find a way to preserve fellowship. Already in 1972, conference minister Roy Koch asked, "Is there something we can do to help bridge the gap between us and our more conservative brothers?"[141] A decade later, Indiana-Michigan was still searching for a solution to the tensions between church and world.

9
Binding and Loosing

The fine, three-story brick building at 1711 Prairie Street in Elkhart, Indiana, had been built in 1915 on the city's south side as the first office for Mennonite Board of Missions (MBM) and home for its administrator, George L. Bender, and his family. As MBM became the largest agency of the Mennonite Church, the building became a vital intersection not just for the denomination but for Mennonites around the globe. Countless important and influential people had offices in it, met there for meetings, and passed through coming and going to mission assignments. But in the early 1970s, MBM, in need of more space, relocated to facilities in downtown Elkhart, and in 1977 Indiana-Michigan Mennonite Conference moved in to establish its first physical office. Even after the conference had begun hiring staff in the 1960s, there was no administrative center, as everyone worked out of their homes, churches, or other locations. But Indiana-Michigan had now matured as an institution, with a single site designated as the conference's home. In 1982, it also left 1711 Prairie Street for a house around the corner on Cleveland Street (but kept the Prairie Street mailing address), where it would remain until establishing its office in Goshen in 1988.

But those weren't the only changes. Conference executive secretary Galen Johns wrote friends in 1984, "The IN-MI office 'isn't what it used to be.' We now have the help of a computer with a 2 million byte capacity and two printers. One is a dot-matrix that prints 140 characters per second and a letter-quality (it printed this letter) that prints about 38 characters per second. Unfortunately this office machinery doesn't solve all the theological, ethical, and leadership concerns!"[1]

And there were numerous concerns demanding Indiana-Michigan's attention. Some were old, such as Goshen College; some were old but manifested themselves differently, such as the role of women in the church; and some were new, such as the sexual activity of conference members. Indiana-Michigan leadership was spending most of its time trying to mediate and manage the different views within the contentious conference. "Our search to be faithful followers of Jesus leads us through honestly differing ways of understanding God," Johns said.[2]

Not everyone agreed, however, resulting in a new Indiana-Michigan dialectic. In the late nineteenth century, conflicts were between traditionalists and progressives, resulting in the creation of the Old Order Amish and Mennonite groups and leaving the progressives in fellowship with each other. A sizable number of progressives would become twentieth-century conservatives, using progressive means to maintain a strong but less severe separation from the world. By the 1960s, they had evolved into two manifestations, one of them culturally conservative; most of them would leave the conference by the 1980s. The theological conservatives, meanwhile, remained alongside their progressive sisters and brothers.[3] Both groups outwardly acculturated, wearing neckties and makeup, singing new worship songs, watching television, and voting in elections. But the conservatives were similar to the traditionalists in the desire for clear lines of demarcation between the righteous faithful and the fallen world. But that led to accusations of authoritarianism and limiting the possibilities of Holy Spirit–inspired change. The progressives did not adhere to such a pronounced separation. They saw the world's collective good as the object of the church's work, and like their progressive predecessors, were receptive to the possibilities of change. Furthermore, they believed, discerning change was the responsibility of the entire fellowship, not just those in leadership positions. As a result, progressives were subject to harsh criticism for tolerating what others considered unacceptable. One dismayed conservative delegate to the 1983 Indiana-Michigan assembly reported "shock at the lukewarmness of conference to sin."[4]

Just as it had been for years, a major factor in the growing distance between conservatives and progressives was geography. While conservatives were found throughout Indiana-Michigan, they were particularly concentrated in southern Indiana and northern Michigan, the two regions farthest away from northern Indiana. But the gap widened as

Elkhart County's prominence grew. By 1990, the Mennonite Church headquarters had moved to Elkhart from Lombard, Illinois, making the county home to all denominational agency headquarters—the boards of Congregational Ministries, Education, and Missions, plus Mennonite Mutual Aid—except the Mennonite Publication Board, which remained in Scottdale, Pennsylvania.[5] Also still in Elkhart County were Associated Mennonite Biblical Seminaries (AMBS) and Goshen College, both of which continued to fuel conservative ire. Meanwhile, at least ten other churchwide organizations, many of them inter-Mennonite, were popping up locally, such as the Mennonite Health Association, Mennonite Medical Association, and the Inter-Mennonite Council on Aging. Even the computerized environment of MennoLink, an online forum for Mennonites to discuss a range of subjects, came out of Goshen. These institutions, as well as the flourishing retirement community around Greencroft, brought people and ideas from outside Indiana-Michigan and added religious and cultural diversity to area congregations.[6] To progressives, their conservative sisters and brother could appear backward and uneducated. For example, a woman was scheduled to colead a workshop with her husband at the 1988 Indiana-Michigan annual assembly, to be held in Washington in southern Indiana, where the conference members still frowned on women in leadership. "These are four churches that are ultra conservative that we have been trying to nurture along toward growth," Indiana-Michigan executive secretary Sherm Kauffman cautioned the presenters from his Elkhart office.[7]

Given their different emphases, members of each group drifted toward competing points on the ideological spectrum.[8] The progressives became aligned, to various degrees, with causes considered liberal, such as advocating for the rights of women and minority groups and demonstrating against nuclear weapons. Many conservatives, however, saw more dangerous threats in what were labeled "moral" issues. Like earlier Indiana-Michigan members who were opposed to ball games, the theater, and parades, they were greatly distressed by the world's rising divorce rate, abortion, and vulgarity in television shows, movies, and music. Yet Indiana-Michigan had ceased adopting resolutions against such vices and traps, while the *Gospel Evangel* was now publishing articles on supporting opposition to war taxes, accepting the charismatic movement, and relating to Muslims.[9]

At the same time, the likes of conservative evangelical leaders Jerry Falwell, Pat Robertson, and James Dobson were surging to cultural and political power in the 1970s and 1980s. Called the religious right because of its place on the ideological spectrum, the movement railed against a morally and spiritually bereft society. Conservative Mennonites found that the religious right, like its fundamentalist forebears, was ready to fortify their faith's essential boundaries. And the religious right was easy to find. The movement's rise was facilitated by the aggressive use of direct mail, television and radio programming, audiovisual materials, the Internet, and other mass media to promote its Christian values and organize the grassroots for action.[10] Their clear and forceful stances came directly into Mennonite homes, often on a daily basis, offering a welcome and easy alternative to the compromised faith seen emanating from Elkhart County. The result was a variation of the concept of separation from the world. This one, however, positioned many of their fellow conference members on the other side of the line while including other Christian groups that previously would have been disregarded. While upholding conservative positions on issues such as abortion and same-sex attraction, the religious right also championed nationalism, military engagement, gun ownership, and a free-market economy as spiritual matters melded with political and cultural ones. That did not go unrecognized by other church members who considered those causes inconsistent with Mennonite beliefs. Indiana-Michigan conference minister John H. Mosemann denounced members' "enchantment with numerous 'messiahs' and the unquestioning loyalty to religious programs and personalities which invade our homes through the radio and TV media."[11]

Adding to the tensions between Elkhart County and other areas was the decision of the conference Mission Commission (the successor to the Indiana-Michigan Mennonite Mission Board) in the mid-1980s to phase out subsidies for congregations. In 1978, the commission paid $164,170 to twenty-three congregations plus pensions to five retired ministers who had served them. The recipients included newer congregations still trying to establish themselves, such as a Latino church plant at Sweetser, Indiana, and an emerging group at Kalamazoo, Michigan. But older congregations such as Germfask Mennonite Church, the first Indiana-Michigan congregation in the Upper Peninsula, had still not achieved financial self-sufficiency after decades of support.[12] At a time when those congregations already felt the conference was marginalizing their religious beliefs, Indiana-Michigan was now also seen as undermining their very viability and producing feelings of abandonment.[13]

Indiana-Michigan was not the only place where conservative Mennonites were rallying to resist the drift toward unfaithfulness they saw in the church. In 1979, twenty-five people gathered at Smoketown, Pennsylvania, to discuss their concerns, including the church's low regard for Scripture and evangelism, overemphasis on social activism, and nonpayment of war taxes. One of the meeting's conveners was Bob Detweiler, pastor at Yellow Creek Mennonite Church of rural Goshen. Also present at the invitation-only meeting was esteemed denominational and conference leader J. C. Wenger. The Smoketown event led to a follow-up public meeting two years later at Berne, Indiana, which drew about 235 people.[14] The churchwide conservative cause put Indiana-Michigan squarely in its crosshairs with the 1983 publication of the twenty-page treatise *A Crisis among Mennonites: In Education, in Publication* by George R. Brunk II. The outspoken conservative, legendary revivalist, and educator at Eastern Mennonite Seminary in Harrisonburg, Virginia, specifically criticized, among others, AMBS and Goshen College and mentioned by name Millard Lind and Willard Swartley of the seminary faculty, Goshen religion professor Don Blosser, and Goshen history professor Theron Schlabach—all members of Indiana-Michigan congregations.[15]

Following the release of *A Crisis among Mennonites*, a group of southern Michigan pastors called on the Mennonite Church General Board and Mennonite Board of Education to evaluate all denominational post–high school educational institutions for "theological orthodoxy."[16] Although no institutions were named in the proposal, it was obvious that the Michigan pastors' targets were AMBS and Goshen. The same pastors the previous year protested the showing of an R-rated movie at Goshen. In 1979, the college board of trustees investigated religion professors Dennis and Diane MacDonald, a married couple, about their views on the virgin birth, Christ's bodily resurrection, and inerrancy of Scripture. The MacDonalds resigned in March 1980 when they were told that they would not be granted tenure.[17] But that didn't eliminate conservative criticism. Remaining on the religion faculty were

268 *In Pursuit of Faithfulness*

Blosser and Marlin Jeschke, who was also considered less than trust-worthy. In making its regular financial contribution to Indiana-Michigan in 1985, English Lake Mennonite Church in northeastern Indiana stipulated that none of the money go to Goshen or AMBS.[18] Even former conference minister Roy Koch said at the 1981 Berne meeting of conservatives, "I've been disturbed for a long time by the liberalism in Bible teaching in our schools."[19]

The Fire Is Ignited

Sexual politics were a recurring theme in the United States during the twentieth century, from women's suffrage in the early 1900s to the Equal Rights Amendment and *Roe v. Wade* in the 1970s to the growing recognition of sexual violence against women in the 1980s. But those were mere skirmishes compared to what came next. Almost without warning, same-sex attraction would enter into the secular mainstream culture in the 1970s, as part of the era's emphasis on social and legal equality as well as reconsideration of sexual mores.[20] Within twenty years the debates in broader society would plunge Indiana-Michigan into a series of fiery battles that would consume much of the conference's time and energy well into the twenty-first century.

In the Mennonite Church, same-sex orientation first publicly surfaced in 1977 in the *Gospel Herald*, the official denominational magazine. An article by Kevin Linehan, a self-described former gay man leading a Mennonite church plant in Reno, Nevada, declared, "There is no such thing as a Christian homosexual."[21] While it was a generally accepted contemporary Christian understanding, a minority of Mennonites as well as Church of the Brethren members disagreed and began mobilizing. A parachurch advocacy and support organization, the Brethren and Mennonite Council for Gay and Lesbian Concerns, was founded in 1978. That same year, Rainbow Mennonite Church in Kansas City, Kansas, a member of both the Mennonite Church and the General Conference Mennonite Church, took the unprecedented position of declaring itself as welcoming noncelibate gays and lesbians as members. In 1980, the Mennonite Church (MC) and General Conference Mennonite Church (GCMC) began work on a joint statement on sexuality, including sexual orientation, which would become incendiary in both groups. (The General Conference Mennonite Church would adopt the statement in 1986, and the Mennonite Church would do likewise the next year.[22]) Also in 1980, in response to student interest, Goshen College held an evening forum featuring presentations on same-sex attraction. "Understanding does not imply approval, but it does increase the likelihood that the answers concerning homosexuality will yet be found in the context of the Christian church," said campus physician Willard S. Krabill, one of the speakers.[23] AMBS hosted a seminar on the topic in 1982.

But the issue had yet to erupt in full fury. That started in 1983, when the Mennonite Church and General Conference Mennonite Church met at Bethlehem, Pennsylvania, for their first joint convention, taking the initial exploratory steps toward a denominational merger. The convention included discussion of the proposed human sexuality statement. Its references to same-sex attraction and relationships were the most controversial, and among Indiana-Michigan members, opinions were decidedly mixed. Wes Culver, one of the conference delegates to the Bethlehem gathering, said, "It is scary to think we may be swayed into condoning homosexuality because Christians should be 'compassionate' or that we should give them a voice in interpreting the scripture and writing the statement 'to be fair.'"[24] New Harvest Ministries, which had been started by Culver, a minister at Goshen's Pleasant View Mennonite Church, hosted a November 1983 seminar for "pastors and helping professionals on the art of Christian counseling and ministry to those desiring recovery from homosexuality."[25] But Indiana-Michigan's Peace, Justice, and Service Commission, at its first meeting after the Bethlehem convention, observed that the church was "often rather quick to judge and allow our feelings to block Christ's love flowing out of our lives."[26]

Two radically different beliefs were emerging, both rooted in Mennonite understandings. One considered sex between two men or two women an earthly abomination that would corrupt God's people and that was expressly forbidden in Scripture. It was a position consistent with the Anabaptist tenet of separation from the world. The second perspective saw people with same-sex attraction as marginalized people deserving respect and compassion, not rejection and condemnation. It was a new expression of the same faith ideals that led Mennonites to advocate for people with mental illness in inhumane asylums, Americans of color in a prejudicial society, or Vietnamese civilians in an unjust conflict. Contributing to that stance was scientific research that posited that same-sex attraction was not a deviant human condition and biblical scholarship that found that Scripture might not be as clear on the matter as was usually believed.

For all the concerns and arguments, however, sexual orientation was largely a theoretical issue for Indiana-Michigan. Neither the conference nor any of its congregations had wrestled with any practical, real-life situations regarding same-sex orientation, church membership, and scriptural interpretation. That soon changed. Using study materials from the General Conference Mennonite Church, Assembly Mennonite Church in Goshen did a comprehensive examination of the proposed joint MC-GCMC sexuality statement, which included the position that sexual activity was reserved for a man and a woman married to each other. That spurred the congregation in 1988 to examine same-sex orientation specifically. It became immediately relevant the next year when an Assembly member came out as a lesbian. But the study process fizzled out in 1990 as the congregation's focus turned elsewhere, particularly on remodeling its church building.[27] Southside Fellowship in Elkhart found itself in a similar situation two years later when a gay man attending the congregation and in a covenanted union wanted to become a member.[28] As was Southside's practice, his request was processed in his small group, which then recommended to the entire congregation that he be granted membership. The small group chose not to make his sexual orientation a criterion for membership, which was consistent with all previous applications to join the congregation. Southside had never asked any prospective members about their sex lives, and it didn't want to start. But this time that approach generated some concern within the congregation, so its leadership decided to begin a congregational study in early 1993.[29]

While the conference and the two congregations would find themselves on the frontlines, they wouldn't be the only ones caught in the conflict. By 1998, five other MC area conferences would discipline six congregations, expelling four, for accepting noncelibate gays and lesbians as members.[30] Within Indiana-Michigan, at least four congregations either had current members who made their same-sex orientation public or had requests for membership by individuals who were already out.[31] But none of these other instances directly challenged the conference, and all were eventually resolved with the congregations.

Discerning Direction

Southside began its congregational discernment in April 1993 and in May asked Indiana-Michigan Mennonite Conference to "walk with us" during the process. But that request, which was repeated at least once, generated no response.[32] In its June meeting, the Indiana-Michigan executive committee had referred the matter to the Church Life Commission (CLC), which was responsible for overseeing spiritual life in the conference. Once Southside's request was in the CLC's care, it disappeared for five months. The congregation finally heard from Indiana-Michigan in a letter dated November 19, 1993, from conference executive secretary Sherm Kauffman, who said he had just learned of Indiana-Michigan's unintentional and long-term silence from Charlotte Holsopple Glick, a conference minister and a former Southside pastor. "You very likely felt alone and abandoned as you addressed this very difficult and emotionally charged issue," Kauffman wrote Southside. "We apologize and ask for your forgiveness. . . . I feel badly that we have dropped the ball with you in the process."[33]

It came too late. Two days after Kauffman penned his letter, Southside held a November 21 congregational meeting to take action on the matter of sexual orientation and membership. During the three-hour session, those present adopted "with some dissent" a statement of acceptance: "While we have differing opinions among us, we affirm that [Southside] will continue to receive into membership, as we always have, anyone who actively affirms the Commitment Statement and signs the annual commitment/pledge form."[34] The congregation would not start making sexual orientation a criterion for membership, nor would it take a position on sexual orientation itself. Thus Southside became the first Indiana-Michigan congregation to accept noncelibate gays as full members.

Southside's decision not to take a position was seen as taking a position, albeit by default. The congregation met in the chapel on the AMBS campus, prompting its president, Marlin Miller, to worry about the effects of the congregation's action on the school.[35] The connections between AMBS and Southside were more than just location, as at least four faculty members were also Southside members. Meanwhile, the conference executive committee didn't address Southside's action until its May 20, 1994, meeting—six months after the congregation made its decision and a year after it first contacted conference officials. The committee decided to initiate conversations with Southside, its overseers, and its council of neighboring Indiana-Michigan congregations. The first meeting between Southside and the conference was in June 1994.

These were deep, turbulent, and unchartered waters. Indiana-Michigan was caught between the congregationalism that had slowly developed over the previous four decades and calls for the authoritarian exercise of conference power of the past to stamp out something that many considered not just obviously unbiblical and sinful but abnormal and perverse. It was a tricky situation of the greatest magnitude. Indiana-Michigan leadership, having fumbled Southside's initial request for counsel, would proceed to be much less than nimble as it struggled to find its way through the theological, ecclesiological, and political hazards now confronting the conference.

Through the spring of 1994, knowledge of Southside's acceptance of noncelibate gay members was not widely known and was largely confined to the congregation and conference leadership. That changed at that summer's delegate assembly in Indianapolis, when the Indiana-Michigan executive committee publicly apologized for its failure to respond to Southside's request of the conference the previous year.[36] After being largely behind the scenes, same-sex orientation now occupied center stage. Indiana-Michigan's reluctance to quickly and forcefully act against Southside left many in the conference bewildered. Jay Miiller, pastor of Michigan Avenue Mennonite Church at Pigeon, Michigan, wrote the executive committee on behalf of his congregation. "We want to begin by clarifying that homosexuality is not an issue," he said. "An issue suggests a point under dispute, something that is not settled or a verdict that is not determined. We are convinced that homosexual behavior is sin and therefore we are convinced that an action of tough love is the only way to respond to this situation."[37]

Miiller and Michigan Avenue were not alone in their beliefs. But there were also a growing number of conference members who were no longer sure the issue was quite so black-and-white. "When I did my senior project on church discipline at Goshen College over ten years ago most issues were clear, and called for certain discipline," Steve Thomas, pastor of Walnut Hill Mennonite Church in Goshen, wrote Indiana-Michigan leaders. "But as a pastor I've come to see that some issues are ambiguous and complex." He proposed that some congregations "led by the Spirit" might come to some controversial positions "as the most loving accommodation to an imperfect situation."[38] The Elkhart Mennonite ministers' council also acknowledged the haziness. After meeting with Southside representatives five times during the winter of 1994–95, council members could not come to agreement on the appropriateness of the congregation's action, but they did conclude, "We want to maintain fellowship and continue mutually open dialogue."[39]

But dialogue was "compromising God's Word," argued Brent Liechty, pastor of Bourbon (Ind.) Chapel. Disregarding the historical Anabaptist understanding of God's will revealed in community, he claimed the problem was the church itself:

> Our structure, albeit unintentional, is designed to maintain spiritual fallenness. As a denomination we have adopted the systems of the world. . . . No matter how overwhelming the majority vote is, if it is not in line with God's word for His Church, it is wrong. The Church has become an organization, led not by anointed apostles, prophets, evangelists, pastors and teachers as Christ intended it to be (Eph. 4:11), but by administrative gifts. . . . When run by the gift of administration, the goal is to keep the Church organization running smoothly. Therefore we are in constant danger of compromise and deception for the sake of ease of the perpetuation of the organization.[40]

As it tried to hold together the quickly polarizing conference, the Indiana-Michigan executive committee was struggling with its own internal differences. In February 1995, moderator Don Delagrange sent a letter to all ministers, delegates, and congregations as well as to conference officials stating, "Congregations and leaders accepting into membership practicing homosexuals and other practicing sins in scripture need to repent, seek truth, and find forgiveness. Our conference of congregations need [sic] to take Biblical steps to call congregations/leaders to repentance in order to maintain fellowship."[41] Four months later, executive committee member Russ Leinbach circulated his own letter, trying to get the conference to back away from a dictatorial stance. A member of Paoli (Ind.) Mennonite Fellowship, he had just come through his congregation's study of the issue. "I still am 'in process' with my own thoughts, and want to continue to look at scripture and discern God's will and leading in conversation with others," Leinbach wrote.[42]

At the 1995 annual assembly, Indiana-Michigan delegates took their first action related to sexual orientation. More than three hundred people packed a Middlebury, Indiana, school auditorium for two and a half hours of debate.[43] That was followed by a vote on a recommendation from the executive committee to give Southside one year to formally adopt the official church position that gay and lesbian sex was sinful or its membership in the conference would "be further evaluated." Proposed amendments to give the congregation three years instead of one and to postpone action indefinitely both failed, and the delegates approved the original proposal with a 71 percent vote. The measure also asked all conference congregations to affirm the denominational stand on human sexuality.[44]

While attention was focused on Southside, Assembly was restarting its own discernment process with little fanfare. After lying dormant for several years, questions about same-sex sexual relations and church membership were resurfacing by 1994, and congregational leadership reluctantly agreed to consider another attempt at finding a resolution. Assembly spent forty days in prayer and fasting during the fall to discern direction, then began a new, more intensive study process in spring 1995. The congregation also notified the Indiana-Michigan executive committee and staff of its plans.

As the saga continued to evolve, some conference members became deeply suspicious. "We have heard the voice of Southside members in support of their action. But I, along with many other persons I have talked to, are wondering if the whole story is being told. I know for a fact that Southside hasn't told the whole story," accused one person in an anonymous letter to the conference office.[45] A group from First Mennonite Church in Middlebury criticized Mennonite Board of Missions (MBM), the denominational mission agency, for sending Willis Breckbill, a former Indiana-Michigan conference minister and a leading advocate for accepting noncelibate gays and lesbians, to Northern Ireland for a six-month assignment. MBM, in fact, played no role in

Breckbill's placement, which had been privately arranged.[46] In October 1995, Maple Grove Mennonite Church of Topeka, Indiana, announced it was placing itself "in a position of non-participation in relationship to Indiana-Michigan Mennonite Conference . . . until such a time that the Conference Executive Committee presents a united statement of agreement and direction for the congregations concerning the issue of church membership for practicing homosexuals."[47] Three months later, Bean Blossom Mennonite Church at Morgantown, Indiana, also decided to withhold its financial support.[48]

But other congregations, particularly Southside's Elkhart County neighbors, expressed trust and support for the fellowship's integrity, even if they did not necessarily share the same position. "We would like to affirm you for the thoroughgoing process of study you followed and your ongoing discernment process around the membership of homosexual persons," the elders of Sunnyside Mennonite Church, Elkhart, told Southside.[49] That was echoed by a conference-appointed task force working with Southside, which observed that it "has probably

Art Smoker, pastor of North Goshen Mennonite Church, speaks on the delegate floor of the 1996 conference assembly. MCUSAA–Goshen.

studied the homosexuality issue more intensely and carefully than many other churches of conference. . . . IN-MI Conference may need their insights in our future continuing attention to this matter, which will likely not go away soon."[50] College Mennonite Church, Goshen, simply asked, "Can we trust God is at work in the process used by Southside Fellowship?"[51]

With Southside's one-year probationary period set to expire, tensions were high when conference members gathered in July for the 1996 assembly at Gaylord in northern Michigan. During one business session, an incensed delegate declared that if the church was going to be soft on same-sex sexual relations, then nothing in Scripture was sacred and the Bible might as well be treated like dirt. And with that he threw his Bible on the floor.[52] The assembly concluded with no action taken against Southside. The conference executive committee the previous month had asked the congregation to consider voluntarily "stepping aside," which it later declined to do.[53] But delegates did approve two measures in an attempt to lessen the acrimony. One was officially establishing as Indiana-Michigan's official position that sex was reserved for a man and woman in a marriage relationship. The second action was approving "Inter-Congregational/Conference Discernment Guidelines" to be used when a congregation took a position at odds with the church and which included the possibility of disciplining and even expelling such congregations. Those provisions had not been previously delineated. But conservatives were not satisfied. Within two months of the Gaylord meeting, Maple Grove and Bourbon Chapel withdrew from the conference, while an emerging congregation at Carson City, Michigan, adopted a wait-and-see approach before deciding whether to become a full conference member.

Anxiety continued to rise when, in September 1996, Assembly finished its study process and chose to grant membership to noncelibate gays and lesbians. The decision was part of a seven-year "sabbatical," developed because a lack of consensus prevented the congregation from making a final decision. Fundamentally, Assembly's position was like Southside's: to not make sexual orientation a criterion for membership. But unlike Southside, the sabbatical agreement explicitly stated Assembly's willingness to welcome noncelibate as well as celibate gays and lesbians until 2003, when the congregation would initiate yet another discernment process. Some Assembly members subsequently left because they could not abide by the contradiction of the congregation enacting a decision they disagreed with while claiming to postpone making that very same decision.

With Assembly and Southside having taken stands that effectively opposed that of the conference, Indiana-Michigan leaders were feeling growing pressure from all sides. Their efforts to manage the situation had not prevented it from becoming a crisis. So at its May 1997 meeting, the executive committee made the bold move of suspending Assembly's and Southside's voting privileges for two years. It was similar to the power struggles of the 1920s, when the conference executive committee acted unilaterally in meting out discipline. The committee claimed such power under the Inter-Congregational/Conference Discernment Guidelines, approved by the delegates the previous year.

The guidelines outlined two procedures. If a congregation was considering a questionable action, it was to request counsel and be in conversation with other congregations, its area council, and, ultimately, the conference. There was no provision for the executive committee to discipline a congregation. Under the second procedure, the conference could step in if the congregation did not follow the first. According to the guidelines, the executive committee "carries the responsibility to bring closure to each situation" and could make recommendations for discipline to the delegates;[54] again, the committee did not have the power to unilaterally punish a congregation, although it did do so.

Assembly and Southside had both been clearly operating according to the first procedure, each having notified Indiana-Michigan leadership of its intentions. Like Southside, Assembly also shared with and sought counsel from area conference congregations. Delegates at the 1997 assembly affirmed the executive committee's disciplinary action.

The 1997 assembly also included public recognition of three congregations—Bourbon, Maple Grove, and First Mennonite Church at Montgomery, Indiana—that had withdrawn from Indiana-Michigan since the previous year's meeting. That disturbed some assembly participants when compared with the treatment Assembly and Southside received. "When the more Conservative churches choose to leave, let them speak, we pray and wish them God's blessing," protested Don Blosser, the Goshen College Bible and religion professor and a favorite target of conservatives. "But when two congregations (who don't want to leave us) are disciplined, we say nothing, do not pray, offer no words of indication that we want to continue to love and care and relate."[55]

Assembly and Southside would remain suspended while Indiana-Michigan continued to struggle with how to deal with the situation. In 1998, Assembly voluntarily yielded its voting privileges for the rest of its sabbatical, which was scheduled to end in 2003. Also in 1998, a conference task force recommended the restoration of Southside's voting privileges, which the executive committee rejected.[56] Southside's suspension was then extended to 2003, to coincide with the end of Assembly's self-imposed hiatus.

Another Firestorm

Another firestorm related to sexual orientation erupted after the 1998 ordination of Southside pastor Jeni Hiett Umble. She had joined the pastoral team in 1995, shortly after graduating from AMBS, and was soon licensed for ministry, a preliminary step toward ordination. Southside and Umble began pursuing ordination by the conference in the spring of 1997. After Southside and Assembly were disciplined by the executive committee, Umble, an avowed progressive, put the process on hold as she considered the prospects of ministering in Indiana-Michigan. She eventually restarted the process and was approved by the conference's Church Leadership Commission (CLC), even though she supported Southside's position on sexual orientation. Umble was ordained October 25, 1998, by Indiana-Michigan conference minister Charlotte Holsopple Glick. Umble was simultaneously ordained by Central District Conference of the General Conference Mennonite Church, of which Southside was also a member.

Brian Arbuckle, an ex-Marine and pastor of Marion Mennonite Church near Shipshewana, Indiana, learned of Umble's ordination when it was announced in the *Gospel Evangel* and soon started vehemently contesting it.[57] He was shocked that so few in Indiana-Michigan saw the same problem he did—the conference sanctioning the ministry of a pastor of a congregation under discipline—and was dissatisfied with the explanations he had received. Although he was not the only theological conservative unhappy with the ordination, Arbuckle was the most active, outspoken, and tenacious crusader against Umble and

Conference minister Charlotte Holsopple Glick (seated) ordains Southside pastor Jeni Hiett Umble, accompanied by husband Art Umble and Lloyd Miller, conference minister for Central District Conference. MCUSAA–Goshen.

the conference. In letters, computer chat room postings, and lengthy and widely distributed emails, Arbuckle repeatedly accused Indiana-Michigan's leadership of heresy and hypocrisy, charging that the executive committee and CLC ignored official church positions by ordaining the pastor of a congregation under discipline. He proposed disciplining the CLC and removing its members, as well as the revocation of Umble's credentials.[58] His initial reason was her leadership of and support for a congregation under Indiana-Michigan discipline. But Arbuckle later added the fact that Umble was one of more than six hundred signatories of "A Welcoming Open Letter on 'Homosexuality,'" a full-page advertisement supporting the inclusion of gays and lesbians that appeared in *Mennonite Weekly Review*, a national, independent, inter-Mennonite newspaper, in February 2000, sixteen months after her ordination. (The "Open Letter" was signed by four additional people with Indiana-Michigan credentials, two in pastoral ministry and two retired, but they were never mentioned by Arbuckle.[59]) Exhausted by the repeated attacks from a fellow minister and the constant struggles over Southside's status, Umble resigned her pastorate in 2001. By then, Arbuckle had led the creation of the Evangelical Anabaptist Network, an organization of Indiana-Michigan congregations disturbed by the direction of the conference and denomination, particularly on same-sex orientation and ministerial credentialing.[60]

While the arguments about her ordination took a toll on Umble, they also contributed to stunning developments in the conference's cornerstone congregation in Michigan. Fairview Mennonite Church was the largest Indiana-Michigan congregation in the state, with well more than three hundred members during the mid-twentieth century. Like most Michigan Mennonites, Fairview was theologically conservative. Yet it was also quite loyal to Indiana-Michigan and the Mennonite Church, sending a number of members into the pastorate, particularly in northern Michigan—six between 1947 and 1958 alone—and into leadership positions in organizations such as Mennonite Central Committee and Mennonite Disaster Service.[61] Fairview actively supported the work in the Upper Peninsula, and the annual Bible school it had helped host had been one of the most successful in the wider Mennonite church.

But relations between Fairview and Indiana-Michigan changed dramatically in 1999. Virgil Hershberger, the congregation's pastor since 1967 and a Goshen College graduate, was a strong supporter of the conference and denomination, which was especially valuable as the gap between Indiana-Michigan and its more conservative members widened. Hershberger was selected as Indiana-Michigan's moderator-elect in 1998, a move that could have helped ease tensions and build trust. In August 1999, however, he suffered a stroke and had to step down from both his congregational and conference positions.

Indiana-Michigan asked Randy Detweiler, pastor at Howard-Miami Mennonite Church near Kokomo, Indiana, to fill the moderator vacancy left by Hershberger's resignation. Detweiler offered some of the same connections as Hershberger, since he was a Fairview native and a former Fairview youth pastor. But in Hershberger's absence, simmering concerns neared boiling, and Fairview quickly started turning away from the conference. During the winter of 1999–2000, the congregation met several times with conference officials to question Umble's ordination more than a year earlier. But the meetings quickly revealed underlying problems such as suspicion of Indiana-Michigan leadership and the conference's unwillingness to "discern Biblical truth."[62] In the summer of 2000, Fairview called Cliff Schrauger as its interim pastor. He was a conservative Calvinist minister who was attending Fairview while serving as director of a nearby Christian camp. Schrauger quickly made it known that in his new position, his goal was to take Fairview out of Indiana-Michigan.[63] That was accomplished in 2001, when the decision to withdraw was made after an emotional and exhausting eight-hour congregational meeting. "Needless to say, it is heartbreaking for some to consider leaving that which has been a part of our identity," Fairview admitted to the conference. But being associated with Indiana-Michigan, with its "apparent tolerance" of same-sex orientation, was "unacceptable."[64]

Indiana-Michigan, burned by the decision to ordain Umble, took an extremely slow approach to the credentialing of another Southside pastor. Rhoda Schrag began her ministry in 2000, and the congregation requested licensing. A conference committee interviewed her in August and recommended to the CLC that she be licensed. The CLC initially agreed, then reversed course, then postponed a final decision until after the 2001 annual conference delegate assembly. The CLC finally rejected the credentialing request for two reasons: Schrag supported the congregation's position on sexual orientation, and the selection of her for the pastorate indicated Southside would continue to maintain that position.[65] Schrag had hoped to be licensed at the same time by both Indiana-Michigan and Central District Conference but was forced to proceed only with the latter.

Adding to the clouds looming over Indiana-Michigan was the illness and death of conference minister Charlotte Holsopple Glick. After ten years of pastoring Waterford Mennonite Church and three years in China on a Mennonite service assignment, Glick in 1993 became Indiana-Michigan's first female conference minister and an inspiration and model for women in the Mennonite Church. In addition to her conference and congregational work, she was an adjunct professor at AMBS, chair of the Mennonite Board of Congregational Ministries (MBCM), and held other churchwide positions. But two years after being diagnosed with cancer, Glick died February 9, 1999, at the age of fifty-one. Her impact on gender roles in the church was evident in the ministers who officiated Glick's funeral, four women and one man, all ordained: Martha Kolb-Wyckoff, a Waterford pastor; Anne Stuckey, an MBCM staff member; Janice Yordy Sutter, a pastor at Kern Road Mennonite Church, South Bend, Indiana; Dee Swartz, a pastor at Zion Mennonite Church, Archbold, Ohio; and Art Smoker, Glick's pastor at North Goshen Mennonite Church.[66]

Earthen Vessel

Sex-related issues would burden Indiana-Michigan in ways other than same-sex relationships.[67] By the 1990s the conference, like the rest of the Mennonite Church, was acknowledging the problem of sexual misconduct against women by men in positions of churchly authority.[68] The *Gospel Herald* was, with alarming frequency, printing articles about ministers disciplined for various forms of sexual misconduct, including several high-profile individuals. In 1992, Indiana-Michigan was responding to charges against four men with conference ministerial credentials.[69] One of those investigations would make the conference the epicenter of seismic upheaval that would send shock waves throughout the denomination and beyond.

If ever there was a Mennonite celebrity, it was John Howard Yoder. The Ohio native attended Goshen College, where his brilliance was soon apparent as he earned his bachelor's degree in just two years, graduating in 1947. He first came to the church's attention in the 1950s as a member of the Concern movement, which had originated with a group of young American Mennonite intellectuals serving and studying in Europe.[70] Yoder had gone to France with Mennonite Central Committee to oversee post–World War II relief and reconstruction work, then stayed to complete his doctorate in theology at the University of Basel in Switzerland. He returned to Indiana in 1957 and was soon teaching part-time at Goshen Biblical Seminary (GBS) while working for Mennonite Board of Missions in Elkhart.[71] He became a full-time seminary faculty member in 1965.

A prolific writer, Yoder's influence exploded beyond Mennonite circles and into wider Christianity with the release of his book *The Politics of Jesus* in 1972, which received tremendous critical acclaim. *Christianity Today*, the leading American evangelical magazine, would rank *The*

Politics of Jesus as the fifth-most influential Christian book of the twentieth century. Other writings and his popularity as a speaker cemented Yoder's status as one of the world's most important theologians and ethicists. All the attention and accolades elevated not just him but the Mennonite faith to unprecedented heights. Yoder attracted new people to the church and influenced countless members of other faith groups.

John Howard Yoder. MCUSAA–Goshen.

But all this celebrity and acclaim obscured a stream of whispered rumors and hushed-up allegations of sexual impropriety against Yoder in the mid-1970s, when such problems in the church were addressed in secrecy—if they were addressed at all. While sex and sexuality began to receive a higher profile in the cultural mainstream in the 1960s, Mennonites were more reactive than proactive, generally condemning the new sexual mores and ignoring their implications.[72] The American judicial system was also slow moving, as the concept of sexual harassment didn't begin to emerge until the mid-1970s. The combination of the church's silence and the lack of legal framework made dealing with sexual impropriety exceedingly difficult. It was even more complicated when those issues pertained to the faith's greatest theologian. As a result, the church not only denied justice to Yoder's victims; it allowed him to continue his predatory ways, resulting in more victims.

Starting perhaps as early as the 1960s and continuing at least until 1991, the well-traveled Yoder sexually harassed and assaulted women, maybe more than one hundred, in Europe, Africa, Latin America, and the Middle East as well as in the United States and Canada.[73] Many but not all were students. The incidents ranged from overt sexual language to indecent exposure to forcible physical acts, even intercourse, although that was rare.[74] Yoder's behavior was based in his belief that because of the intimacy that Christian women and men were supposed to share, even when not married to each other, sexual relations were appropriate. He made a distinction between nonerotic and erotic sex, the latter being unacceptable outside marriage.[75] Saying he was doing pioneering work on a new Christian ethic of sex, Yoder sought women to participate in experiments or to counsel them. He targeted some of the best and brightest women he encountered, appealing to their intellect and friendship. Thus his sexual advances were also abuses of his power as their professor and mentor.[76] An unknown number of women were able to ward off Yoder, but for those who were manipulated into his forays, he demanded total secrecy, even to the point of using addresses other than his home or office for correspondence. "We do it, as did the apostle Paul, out of respect for the integrity of those who could not help but misunderstand this liberty and who therefore would be harmed by seeing it lived out in front them," he told the women.[77] Yoder considered himself a radical Christian intellectual, duly authorized by the church, and felt he shouldn't be constrained by conventional expectations of religious conduct or scholarship.[78]

Yoder had served a term as GBS president and was succeeded in 1975 by Marlin Miller, one of his former students, who quickly heard of Yoder's conduct. Miller's approach was not disciplinary, however, and he didn't order Yoder to stop until 1979.[79] Rather, he held secret disputations with Yoder to try to convince him not that he was hurting women but that his theology was flawed. That played to Yoder's strength, as he was able to intellectually bully Miller as well as another faculty member and two GBS board members who later joined the discussions. But when Miller realized Yoder hadn't ceased his activities as ordered, he forced his resignation in 1984.[80] Without any fanfare, Yoder immediately moved to the University of Notre Dame in South Bend, Indiana. While at GBS, he had started teaching at the university in the late 1960s. The roles were reversed in 1977, when he became a full-time, tenured Notre Dame professor, with part of his teaching load seconded to the seminary. Yoder's departure from AMBS puzzled students and a few observers, but no explanation or statement was ever provided, per an agreement between president and professor. To most observers, Yoder simply appeared to be shifting to a larger, wealthier, and more prestigious school barely twenty miles away.[81] That it was a Catholic school could be seen as an expression of Yoder's robust ecumenism.[82]

Although the public knew virtually nothing, Mennonite Church leadership was aware, at least in a general way, of Yoder's inappropriate relations with women, but nothing was substantiated. Prairie Street Mennonite Church, where Yoder was a member, included a number of people who did work or had worked in a variety of church institutional capacities and had heard concerns about their fellow congregational member.[83] In the early 1980s, female faculty and staff from Notre Dame and Saint Mary's College (a South Bend women's school affiliated with Notre Dame) began sharing incidents and rumors about Yoder with women from AMBS and Goshen College. They subsequently started informing administrators at Notre Dame, who never took action against him and would remain mum even after the news became public.[84] Yoder's misconduct was also known among his colleagues within ecumenical Christian academia, including the Society for Christian Ethics, which nevertheless selected him in 1987 for a term as its president.[85]

Despite their knowledge, Mennonite leaders were unwilling to take action against Yoder. There were, however, a few exceptions. In 1983, Mennonite Board of Missions privately urged other church institutions to not use Yoder as a resource person or invite him to events.[86] In the mid-1980s, Goshen College barred him from campus events and from speaking or guest lecturing, including revoking an invitation for him to speak at a peace convocation.

About the same time, Prairie Street tried again to address the allegations against him. Before Yoder left GBS, pastor Phil Bedsworth had several conversations with him, but they quickly fizzled.[87] But a new pastor and new pressures prompted Prairie Street to try again in 1986 when a group of women contacted Prairie Street with complaints.[88] About the same time, Herald Press, the Mennonite Church book publisher, was wanting to know if Yoder was a church member in good standing, after receiving requests to cease publication of his books because of the unconfirmed charges of sexual improprieties.[89] New pastor Charlie Cooper led an effort to determine their veracity and nature but was left dizzy by Yoder's loquacious verbal gymnastics.[90] Miller, the only other person who knew specifics of Yoder's offenses, wasn't helpful, either, as he considered himself bound by his confidentiality agreement with Yoder when he was terminated.[91] As Prairie Street tried to continue its investigation, Yoder demanded, and the elders agreed, that he be allowed to meet individually with each of his accusers. While grounded in Scripture, particularly Matthew 18, the idea was threatening to the women, who flatly rejected it.[92] They had already been victimized by Yoder in private and weren't going to risk putting themselves in such a situation again. So the Prairie Street investigation foundered.[93] In the absence of any solid evidence of wrongdoing, Herald Press felt it had no choice but to continue publishing Yoder's books, which didn't make Miller happy.[94] Even though he felt he could not provide assistance, he now regretted his confidentiality agreement with Yoder and was encouraging others to do their own investigations.[95]

Prairie Street would get yet a third chance to look into Yoder's conduct. It would be part of a confluence of events over two years that would bring the famous theologian more, albeit unwelcome, attention. The husband-and-wife team of Harold and Ruth Yoder followed Cooper as Prairie Street pastors in 1990 and were soon receiving inquiries from across the church regarding rumors about John Howard Yoder and asking if he could or should be invited to speak and teach at conferences and workshops. This was nothing new to Harold and Ruth. As AMBS students before arriving at Prairie Street, they knew questions had been raised about using Yoder's books in the school's courses.[96] In July 1991, the pastors convened a congregational task force for yet another investigation into the long-circulating allegations.

As the task force began its work, AMBS hosted an October conference on "Peace Theology and Violence against Women," where several of Yoder's victims met for the first time.[97] That spawned a network of women who had been victimized by Yoder, finally giving them a place of mutual support and a platform for advocacy. Meanwhile in 1991, Goshen College was also preparing to hold a conference, this one on church discipline, for which the school lifted its ban on Yoder by appointing him to the planning committee. Miller urged Goshen to first address the charges against Yoder for the sake of "a modest measure of integrity," but the school declined to do so.[98] With the Prairie Street task force not yet ready to release any information or make any statements, Yoder's behavior remained hidden.

That changed in early 1992. Yoder was to be the keynote speaker at an April peace conference at Bethel College, the General Conference Mennonite Church school in North Newton, Kansas. Individuals familiar with the accusations and investigations, including victims, protested the invitation, and Bethel dropped Yoder from the program about six weeks before it was scheduled to be held. The March 5 issue of the campus newspaper declared "Yoder Disinvited to Conference" with a front-page banner headline. The article did not provide any details of his misdeeds except to say that he was being accused of "sexual harassment" by "a number of women." Bethel president John E. Zehr called the misconduct "inconsistent with the nonviolent topic" of the conference.[99] It was the first time Yoder's conduct was publicly acknowledged in any way. The Mennonite media quickly disseminated the news throughout the church.

The Bethel newspaper story broke just a few days after a group of eight of Yoder's victims, finally connected after years of isolation across the country, met in Elkhart to share, commiserate, and strategize. Their agenda also included meeting with the Prairie Street task force to recount their experiences with the famous theologian. After years of being ignored, the women heard the task force members say they believed them. The task force concluded its work in June by recommending to Indiana-Michigan Mennonite Conference that Yoder's ministerial credentials be suspended due to thirteen counts of sexual offenses against women. The CLC immediately affirmed the task force's findings and withdrew Yoder's ordination. Yoder never denied the accusations and even said he regretted the pain the women suffered, but he repeatedly claimed that his error was not recognizing when they tried to refuse his advances.[100] Yoder continued to argue that it was all just misunderstandings and that, fundamentally, there was no moral or religious problem with his sexual pursuits.

Although the shroud of secrecy had been partially lifted after more than fifteen years and was expected to lift even more, Indiana-Michigan leaders tried to prevent it. Shortly before the conference suspended Yoder's credentials, a reporter for the *Elkhart Truth* newspaper had written an article that the decision had been made. A CLC member threatened him with repercussions should his story be published, which it was. The CLC also tried to squelch those who were leaking information to the reporter.[101]

News of the superstar's discipline was explosive. After the *Gospel Herald* reported Indiana-Michigan's suspension of Yoder's ordination, one female member of Fairview (Mich.) Mennonite Church wrote in a letter to the editor, "I don't buy the women accusing our leaders when they aren't open to being named as well. I hope you can repent rather than continually justify your printing names of leaders that you could humiliate churchwide. That's abuse!"[102] Vitriolic accusations of the women trying to "seduce an innocent man" and "giving the church a bad name" left the victims again feeling battered by the church. "I had not anticipated the level of anger & disgust & yes, hatred that would be directed towards us," one of the women wrote.[103] That nobody publicly rose to the women's defense compounded the years of ill treatment by the church, even though both Prairie Street and Indiana-Michigan had substantiated the women's claims. Nevertheless, falsehoods such as that none of the women were willing to confront Yoder directly (several had since the early 1980s) and that they were hiding their identities (individuals at AMBS, Prairie Street, and Indiana-Michigan knew who at least some of the women were) went unchecked.[104]

The Prairie Street task force, in addition to recommending the suspension of the theologian's credentials, also called for therapy and ongoing monitoring given the egregiousness of his conduct. Having assumed responsibility for Yoder, Indiana-Michigan began work during the summer of 1992, opening a new chapter that would exacerbate the existing contentiousness and anguish surrounding his case. The CLC appointed an Accountability and Support Group (ASG) to lead the conference's efforts, with the goal of rehabilitation and reconciliation. The ASG's assignment was herculean, wrestling with a situation no one in the church had ever faced before and with a person who was notoriously difficult to deal with, as Miller, seminary employees, Prairie Street pastors, and many others in the church could attest. In fact, Yoder initially refused to participate in the process, almost thwarting the ASG before it could even start. Disgusted at his treatment by the church, he and his wife, Anne, left Prairie Street and were soon worshiping with a Lutheran congregation in Elkhart. Yoder relented and agreed to the process after three friends and colleagues intervened. Jim McClendon and Glen Stassen, professors at Fuller Theological Seminary in Pasadena, California, and Stanley Hauerwas, who taught ethics at Duke University in Durham, North Carolina, and previously was at Notre Dame with Yoder, all had their views greatly shaped by him. In a conference call with Yoder, they were able to convince him to submit to the discipline process and live out what he had taught them about love, peace, and community.[105]

The ASG's primary responsibilities were to secure therapy for Yoder, establish a "safe plan" to monitor his interactions with others, develop a victims' restitution fund, and ultimately restore him to his academic ministry.[106] The ASG met thirty times between November 1992 and July 1994, all but a couple of times with John and Anne. It turned out to be mostly an exercise in futility and frustration. Yoder fought the idea of counseling—which would have been best done at an in-treatment group setting beyond the region—until a compromise of sorts was reached with the weary ASG, and he started sessions with a fellow Notre Dame faculty member; the counselor's findings were favorable to Yoder. Later, the CLC stepped in and sent Yoder to a psychiatrist in Chicago for a second opinion. When it was more critical, Yoder revoked conference access to it, rendering it moot.[107]

Because it wasn't a charitable organization and so had no legal standing to create and manage a restitution fund, the ASG could only recommend to the conference that one be started. Prairie Street was already holding $1,500—$1,000 from Yoder and $500 from the congregation—in escrow for such purposes.[108] Indiana-Michigan wanted Mennonite Central Committee to assume responsibility for the fund, which could be used to reimburse victims for mental healthcare costs, victims' travel, or seminars on sexual abuse. MCC, which had a Women's Concerns desk and was producing resources on domestic abuse, had already started compiling a list of victims of Mennonite pastoral abuse. But MCC instead recommended that Indiana-Michigan turn to the denominational Mennonite Board of Congregational Ministries, and the idea eventually died.[109] Prairie Street would send $900 of the money in escrow to a domestic violence center in Seattle, as suggested by Yoder, while the remainder went into the congregation's mutual aid fund. None of Yoder's victims were ever told of the fund's existence.[110]

Hopes for a "safe plan" to protect others from Yoder were dashed when he revealed in 1995 that he had no interest in having his ministerial credentials restored. He never sought to be ordained in the first place, as he believed "there is no hierarchy of value" of roles in the body of believers because they all come from God and are all "uniquely indispensable."[111] But Yoder had agreed to be ordained in 1973, after he was named GBS president and at the urging of seminary professor J. C. Wenger. In addition, the man who raised Anabaptism to new heights but had stopped attending a Mennonite congregation was questioning his continued affiliation with the church.[112] So it should not have been surprising that Yoder relinquished his credentials. But when he did so, Indiana-Michigan lost not only leverage with Yoder but also its jurisdiction over him. The conference could not demand or enforce a safe plan for someone who did not hold conference credentials.[113]

So in June 1996, Indiana-Michigan, exhausted from futilely battling Yoder for four years, released a statement announcing the end of the process. The conference commended Yoder for his participation and encouraged the church to again use his gifts as a speaker, teacher, and writer.[114] Having seen his invitations and opportunities to do so dry up during the previous several years, Yoder was restored to do what first brought him acclaim. In 1997, thirteen years after being barred from campus, he returned to the AMBS campus to teach a class, and he resumed itinerating, including an appearance at Eastern Mennonite Seminary in Harrisonburg, Virginia. It was Yoder's first speaking engagement in a Mennonite setting since his discipline was lifted, and some at the school protested the invitation because of the lack of an apology or evidence of reconciliation with his victims.[115]

The restoration process was indisputably imperfect and probably impossible. After a promising start with the Prairie Street task force, the women felt left out of Indiana-Michigan's work and maintained that its focus was not on justice and accountability but on the rehabilitation of Yoder's reputation and returning him to prominence. As evidence, the victims cited Yoder's lack of remorse. One attempted apology from him, in letter form, was circulated among a group of victims, who found it "reflected considerable self-justification by explaining the situation as misunderstanding or misinterpreting his motives and approaches rather than clearly reflecting a confessional and repentance position."[116] Yoder, meanwhile, always maintained that he tried to apologize but was denied the opportunity by both Prairie Street and Indiana-Michigan.[117] Meanwhile, the Yoders were also suffering and felt victimized by the process.[118] While her husband addressed it with cold rationalism, Anne felt it with deep emotion.[119] When she saw a draft of the statement about the end of the process in 1996, she pleaded with conference officials to soften its tone. "Should we, as a family, be subjected to such punishment once more after the vast, devastating publicity of 1992?" she wrote.[120]

Amid all the trials and errors were lessons that were slow to be learned. In a series of exchanges between Eastern Mennonite Seminary and Indiana-Michigan about the advisability of Yoder speaking on campus, dean George R. Brunk III tactfully chided the conference for not mentioning that "we are corporately participants in the evil perpetrated—silence, institutional interests, damage control and the like. Our public statements could acknowledge the corporate guilt." The damage caused by one individual was compounded by the gross shortcomings of the responses by those responsible for holding Yoder accountable and extending care to his victims. Brunk's point, however, perplexed Indiana-Michigan executive secretary Sherm Kauffman, who called it "a little hard to understand."[121]

While Indiana-Michigan wrangled with the Yoders, Prairie Street Mennonite Church also remained in contact with them, even as the couple had stopped attending their longtime congregation. But they remained members, and the pastors and elders sought to rebuild relationships with them. In September 1997, the Yoders met with their Prairie Street Sunday school class for the first time in more than five years. But they didn't attend a Sunday morning worship service until December 28, ending their self-imposed exile.[122] Two days later, and one day after his seventieth birthday, John Howard Yoder died from an aortic aneurysm while in his office at Notre Dame. Visitation was held at Prairie Street but the funeral was at the larger College Mennonite Church in Goshen. Yoder's son-in-law Tom Yoder Neufeld, himself a Mennonite theologian of note at Conrad Grebel University College in Waterloo, Ontario, gave a meditation on 2 Corinthians 4:7. He said that "in the best of times earthen vessels have rough edges" and "in the worst of times they fall and break and have shards that cut deeply and wound."[123]

Other Developments

Although the most visible and most contentious, same-sex sexual relations and sexual misconduct were not the only issues challenging Indiana-Michigan. Well into the 1980s, the conference was still trying

Simon Mungai and Gladys Maina.
MCUSAA–Goshen.

to develop institutional structures in order to do its work in the most effective and efficient manner possible. A major step had been the creation of the paid staff position of conference minister in 1968, which was followed the next year with the adoption of a new constitution. For the first time, all the work being done in the name of Indiana-Michigan Mennonite Conference was brought together into one organization. The executive committee, long the seat of conference power, assumed more of a coordinating and counseling role, with many of its former responsibilities delegated to five new commissions. One of them was the Mission Commission, formerly the Indiana-Michigan Mennonite Mission Board, which officially had been a separate entity since its creation in 1912. The board's *Gospel Evangel* subsequently became the official publication for the entire conference. But with the emergence of organizations came the need to finance them, which became more difficult to do starting in the 1980s. In 1982, Indiana-Michigan was facing a $100,000 shortfall, prompting the elimination of deaf ministries, its disabilities committee, and the victim-offender reconciliation program. The conference had to again slash the budget five years later and yet again in 1991. An abbreviated *Gospel Evangel* came out in December 1996 with a handwritten note reproduced across the top of the first page: "Sorry about the missing pages, we're trying to balance the budget."

Money was not the only problem vexing the conference. The old bishop system was fading away, requiring new methods of congregational oversight and accountability. By 1980, Indiana-Michigan was employing a hodgepodge of approaches: area councils of congregations, congregation-selected overseers, and the CLC, as well as a few remaining traditional bishops. The ambiguous relationships and lack

Conferring during the 1991 joint CDC-IM assembly in Fort Wayne are (left to right): Ruth Naylor, conference minister for Central District Conference; Rachel Fisher, first woman moderator; and Sherm Kauffman, conference minister for Indiana-Michigan. MCUSAA–Goshen.

of accountability translated into a loss of corporate identity and mission. In 1965, during their conference-wide travels, Alta and Paul Erb warned of the still-evolving congregational autonomy going too far, undermining unity and thwarting discipline.[124] The Erbs' predictions were coming true fifteen years later. In his address to the 1980 Indiana-Michigan annual assembly, conference minister John H. Mosemann denounced congregational "islands of independent purpose. We see our own visions and dream our own dreams with a minimal interest in testing these with our neighboring congregations." There was no structure in place to adequately combat that tendency, he said. Of the conference's 101 congregations, 40 were under direct CLC oversight, which Mosemann called "unrealistic" and "absurd," while area councils were ineffective. "The result," he said, "is that many churches have no functional frame of reference in which to maintain the kind of relationships needed truly to remain a conferring people."[125] In 1987 Indiana-Michigan implemented a system of overseers for each congregation and eliminated the other oversight options.

Other changes, however, were celebrated. Tim Atwood left the pastorate at Ninth Street Mennonite Church in Saginaw, Michigan,

Marie (seated) and Tim Atwood and daughter Latoya. MCUSAA–Goshen.

to assume the pulpit at Amish Mennonite–originated North Leo (Ind.) Mennonite Church in 1992. "To my knowledge this is the first African-American pastor in an all Anglo traditionally ethnic Mennonite church," Indiana-Michigan executive secretary Sherm Kauffman told the conference executive committee. "Our prayer is that this can be a successful and mutually beneficial journey together."[126] Three years later, married couple Gladys Maina and Simon Mungai from Kenya began pastoring Morningstar Mennonite Church in Muncie, Indiana, where they had attended while studying at Ball State University. They weren't the first people of color to lead Anglo Indiana-Michigan Mennonites. In 1976, Mario Bustos Jr., son of an early minister at Iglesia del Buen Pastor in Goshen, became pastor of Hudson Lake Mennonite Church, a small congregation in northwestern Indiana. Bethany Christian High School scored a win for racial justice in 1992 when it changed the nickname of its athletic teams from the Braves to the Bruins. The school said the old name was "a derogatory symbol to many and contributes to the stereotypical image of the Native American as a savage. Out of respect for all people as a part of God's creation this use is inappropriate." Bethany also noted that the image of braves was often used to represent violence, which was inconsistent with the school's peace and justice values.[127]

Meanwhile, women continued to rise in the conference. From 1980, when Wilma Bailey was licensed for congregational ministry, to 1996, Indiana-Michigan credentialed forty-six women, half of them between 1992 and 1996.[128] Bailey in 1982 became the first woman—and person of color—on the Indiana-Michigan executive committee. Five years later, eleven of the conference's twenty-five delegates to the Mennonite Church convention were women. But the top position remained out of reach until 1991, when College Mennonite Church pastor Rachel Fisher became the first woman to serve as Indiana-Michigan moderator. A member of North Goshen Mennonite Church who had earlier served in Africa with Mennonite Board of Missions and Mennonite Central Committee, Fisher was also executive secretary of the Mennonite Church's Women's Missionary and Service Commission. That same year, Goshen College English professor and College Mennonite Church member Shirley Showalter broke through Mennonite academia's glass ceiling when she assumed the school's presidency, becoming the first woman to lead a Mennonite Church college.[129]

A New Church

Following the 1983 joint Mennonite Church-General Conference Mennonite Church convention at Bethlehem, Pennsylvania, delegate and longtime Indiana-Michigan leader Russell Krabill correctly predicted: "It is my impression that this will hasten the day when we will experience a merger. The meeting demonstrated that there are actually not as many differences as there were 40 years ago."[130] The changes in Indiana-Michigan and in much of the rest of the Mennonite Church since World War II had indeed underscored the commonalities of faith between the Mennonite Church and the General Conference Mennonite Church. In some areas of the conference, distinctions between the two had become increasingly blurred by century's end. Indianapolis's two congregations, First and Shalom, included a number of members from GCMC background who had come to the city for work or school. In Elkhart County, MC institutions such as Mennonite Board of Missions and Goshen College had employees who were GCMC members. Pastors were even crossing denominational lines. For example, Mick Sommers, who grew up in and later pastored at Howard-Miami Mennonite Church near Kokomo, in 1996 began as pastor of Hively Avenue Mennonite Church, the Central District Conference congregation in Elkhart, and later served as conference president. Meanwhile, James Waltner, a born-and-bred General Conference Mennonite from South Dakota and previously pastor of GCMC congregations in California and Kansas and a dual-conference congregation in Illinois, became lead pastor at Goshen's College Mennonite Church.[131] He was Indiana-Michigan moderator from 1998 to 2000. Meanwhile, Indiana-Michigan and fellow MC area conferences Illinois and Ohio joined with Central District in 1986 to create the East Central States Inter-Mennonite Council (ECSIMC) to work on cooperative initiatives.

The Mennonite Church and General Conference Mennonite Church were able to draw closer because, in part, the former gradually decreased its traditional emphasis on attire, accepted higher education and a professional pastorate, and became more congregational in polity, all of which had historically been more common in the General Conference Mennonite Church. But while increasing in congregationalism, the influence of Indiana-Michigan's bishop-centric past remained, as some members contended that the conference still had a responsibility to define and enforce right belief and practice, at least on some issues. That was even more pronounced when compared with the Central District Conference. Indiana-Michigan's GCMC neighbors were passionately congregational and distrustful of centralized power, characteristics resulting from the fact that many members, both individuals and congregations, joined Central District after being disciplined in the more authoritarian Mennonite Church in the late nineteenth and early twentieth centuries. In fact, six congregations that were Central District members at the time were formed out of schisms in Indiana-Michigan congregations.[132]

With that background, Central District was loath to take action against Southside and Assembly for their stances on same-sex sexual relations and church membership, favoring the primacy of local congregational discernment over conference judiciary enforcement. Even though Central District had decidedly conservative segments of its membership, critics in Indiana-Michigan accused the GCMC area conference of being soft on sin by not taking action against the two congregations, which hampered regional merger explorations. "In light of Central District's . . . polity (or lack thereof) for disciplining congregations, I cannot help but think that our 'merger' will result in yet another round of agonizing debate on this matter," Charles Buller, pastor of Communion Fellowship in Goshen, told the conference executive committee. "How tragic when a needy world so awaits the gospel."[133] His congregation would eventually withdraw from Indiana-Michigan.

In 1995, twelve years after their initial joint convention at Bethlehem, the Mennonite Church and General Conference Mennonite

By the 1980s, members of Indiana-Michigan Mennonite Conference had been credentialed for a range of work, such as denominational administration and prison ministry, in addition to the congregational pastorate. Such an expanded idea of ministry would also include spiritual deliverance in 1986.

Dean Hochstetler was a welder by profession and a member of North Main Street Mennonite Church in Nappanee, Indiana, when he began studying demon possession in 1962. The Hochstetlers had been hearing strange noises in their house, and one night they were especially pronounced in his son's room. Dean entered, had an oppressive feeling of Satan, and declared, "In Jesus' name, I order you out of this house and off these premises." Calm quickly returned.[1]

Hochstetler subsequently heard a call to spiritual deliverance as a ministry, and in the 1970s he began delivering people from evil spirits. In 1978, Indiana-Michigan created a "support and discernment" group for Hochstetler's work because of its uniqueness and controversy. The group recommended that the church give more concerted study to the topic, including Mennonite seminaries incorporating teaching on the occult, demon possession, and deliverance ministry into their curricula.[2] While receiving support within the conference, Hochstetler had to also endure opposition. After being denied opportunity to speak at Goshen College, he complained, "One learns from experience that Mennonite institutions have 'black lists' too. While they proclaim brotherhood loudly, practice is another matter."[3]

The conference ordained Hochstetler in 1986, making him the first person to be officially recognized in the Mennonite Church for spiritual deliverance. He died in 2006 at the age of seventy-eight.

1. Ben Snyder, ed., *The Ministry of Dean Hochstetler*, 1974–2005 (privately published, 2010), 4–5.
2. Recommendations by the Dean Hochstetler Support & Discernment Group, September 4, 1985, Indiana-Michigan Mennonite Conference collection (II-5-20), box 6, folder 15, MCUSAA–Goshen.
3. Dean Hochstetler to Bro. Galen, February 22 [no year given], Indiana-Michigan Mennonite Conference collection (II-5-20), box 6, folder 2, MCUSAA–Goshen.

Church met together again in 1995 in Wichita, Kansas, where they officially agreed to unite. The decision accelerated discussions about regional mergers in MC and GCMC area conferences across the country. In 1998, the ECSIMC called for the creation of a committee to develop a plan for a merger of its four conferences, and its proposal was presented in 2000.[134] The plan was to unite Indiana-Michigan, Illinois, Ohio, and Central District into one supersized Great Lakes area conference. But it would be organized into "mission cells" of five to nine congregations each and into larger mission districts of thirty-five to forty congregations each. The districts, in effect, would be mini-conferences that would meet annually, while the entire conference would hold biennial assemblies as a sort of mini-denomination.

In July 2001, U.S. MC and GCMC delegates meeting in Nashville, Tennessee, approved the final details necessary to join their denominations into a new one, to be called Mennonite Church USA, effective the following February.[135] At Indiana-Michigan's annual assembly before the Nashville convention, delegates approved joining the new denomination with a 93 percent vote, pending action in Nashville.[136] That left one more matter to be addressed. On October 13, 2001, a special one-day meeting of Indiana-Michigan, Illinois, Ohio, and Central District was held at First Mennonite Church in Berne to vote on the ECSIMC plan for a regional merger. A two-thirds vote of each conference's delegates was necessary for passage. Seventy-two percent of Indiana-Michigan's representatives affirmed the plan. Central District and Illinois approved the proposal with a 91 percent vote and 83 percent vote, respectively. But the Great Lakes conference idea died when only 55 percent of Ohio delegates supported it. Conference leaders attributed the vote to prevailing concerns about polity and membership—in other words, Central District's inaction against Assembly and Southside.[137] The eighty-five-year-old Indiana-Michigan Mennonite Conference would remain in existence to work, worship, fellowship, and serve in the twentieth-first century.

Epilogue:
Relations at the Crossroads

First Mennonite Church and Pleasant Oaks Mennonite Church, both in Middlebury, Indiana, celebrated the Lord's Supper together on Worldwide Communion Sunday, October 4, 2009. While an important practice in the life of the church, it's rarely a newsworthy event. But when the congregations joined in the Lord's Supper that day, it symbolized the successful resolution of a schism that resulted in two separate fellowships after a communion service eighty-six years earlier. In 1923, a group of young women at First Mennonite Church were denied the bread and cup because, according to the officiating bishop, their prayer coverings lacked strings and thus didn't meet Indiana-Michigan Mennonite Conference standards. Progressives soon left the first congregation and established what came to be called Pleasant Oaks and joined the General Conference Mennonite Church.[1]

The 2002 merger of the General Conference Mennonite Church and Mennonite Church brought the two congregations into the same denomination. So the communion service seven years later rightly recognized First and Pleasant Oak's unity in faith. But the two congregations took it a step further. Not only had their denominations become one, but now First and Pleasant Oaks did as well. After months of discussion and negotiation, First Mennonite Church approved a "reunion" of the two congregations at a September 2009 congregational meeting.[2] Pleasant Oaks would do likewise shortly after the joint communion service. Both votes were unanimous.

Their actions could easily be considered cynically. The two congregations were experiencing decreasing membership, especially Pleasant Oaks, which was about ready to dissolve entirely. But this wasn't simply a matter of practicality; it was one of reconciliation. Pleasant Oaks could have locked its doors for good and let its members choose new church homes on their own. But both groups agreed to testify to the power of God to repair divisions, no matter how old.

The Middlebury merger appeared indicative of a new mood emerging as Indiana-Michigan moved through the first decade of the twenty-first century. In 2003, six years after Assembly Mennonite Church in Goshen, Indiana, and Southside Fellowship in Elkhart, Indiana, were suspended for their positions on sexual orientation and church membership, 92 percent of Indiana-Michigan delegates voted to restore the two congregations to full membership. There had been no grand revelations about human sexuality, no groundbreaking understandings about church membership, no new consensus on scriptural interpretation. Rather, said conference executive committee member Terry Diener, the time had come to focus not on divisions but on Christ "and move ahead with the missional agenda of Mennonite Church USA."[3]

The level of agreement was largely possible due the exodus of conservative Indiana-Michigan members fearful of the prospects of legitimizing same-sex attraction but also afraid of the merger of the Mennonite Church and General Conference Mennonite Church. The GCMC congregational polity and mind-set meant little disciplinary action against offending congregations, which was often interpreted as liberal laxness that could infect the Mennonite Church. "We have been concerned for some time at the departure from our anabaptist [sic] perspective, and the authority of the scripture," Bethel Mennonite Church of Odon, Indiana, explained when it pulled out of Indiana-Michigan in 2001. "Now with the merger of the two [denominations], of which we do not feel comfortable with, we have officially with the voice of the congregation voted to withdraw our relationship with conference."[4] Indiana-Michigan membership dropped from 12,744 in 102 congregations in 1990 to 11,699 in 96 congregations in 2001, the year of both Mennonite Church USA's final approval and the failure of the Great Lakes area conference proposal. By 2005, the conference had 10,283 members in 85 congregations.

The remaining conference members were seemingly comfortable with the new environment and were committed to working and serving together, despite their disagreements. But that impression was shattered by events in Colorado. In February 2014, Mountain States

Mennonite Conference became the first in Mennonite Church USA to credential an openly gay pastor when it licensed Theda Good, a lesbian in a committed relationship, for congregational ministry at First Mennonite Church in Denver. Mountain States's decision, which came after a year of discernment and discussion, generated a barrage of opposition and demands for punishment from across the denomination. Forty-seven Indiana-Michigan ministers—pastors of twenty-four congregations, retired ministers, and ministers in other roles, plus the pastor of a former conference congregation—wrote to the Mennonite Church USA Executive Board: "We believe it is time for clear decisions by the denominational leadership so we can determine the best direction for our congregations. We recognized that some in our conference and denomination feel differently. We do not seek to change or force our beliefs on other congregations or conferences. At the same time, we are committed to identifying with congregations, a conference, and a denomination that unite us in a common witness to the transforming power of Jesus Christ. Our desire is that our current affiliations could be that place."[5]

It would remain so for some. But between June 2014 and June 2015, eight congregations severed their ties with Indiana-Michigan; seven of them had been represented in the letter to the denominational executive board, all citing issues pertaining to the acceptance of lesbian, gay, bisexual, and transgender (LGBT) Christians.[6] The most shocking was Clinton Frame Mennonite Church in 2014. Its lead pastor was Terry Diener, the same person who thirteen years earlier had urged the conference to concentrate on the work of the church and not on the conflicts surrounding sexual orientation. Clinton Frame, the first Amish Mennonite congregation in northern Indiana, had long been a pillar in Indiana-Michigan. Its history included an impressive roster of leaders, such as D. J. Johns, Ira S. Johns, D. D. Troyer, and Vernon Bontreger, the great-great-grandson of Amish Mennonite pioneer settler Joseph Borntreger and Clinton Frame's pastor for forty years until his retirement in 1990.[7] These individuals' impact was felt not just in the congregation but also at the conference and denominational levels. In addition, a number of current Clinton Frame members were employed by Mennonite Church USA organizations, including the executive director of the Mennonite Education Agency, which at one time had its offices in the church. All these connections made Clinton Frame's withdrawal, with the support of 95 percent of the congregation, even more stunning than that of Fairview (Mich.) Mennonite Church in 2001.[8]

When it withdrew, Clinton Frame had declared its intention to transfer to South Central Mennonite Conference, which was considered more conservative than Indiana-Michigan, and thus remain with Mennonite Church USA. But less than a year later, Clinton Frame changed course and announced it would not join South Central but cut all ties to the denomination and become the first congregation to join a new Mennonite group created in the summer of 2015 in the aftermath of Mountain States's licensure decision. Called Evana—a combination of the words *evangelical* and *Anabaptist*—it claimed it was not a competing denomination, although it would be a credentialing body, but a fellowship of like-minded congregations that would be able to also maintain any existing affiliations.[9] Indiana-Michigan members and former members were instrumental in Evana's development. Its first executive was John Troyer, who had been a pastor at Locust Grove Mennonite Church, Sturgis, Michigan, and more recently at Clinton Frame, and among its board members were Virginia Leichty and Tyler Hartford, pastors at Valparaiso (Ind.) Mennonite Church and Pleasant View Mennonite Church of Goshen, respectively. Pleasant View, which also severed connections with Indiana-Michigan, did transfer to South Central in 2015. But the congregation abruptly pulled out later that year to affiliate solely with Evana.

Adding to the discontent was Indiana-Michigan's light discipline of Assembly Mennonite Church pastor Karl Shelly.[10] In 2014, Shelly, an outspoken LGBT supporter, became one of the few Mennonite Church USA ministers to marry a same-sex couple, in violation of denominational regulations. The next year, the conference ministerial committee voted to note in his official file his "variance" from church policy. Two members of the five-person committee wanted stronger action taken against Shelly. "When we realized we could not follow our normal practice of consensus, we went with a simple majority vote," the committee explained in a prepared statement.[11] Shelly had earlier participated in a same-sex wedding, although he did not officiate, and was reprimanded by Indiana-Michigan. His punishment the second time was no worse. "The conference did nothing significant about it," argued

David Araujo, pastor of Goshen's Iglesia Menonita del Buen Pastor, one of the departing congregations.[12] The latest round of withdrawals left Indiana-Michigan with 8,370 members in sixty-six congregations.

The congregational approach that had allowed Indiana-Michigan to manage many significant changes did not work with same-sex attraction. Discussing what women wear on their heads, for example, was more of an exercise in logic, involving biblical interpretation, notions of nonconformity, the locus of authority, and more. In contrast was the visceral nature of sex, with its innate urges and feelings that defy reason, which frequently produced intensely emotional reactions. Those on opposing sides grew bolder and more outspoken. Subsequently, Good's licensure and Shelly's wedding officiating, the former unprecedented and the latter highly irregular, poured even more gasoline on the already explosive issue.[13] Much to the conservatives' dismay, the Mennonite Church and Indiana-Michigan already had noncelibate gays and lesbians in their midst. But that ministers of the gospel, the very people called to lead Christians away from sin, would blatantly condone what some considered obvious sin was too much for some members.

At the same time, the cultural and political heat was increasing, and in no place was it hotter than in Indiana. The state had outlawed same-sex marriage in 1997, and in the 2000s, legislators regularly but unsuccessfully tried to add the ban to the Indiana Constitution. Such attempts always generated controversy in a state that has been traditionally Republican but with a strong enough Democratic presence to create political volatility, to which the church wasn't immune.[14] Prohibitions on same-sex marriage were overturned nationwide by the U.S. Supreme Court in 2015, the same year Indiana approved legislation that allowed businesses to refuse service to LGBT individuals for religious reasons. After a fierce public backlash, particularly from Indiana business and groups threatening to boycott the state, including cancelling conventions, the law was amended to cancel the discriminatory provision.[15] Like their fellow Hoosiers and fellow Christians, Indiana-Michigan members were on all sides of the issue.

While issues pertaining to same-sex attraction continued to bedevil the conference and the rest of Mennonite Church USA, steps were taken in 2015 to exorcise some old demons from John Howard Yoder's years of sexual abuse and assault.[16] Sara Wenger Shenk became president of

AMBS president Sara Wenger Shenk speaking at the John Howard Yoder service of lament, March 2015. Mary Klassen, AMBS.

Associated Mennonite Biblical Seminary, Elkhart, Indiana, in the fall of 2010, the first woman to hold the position. She moved to AMBS from Eastern Mennonite Seminary in Harrisonburg, Virginia, where, as associate dean, she had witnessed the complexities surrounding Yoder and his discipline when the school invited him to speak on campus in 1997. Arriving at AMBS, she quickly became aware of the seminary's unfinished business regarding Yoder. In 2011, the seminary began concerted conversations about his legacy, which the next year produced a faculty statement on the limitations of using Yoder in their teaching.[17] Mennonite Church USA joined the seminary in 2013 to do what hadn't been done before: formally document both complaints against Yoder and, more importantly, how the responses of church institutions had often compounded problems. The process culminated in a public service on March 22, 2015, in which AMBS officially apologized for its complicity by allowing Yoder to continue violating women, and for ignoring the victims' cries for justice. "I am sorry that we neglected to genuinely listen to your reports of violation and that even after hearing your warnings, we failed to raise the alarm," Shenk said. AMBS and Mennonite Church USA also announced the creation of a restitution fund.[18] Indiana-Michigan, meanwhile, remained silent, despite its failures in disciplining and restoring Yoder.

But not all in Indiana-Michigan was contentious. The twenty-first century also saw conference members in new pursuits of faithfulness as the church adjusted to changing religious and cultural dynamics, sometimes posing some unsettling challenges.[19] The crossroads continued to lead to new possibilities. As denominational loyalties waned, congregations were no longer relying solely on Mennonite Church USA–related organizations to do international ministry. For example, North Leo (Ind.) Mennonite Church began a partnership with Kenyan Christians in 2000. Two years later Emma (Ind.) Mennonite Church helped build a medical clinic in India in the home community of a congregational member who had come to faith at Emma. Other Indiana-Michigan congregations and groups established one-to-one connections with people in places such as Pakistan, Iran, Iraq, Botswana, and West Africa. Domestically, the continuing arrival of immigrants from Latin America to the region of Indiana-Michigan became a source of vehement contention. Indiana-Michigan individuals and congregations responded in a variety of ways, such as engaging in political advocacy and providing social services. North Goshen (Ind.) Mennonite Church began conducting all its worship services in both English and Spanish, while several Elkhart congregations joined together to provide English-language instruction to Spanish-speaking newcomers. Cross-cultural sensitivity was also heightened after the September 11, 2001, terrorist attacks against the United States by radical Islamists. Some conference members felt called to apply their beliefs in Christian peace and justice and seek relationships with area Muslims as a way to get beyond stereotyping and demonizing.

In all activities and in all situations, Indiana-Michigan has pursued faithfulness to the Lord and right relations with God's creation.[20] That has generated both vibrant discipleship and intense dissension through the years. In fact, the conference's difficulties in the early 2000s have been strikingly similar to those of a century earlier. The 1960s and 1970s, like the 1860s and 1870s, saw the departure of the most conservative members. While painful, the withdrawals also left conference members at the turn of each century looking toward a future of promise and possibilities. But in both cases, however, appearances of unity in mission were much too quickly overshadowed by discord. The issues and the buzzwords changed—*modernism* and *fundamentalism* in the first couple of decades of the twentieth century, *family values* and *tolerance* a hundred years later—but for Indiana-Michigan Mennonite Conference, the conflicts were still rooted in differing understandings of separation from the world.

While it may appear that the conservatives and progressives shall never meet and the church shall remain divided, consider C. Henry Smith.[21] He was the young progressive professor who, tired of conservative intrusions at Goshen College, left the school in 1913 for a more hospitable climate at Bluffton (Ohio) College. Initially, Smith was filled with the glorious optimism of the era's progressive movement. But a funny thing happened on the way to becoming the first preeminent American Mennonite historian. His progressivism was tempered, in no small part, by those in the church with whom he debated and argued. In the end, the liberal scholar (at least by Mennonite standards) needed the more conservative members in the church, such as John Horsch and Harold S. Bender, to challenge some of his beliefs and perceptions. And they likewise needed him. The benefits of the refining fire generated by heated disagreement is one of history's teachings.

But there is another lesson in the annals of the church, one without ups and downs. It is the constancy of God's faithfulness through the ages—and it will continue in the ages to come. "But the steadfast love of the Lord is from everlasting to everlasting on those who fear him," the psalmist says.[22] For those who choose to follow and serve God, that is the most important history lesson of all.

Appendix A

Indiana-Michigan Mennonite Conference Congregations
1917–2015

* Dual-conference affiliation

C = Closed

W = Withdrew

T = Transfer from Indiana-Michigan to another Mennonite Church or Mennonite Church USA area conference

D = Congregation was a member of both Indiana-Michigan Mennonite Conference and Central District Conference who dropped its Indiana-Michigan membership

Congregation	Location	Start	End	
Agape Fellowship	Kendallville, Indiana	1953	1989	W
Previous name: Elmwood Mennonite Church				
*Ann Arbor Mennonite Church	Ann Arbor, Michigan	1964		
*Assembly Mennonite Church	Goshen, Indiana	1974		
Barker Street Mennonite Church	Mottville, Michigan	1863	1923	W
Previous name: Joseph Yoder Church				
Bean Blossom Mennonite Church	Morgantown, Indiana	1945	2003	W
Belmont Mennonite Church	Elkhart, Indiana	1929		
Belmont Neighborhood Fellowship	Elkhart, Indiana	1991		
Benton Mennonite Church	Benton, Indiana	1944		
Berea Mennonite Church	Montgomery, Indiana	1921	2004	W
Berkey Avenue Mennonite Fellowship	Goshen, Indiana	1979		
Previous name: West Goshen Fellowship				
Bethany Mennonite Church	Imlay City, Michigan	1918	1999	C
Bethel Mennonite Church	Ashley, Michigan	1920		
Bethel Mennonite Church	Odon, Indiana	1964	2002	W

Big Branch Mennonite Church	Bareville, Kentucky	1956	1961	C
Bonneyville Mennonite Church	Bristol, Indiana	1962		
Bowne Mennonite Church	Clarksville, Michigan	1866	1974	W
Burr Oak Mennonite Church	Rensselaer, Indiana	1918		
Cady Mennonite Church	Midland, Michigan	1945	1967	C
Caledonia Mennonite Church	Kent County, Michigan	1864	1910	C
California Mennonite Church	Montgomery, Michigan	1956	1975	C
Campus Mennonite Church	Mount Pleasant, Michigan	1967	1968	C
Caney Creek Mennonite Church	Lost Creek, Kentucky	1952	1968	W
Carroll Community Worship Center	Anderson / Fort Wayne, IN	1933		
Previous name: Anderson Mennonite Church				
Carson City Fellowship	Carson City, Michigan	1992	1997	C
Cedar Grove Mennonite Church	Manistique, Michigan	1951		
Central Mennonite Church	Fort Wayne, Indiana	1969	2002	W
Christian Fellowship Center	Sturgis, Michigan	1987	2008	W
Church Without Walls	Elkhart, Indiana	1991		
Clarion Mennonite Church	Boyne Falls, Michigan	1957	1967	C
Clinton Brick Mennonite Church	Goshen, Indiana	1854	2014	W
Clinton Frame Mennonite Church	Goshen, Indiana	1854	2014	W
Cold Springs Mennonite Church	Mancelona, Michigan	1948	2010	W
College Mennonite Church	Goshen, Indiana	1903		
Previous name: Goshen College Mennonite Church				
Community Bible Chapel	Giles, Wisconsin	1976	1980	C
Previous name: Ironwood Mennonite Church				
Community Christian Fellowship	Detroit, Michigan	1991		
Community Mennonite Church	South Bend, Indiana	1958	1991	C
Crumstown Mennonite Church	North Liberty, Indiana	1933	1986	C
East End Covenant Church	Goshen, Indiana	1985	1987	C
East Goshen Mennonite Church	Goshen, Indiana	1947		
Emma Mennonite Church	Topeka, Indiana	1903		
English Lake Mennonite Church	North Judson, Indiana	1949	1993	W
Fairhaven Mennonite Church	Fort Wayne, Indiana	1954		
Fairview Mennonite Church	Fairview, Michigan	1904	2002	W
*Faith Mennonite Church	Goshen, Indiana	1997	2015	D
Family Worship Center at the Lighthouse	Goshen, Indiana	1950		
Previous names: Gospel Lighthouse, Twenty-Seventh Street Chapel				
Fellowship of Hope	Elkhart, Indiana	1970		

First Mennonite Church	Fort Wayne, Indiana	1903		
First Mennonite Church *Previous name: Middlebury Mennonite Church*	Middlebury, Indiana	1903		
First Mennonite Church *(New York Mennonite Conference)*	New Bremen, New York	1941#	1973	T
First Mennonite Church	Indianapolis, Indiana	1954		
First Mennonite Church	Montgomery, Indiana	1980	1997	W
Fish Lake Mennonite Church	Walkerton, Indiana	1950	1995	W
Forks Mennonite Church	Middlebury, Indiana	1857		
Gay Mennonite Church	Gay, Michigan	1951	1959	C
Germfask Mennonite *Previous name: Fernland Mennonite Church*	Germfask, Michigan	1937	2015	W
Good News Community Chapel *Previous name: Calvary Mennonite Church*	Pinckney, Michigan	1941		
Good Samaritan Mennonite Church	Cumberland, Kentucky	1991	2010	C
Grace Chapel *Alternate name: East Side Mennonite Church*	Saginaw, Michigan	1951		
Grand Marais Mennonite Church	Grand Marais, Michigan	1948		
Harlan Mennonite Church	Harlan, Kentucky	1977##	2011	C
Harmony Mennonite Church *Previous name: Harmony Christian Fellowship*	Nashville, Tennessee	1991	2013	C
Herrick Mennonite Church	Clare, Michigan	1952	1977	C
Hilltop Mennonite Fellowship *Previous name: Petoskey Mennonite Church*	Petoskey, Michigan	1950	2015	C
Holdeman Mennonite Church	Wakarusa, Indiana	1851		
Hopewell Mennonite Church	Kouts, Indiana	1918		
Howard-Miami Mennonite	Church Kokomo, Indiana	1854		
Hudson Lake Mennonite Church	New Carlisle, Indiana	1950		
Iglesia Evangelica Emanuel *Previous name: Iglesia Anabautista Emanuel*	South Bend, Indiana	1986	2001	C
Iglesia Menonita del Buen Pastor	New Paris / Goshen, Indiana	1970	2015	W
Iglesia Menonita Emanuel	Marion, Indiana	1980	1989	C
Jefferson Avenue Mennonite Church	Kalamazoo, Michigan	1986	1987	C

First Mennonite Church broke from a Conservative Mennonite Conference congregation in 1941 and joined Indiana-Michigan in 1959

Harlan Mennonite Church was under the auspices of the Mennonite Church General Board before it joined Indiana-Michigan in 1994

Kalamazoo Mennonite Church	Kalamazoo, Michigan	1960	1979	C
Kalamazoo Mennonite Fellowship	Kalamazoo, Michigan	2010		
Kern Road Mennonite Church *Previous name: Kern Road Chapel*	South Bend, Indiana	1961		
*Lafayette Mennonite Fellowship	Lafayette, Indiana	1983	2009	C
Lake Bethel Mennonite Church	LaGrange, Indiana	1983		
Leo Mennonite Church	Leo, Indiana	1861	1990	C
Liberty Christian Fellowship *Previous name: Liberty Mennonite Church*	Somerset Center, Michigan	1946		
*LifeSpring Community Church *Previous name: Communion Fellowship*	Goshen, Indiana	1984	1995	W
Locust Grove Mennonite Church	Burr Oak, Michigan	1941		
Locust Grove Mennonite Church	Elkhart, Indiana	1943	1993	C
Madison Union Chapel	Wakarusa, Indiana	1906	1936	C
Maple Grove Mennonite Church	Topeka, Indiana	1854	1997	W
Maple Grove Mennonite Church	Gulliver, Michigan	1942	2004	W
Maple River Mennonite Church *Previous name: Dettwiler Church*	Brutus, Michigan	1879		
Maranatha Mennonite Church	Nappanee, Indiana	1981	2003	W
Marion Mennonite Church	Shipshewana, Indiana	1944		
Mennonite Fellowship of Bloomington	Bloomington, Indiana	1993		
Menominee River Fellowship	Menominee, Michigan	1991	2005	C
Michigan Avenue Mennonite Church *Previous name: Pigeon Mennonite Church*	Pigeon, Michigan	1894		
*MSU Fellowship East	Lansing, Michigan	1972		
Milan Center Mennonite Church	New Haven, Indiana	1962	1972	C
Milford Chapel	Milford, Indiana	1974	1981	W
Moorepark Mennonite Church	Moorepark, Michigan	1947	2000	W
*Morning Star Mennonite Church	Muncie, Indiana	1991		
Mount Pleasant Mennonite Church	Martinsville, Indiana	1951	1983	C
Naubinway Christian Fellowship *Previous name: Naubinway Mennonite Church*	Naubinway, Michigan	1943	2015	W
New Bethel Mennonite Church	Ossian, Indiana	1949	1967	C
New Foundation United in Christ Mennonite Fellowship *Previous name: House of Power*	Elkhart, Indiana	1994		

New Hope Community Church *Previous name: Midland Mennonite Church*	Midland, Michigan	1913		
New Life Fellowship *Previous name: Osceola Mennonite Church*	Osceola, Indiana	1951	1987	W
New Wine Chapel *Previous names: Bremen Mennonite Church, Bourbon Chapel*	Bremen, Indiana	1962	1996	W
Ninth Street Community Church *Previous name: Saginaw Mennonite Church*	Saginaw, Michigan	1950		
North Goshen Mennonite Church	Goshen, Indiana	1936		
North Leo Mennonite Church	Leo, Indiana	1966		
North Main Street Mennonite Church	Nappanee, Indiana	1867		
North Park Mennonite Church	Grand Rapids, Michigan	1969	1989	C
Noxubee Mennonite Church	Noxubee, Mississippi	1967	1968	C
Oak Terrace Mennonite Church *(Southeast Mennonite Conference)*	Blountstown, Florida	1953	1978	T
Olive Mennonite Church	Elkhart, Indiana	1850		
Open Door Fellowship	Kouts, Indiana	1995	1997	W
*Paoli Mennonite Fellowship	Paoli, Indiana	1974		
Parkview Mennonite Church *Previous name: Bon Air Mennonite Church*	Kokomo, Indiana	1947		
Peace Community Church *Previous name: Detroit Mennonite Fellowship*	Detroit, Michigan	1980	1997	C
Pine Grove Mennonite Church *Previous name: Heath Street Mennonite Church*	Battle Creek, Michigan	1952		
Plato Mennonite Church	Lagrange, Indiana	1949	2003	C
Pleasant Valley Mennonite Church	DeKalb County, Indiana	1867	1917	C
Pleasantview *Previous name: Union Congregation*	Brethren, Michigan	1906	1975	C
Pleasant View Mennonite Church *(South Central Mennonite Conference)*	Goshen, Indiana	1936	2015	T
Prairie Street Mennonite Church *Previous name: Elkhart Mennonite Church*	Elkhart, Indiana	1871		
Praise Chapel	Goshen, Indiana	2003	2006	C
Providence Mennonite Church	Washington, Indiana	1953	2008	W
Restoration Fellowship	South Bend, Indiana	1992	2003	C
Rexton Mennonite Church	Rexton, Michigan	1948	2015	W
Rich Valley Mennonite Church	Kokomo, Indiana	1963	1972	W
Ridgeview Mennonite Church *Previous name: Morgantown Mennonite Church*	Morgantown, Kentucky	1952	2006	C

River of Life Mennonite Church	Warsaw, Indiana	1990	2013	C

Previous names: Warsaw Mennonite Church, North Pointe Fellowship

Salem Mennonite Church	New Paris, Indiana	1889	1981	W
Santa Fe Mennonite Church	Peru, Indiana	1960	1989	C
Seney Mennonite Church	Seney, Michigan	1946	1967	W
Shalom Mennonite Church	Indianapolis, Indiana	1994		
*Shalom Community	Ann Arbor, Michigan	1978	2003	D

Previous name: Ann Arbor Mennonite Fellowship

Shore Mennonite Church	Shipshewana, Indiana	1865	2016	W
Smith School Mennonite Church	Jetson, Kentucky	1959	1968	C
Soo Hill Mennonite Church	Escanaba, Michigan	1952	2008	C
South Colon Mennonite Church	Colon, Michigan	1954	2000	W
*Southside Fellowship	Elkhart, Indiana	1966	2005	D
Stutsmanville Chapel	Harbor Spring, Michigan	1957	2015	W

Previous name: Stutsmanville Mennonite Church

Sunnyside Mennonite Church	Montmorency County, Michigan	1907	1919	C
Sunnyside Mennonite Church	Elkhart, Indiana	1947		
Talcum Mennonite Church	Talcum, Kentucky	1952		
Templo Menonita de La Hermosa	Kalamazoo, Michigan	1984	1989	C
Toto Mennonite Gospel Mission	Toto, Indiana	1948	1981	W
Tri-Lakes Mennonite Church	Mottville, Michigan / Bristol, Indiana	1960	1998	W
True Vine Tabernacle	Elkhart, Indiana	1949		

Previous name: Roselawn Mennonite Church

Valparaiso Mennonite Church	Valparaiso, Indiana	1966		
Walnut Hill Mennonite Church	Goshen, Indiana	1956		

Previous name: Walnut Hill Chapel

Wasepi Mennonite Church	Centreville, Michigan	1966		

Previous name: Oak Grove Mennonite Church

Waterford Mennonite Church	Goshen, Indiana	1959		
Wawasee Lakeside Chapel	Syracuse, Indiana	1947		
Wayside Mennonite Church	Brimley, Michigan	1948	2004	C
Wellington Mennonite Church	Lachine, Michigan	1955	1975	C
West Odessa Mennonite Church	Lake Odessa, Michigan	1982	1999	C
White Cloud Mennonite Church	White Cloud, Michigan	1899	1975	W
Wildwood Mennonite Church	Engadine, Michigan	1939		
Yellow Creek Mennonite Church	Goshen, Indiana	1845		
Zion Mennonite Church	Vestaberg, Michigan	1913	1971	C

Appendix B

Indiana-Michigan Mennonite Conference Moderators
1917–2015

1917	D. D. Miller	1964–76	Russell Krabill
1918–19	J. K. Bixler	1976–79	John H. Mosemann
1919–20	D. A. Yoder	1979–85	Arnold C. Roth
1920–21	D. D. Miller	1985–91	Del Glick
1921–22	J. K. Bixler	1991–92	Rachel S. Fisher
1922–24	D. A. Yoder	1992–94	John C. Murray
1925–29	D. D. Miller	1994–96	Don Delagrange
1929–30	J. K. Bixler	1996–98	Marian Hostetler
1930–39	O. S. Hostetler	1998–2000	James Waltner
1940–44	D. A. Yoder	2000–2002	Dale Shenk
1944–47	Paul Mininger	2002–4	Randy Detweiler
1947–49	R. F. Yoder	2004–6	David Sutter
1949–51	Anson G. Horner	2006–8	Mary Swartley
1951–52	T. E. Schrock	2008–11	Brent Eash
1952–53	Paul M. Miller	2001–13	Wes Bontreger
1952–64	John C. Wenger	2013–15	Jane Stoltzfus Buller

Notes

Introduction: Crossroads of Faithfulness

1. "Indianapolis Union Railroad Station," National Park Service, accessed March 15, 2013, http://www.nps.gov/nr/travel/indianapolis/unionstation.htm.
2. "History of the Soo Locks," Sault Ste. Marie Convention and Visitors Bureau, accessed March 15, 2013, http://www.saultstemarie.com/soo-locks-46/.
3. Mennonite Church USA is the largest Mennonite denomination in the United States, created in 2002 by the merger of the Mennonite Church—Indiana-Michigan's original denomination—and the General Conference Mennonite Church. See chap. 9.
4. The General Conference Mennonite Church was founded in 1860, thirty-eight years before the birth of the Mennonite Church. It originally consisted of recent European immigrants who settled in Iowa, Illinois, and Ohio and who never affiliated with the Old Mennonites, plus a splinter group that used to be part of Franconia Mennonite Conference in eastern Pennsylvania.
5. Both my maternal grandparents and my paternal grandfather were Swiss-Volhynian. They were descendants of Amish Mennonites from the Alsace who, instead of going west to the New World in search of religious security and opportunity, went east, eventually settling in Volhynia (present-day northwestern Ukraine and southeastern Poland) starting in the late eighteenth century. The Swiss-Volhynians moved to the United States as part of the great Russian Mennonite and Hutterite migrations of the mid-1870s, initially settling at what is now Freeman, South Dakota, and Moundridge, Kansas.
6. Indiana-Michigan Mennonite Conference, *Minutes of the Indiana-Michigan Mennonite Conference, 1864–1929*, comp. Ira S. Johns, J. S. Hartzler, and Amos O. Hostetler (Scottdale, PA: Mennonite Publishing House, [1929?]), 8–9. As the title indicates, conference minutes for 1864–1929 are combined in one bound volume. Those after 1929 are located in several places and formats: as annually issued pamphlets and, later, report books, found in the Mennonite Church USA Archives–Goshen and the Mennonite Historical Library (and presumably elsewhere) and as part of the *Gospel Evangel*. Hereafter, minutes for the 1930 meeting and later are cited by title and, when not included in the title itself, the year.
7. Genesis 9:21; Matthew 26:69-75; Mark 14:66-72; Luke 22:54-60; John 18:15-18, 25-27.
8. See Mennonite Church USA and Mennonite Church Canada, *A Shared Understanding of Church Leadership: Polity Manual for Mennonite Church*

Canada and Mennonite Church USA [working document] (Harrisonburg, VA: MennoMedia, 2014).

9. J. Winfield Fretz and Harold S. Bender, "Mutual Aid," *Mennonite Encyclopedia*, vol. 3 (Scottdale, PA: Mennonite Publishing House, 1957).

Chapter 1: Beginnings, Both Anabaptist and American

1. Amish Heritage Committee, *Amish and Mennonites in Eastern Elkhart and LaGrange Counties, 1841–1991* (Goshen, IN: privately published, 1992), xiii.
2. John E. Borntreger, *A History of the First Settlers of the Amish Mennonites and the Establishment of Their First Congregation in the State of Indiana: Along with a Short Account of the Division Which Took Place in This Church* (Topeka, IN: privately published, 1988), 4–5.
3. Amish Heritage Committee, *Amish and Mennonites*, 8. The cabins might have been built by hunters or trappers who had left the area.
4. J. C. Wenger, *Anniversary Celebration Clinton Frame Mennonite Church, 1863–1988* (Goshen, IN: privately published, 1988), 6.
5. The Easter 1842 service also marks the beginning of the local Old Order Amish worshiping community.
6. The classic general historical survey of the faith is Cornelius J. Dyck, ed., *An Introduction to Mennonite History: A Popular History of the Anabaptists and the Mennonites*, 3rd ed. (Scottdale, PA: Herald Press, 1993).
7. 1 Corinthians 10:21: "You cannot drink the cup of the Lord and the cup of demons. You cannot partake of the table of the Lord and the table of demons"; Romans 12:2: "Do not be conformed to this world, but be transformed by the renewing of your minds, so that you may discern what is the will of God—what is good and acceptable and perfect."
8. J. C. Wenger, "Schleitheim Confession," *Mennonite Encyclopedia*, vol. 4 (Scottdale, PA: Mennonite Publishing House, 1959).
9. See Steven M. Nolt, *A History of the Amish*, 2nd ed. (Intercourse, PA: Good Books, 2003), chap. 2; and Leroy Beachy, *Unser Leit: The Story of the Amish*, vol. 1 (Millersburg, OH: Goodly Heritage Books, 2011), chap. 2.
10. The Anabaptists of Switzerland, South Germany, and the Alsace would not adopt the Mennonite name until much later, choosing instead to call themselves Swiss Brethren. Nevertheless, I have chosen to call them Mennonites here for convenience.
11. H. S. K. Bartholomew, *Stories and Sketches of Elkhart County* (Nappanee, IN: privately published, c. 1936), 170. The exact date of the origin of the Yellow Creek Mennonite Church and community is unknown. Accounts vary widely on the identities and dates of the area's first Mennonite settlers, ranging from 1839 to 1843.
12. J. C. Wenger, "Jacob Wisler and the Old Order Mennonite Schism of 1872 in Elkhart County, Indiana," pt. 1, *Mennonite Quarterly Review* (hereafter abbreviated *MQR*) 33, no. 2 (April 1959): 108.
13. J. C. Wenger, *The Yellow Creek Mennonites: The Original Mennonite Congregations of Western Elkhart County* (Goshen, IN: privately published, 1985), 20.

14. Indiana-Michigan Mennonite Conference, *Minutes of the Conference, 1864–1929*, 7.

15. Not only were the Elkhart-LaGrange Amish Mennonites and Yellow Creek Mennonites not the first Anabaptists in Indiana; they were not the first in northern Indiana. A Dunkard (Brethren) minister built a home at what is now Goshen in 1829, according to H. S. K. Bartholomew in *Pioneer History of Elkhart County* (Goshen, IN: privately published, 1930).

16. Eva F. Sprunger, *The First Hundred Years: A History of the Mennonite Church in Adams County, Indiana, 1838–1938* (Berne, IN: privately published, 1938), 4.

17. For more on Mennonite and Amish Mennonite westward migrations, see Theron F. Schlabach, *Peace, Faith, Nation: Mennonites and Amish in Nineteenth Century America*, Mennonite Experience in America, vol. 2 (Scottdale, PA: Herald Press, 1988), chaps. 1–2. For the broader American context, see John D. Unruh Jr., *The Plains Across: The Overland Emigrants and the Trans-Mississippi West, 1840–60* (Urbana, IL: University of Illinois Press, 1979).

18. Mary Beth Norton et al., *A People and a Nation: A History of the United States*, 2nd ed., vol. 1, *To 1877* (Boston: Houghton Mifflin, 1986), 346.

19. Ivan J. Miller, "Somerset County," *Mennonite Encyclopedia*, vol. 4.; Amish Heritage Committee, *Amish and Mennonites*, 6.

20. Lynn Bender, "The Yellow Creek Mennonite Settlers: A Study of Land and Family," *MQR* 46, no. 1 (January 1972): 72.

21. James H. Madison, *The Indiana Way: A State History* (Bloomington: Indiana University Press and Indianapolis: Indiana Historical Society, 1986), 37–39.

22. Howard Zinn, *A People's History of the United States, 1492–Present* (New York: HarperPerennial, 1995), 124.

23. No documentation has been discovered that adequately illuminates Mennonite and Amish Mennonite settlers' perspectives on inhabiting U.S. lands that had belonged to Native Americans who had been forcibly relocated by whites. We simply do not know whether they agreed with the prevailing understanding of Native Americans as uncivilized, violent, and obstacles to progress. Because of the absence of correspondence, diaries, and other materials on the matter, it might be safely extrapolated that the Mennonites and Amish Mennonites probably didn't give it much if any thought. Holly Blosser Yoder notes that in Iowa, several generations after the initial white settlers used phrases such as "empty lands" and "sparsely populated plains" to describe what had been Native American territories. *The Same Spirit: History of Iowa-Nebraska Mennonites* (Freeman, SD: privately published, 2003), 10. Earlier, Mennonites in colonial Pennsylvania demonstrated a desire to peaceably live with their Native American neighbors; see Richard K. MacMaster, *Land, Piety, Peoplehood: The Establishment of Mennonite Communities in America, 1683–1790*, Mennonite Experience in America, vol. 1 (Scottdale, PA: Herald Press, 1985), 239–42.

24. R. David Edmunds, *The Potawatomis: Keepers of the Fire* (Norman: University of Oklahoma Press, 1978), 266–68.

25. Howard-Miami Mennonite Church, *History of Howard-Miami Mennonite Church* (Greentown, IN: privately published, 1999), 7.

26. Indiana-Michigan Mennonite Conference, *Minutes of the Conference, 1864–1929*, 7.

27. John F. Funk diary, 1867, John F. Funk collection (HM 1-1), box 2, Mennonite Church USA Archives–Goshen, Goshen, IN (hereafter MCUSAA–Goshen).

28. Wanda Kauffman Hoffman, *Brick by Brick: The Story of Clinton Brick Mennonite Church, 1854–2004* (Goshen, IN: privately published, 2004), 10.

29. The reasons for the move by the Balk group move are unclear. Some historians have argued that it was to avoid compulsory military service. But Dutch Mennonite historian Carl F. Brusewitz writes, "There is no indication anywhere of the source from which these brethren got the idea of going to the United States." "The Mennonites of Balk, Friesland," *MQR* 30, no. 1 (January 1956): 27.

30. Marie Yoder, "The Balk Dutch Settlement Near Goshen, Indiana, 1853–1889," *MQR* 30, no. 1 (January 1956): 34.

31. Grietja Jacobs Symensma diary, 16 (English translation), Smid Family collection (HM 1-86), box 7, folder 4, MCUSAA–Goshen. *Doopsgezinde* is the Dutch term for Mennonites, meaning "baptism minded."

32. The earliest reference to such meetings is 1855, found in Greitja Jacobs Symenmsa's diary. Secondary sources have cited earlier years, but original documentation has not been found to verify those claims. Symensma's diary also notes that the 1857 meeting was the "10th baptism service, and the 11th breadbreaking [communion]." If those were annual occurrences, then the Yellow Creek Mennonites had been gathering since 1847. The earliest recorded conference minutes are from the 1864 meeting.

33. Indiana-Michigan Mennonite Conference, *Minutes of the Conference, 1864–1929*, 8–9.

34. Symensma diary, 20.

35. See Indiana-Michigan Mennonite Conference, *Minutes of the Conference, 1864–1929*, 8, 10; and John F. Funk, "My Journey to Ohio—Conference," *Herald of Truth*, June 1867, 89.

36. Indiana-Michigan Mennonite Conference, *Minutes of the Conference, 1864–1929*, 14, 42.

37. Ibid., 9.

38. See Willis Frederick Dunbar, *Michigan: A History of the Wolverine State* (Grand Rapids, MI: Wm. B. Eerdmans, 1965).

39. David Sherk, "A Letter from Canada," *Herald of Truth*, June 1864, 33.

40. Paton Yoder, *Tradition and Transition: Amish Mennonites and Old Order Amish, 1800–1900* (Scottdale, PA: Herald Press, 1991), 44.

41. Borntreger, *History of the First Settlers*, 8.

42. Now North Danvers Mennonite Church of Danvers, Illinois.

43. Genevieve Yoder Friesen, "The History of Maple Grove Mennonite Church, Topeka, Indiana" (research paper, Goshen College, 1935), 1.

44. J. C. Wenger, *The Mennonites in Indiana and Michigan* (Scottdale, PA: Herald Press, 1961), 161.

45. Borntreger, *History of the First Settlers*, 12.

46. The historical record has conferred upon Isaac and Jonathan different spellings of their last names, even though they were father and son. Both initially signed their names as Smoker, although the *Herald of Truth* and its German-language counterpart, *Herold der Wahrheit*, usually spelled it Schmucker.

According to family tradition, when Jonathan was ordained to the ministry, he changed the spelling of his last name to Smucker because a preacher should not be a "smoker." Paton Yoder and Silas J. Smucker, *Jonathan P. Smucker: Amish Mennonite Bishop* (Goshen, IN: privately published, 1990), 19.

47. Herbert L. Osborne, "Howard and Miami Counties Mennonites and Amish" (research paper, Goshen College, 1948), 13–14.

48. William C. Ringenberg, "Development and Division in the Mennonite Community in Allen County, Indiana," *MQR* 50, no. 2 (April 1976): 114–31.

49. The Apostolic Christian Church was born in Switzerland in the 1830s, and its first U.S. congregation was founded in 1852. Its success in attracting converts from among the Amish Mennonites resulted in the group being nicknamed the New Amish. See Tillman R. Smith, "Apostolic Christian Church of America," *Mennonite Encyclopedia*, vol. 1 (Scottdale, PA: Mennonite Publishing House, 1955).

50. The Egly group, initially known as the Egli Amish, would adopt the name Defenseless Mennonite Church and eventually Evangelical Mennonite Church. The denomination changed its name to the Fellowship of Evangelical Churches in 2003.

51. Paton Yoder and Steven R. Estes, *Proceedings of the Amish Ministers' Meetings, 1862–1878* (Goshen, IN: Mennonite Historical Society, 1999), 401–5.

52. Ibid., 3–21.

53. Ibid., 48.

54. Nolt, *History of the Amish*, 170.

55. Yoder and Estes, *Proceedings*, 58–60.

56. Paton Yoder, *Tradition and Transition*, 201.

57. Nolt, *History of the Amish*, 203.

58. Yoder and Estes, *Proceedings*, 231, n. 6.

59. Progressives from Illinois to the Pacific coast would organize the Western Amish Mennonite Conference in 1890. Three years later the Amish Mennonite Conference of Ohio would be formed and eventually renamed the Eastern Amish Mennonite Conference as it grew to include congregations in Pennsylvania, Maryland, and Virginia. The Eastern and Western Amish Mennonite conferences would discontinue in the 1920s when they were incorporated into the Mennonite Church. In addition to the Indiana, Eastern, and Western conferences, another group was the Conservative Amish Mennonite Conference, organized in 1910. It was less progressive than the other three conferences but more open to change than the Old Order Amish. It was renamed the Conservative Mennonite Conference in 1957. See Nathan E. Yoder, *In the Work of the Lord: A History of the Conservative Mennonite Conference* (Harrisonburg, VA: Herald Press, 2014). Indiana bishops Daniel J. Johns and Jonathan Smucker were the first moderator and assistant moderator, respectively, of the Ohio conference; see Eastern Amish Mennonite Conference, *Report of the Eastern Amish Mennonite Conference from the Time of Its Organization to the Year 1911* (Sugarcreek, OH: privately published, 1911), x.

60. Indiana-Michigan Mennonite Conference, *Minutes of the Conference, 1864–1929*, 140.

61. Paton Yoder, *Tradition and Transition*, 214.

62. Paton Yoder, "Joseph Yoder: Amish Mennonite Bishop" (paper presented to Michiana Anabaptist Historians, April 1, 2000), 6.

63. Quoted in J. C. Wenger, *Mennonites in Indiana and Michigan*, 200.

64. Ibid.

65. Grant Stoltzfus, *Mennonites of the Ohio and Eastern Conference from the Colonial Period in Pennsylvania to 1968* (Scottdale, PA: Herald Press, 1969), 111; Indiana-Michigan Mennonite Conference, *Minutes of the Conference, 1864–1929*, 175. The West Liberty congregation apparently died out before it could join the Eastern Amish Mennonite Conference.

66. Indiana-Michigan Mennonite Conference, *Minutes, 1864–1929*, 146.

67. Ibid., 149.

68. Hope Kauffman Lind, *Apart and Together: Mennonites in Oregon and Neighboring States, 1876–1976* (Scottdale, PA: Herald Press, 1990), 41–44. Several Amish Mennonite congregations were started in the region in the 1880s, but it is unclear which one or ones affiliated with Indiana-Michigan and for how long.

69. Indiana-Michigan Mennonite Conference, *Minutes of the Conference, 1864–1929*, 159; Eastern Amish Mennonite Conference, *Report of the Conference*, 15; Silas Hertzler, "Long Green Mennonite Church," *Mennonite Encyclopedia*, vol. 3 (Scottdale, PA: Mennonite Publishing Company, 1957).

70. John Ringenberg, "Letter from Lock, Ind.," *Herald of Truth*, July 1864, 43. *Amonite* was another name for Amish.

71. Paton Yoder, *Tradition and Transition*, 240.

72. Yoder and Smucker, *Johnathan P. Smucker*, 7.

73. Indiana-Michigan Mennonite Conference, *Minutes of the Conference, 1864–1929*, 38–39.

74. J. S. Coffman diary, 1889, J. S. Coffman collection (HM 1-19), box 1, MCUSAA–Goshen.

75. J. D. Troyer, "Correspondence," *Herald of Truth*, March 1, 1886, 74.

76. Indiana-Michigan Mennonite Conference, *Minutes, 1864–1929*, 25.

77. Ibid., 63.

78. For more on Amish Mennonite polity, see Paton Yoder, *Tradition and Transition*, especially chaps. 3 and 11.

79. Indiana-Michigan Mennonite Conference, *Minutes of the Conference, 1864–1929*, 147.

80. Ibid., 157.

81. Ibid., 171.

82. Ibid., 140.

83. Ibid., 179.

84. Ibid., 141–42.

85. "Do not be yoked together with unbelievers. For what do righteousness and wickedness have in common? Or what fellowship can light have with darkness?" This verse, 2 Corinthians 6:14 (NIV), was often cited as a rationale for a strict separation from the world.

86. Indiana-Michigan Mennonite Conference, *Minutes of the Conference, 1864–1929*, 66.

87. Ibid., 185.

88. Ibid., 19.
89. Ibid., 235.
90. C. Norman Kraus, "American Mennonites and the Bible," *MQR* 41, no. 4 (October 1967): 313–18.
91. Indiana-Michigan Mennonite Conference, *Minutes of the Conference, 1864–1929*, 45.
92. *The Revelation of Barbara Stutzman, Deceased, to All Mankind* (n.p., n.d.).
93. Ibid.
94. Ibid.
95. *History of Elkhart County, Indiana, Together with Sketches of Its Cities and Biographies of Representative Citizens* (Chicago, IL: Chas. C. Chapman, 1881), 640.
96. James C. Juhnke, *Vision, Doctrine, War: Mennonite Identity and Organization in America, 1890–1930*, Mennonite Experience in America, vol. 3 (Scottdale, PA: Herald Press, 1989), 21–25.

Chapter 2: The John F. Funk Era

1. "Our New Home," *Herald of Truth*, May 1867, 72.
2. Norton et al., *A People and a Nation*, vol. 1, 326–27.
3. Theron F. Schlabach, "Nineteenth-Century Humility: A Vital Message for Today?" *Mennonite Historical Bulletin*, January 2002, 3; MacMaster, *Land, Piety, Peoplehood*, chap. 8; Schlabach, *Peace, Faith, Nation*, chaps. 4 and 8; Juhnke, *Vision, Doctrine, War*, 71, 107–8.
4. J. C. Wenger, *Mennonites in Indiana and Michigan*, 321.
5. Indiana-Michigan Mennonite Conference, *Minutes of the Conference, 1864–1929*, 14.
6. *An Historical 75th Anniversary Publication* (Elkhart, IN: Indiana Conference of the United Missionary Church, 1958), 10.
7. It is unknown how many Mennonites and Amish Mennonites supported the American Civil War. J. C. Wenger says "a number" of young men from Indiana who were probably not yet church members joined the Union army. *Mennonites in Indiana and Michigan*, 23. There is little indication of Michigan church members' positions or involvements.
8. See James O. Lehman and Steven M. Nolt, *Mennonites, Amish, and the American Civil War* (Baltimore: Johns Hopkins Press, 2007), chap. 5.
9. Madison, *Indiana Way*, 197.
10. See Edwin L. Weaver, *Holdeman Descendants: A Compilation of the Genealogical and Biographical Record of the Descendants of Christian Holdeman, 1788–1846* (Nappanee, IN: E. V. Publishing House, 1937).
11. Symensma diary, 53, Smid Family collection (HM 1-86), box 7, folder 4, MCUSAA–Goshen.
12. Rufus Martin and Thelma Martin, *They Had a Vision: A Guide to Some of the Early Mennonite Pioneers in the Yellow Creek Area, Elkhart County, Indiana* (Goshen, IN: privately published, 1995), n.p.
13. Howard Miami Mennonite Church, *History of Howard-Miami Mennonite Church*, 24.
14. George Funk, "A Visit," *Herald of Truth*, March 1865, 19.

15. John F. Funk, *Warfare: Its Evils, Our Duty* (Markham, IL: privately published, 1863), 1, 14.

16. In 1847, John H. Oberholtzer led a group of progressives, including Abraham Hunsicker, in a split from Franconia Mennonite Conference to create the Eastern Conference of Mennonites. The group eventually became the Eastern District Conference of the General Conference Mennonite Church and then of Mennonite Church USA. By the time Funk attended Freeland Seminary, a faction led by Hunsicker had been expelled from the Eastern Conference because of its liberal beliefs. Freeland was later sold and became Ursinus College in 1869.

17. Joseph Liechty and James O. Lehman, "From Yankee to Nonresistant," *MQR* 59, no. 3 (July 1985): 204.

18. Helen Kolb Gates et al., *Bless the Lord O My Soul: A Biography of John Fretz Funk* (Scottdale, PA: Herald Press, 1964), 48.

19. Gates et al., 43. For more on Moody and the Sunday school movement, see David W. Beddington, *The Dominance of Evangelicalism: The Age of Spurgeon and Moody* (Downers Grove, IL: InterVarsity Press, 2005), chap. 1.

20. Liechty and Lehman, "From Yankee to Nonresistant," 210–12.

21. John F. Funk diary, 1862, John F. Funk collection (HM 1-1), box 2, MCUSAA–Goshen.

22. Harold S. Bender, *Two Centuries of American Mennonite Literature: A Bibliography of Mennonitica Americana, 1827–1928* (Goshen, IN: Mennonite Historical Society, 1929), 159–60. John H. Oberholtzer, Franconia Mennonite Conference maverick and General Conference Mennonite Church pioneer, began the *Religioser Botschafter*, the first successful Mennonite periodical, five years after he split from Franconia. Obviously it served a readership that wasn't Old Mennonite. The *Religioser Botschafter* went through a number of incarnations as a GCMC periodical until 2008 when, as *Der Bote*, it ceased operation.

23. Daniel Brenneman to John F. Funk, August 6, 1863, John F. Funk collection (HM 1-1), box 6, folder 2, MCUSAA–Goshen.

24. John McMullen captioned photograph in Constance Sykes collection (HM 4-111), box 1, folder 11, MCUSAA–Goshen.

25. Note in J. C. Wenger collection (HM 1-337), box 37, folder 135, MCUSAA–Goshen.

26. "To the Readers of the Herald," *Herald of Truth*, November 1865, 95.

27. John M. Brenneman to John F. Funk, June 17, 1863, John F. Funk collection (HM 1-1-3), box 6, folder 3, MCUSAA–Goshen.

28. John M. Brenneman to John F. Funk, November 25, 1863, John F. Funk collection (HM 1-1-3), box 6, folder 3, MCUSAA–Goshen.

29. "Sixty Years in the Mennonite Church," 5, John F. Funk collection (HM 1-1-3), box 49, folder 3, MCUSAA–Goshen.

30. A. S. Overholt to Funk, April 12, 1866, John F. Funk collection (HM 1-1-3), box 6a, folder 1, MCUSAA–Goshen.

31. "Book Lists, Autobiography, Convent" notebook, John F. Funk collection (HM 1-1-24), box 138, folder 3, MCUSAA–Goshen.

32. See Richard S. Simons and Francis H. Parker, *Railroads of Indiana* (Bloomington: Indiana University Press, 1997); Dave McLellan and Bill Warrick, *The Lake Shore and Michigan Southern Railway* (Polo, IL: Transportation Trails, 1989).

33. John M. Brenneman to John F. Funk, March 18, 1867, John F. Funk collection (HM 1-1-3), box 6a, folder 3, MCUSAA–Goshen.

34. Ibid.

35. J. C. Wenger, "Jacob Wisler and the Schism of 1872," pt. 1, 116–17.

36. Jesus Christ's words in Matthew 18:15-17 have traditionally been upheld as biblical instructions for addressing disputes among church members: "If another member of the church sins against you, go and point out the fault when the two of you are alone. If the member listens to you, you have regained that one. But if you are not listened to, take one or two others along with you, so that every word may be confirmed by the evidence of two or three witnesses. If the member refuses to listen to them, tell it to the church; and if the offender refuses to listen to even the church, let such a one be to you as a Gentile and a tax collector."

37. "A synopsis of testimonies presented before Conference," John F. Funk collection (HM 1-1-6), box 63, folder 5, MCUSAA–Goshen.

38. J. C. Wenger, "Jacob Wisler and the Schism of 1872," pt. 1, 118.

39. Symensma diary, 65.

40. "Dear Brethren" letter, July 20, 1880, David Sherk Regarding Wisler Schism collection (HM 1-84 SC), MCUSAA–Goshen.

41. Amos B. Hoover, *The Jonas Martin Era* (Denver, PA: privately published, 1982), 622.

42. Common practice at the time was for a congregation to meet every other week. It continues to be the practice of the Old Order groups.

43. John M. Brenneman to Samuel Coffman, February 8, 1870, J. S. Coffman collection (HM 1-19), box 9, folder 10, MCUSAA–Goshen.

44. Symensma diary, 70.

45. Indiana-Michigan Mennonite Conference, *Minutes of the Conference, 1864–1929*, 14.

46. See Philipp Gollner, "Against the Warlike Churches: The Mennonite Sunday School Conflict in Civil War America" (master's thesis, University of Chicago, 2010).

47. J. C. Wenger, "Jacob Wisler and the Schism of 1872," pt. 1, 128.

48. Hoover, *The Jonas Martin Era*, 944.

49. J. C. Wenger, "Jacob Wisler and the Schism of 1872," pt. 2, *MQR* 33, no. 3 (July 1959): 219.

50. J. C. Wenger, *Mennonites in Indiana and Michigan*, 142.

51. Stephen Scott, *An Introduction to Old Order and Conservative Mennonite Groups* (Intercourse, PA: Good Books, 1996), 17–18.

52. Gates et al., *Bless the Lord O My Soul*, 49.

53. Gollner, "Against the Warlike Churches."

54. "Early Life" notebook, John F. Funk collection (HM 1-1-3), box 48, folder 4, MCUSAA–Goshen.

55. "Daniel Brenneman Autobiography," n.d., C. Henry Smith collection (MS 1), box 23, folder 17, Bluffton University Archives and Special Collections, Bluffton, OH.
56. Ibid.
57. John F. Funk diary, 1874, John F. Funk collection (HM 1-1), box 2, MCUSAA–Goshen.
58. John M. Brenneman to John F. Funk, February 21, 1874, John F. Funk collection (HM 1-1-2), box 7, folder 3, MCUSAA–Goshen.
59. Wayne Brenneman, "Daniel Brenneman: The Birth of a Church," *Reflections*, Summer 1993, 29.
60. "Research Source," *Mennonite Historical Bulletin*, July 1947, 3. The Mennonite Brethren in Christ changed its name to the United Missionary Church in 1947. In 1969, it merged with the Missionary Church Association, an offshoot of the Egli Amish (Evangelical Mennonite Church), to create the Missionary Church. Eby and Brenneman's Reforming Mennonite Society should not be confused with the Reformed Mennonite Church, a conservative group that split from Lancaster Mennonite Conference in 1812 and is still in existence.
61. Timothy Brenneman, "Reminiscences of J. F. Funk." *Mennonite Historical Bulletin*, July 1948, 2.
62. "Daniel Brenneman Autobiography."
63. John A. Hostetler, *God Uses Ink: The Heritage and Mission of the Mennonite Publishing House after Fifty Years* (Scottdale, PA: Herald Press, 1958), 220–28.
64. John S. Umble, "John S. Coffman as an Evangelist," *MQR* 23, no. 3 (July 1949): 139.
65. J. S. Coffman diary, 1880, J. S. Coffman collection (HM 1-19), box 1, MCUSAA–Goshen.
66. J. S. Coffman diary, 1881, J. S. Coffman collection (HM 1-19), box 1, MCUSAA–Goshen.
67. Albert N. Keim, *Harold S. Bender, 1897–1962* (Scottdale, PA: Herald Press, 1998), 88.
68. The Hutterites were another Anabaptist group, founded in eastern Europe in the 1520s. The name was taken from their early leader Jakob Hutter. The Hutterites, or Hutterian Brethren, are known for their communal life, living and working in self-supporting colonies in the central and western United States and Canada.
69. Dyck, ed., *Introduction to Mennonite History*, 180.
70. "From Germany," *Herald of Truth*, April 1870, 56.
71. "The Mennonites in Russia. A Visit from There," *Herald of Truth*, August 1872, 122.
72. Gates et al., *Bless the Lord O My Soul*, 101.
73. "The Present Number," *Herald of Truth*, February 1873, 25.
74. The Krimmer Mennonite Brethren was formed in 1869, the result of a revival movement among Mennonites living in the Crimea (or *Krim* in German) in southern Russia. The group merged with the Mennonite Brethren in 1960.
75. John F. Funk diary, 1874, John F. Funk collection (HM 1-1), box 2, MCUSAA–Goshen; Charles Rittenhouse, "An Interview with John F. Funk," *Mennonite Historical Bulletin*, October 1984, 4; Harold S. Bender, "Krimmer Mennonite

Brethren," *Mennonite Encyclopedia*, vol. 3 (Scottdale, PA: Mennonite Publishing House, 1957).

76. J. C. Wenger, *Mennonites in Indiana and Michigan*, 147–48. Little more is known about the fate of the Okemos Russian Mennonites. Testimony before the grand jury investigating the 1918 burning of Fairview (Mich.) Mennonite Church (see chap. 4) includes passing reference to a "Russian Mennonite" by the name of Peter "Bushman," perhaps Boschmann, which is a Russian Mennonite name. While it cannot be assumed that he had been part of the Okemos community, about 180 miles south of Fairview, the possibility nevertheless remains.

77. Henry Eyman, "From Kent Co., Michigan," *Herald of Truth*, May 1878, 85.

78. Melvin Gingerich, "Research Notes: Jantz-Jontzen-Johnson-Yontz and Smith," *MQR* 33, no. 4 (October 1959): 347.

79. *The Mennonites in Indiana and Michigan* book notes, J. C. Wenger collection (HM 1-337), box 37, folder 100, MCUSAA–Goshen.

80. The Mennonite Brethren was started in 1860 as a renewal movement among the Mennonites in Russia. Following their immigration to North America starting in the 1870s, most Russian Mennonites affiliated with the General Conference Mennonite Church. But the Mennonite Brethren, Krimmer Mennonite Brethren, and several other smaller, more conservative groups remained separate and distinct after resettling in the United States and Canada.

81. Funk sold *Die Mennonitische Rundschau* and his other periodicals to the new Mennonite Publishing House in 1908 (see chap. 3). It was purchased from Mennonite Publishing House by private Canadian Mennonite Brethren interests in 1945, and in 1960 it became an official publication of the Canadian Conference of Mennonite Brethren Churches. When it was discontinued in 2007, *Die Mennonitische Rundschau* was the oldest Mennonite periodical published continuously under one name.

82. Orlando Harms, *Pioneer Publisher: The Life and Times and J. F. Harms* (Winnipeg, MB: Kindred Press, 1984), 27, 31.

83. "Elkhart Mennonite Church Missionary Collections Book," Prairie Street Mennonite Church collection (III-14-2), box 1, folder 2, MCUSAA–Goshen.

84. "Amish Mennonite Conference," *Herald of Truth*, June 15, 1891, 188.

85. "Foreign Mission Work," *Herald of Truth*, November 15, 1898, 338; IN/MI Conference History Notebook H, J. C. Wenger collection (HM 1-337), box 38a, folder 9, MCUSAA–Goshen. The Old Mennonites were not the only ones responding to the disaster in India. It also prompted the General Conference Mennonite Church and the Mennonite Brethren to send their first overseas workers, both in 1899.

86. J. S. Hartzler, unpublished autobiography, J. S. Hartzler collection (HM 1-3-3), box 3, folder 1, MCUSAA–Goshen. For more on the growing acceptance of higher education in the church in the late nineteenth century, see also Susan Fisher Miller, *Culture for Service: A History of Goshen College, 1894–1994* (Goshen, IN: privately published, 1994), chap. 2.

87. Interview with Huber Yoder, J. S. Hartzler collection (HM 1-3-3), box 3, folder 4, MCUSAA–Goshen. Boller was a minister in the National Council of the

Congregational Churches of the United States, one of several denominations in the Congregational tradition and now part of the United Church of Christ.

88. Susan Fisher Miller, *Culture for Service*, 17.

89. Juhnke, *Vision, Doctrine, War*, 109.

90. In its earliest usage among Old Mennonites and Amish Mennonites, "conference" referred to an event and not an organization. A "general" conference was meant to be a meeting that was broadly inclusive in composition and agenda. For more on the midcentury attempt to organize an Old Mennonite general conference, see Elwood Yoder, *The Bishop's Letters: The Writings, Life and Times of Virginia Mennonite Bishop Martin Burkholder, 1817–1860* (Harrisonburg, VA: Shenandoah Valley Mennonite Historians, 2011), 17–30.

91. Mennonite Church, *Proceedings of Mennonite General Conference Including Discussions Leading to Its Origination* (Scottdale, PA: Mennonite Publishing House, 1921), 46.

92. Sewing circles were congregation-based women's organizations that made clothing and bedding for missionary and relief work, both domestically and overseas. The first Mennonite sewing circles were founded in Lancaster Mennonite Conference in the 1890s.

93. Gates et al., *Bless the Lord O My Soul*, 89.

94. Elaine Sommers Rich, *Mennonite Women: A Story of God's Faithfulness, 1683–1983* (Scottdale, PA: Herald Press, 1983), 191.

95. Ibid.

96. Similar to Catholic nuns, Mennonite deaconesses were usually single women who chose a career of church work, often nursing or some other occupation in healthcare. They were more common in the General Conference Mennonite Church. See Christian Neff and Lena Mae Smith, "Deaconess," *Mennonite Encyclopedia*, vol. 2 (Scottdale, PA: Mennonite Publishing House, 1956).

Chapter 3: Coming Together, Coming Apart

1. Paton Yoder, *Tradition and Transition*, 17.

2. Indiana-Michigan Mennonite Conference, *Minutes of the Conference, 1864–1929*, 138.

3. "Our Indiana Meetings," *Gospel Herald*, September 6, 1917, 419.

4. John S. Coffman, "The Spirit of Progress," pts. 1 and 2, *Young People's Paper*, February 29, 1896, 35; March 14, 1896, 43. Coffman's address was serialized in three consecutive issues.

5. Coffman, "The Spirit of Progress," pt. 2, 43.

6. Coffman, "The Spirit of Progress," pt. 3, *Young People's Paper*, March 28, 1896, 51.

7. Indiana-Michigan Mennonite Conference, *Minutes of the Conference, 1864–1929*, 169.

8. Ibid., 45.

9. Ibid., 66.

10. Ibid., 68.

11. Marvin Eash, "The Clinton Frame Split of 1892" (research paper, Goshen College, 1964), 2.

12. Ibid., 3.

13. Ibid., 7.
14. In the 1980s, Silver Street Mennonite Church moved into Goshen and changed its name to Silverwood Mennonite Church. The Central Conference of Mennonites originated in the 1870s as a fellowship of progressive Amish Mennonites in Illinois under the leadership of bishop Joseph Stuckey. By the time it was formally organized as a conference in 1908, it had congregations from Indiana to Nebraska. It joined the General Conference Mennonite Church in 1945 as an area conference, then twelve years later merged with the denomination's Middle District Conference to form the Central District Conference.
15. Raymond Mark Yoder, "The Story of Daniel J. Johns' Life" (research paper, Goshen College, 1935), 27.
16. See chap. 2.
17. John A. Hostetler, *God Uses Ink*, 71.
18. G. L. Bender to M. S. Steiner, July 28, 1897, Menno S. Steiner collection (HM 1-33), box 3 folder 11, MCUSAA–Goshen.
19. G. L. Bender to M. S. Steiner, November 2, 1897, Menno S. Steiner collection (HM 1-33), box 3, folder 11, MCUSAA-Goshen; G. L. Bender to M. S. Steiner, March 2, 1900, Menno S. Steiner collection (HM 1-33), box 4, folder 9, MCUSAA-Goshen.
20. Aaron Loucks to J. S. Coffman, June 13, 1898, J. S. Coffman collection (HM 1-19), box 4, folder 5, MCUSAA–Goshen.
21. Untitled document, June 11, 1899, John F. Funk collection (HM 1-1-5), box 57, folder 15, MCUSAA–Goshen.
22. Undated, untitled document, John F. Funk collection (HM 1-1-6), box 64, folder 3, MCUSAA–Goshen.
23. Susan Fisher Miller, *Culture for Service*, 18–19.
24. Barbara F. Coffman, *His Name Was John: The Life Story of an Early Mennonite Leader* (Scottdale, PA: Herald Press, 1964), 292–94.
25. John F. Funk to Marlin Blosser, December 12, 1900, John F. Funk collection (HM 1-1), box 46, folder 1, MCUSAA–Goshen.
26. Undated, untitled document. Mennonite Board of Education collection (V-4-1), box 3, folder 35, MCUSAA–Goshen.
27. "Conference" document, John F. Funk collection (HM 1-1-6), box 64, folder 11, MCUSAA–Goshen.
28. J. C. Wenger, *Mennonites in Indiana and Michigan*, 94.
29. Quoted in Gates et al., *Bless the Lord O My Soul*, 177–78. The passage is the text of a letter from A. C. Kolb to nephew J. Clemens Kolb, who was a son of A. B. Kolb and a grandson of John F. Funk. A. B. Kolb and A. C. Kolb, brothers from Ontario, had come to Elkhart to work at the Mennonite Publishing Company. A. B. married Funk's daughter Phoebe, while A. C. married a daughter of institute founder Henry A. Mumaw, also named Phoebe.
30. *Housekeeping* was a common term referring to Amish Mennonite and Mennonite polity, or how they conducted the affairs of the church, such as selecting leaders and accepting and disciplining members. "Whereas complicasions [*sic*] and dissatisfactions have arisen," John F. Funk collection (HM 1-1-6), box 64, folder 13, MCUSAA–Goshen.

31. Mennonite General Conference, *Proceedings of the Mennonite General Conference Including Discussions Leading to Its Origination*, 81.

32. Indiana-Michigan Mennonite Conference, *Minutes of the Conference, 1864–1929*, 87–89.

33. "Plain Facts!" John F. Funk collection (HM 1-1-6), box 62, folder 21, MCUSAA–Goshen.

34. John F. Funk to various ordained men, October 18, 1900, John F. Funk collection (HM 1-1-6), box 62, folder 17, MCUSAA–Goshen.

35. Ibid.

36. Amos Cripe to John F. Funk, October 22, 1900, John F. Funk collection (HM 1-1-6), box 62, folder 17, MCUSAA–Goshen.

37. Noah Metzler to John F. Funk, October 22, 1900, John F. Funk collection (HM 1-1-6), box 62, folder 17, MCUSAA–Goshen.

38. "Charges against John F. Funk," January 31, 1902, J. S. Coffman collection (HM 1-19), box 11, folder 3, MCUSAA–Goshen.

39. Indiana-Michigan Mennonite Conference, *Minutes of the Conference, 1864–1929*, 75. Counsel meetings were congregational meetings prior to the scheduled observance of communion to determine if members were "at peace with God, fellow man, and the church" and could proceed with the service. Harmony and unity were requirements for participation in the Lord's Supper. Counsel meetings have since disappeared among mainstream Mennonite groups.

40. Ibid., 76–77.

41. "Diaries 26 Feb. 1903–23 March 1903," John F. Funk collection (HM 1-1-18), box 128, MCUSAA–Goshen.

42. Indiana-Michigan Mennonite Conference, *Minutes of the Conference, 1864–1929*, 109.

43. Daniel Kauffman, *Fifty Years in the Mennonite Church* (Scottdale, PA: Mennonite Publishing House, 1941), 39–40.

44. Ellrose Zook, "Mennonite Publishing: A Church Institution" (unpublished manuscript, n.d.), 29–36.

45. The *Gospel Herald* merged with *The Mennonite*, the magazine of the General Conference Mennonite Church, in 1998 to create a new publication, also called *The Mennonite*, to serve Mennonite Church USA, formed by the union of the two denominations.

46. Gates et al., *Bless the Lord O My Soul*, 221. The veracity of the charges is yet to be proved. *Bless the Lord O My Soul* is a rather hagiographic account of Funk written by four of his grandchildren, which must be taken into account when considering its assertions. According to the book, a family-initiated attempt in 1961 to determine whether Funk was owed support was fruitless because pertinent ledger pages were missing. But that had also been John A. Hostetler's finding several years earlier when researching *God Uses Ink*, which includes a history of the Mennonite Publication Board.

47. Susan Fisher Miller, *Culture for Service*, 24–25.

48. John S. Umble, *Goshen College, 1894–1954: A Venture in Christian Higher Education* (Goshen, IN: privately published, 1955), 40, 200.

49. J. C. Wenger, *Mennonites in Indiana and Michigan*, 201.

50. Umble, *Goshen College, 1894–1954*, 48.

51. Indiana-Michigan Mennonite Mission Board executive committee minutes, May 25, 1912, Indiana-Michigan Mennonite Conference collection (II-5-3), box 1, folder 3, MCUSAA–Goshen.
52. Indiana-Michigan Mennonite Mission Board executive committee minutes, January 8, 1913, Indiana-Michigan Mennonite Conference collection (II-5-3).
53. George M. Marsden, *Fundamentalism and American Culture*, 2nd ed. (New York: Oxford University Press, 2006), 3, 38.
54. N[oah] E. Byers, "Missionary Work in the Foreign Field," *Herald of Truth*, October 1, 1897, 294.
55. Jacob C. Meyer to Levi W. Yoder, July 9, 1919, Jacob C. Meyer collection (HM 1-44), box 1, folder 11, MCUSAA–Goshen.
56. Christian Neff, "James, Epistle of," *Mennonite Encyclopedia*, vol. 3 (Scottdale, PA: Mennonite Publishing House, 1957).
57. Daniel Brenneman, "A Visit—Thoughts and Suggestions in Relation to a Reunion," *Herald of Truth*, January 1867, 11–12.
58. Amos O. Hostetler, *Emma Mennonite Church since 1969* (privately published, n.d.), 2, 7.
59. A Mennonite Brethren in Christ congregation had been located in Goshen since 1885, but it obviously was not an acceptable option for Indiana-Michigan Mennonites and Amish Mennonites.
60. Indiana-Michigan Mennonite Conference, *Minutes of the Conference, 1864–1929*, 112.
61. Ibid., 209.
62. Indiana-Michigan Mennonite Conference, *Constitution and Discipline of the Indiana-Michigan Mennonite Conference* (n.p., 1909), 2.
63. Amish Mennonite Conference of Indiana and Michigan, *Constitution, Rules and Discipline of the Amish Mennonite Conference of Indiana and Michigan* (n.p., 1905), 4.
64. Indiana-Michigan Mennonite Conference, *Constitution, Rules and Discipline of the Indiana-Michigan Mennonite Conference, 1915* (n.p., [1915?]), 6–7.
65. Ibid., 15.
66. Ibid., 16.
67. Indiana-Michigan Mennonite Conference, *Minutes of the Conference, 1864–1929*, 138.

Chapter 4: Threats from Without and Within

1. Quoted in Bob Hammel, *Hoosiers Classified: Indiana's Love Affair with One-Class Basketball* (Indianapolis, IN: Masters Press, 1997), xii.
2. Niles Slabaugh to Ira Johns, February 24, 1926, Indiana-Michigan Mennonite Conference collection (II-5-2), box 2, folder 10, MCUSAA–Goshen.
3. Ibid.
4. Zinn, *People's History of the United States*, 355–64; Norton et al., *A People and a Nation*, vol. 2, *Since 1865*, 665–66.
5. J. S. Hartzler, *Mennonites in the World War, or Nonresistance under Test* (Scottdale, PA: Mennonite Publishing House, 1921), 59–60.
6. "Field Notes," *Gospel Herald*, August 30, 1917, 408.

7. F. J. Dunten to Will H. Hays, June 29, 1917, Indiana State Council of Defense collection (HM 8-22), MCUSAA–Goshen. County and state councils of defense were part of a national system to coordinate support for the war, including farm and industrial production, transportation, and financial backing.

8. F. J. Dunten to State Council of Defense, August 4, 1917, Indiana State Council of Defense collection (HM 8-22), MCUSAA–Goshen.

9. Mennonite General Conference, *Proceedings of the Mennonite General Conference Including Discussions Leading to Its Origination*, 186.

10. Juhnke, *Vision, Doctrine, War*, 213.

11. "Church Heads Called to Goshen Monday," *Middlebury Independent*, August 23, 1918, typed transcript in W. Richard and Hazel (Nice) Hassan collection (HM 1-876), box 1, folder 3, MCUSAA–Goshen.

12. Edwin S. Wertz to U.S. Attorney General, telegram, August 20, 1918, Allan Teichroew World War I collection, box 155-4, folder R660, Mennonite Church USA Archives–North Newton, North Newton, KS (hereafter MCUSAA–North Newton). The collection comprises copies of official government documents from the National Archives in Washington, DC.

13. Col. R. H. Van Deman to A. Bruce Bielaski, April 12, 1918, Allan Teichroew World War I collection, box 155-3, folder R6165, MCUSAA–North Newton.

14. "Autobiography," J. S. Hartzler collection (HM 1-3-3), box 3, folder 2, MCUSAA–Goshen; J. A. Ressler, ed., "The Real Facts about the Attitude of the Mennonite Church on the Issues of the Late War," *Mennonite Year-Book and Directory 1921* (Scottdale, PA: Mennonite Publishing House), 22.

15. Ethel Lind, "Biography of J. S. Hartzler" (research paper, Goshen College, n.d.), 20–21; James R. Krabill, "Jonas S. Hartzler (1857–1953): The Makings and Methods of a Peacemaker" (research paper, Goshen College, 1973), 32.

16. There exists no reasonably comprehensive compilation of men from Indiana-Michigan Mennonite Conference who served in the military during World War I. A survey by Guy F. Hershberger showed that of fifty-five conference draftees, only two entered regular military duty, while six accepted noncombatant service. But his survey did not include every congregation. Anecdotal evidence indicates at least a handful more Indiana-Michigan young men entered regular military service or held noncombatant positions. Nevertheless, it is apparent that a sizable number adhered to the church's nonresistant beliefs.

17. See Gerlof D. Homan, *American Mennonites and the Great War, 1914–1918* (Scottdale, PA: Herald Press, 1994). Homan addresses the legislative and legal dynamics quite extensively in his book.

18. Ray F. Yoder to Aaron Loucks, August 24, 1918, Mennonite Church Peace Problems Committee collection (I-3.5.1), box 2, file 3, MCUSAA–Goshen.

19. Homan, *American Mennonites and the Great War*, 165–66.

20. "Case No. 24: Proceedings of a general court-martial which convened at Camp Zachary Taylor, Kentucky," May 5, 1918, Allen B. Christophel collection (HM 1-319 SC), MCUSAA–Goshen.

21. "Religious C.O.'s Imprisoned at the U.S. Disciplinary Barracks, Ft. Leavenworth, Kansas," n.d., J. D. Mininger collection (HM 1-11-2), box 22, folder 14, MCUSAA–Goshen.

22. Payson Miller to "Raymond," March 31, 1918, Payson Miller collection (HM 1-670), box 1, folder 1, MCUSAA–Goshen.

23. Hartzler, *Mennonites in the World War*, 46. In church circles, tobacco use was generally considered a vile, worldly vice and had been officially prohibited by Indiana-Michigan Mennonite Conference.

24. Robert E. Proctor to M. E. Foley, October 22, 1918, typed copy in Payson Miller collection (HM 1- 670), box 1, MCUSAA–Goshen.

25. "Church Heads Called to Goshen Monday."

26. Ora Troyer, *Fairview Mennonite Church* (Fairview, MI: privately published, 1990), 109–110.

27. D. D. Miller interview, March 1940, Guy F. Hershberger collection (HM 1-171), box 65b, folder 9, MCUSAA–Goshen.

28. "Rev. D. D. Miller Says Reports Are Exaggerated," *Goshen Democrat*, September 25, 1918, 4.

29. D. D. Miller interview.

30. Mennonite Church, *Proceedings of Mennonite General Conference*, 186.

31. "Erect Flag Pole and Fly Flag at College," *Goshen Daily News-Times*, April 27, 1918, 1.

32. Elkhart County Council of Defense minutes, July 19, 1918, Elkhart County Council of Defense collection (1978.075), Elkhart County Historical Society, Bristol, IN.

33. B. F. Deahl to Will H. Wade, October 18, 1918, Indiana State Council of Defense collection (HM 8-22), MCUSAA–Goshen.

34. Indiana-Michigan Mennonite Conference, *Minutes of the Conference, 1864–1929*, 240–42.

35. "Middlebury Should be 100% Patriotic," *Middlebury Independent*, April 5, 1918, typed transcript in W. Richard and Hazel (Nice) Hassan collection (HM 1-876), box 1, folder 3, MCUSAA–Goshen.

36. H. S. K. Bartholomew, *Elkhart County, Indiana, in World War I* (Goshen, IN: n.p., 1924), 49–51.

37. Niles Slabaugh to Aaron Loucks, August 9, 1918, Mennonite Church Peace Problems Committee collection (I-3-5.1), box 1, folder 11, MCUSAA–Goshen.

38. Quoted in Gerlof Homan, "Niles M. Slabaugh's Ordeal in 1918," *Mennonite Historical Bulletin*, October 1989, 4–5.

39. W. F. McNeely broadside, J. N. Mast collection (HM 1-331 SC), MCUSAA–Goshen.

40. "Grand Jury Proceedings, Held at Mio, Oscoda County, April 14–15," Fairview Mennonite Church collection (III-2-7 SC), box 1, 55, MCUSAA–Goshen.

41. Gerlof D. Homan, "The Burning of the Mennonite Church, Fairview, Michigan, in 1918," *MQR* 64, no. 2 (April 1990): 106–7; "Grand Jury Proceedings," 74.

42. "Grand Jury Proceedings," 32, 67–68.

43. Herman Dehnke to Alex J. Grossbeck, April 22, 1920, Fairview Mennonite Church collection (III-22-7 SC), MCUSAA–Goshen.

44. "Grand Jury Proceedings," 77, 81–82.

45. Ora Troyer, *Fairview Mennonite Church*, 130.

46. Ora Troyer to Galen Johns, May 7, 1979, Fairview Mennonite Church collection (III-22-7), MCUSAA–Goshen; Homan, *American Mennonites and the Great War*, 112.

47. "Mennonite Ladies Ship Red Cross Supplies Tuesday," *Middlebury Independent*, September 20, 1918; typed transcript in W. Richard and Hazel (Nice) Hassan collection (HM 1-876), box 1, folder 3, MCUSAA–Goshen.

48. "Memorandum of Conference," September 13, 1918, Mennonite Church Peace Problems Committee collection (HM 1-3-5.1), box 2, folder 10, MCUSAA–Goshen

49. "Mennonites Devise Bond Buying Plan," *Goshen Daily News-Times*, September 14, 1918, 7.

50. Guy F. Hershberger, "Mennonite Relief Commission for War Sufferers," *Mennonite Encyclopedia*, vol. 3 (Scottdale, PA: Mennonite Publishing House, 1957).

51. Orie O. Miller, interview by John S. Miller, September 4, 1972, transcript, Mennonite Board of Missions History Project interviews collection (HM 6-81), box 1, folder 3, MCUSAA–Goshen.

52. C. Henry Smith, *Mennonite Country Boy* (Newton, KS: Faith & Life Press, 1962), 211; Susan Fisher Miller, *Culture for Service*, 51. Bluffton College changed its name to Bluffton University in 2004.

53. "Synopsis of Inaugural Address," *Goshen College Record*, November 1913, 7–12.

54. Ibid.

55. John Horsch to J. E. Hartzler, January 11, 1914; and Hartzler to Horsch, January 15, 1914, both in J. E. Hartzler collection (HM 1-62), box 22, folder 4, MCUSAA–Goshen.

56. For more on modernism and its opposite, fundamentalism, see Marsden, *Fundamentalism and American Culture*, 2nd ed.; and Nathan E. Yoder, "Mennonite Fundamentalism: Shaping an Identity for an American Context" (PhD diss., University of Notre Dame, 1999). The former has become the standard history of American fundamentalism, while the latter explores fundamentalism as it specifically affected Mennonites.

57. John Horsch, *The Mennonite Church and Modernism* (Scottdale, PA: Mennonite Publishing House, 1924), 7–8.

58. Theron Schlabach, *Gospel versus Gospel* (Scottdale, PA: Herald Press, 1980), 114. Schlabach has famously called the era's conservative attacks on modernists in the Mennonite Church as "aiming elephant guns to kill flies." Nathan Yoder sees unmistakable modernist influences at Goshen College at the time but also says that none of the faculty "were full-blown modernists." "Mennonite Fundamentalism," 206.

59. Marsden, *Fundamentalism and American Culture*, 146; William R. Hutchison, *The Modernist Impulse in American Protestantism* (Cambridge, MA: Harvard University Press, 1976), 2; Nathan E. Yoder, "Mennonite Fundamentalism," 192–207.

60. Harold S. Bender, "Fundamentalism," *Mennonite Encyclopedia*, vol. 2 (Scottdale, PA: Mennonite Publishing House, 1957).

61. John Horsch, *Modern Religious Liberalism: The Destructiveness and Irrationality of the New Theology* (Scottdale, PA: Fundamental Truth Depot, 1920), 17.

62. The word *foundation* appears in the minutes of the 1867 Indiana-Michigan Mennonite Conference assembly (Indiana-Michigan Mennonite Conference, *Minutes of the Conference, 1864–1929*, 11) and frequently in subsequent minutes. Also used are related phrases such as "building on the rock" and "cornerstone." Nathan Yoder notes the similarities in word usage between the English translation of Menno Simons's book *Foundation of Christian Doctrine* and its German-language version *Ein Fundament und Klare Anweisung von der Seligmachenden Lehre unsers Herr Jesu Christi.* Nathan E. Yoder, "Mennonite Fundamentalism," 114.

63. Indiana-Michigan Mennonite Conference, *Minutes of the Conference, 1864-1929*, 245.

64. Marsden, *Fundamentalism and American Culture*, 3, 38.

65. Quoted in ibid., 36.

66. Daniel Kauffman, ed., *Mennonite Cyclopedic Dictionary: A Compendium of the Doctrines, History, Activities, Literature and Environments of the Mennonite Church, Especially in America* (Scottdale, PA: Mennonite Publishing House, 1937), 116.

67. Leonard Gross, "The Doctrinal Era of the Mennonite Church," *MQR* 60, no. 1 (January 1986): 83–87.

68. Harold S. Bender, "Bible," *Mennonite Encyclopedia*, vol. 1 (Scottdale, PA: Mennonite Publishing House, 1955).

69. Marsden, *Fundamentalism and American Culture*, 4.

70. Chester Weaver, "Fundamentalism and the Followers of Menno" (paper presented at the Anabaptist Identity Conference, Nappanee, IN, March 12–14, 2015). Weaver, a member of the Beachy Amish, provides a powerful critique of fundamentalism's impact from a plain people's perspective that is also relevant to more mainstream Mennonite groups, particularly the Mennonite Church in the early twentieth century.

71. "Minutes of the Ninth Annual Meeting of the Mennonite Board of Missions and Charities Held Near Newton, Kans., May 18–20, 1915," *Gospel Herald*, July 1, 1915, 237.

72. Indiana-Michigan Mennonite Conference, *Minutes of the Conference, 1864–1929*, 237.

73. Kauffman, *Mennonite Cyclopedic Dictionary*, 82; Galen Johns, interview by author, June 2, 2006, Goshen, IN, recording in author's possession.

74. Eric Yordy, "The 1922 Investigation of Bishop Jacob K. Bixler: The Preservation of Conservatism" (research paper, Goshen College, 1993), 8.

75. Mattie Brubaker Babcock, interview by Leonard Gross, Leonard Gross oral interview collection (HM 6-241), MCUSAA–Goshen.

76. Ibid.

77. Indiana-Michigan Mennonite Conference, *Minutes of the Conference, 1864–1929*, 231.

78. Susan Fisher Miller, *Culture for Service*, 64.

79. Pennsylvania Mennonite Church, named after the home state of many of its founders, in 1964 moved from its rural location between Hesston and Newton, Kansas, into Hesston, where it was renamed Whitestone Mennonite Church.

80. J. E. Hartzler to T. M. Erb, November 20, 1920, J. E. Hartzler collection (HM 1-62), box 24, folder 2, MCUSAA–Goshen.

81. T. M. Erb to J. E. Hartzler, November 16, 1920, J. E. Hartzler collection (HM 1-62), box 24, folder 2, MCUSAA–Goshen.

82. Witmarsum board members also came from the General Conference Mennonite Church, Central Conference of Mennonites, Mennonite Brethren in Christ, Defenseless Mennonite Church, and Mennonite Brethren. While Witmarsum intended to serve all those groups, students and support came mostly from the General Conference Mennonite Church and Central Conference of Mennonites. See C. Henry Smith and E. J. Hirschler, eds., *The Story of Bluffton College* (Bluffton, OH: privately published, 1925), especially chap. 7. Witmarsum—which was named after Menno Simons's hometown—closed in 1931.

83. D. A. Yoder, D. J. Johns, J. S. Hartzler, J. W. Christophel, and D. D. Troyer "to whom it may concern," October 23, 1922, Indiana-Michigan Mennonite Conference collection (II-5-1), box 2, folder 7, MCUSAA–Goshen. The All-Mennonite Convention was held between 1913 and 1936, usually every three years, bringing together representatives from various U.S. groups to address matters of common concern. Because of the Mennonite Church's cool attitude toward inter-Mennonite relations, no one from the denomination attended the 1919 convention, which was held at Bluffton, Ohio. Eight years earlier, the Indiana-Michigan Mennonite Conference expressed its support for the first convention, "provided such union can be brought about strictly on Gospel principles." Indiana-Michigan Mennonite Conference, *Minutes of the Conference, 1864–1929*, 111. The first convention was held in at Berne, Indiana, and the last one at Topeka, Indiana.

84. Yoder, Johns, Hartzler, Christophel, and Troyer "to whom it may concern."

85. J. E. Hartzler to A. J. Steiner, March 2, 1925; and Hartzler to John Y. King, June 2, 1925, both in J. E. Hartzler collection (HM 1-62), box 24, folder 3, MCUSAA–Goshen.

86. John Y. King to J. E. Hartzler, June 8, 1925, J. E. Hartzler collection (HM 1-62), box 24, folder 4, MCUSAA–Goshen.

87. W. B. Weaver to J. E. Hartzler, April 13, 1921, J. E. Hartzler collection (HM 1-62), box 24, folder 1, MCUSAA–Goshen.

88. Ordination by a bishop did not automatically give a minister a voice in conference affairs. He also needed to be officially received into the conference by the conference's ordained men. Ordination and membership usually went hand in hand, but not always, as the Wilbur Miller case illustrates.

89. Rudy Senger to J. E. Hartzler, May 16, 1922, J. E. Hartzler collection (HM 1-62), box 24, folder 3, MCUSAA–Goshen.

90. W. B. Weaver to Hartzler, April 13, 1921, J. E. Hartzler collection (HM 1-62), box 24, folder 1, MCUSAA–Goshen.

91. Mary Schantz Zook to Vesta Zook, April 23, 1922, Vesta Zook Slagel collection (HM 1-403), box 2, folder 1, MCUSAA–Goshen.

92. Mary Zook to Vesta Zook, April 2, 1922, Vesta Zook Slagel collection (HM 1-403), box 2, folder 1, MCUSAA–Goshen.

93. Orie O. Miller and Arthur Slagle were two of the first three Mennonite Central Committee workers. Joining Miller and Slagle was Clayton Kratz, a Goshen College student who disappeared while in the Ukraine and was never seen or heard from again.

94. Vesta Zook to Mary Zook, May 5, 1921, Vesta Zook Slagel collection (HM 1-403), box 1, folder 2, MCUSAA–Goshen.

95. Vinora Weaver Salzman, *Day by Day, Year by Year* (Elkhart, IN: privately published, 1982), 18.

96. Ibid., 26.

97. Mary Zook to Vesta Zook, June 19, 1921, Vesta Zook Slagel collection (MH 1-403), box 1, folder 2, MCUSAA–Goshen.

98. Mary Zook to Vesta Zook, July 1922 [no day given], Vesta Zook Slagel collection (HM 1-403), box 2, folder 1, MCUSAA–Goshen.

99. According to Melvin Gingerich, many Mennonite and Amish Mennonite groups had earlier banned bonnets in favor of unadorned broad-brimmed hats. Plain bonnets seem to have become acceptable starting in the late nineteenth century, when they were began falling out of style in "worldly" society. See chap. 2 of Melvin Gingerich, *Mennonite Attire through Four Centuries* (Breinigsville, PA: Pennsylvania Germany Society, 1970).

100. Mary Zook to Vesta Zook, January 30, 1922, Vesta Zook Slagel collection (HM 1-403), box 2, folder 1, MCUSAA–Goshen. It is interesting that both Vesta Zook and Vinora Weaver would both join the General Conference Mennonite Church. Vesta married Arthur Slagle, another early Mennonite Central Committee worker. After living in Chicago for seven years, they moved to her home community and joined Topeka Mennonite Church. Weaver married Earl Salzman, a minister in the Central Conference of Mennonites and General Conference Mennonite Church. As a minister's wife, she would even occasionally preach.

101. Rudy Senger to J. E. Hartzler, May 16, 1922, J. E. Hartzler collection (HM 1-62), box 24, folder 3, MCUSAA–Goshen.

102. "A Report: Glossed Over," undated, J. E. Hartzler collection (HM 1-62), box 24, folder 17, MCUSAA–Goshen.

103. J. S. Hartzler to J. E. Hartzler, August 5, 1922, J. E. Hartzler collection (HM 1-62), box 24, folder 16, MCUSAA–Goshen.

104. J. E. Hartzler to Sophia Weber, August 6, 1922; and Sophia Weber to J. E. Hartzler, August 9, 1922, both in J. E. Hartzler collection (HM 1-62), box 24, folder 16, MCUSAA–Goshen.

105. J. E. Hartzler to W. W. Oesch, July 20, 1922, J. E. Hartzler collection (HM 1-62), box 24, folder 16, MCUSAA–Goshen.

106. Indiana-Michigan Mennonite Conference, *Report of Committee Called to Investigate and Adjust Difficulties in the Indiana-Michigan Conference District*, 1923, J. E. Hartzler collection (HM 1-62), box 14, folder 27, MCUSAA–Goshen.

107. J. S. Hartzler to Violet Bender, October 24, 1923, D. A. Yoder collection (HM 1-314), box 3, folder 9, MCUSAA–Goshen.

108. Violet Bender to J. S. Hartzler, October 21, 1923, D. A. Yoder collection (HM 1-314), box 3, folder 9, MCUSAA–Goshen.

109. Rudy Senger to J. E. Hartzler, May 10, 1922, J. E. Hartzler collection (HM 1-62), box 24, folder 17, MCUSAA–Goshen.

110. See Susan Fisher Miller, *Culture for Service*, especially chap. 4; and Nathan E. Yoder, "I Submit: Daniel Kauffman and the Legacy of a Yielded Life," 121–55, in Jared S. Burkholder and David C. Cramer, eds., *The Activist Impulse: Essays on the Intersection of Evangelicalism and Anabaptism* (Eugene, OR: Pickwick Publications, 2012).

111. Nathan E. Yoder, "Mennonite Fundamentalism," 189.

112. John Horsch, *Is the Mennonite Church of American Free from Modernism?* (Scottdale, PA: 1926), 121, 123.

113. Nathan E. Yoder, "Mennonite Fundamentalism," 192–205.

114. Susan Fisher Miller, *Culture for Service*, 100.

115. The current evidence of modernism at Goshen College is scant. Only a few scholars, most notably Nathan E. Yoder, have offered any proof, and then only in retrospect. Goshen critics in the 1910s and '20s, while frequently couching their arguments as antimodernist, were in reality upset at what they perceived as violations of Mennonite cultural sensibilities. John S. Umble and Susan Fisher Miller, in their respective histories of the school, identify no explicit modernist influences as contributing to Goshen's preclosure struggles. Not even Horsch, one of the college's fiercest critics at the time, could provide examples. His 1920 booklet *What Ails Our Colleges and Seminaries?* doesn't even mention Goshen (or any other Mennonite schools, for that matter), much less how it succumbed to modernism. Horsch's *Is the Mennonite Church of America Free from Modernism?* is mostly rejoinders to former presidents Noah Byers and J. E. Hartzler, with nothing on how their progressivism turned Goshen modernist. Horsch wrote *The Mennonite Church and Modernism* in 1924 while the college was closed and devoted a section to the situation. Yet his charges of modernism at the school—e.g., "Even some of the more conservative Bible teachers held modernized views"—are unsubstantiated.

116. James C. Juhnke, "Mennonite Church Theological and Social Boundaries, 1920–1930: Loyalists, Liberals, and Laxitarians," *Mennonite Life*, June 1983, 18; Paul Toews, "Fundamental Conflict in Mennonite Colleges: A Response to Cultural Transitions," *MQR* 57, no. 3 (July 1983): 244.

117. Quoted in Umble, *Goshen College, 1894–1954*, 89–90.

118. Susan Fisher Miller, *Culture for Service*, 65.

119. "Minutes of Special Session of Ind.-Mich. Conference, June 3, 1920 at home of I. S. Long," S. C. Yoder collection (HM 1-162), box 2, folder 1, MCUSAA–Goshen.

120. Susan Fisher Miller, *Culture for Service*, 71; Indiana-Michigan Mennonite Conference, *Minutes of the Conference, 1864–1929*, 255.

121. Indiana-Michigan Mennonite Conference, *Report of Committee Called to Investigate and Adjust Difficulties in the Indiana-Michigan Conference District*, 1923.

122. Susan Fisher Miller, *Culture for Service*, 87.

123. Anna Showalter, "The Rise and Fall of the Young People's Conference, 1918–1923," *Mennonite Historical Bulletin,* January 2011, 4–11.

124. Susan Fisher Miller, *Culture for Service,* 62.

125. Minutes, Mennonite Board of Education special session, July 6, 1921, Mennonite Board of Education collection (V-I-8), box 14, folder 8, MCUSAA–Goshen.

126. Statement, April 4, 1923, Mennonite Board of Education collection (V-1-8), box 14, folder 8, MCUSAA–Goshen.

127. The closing of Goshen College was an event of seismic proportions in the Mennonite Church, with great ramifications for the Central Conference of Mennonites and General Conference Mennonite Church, as they welcomed former Goshen administrators and faculty and others forced out of Indiana-Michigan by the school difficulties. For a more thorough treatment of the subject, see Susan Fisher Miller, *Culture for Service,* especially chap. 4. For its context in the broader church, see Nathan E. Yoder, "Mennonite Fundamentalism"; and Juhnke, *Vision, Doctrine, War,* chaps. 9–11.

128. J. H. Eigsti to S. C. Yoder, August 7, 1923, S. C. Yoder collection (HM 1-162), box 2, folder 1, MCUSAA–Goshen.

129. Elva May Schrock to Committee for Goshen College, July 27, 1923, S. C. Yoder collection (HM 1-162), box 2, folder 1, MCUSAA–Goshen.

130. Susan Fisher Miller, *Culture for Service,* 85.

131. Notebook #5, Indiana-Michigan Mennonite Conference collection (II-5-1), box 2, folder 7, MCUSAA–Goshen.

132. Life insurance was impermissible for several reasons: it reflected more trust in human efforts than reliance on God, it unequally yoked Mennonites with non-Mennonites, and, as a practical matter, it usually benefited the wealthy more than the needy.

133. "The following are the statements," undated, Indiana-Michigan Mennonite Conference collection (II-5-2), box 2, folder 8, MCUSAA–Goshen.

134. W. W. Oesch to L. S. Nafziger, December 19, 1922, W. W. and Elva Garver Oesch collection (HM 1-428), box 1, folder "Barker Street Problems; J. K. Bixler", MCUSAA–Goshen.

135. Orie O. Miller interview; J. C. Wenger, *The Story of the Forks Mennonite Church* (privately published, 1982), 29.

136. Theron F. Schlabach, "History," chap. 1 in *College Mennonite Church, 1903–2003* (Goshen, IN: privately published, 2003), 29.

137. After changing denominational affiliations, West Market Street was renamed First Mennonite Church.

138. Rachel Nafziger Hartzler, *No Strings Attached: Boundary Lines in Pleasant Places: A History of Warren Street/Pleasant Oaks Mennonite Church* (Eugene, OR: Resource Publications, 2013), 92.

139. "To Whom This May Concern," undated, Indiana-Michigan Mennonite Conference collection (II-5-18), box 1, folder 20, MCUSAA–Goshen.

140. Indiana-Michigan Mennonite Conference, *Report of Committee Called to Investigate and Adjust Difficulties in the Indiana-Michigan Conference District,* 1923.

141. A convention of disenfranchised Mennonite Church members was held at West Market Street Mennonite Church in 1924. Among those in attendance were

representatives from five congregations with Indiana-Michigan origins: Warren Street in Middlebury; Raymond L. Hartzler's group at Topeka, Indiana; College in Goshen, Indiana; and Barker Street, Mottville, Michigan, in addition to West Market Street. Also present were members of three Ohio congregations and one from Ontario. See Elden Schrock, *100th Anniversary Edition of the History and a Pictorial Directory of the First Mennonite Church, Nappanee, Indiana* (n.p., [1975?]), 11.

142. Notebook #5, Indiana-Michigan Mennonite Conference collection (II-5-1), box 2, folder 7, MCUSAA–Goshen.

Chapter 5: Expanding the Boundaries

1. James L. Troyer, "History of the Wildwood Mennonite Church" (research paper, Goshen Biblical Seminary, 1968), 1.
2. J. D. Livermore, interview by author, June 21, 2006, Germfask, MI, recording in author's possession.
3. James L. Troyer, "History of the Wildwood Mennonite Church," 2.
4. Edwin J. Yoder, "Northern Peninsula of Michigan," *Rural Evangel*, March 1935, 4.
5. Ira S. Johns, "Colonization as a Factor in Rural Missions," *Rural Evangel*, October 1, 1921, 3.
6. "Editorials," *Rural Evangel*, November 1933, 1.
7. Guy F. Hershberger, *War, Peace, and Nonresistance* (Scottdale, PA: Herald Press, 1981), 213–14.
8. Johns, "Colonization as a Factor."
9. Edwin J. Yoder, "Northern Peninsula of Michigan," *Rural Evangel*, September 1934, 3.
10. Schlabach, *Gospel versus Gospel*, 89.
11. Historical Notebook #2, First Mennonite Church (Fort Wayne, Ind.) collection (III-14-22), box 1, folder 6, MCUSAA–Goshen. Other urban workers from Fort Wayne were Perry Heller, who went to the Mennonite mission in Los Angeles; Norman Hobbs, who went to Iowa City, Iowa; and Frank Martin, who stayed home and become superintendent of the Fort Wayne mission, where he had become a Christian. See John R. Smucker, "One Hundred Years of a Mennonite Presence in Fort Wayne, Indiana" (unpublished paper in Mennonite Historical Library, Goshen, IN, 2004), 4.
12. Herbert L. Osborne, comp., *History of the First Mennonite Church in Fort Wayne, Indiana, 1903–1978* (Fort Wayne, IN: privately published, 1978), 5–6.
13. Henry Ford started building automobiles in Detroit in the late 1890s and would be followed by dozens more manufacturers over the next several decades.
14. C. C. King, "Detroit as a Mission Field," *Rural Evangel*, July 1, 1927, 3.
15. "Editorials," *Rural Evangel*, March 1935, 1.
16. James L. Troyer, "History of the Wildwood Mennonite Church," 3.
17. C. A. Shank, "Mission Board Request," *Rural Evangel*, July 1934, 2.
18. James Troyer, interview by author, June 23, 2006, Manistique, MI, recording in author's possession; Rosella Prater, *Mennonite Stirrings in America's Playland* (Naubinway, MI: privately published, 1987), 9.
19. Prater, *Mennonite Stirrings*, 9.

20. Chester Osborne to Brother Yoder, April 21, 1937, Indiana-Michigan Mennonite Conference collection (II-5-3), box 3, folder 2, MCUSAA–Goshen.

21. Clarence Troyer, *The Mennonite Church in the Upper Peninsula* (Nappanee, IN: Evangel Press, 1986), 12.

22. Chester C. Osborne, "Fernland Congregation," *Rural Evangel*, January 1941, 4. Fernland was the congregation's original name.

23. Adding to Clarence and Wavia Troyer's legacy were five children who would also make the Upper Peninsula their homes as adults, including three sons who, like their father, would also become ministers of Upper Peninsula Indiana-Michigan congregations.

24. James Troyer interview.

25. Prater, *Mennonite Stirrings*, 41, 73.

26. Ibid., 40

27. Ibid., 27, 70.

28. Daniel Hertzler, "Twenty Years, Ten Churches: A Report on the Mennonite Churches in Michigan's Upper Peninsula," *Christian Living*, December 1958, 33.

29. James Troyer interview.

30. Clarence Troyer, *The Mennonite Church in the Upper Peninsula*, 15.

31. George Mark, interview by author, June 16, 2006, Elkhart, IN.

32. Elno Steiner, "History of the Indiana-Michigan Mennonite Mission Board" (research paper, Goshen College, 1951), 25.

33. Ibid., 18.

34. Dorsa Mishler and Russell Krabill, *The Prairie Street Mennonite Church Story, 1871–1996* (Elkhart, IN: privately published, 1996), 57–58.

35. Erie E. Bontrager, "Zion Congregation," *Rural Evangel*, November 1938, 4.

36. "Gleanings from the Conference Secretary's Report of the Congregations," *Rural Evangel*, July 1928, 3.

37. "Echoes from the Field," *Rural Evangel*, January 1935, 4.

38. Orlin Reedy, "The History of the North and East Goshen Sunday Schools" (research paper, Goshen College, 1932), 23–24.

39. J. C. Wenger, *North Goshen Mennonite Church* (Goshen, IN: privately published, 1986), 28.

40. Luella Friesen, interview by author, September 18, 2012, Goshen, IN.

41. The Friesens were not typical Mennonite Board of Missions workers or Mennonite Church members. They were children of Russian Mennonite immigrants who settled at Mountain Lake, Minn., and were part of the Evangelical Mennonite Brethren (which changed its name to the Fellowship of Evangelical Bible Churches in 1987), which did not have its own mission agency. The Friesens chose to follow God's call by joining MBM.

42. Jonathan Yoder, *Jungle Surgeon* (Goshen, IN: privately published, 1986), 8.

43. Nona Kauffman interview, Indiana-Michigan Mennonite Conference collection (II-5-13), box 3, folder "Retired Ministers Interviews, B-L," MCUSAA–Goshen.

44. "Questions for the Examination" in minutes of the Indiana-Michigan Mennonite Mission Board, November 14, 1912, Indiana-Michigan Mennonite Conference collection (II-5-3), box 1, folder 3, MCUSAA–Goshen.

45. Ira Johns to D. A. Yoder, January 24, 1935, D. A. Yoder collection (HM 1-314), box 3, folder 49, MCUSAA–Goshen.

46. "Minutes of the Ind.-Mich. Mennonite Conference Held with the Salem Congregation Near New Paris, Ind., on June 4, 5, 1931," Indiana-Michigan Mennonite Conference collection (II-5-1), box 2, folder 8, MCUSAA–Goshen.

47. Ibid.

48. John R. Smucker, "One Hundred Years of a Mennonite Presence in Fort Wayne, Indiana." It is unclear whether Perry Heller was ever placed under discipline for hairstyling. According to Smucker, one of his sons may have taken the punishment in place of Heller and ceased his affiliation with the church. See Smucker, 4n12.

49. Indiana-Michigan Mennonite Conference, *Report of the Indiana-Michigan Church Conference* 1938, 4.

50. Ledger, 1918–1951, Salem Mennonite Church collection (III-14-25), box 1, folder 2, MCUSAA–Goshen.

51. J. C. Wenger, *Mennonites in Indiana and Michigan*, 32.

52. Melvin Gingerich, "The Mennonite Women's Missionary Society," *MQR* 37, no. 3 (July 1963): 221. The leadership of Mennonite Board of Missions—all male, of course—started its own women's group in 1926 and in two years had shut down the original organization.

53. Sharon Klingelsmith, "Women in the Mennonite Church, 1900–1930," *MQR* 54, no. 3 (July 1980): 169.

54. Indiana-Michigan Mennonite Conference, *Minutes of the Conference, 1864–1929*, 137.

55. J. K. Bixler, "Women's Spiritual Service in the Church," *Gospel Herald*, January 17, 1929, 887–88.

56. "Editorials," *Rural Evangel*, March 1937, 1.

57. "Depression and Spirituality," *Rural Evangel*, March 1933, 4.

58. J. E. S., "Clinton Frame Congregation," *Rural Evangel*, January 1938, 4.

59. "Editorials," *Rural Evangel*, July 1936, 1.

60. George R. Brunk, "Evils of a Fractional Gospel," *Rural Evangel*, January 1937, 2–3.

61. Yellow Creek Mennonite Business Meeting Records, Book #1, Yellow Creek Mennonite Church collection (III-14-3), box 2, folder 4, MCUSAA–Goshen.

62. Journal, n.d., 61–65, Zion Mennonite Church collection (III-22-25), box 1, MCUSAA–Goshen.

63. "Editorials," *Rural Evangel*, September 1933, 1.

64. C. C. Culp to Silas Weldy, March 14, 1934, Indiana-Michigan Mennonite Conference collection (II-5-3), box 3, folder 1, MCUSAA–Goshen.

65. J. S. Hartzler to E. F. Martin, March 24, 1938, Indiana-Michigan Mennonite Conference collection (II-5-3), box 3, folder 3, MCUSAA–Goshen.

66. Poor Fund Book, Leo Mennonite Church collection (III-14-38), box 6, folder 2, MCUSAA–Goshen.

67. Indiana-Michigan Mennonite Conference, *Report of the Indiana-Michigan Church Conference* 1932, 8.

68. Ora Troyer, *Fairview Mennonite Church*, 154–55.

69. Ledger, 1918–1951, Salem Mennonite Church collection (III-14-25), box 1, folder 2, MCUSAA–Goshen.

70. Schlabach, *Gospel versus Gospel*, 244.

71. Chester Osborne to Homer North, December 29, 1937, Indiana-Michigan Mennonite Conference collection (II-5-3), box 3, folder 2, MCUSAA–Goshen.

72. Mark A. Noll, *A History of Christianity in the United States and Canada* (Grand Rapids, MI: Wm. B. Eerdmans, 1992), 304–7.

73. Juhnke, *Vision, Doctrine, War*, 175.

74. D. D. Troyer to Silas Weldy, January 11, 1932, Indiana-Michigan Mennonite Conference collection (II-5-3), box 3, folder 1, MCUSAA–Goshen.

75. "Depression and Spirituality," *Rural Evangel*, March 1933, 4.

76. Membership numbers from the annual *Mennonite Yearbook and Directory*, 1923–1940 (Scottdale, Pa: Mennonite Publishing House) and Indiana-Michigan Mennonite Conference collection (II-5-1), box 2, folders 7 and 8, MCUSAA–Goshen.

77. Herbert L. Osborne, "Howard-Miami Mennonites and Amish," 23; Ora Troyer, *Fairview Mennonite Church*, 136.

78. Tabulations in Indiana-Michigan Mennonite Conference collection (II-5-1), box 2, folders 7, 8, MCUSAA–Goshen.

79. Keim, *Harold S. Bender*, 165–66.

80. Leonard Gross, "Conversations with Elizabeth Bender IV," *Mennonite Historical Bulletin*, July 1986, 9.

81. Keim, *Harold S. Bender*, 265.

82. Ida Yoder, ed., *Edward: Pilgrimage of a Mind* (Wadsworth, OH and Irwin, PA: privately published, 1985), 305–6.

83. Harold S. Bender, "In Time of Peace Prepare for War," *Christian Doctrine*, supplement to *Gospel Herald*, April 21, 1932, 70–71.

84. Ida Yoder, *Edward: Pilgrimage of a Mind*, 219.

85. Ibid., 220.

86. Juhnke, "Mennonite Church Theological and Social Boundaries, 1920–1930," 21–22.

87. Carol Miller, interview by author, March 24, 2006, Elkhart, IN.

88. Indiana-Michigan Mennonite Conference, *Report of the Indiana-Michigan Church Conference 1932*, 3–4.

89. Indiana-Michigan Mennonite Conference, *Report of the Indiana-Michigan Church Conference 1941*, 7.

90. "The Radio," *Rural Evangel*, May 1934, 3.

91. Ernest E. Miller, "The Use of the Radio among the Mennonites of the Indiana-Michigan Conference," *MQR* 14, no. 3 (July 1940): 134.

92. Ibid., 142–43, 147.

Chapter 6: The End of Isolationism

1. Mennonite Central Committee, representing the Mennonite Church and all other U.S. Mennonite and Amish bodies, joined with the Church of the Brethren, Quakers, and other denominations to negotiate with the federal government to create Civilian Public Service. See Melvin Gingerich, *Service for Peace: A History of Mennonite Civilian Public Service* (Akron, PA: Mennonite

Central Committee, 1949). Despite its age, the book remains a valuable work because of its comprehensive coverage of Mennonite involvement in CPS.

2. For more on the history and principles of mutual aid among Anabaptists, including the origins of Mennonite Mutual Aid, see Willard M. Swartley and Donald B. Kraybill, eds., *Building Communities of Compassion: Mennonite Mutual Aid in Theory and Practice* (Scottdale, PA: Herald Press, 1998).

3. Orie Miller was a member of Lancaster Mennonite Conference, which at the time was not officially a member of the Mennonite Church. But fraternal relations and cooperation made Lancaster in many ways functionally part of the Mennonite Church.

4. MMA Committee minutes, March 15, 1945, Mennonite Mutual Aid Association [Everence] collection (XII-9), box 1, folder 1, MCUSAA–Goshen.

5. Mennonite Mutual Aid was renamed Everence in 2010.

6. The Mennonite Aid Plan would increasingly serve members from beyond Indiana and Michigan and from other Mennonite denominations, so much so that Indiana-Michigan Mennonite Conference in 1911 started another mutual aid organization to specifically serve its own members. The original Mennonite Aid Plan relocated its headquarters to Freeman, S. Dak., in 1912.

7. Hesston College, like Goshen, was under the auspices of Mennonite Board of Education, while Eastern Mennonite School in Harrisonburg initially was not.

8. Of the three Mennonite Church General Conference moderators or preachers not associated with Mennonite Board of Education or Mennonite Publication Board during that time, one was Noah Mack of the Lancaster Mennonite Conference, which generally opposed the progressivism it saw in Indiana-Michigan and elsewhere. A second person was rising church leader Allen Erb, son of Kansas bishop Tillman Erb, who had helped thwart J. E. Hartzler's communion attempts (see chap. 4). The third man was longtime Mennonite Board of Missions member S. E. Allgyer from Ohio.

9. See Susan Fisher Miller, *Culture for Service*, chap. 6.

10. Bender, "In Time of Peace Prepare for War," 70–71.

11. Keim, *Harold S. Bender*, 275–76.

12. Indiana-Michigan Mennonite Conference, *Report of the Indiana-Michigan Church Conference* 1941, 3.

13. "Editorials," *Rural Evangel*, November 1940, 1.

14. Guy F. Hershberger, *The Mennonite Church in the Second World War* (Scottdale, PA: Mennonite Publishing House, 1951), 29.

15. Ibid., 153.

16. James Troyer interview.

17. Ibid.

18. "Some of My Memories of No. 135," Chester C. and Eva Osborne collection (HM 1-915), box 1, yellow binder "Civilian Public Service Camp No. 135, Germfask Michigan," MCUSAA–Goshen.

19. "The Tobacco Road Gang," *Time*, February 19, 1945, 21.

20. "Some of My Memories of No. 135," Chester C. and Eva Osborne collection.

21. Ibid.

22. "An Explanation of My Resignation from the Civilian Public Service Camp 135," July 25, 1944, Chester C. and Eva Osborne collection (HM 1-915), box

1, yellow binder "Civilian Public Service Camp No. 135, Germfask Michigan," MCUSAA–Goshen.

23. C. S. Johnson to Chester Osborne, February 25, 1948, Chester C. and Eva Osborne collection (HM 1-915), box 1, yellow binder "Civilian Public Service Camp No. 135, Germfask Michigan," MCUSAA–Goshen.

24. Mennonite General Conference, *Mennonite General Conference Report, August 23–26, 1949* (Scottdale, PA: Mennonite Publishing House, 1949), 62.

25. Hershberger, *Mennonite Church in the Second World War*, 76–77.

26. Robert Wuthnow, *The Restructuring of American Religion: Society and Faith since World War II* (Princeton, NJ: Princeton University Press, 1988), 15.

27. See Gingerich, *Service for Peace*, chap. 19.

28. Ibid., 302.

29. Rachel Waltner Goossen, *Women against the Good War: Conscientious Objection and Gender on the American Home Front, 1941–1947* (Chapel Hill: University of North Carolina Press, 1997), 101–2, 105.

30. Mennonite General Conference, *Mennonite General Conference Report, August 23–26, 1949*, 62-65.

31. Laura Rheinheimer, "Close to the Center, Far from the Heart: The Experiences of Mennonite Veterans of World War II from the Indiana-Michigan Conference," (research paper, Goshen College, 2005), 15.

32. Rodney James Sawatsky, "The Influence of Fundamentalism on Mennonite Nonresistance, 1908–1944" (master's thesis, University of Minnesota, 1973), 42; Perry Bush, "Military Service, Religious Faith and Acculturation: Mennonite G.I.s and Their Church, 1941–1945," *MQR* 62, no. 3 (July 1993): 266–67.

33. Rheinheimer, "Close to the Center," 15–16.

34. Ibid., 22–23.

35. Mennonite General Conference, *Mennonite General Conference Report, August 23–26, 1949*, 62.

36. Rheinheimer, "Close to the Center," 24–25.

37. Indiana-Michigan Mennonite Conference, *Report of the Indiana-Michigan Church Conference 1941*, 4–5.

38. Indiana-Michigan Mennonite Conference, *Report of the Indiana-Michigan Church Conference 1942*, 5.

39. "Minutes of the Indiana-Michigan Mennonite Church Conference," 1943.

40. Melvin Gingerich, "Rural Life Problems and the Mennonites," *MQR* 16, no. 3 (July 1942): 168.

41. "Editorials," *Rural Evangel*, September–October 1945, 2.

42. See Harold S. Bender, *The Anabaptist Vision* (Scottdale, PA: Herald Press, 1944).

43. Wuthnow, *Restructuring of American Religion*, 37. He argues that much of American Christianity experienced a movement from prewar factionalism and contentiousness to a renewed emphasis on the basics of belief and practice.

44. For a concise and readable analysis of Hershberger's book, see Theron F. Schlabach, "War, Peace, and Nonresistance (1944): Background, Genesis, Message," *MQR* 80, no. 3 (July 2006).

45. Mennonite Church, "Mennonite General Conference Report, Goshen, Ind., August 18–24, 1943," 52.

46. Willard H. Smith, *Mennonites in Illinois* (Scottdale, PA: Herald Press, 1983), 206–7.

47. Sanford G. Shetler, "The Mennonite Church Today," *Gospel Herald*, August 11, 1944, 369.

48. From the editor, "The Meetings in Indiana," *Gospel Herald*, August 25, 1944, 412.

49. Guy F. Hershberger, introduction to *Edward: Pilgrimage of a Mind*, edited by Ida Yoder (Wadsworth, OH: privately published, 1985), xix–xx.

50. From the editor, *Gospel Herald*, 412.

51. Ibid., 420.

52. Mennonite General Conference, *Prophecy Conference: Report of Conference Held at Elkhart, Indiana, April 3–5, 1952* (Scottdale, PA: Mennonite Publishing House, 1953), 156.

53. Minutes of the Indiana-Michigan Mennonite Conference (1947), Indiana-Michigan Mennonite Conference collection (II-5-1), box 2, folder 9, MCUSAA–Goshen.

54. For more on Guy F. Hershberger and the Mennonite Community movement, see Theron F. Schlabach, *War, Peace, and Social Conscience: Guy F. Hershberger and Mennonite Ethics* (Scottdale, PA: Herald Press, 2009), especially chap. 6.

55. Minutes of the Indiana-Michigan Mennonite Conference (1948), Indiana-Michigan Mennonite Conference collection (II-5-1), box 2, folder 10, MCUSAA–Goshen.

56. "A Change of Name," *Rural Evangel*, September–October 1947, 3.

57. Untitled, *Rural Evangel*, May–June 1944, 6.

58. Tobin Miller Shearer, *Daily Demonstrators: The Civil Rights Movement in Mennonite Homes and Sanctuaries* (Baltimore: Johns Hopkins University, Press, 2010), 9–13.

59. Irene Bechler and LeRoy Bechler, interview by author, October 2, 2013, Goshen, IN, recording in author's possession; LeRoy Bechler, "Answering the Call: Telling the Story" (unpublished paper), 31–33.

60. In 1952, Camp Ebenezer joined with the Young People's Institute, an annual Ohio Mennonite program that had been meeting at various camps in the region, to start Camp Luz near Kidron, Ohio.

61. Bechler and Bechler interview.

62. LeRoy Bechler, "Saginaw Service Unit," *Gospel Evangel*, September 1949, 6; LeRoy Bechler, *The Black Mennonite Church in North America, 1886–1986* (Scottdale, PA: Herald Press, 1986), 96.

63. Bechler and Bechler interview.

64. LeRoy Bechler, "Summer Activities at Saginaw," *Gospel Evangel*, September–October 1951, 5–6.

65. Untitled clipping, undated, LeRoy Bechler collection (HM 1-723), box 1, folder 34, MCUSAA–Goshen.

66. Daniel Zook, "The Mission Station in Battle Creek," *Gospel Evangel*, July–August 1953, 7; Harold Christophel, "A New Church Building at Battle Creek," *Gospel Evangel*, March–April 1954, 9.

67. J. C. Wenger, *Mennonites in Indiana and Michigan*, 226–27.

68. See Tobe Schmucker, *Beacon of Hope: The Story of an Inner-City Rescue Mission* (South Bend, IN: privately published, 1991).

69. J. C. Wenger, *Mennonites in Indiana and Michigan*, 236.

70. Harold J. Sherk, "I-W Service," *Mennonite Encyclopedia*, vol. 3 (Scottdale, PA: Mennonite Publishing House, 1956).

71. Cleo Mann, "Indianapolis Our Samaria," *Gospel Evangel*, March–April 1954, 3.

72. Schlabach, *War, Peace, and Social Conscience*, 210–11.

73. Bethel and Bluffton were colleges affiliated with the General Conference Mennonite Church, while Tabor, in Hillsboro, Kansas, was a Mennonite Brethren school.

74. Willard Roth, "J. D. Graber Leaves Mission Legacy," *Gospel Herald*, February 7, 1978, 118.

75. "How Can I Be a Missionary in My Home Community?" *Rural Evangel*, July 1, 1922, 1.

76. "Editorial," *Rural Evangel*, October 1, 1929, 1.

77. Edwin L. Weaver, "The Stronger Congregations and the Unchurched Rural Communities," *Rural Evangel*, November 1, 1930, 2.

78. 1944 conference report, Indiana-Michigan Mennonite Conference collection (II-5-1), box 2, folder 9, MCUSAA–Goshen.

79. "A Mission Outpost for Every Congregation," *Rural Evangel*, March–April 1956, 4; Wayne Wenger, "Developments and Trends in Our Summer Bible Schools," *Rural Evangel*, March–April 1950, 2.

80. Homer F. North, "A Resolution Passed at Our Last Annual Meeting," *Rural Evangel*, September 1941, 3.

81. "Voluntary Service under District Mission Board," *Rural Evangel*, November–December 1952, 5.

82. Kathleen Zehr, "History of the First Mennonite Church, New Bremen, New York" (unpublished paper), D. A. Yoder Wenger collection (HM 1-314), box 4, folder 48, MCUSAA–Goshen.

83. J. C. Wenger, *Mennonites in Indiana and Michigan*, 257; J. Kore Zook, "Blountstown Tidings," *Gospel Evangel*, November–December 1957, 10.

84. Mennonite World Conference was an international gathering of all Mennonite groups held every five or six years. By the late twentieth century, MWC had grown into a programmatic organization, in addition to continuing to hold the regular assemblies.

85. Hershberger, *Mennonite Church in the Second World War*, 263. The Mennonite Church–only CPS unit was located at Malcolm, Neb., on a farm owned by the Mennonite Publication Board and had about thirty-five men.

86. Keim, *Harold S. Bender*, 159. Virtually all Mennonite and related groups at the time were in North America and Europe, as churches in Africa, Asia, and Latin America were still under the auspices of Western Mennonite mission boards. There were two exceptions: One was several colonies of conservative Mennonites of Russian background, who moved from Canada to Mexico and Paraguay in the 1920s. The second exception was refugees from Communist Russia who settled in Brazil and Paraguay in the 1920s and 1930s.

87. Ibid., 252.

88. Mennonite World Conference, *Proceedings of the Fourth Mennonite World Conference* (Akron PA: Mennonite Central Committee, 1950), viii–ix.
89. Rich Preheim, "Cooperation's Harvest: The Growth of Inter-Mennonite Relations on 55 Acres," *Mennonite Historical Bulletin*, October 2008, 5–7.
90. Samuel Floyd Pannabecker, *Ventures in Faith: The Story of Mennonite Biblical Seminary* (Elkhart, IN: privately published, 1975), 55–57.
91. Ibid, 7.
92. Associated Mennonite Biblical Seminaries, which largely functioned as a single operation, officially became one institution in 1994, legally joining together Goshen Biblical Seminary and Mennonite Biblical Seminary as Associated Mennonite Biblical Seminary. It then changed its name to Anabaptist Mennonite Biblical Seminary in 2012.
93. See chap. 1.
94. See chap. 3, n. 14 for an explanation of Stuckey Amish and the Central Conference of Mennonites.
95. Harold S. Bender, "Washington Center Mennonite Church," *Mennonite Encyclopedia*, vol. 4 (Scottdale, PA: Mennonite Publishing House, 1959).
96. Indiana-Michigan Mennonite Conference, *Report of the Indiana-Michigan Church Conference* 1940, 3–5, 7.
97. Silas Hertzler, "Mennonite Parochial Schools: Why Established and What They Have Achieved," in *Proceedings of the Seventh Annual Conference on Mennonite Cultural Problems* (Hillsboro, KS: 1949), 79.
98. Indiana-Michigan Mennonite Conference, *Report of the Annual Sessions of the Indiana-Michigan Mennonite Conference*, 25–26.
99. Verle Hoffman to Indiana-Michigan High School Planning Committee, May 8, 1953, Bethany Christian Schools collection (III-5-8), box 1, folder "Correspondence 1953," MCUSAA–Goshen.
100. H. S. Bender to "Brothers" (form letter), May 6, 1953, Bethany Christian Schools collection (III-5-8) box 1, folder "Correspondence 1953," MCUSAA–Goshen.
101. Jess Kauffman, *A Vision and a Legacy: The Story of Mennonite Camping, 1920–80* (Newton, KS: Faith & Life Press, 1984), 58.
102. Cheryl Mast, *Amigo Centre: In Harmony with God and Nature* (Sturgis, MI: privately published, 2007), 3.
103. Russell Krabill, "With Our Youth," *Gospel Evangel*, July–August 1955, 6.
104. Mast, *Amigo Centre*, 3–4.
105. Levi Hartzler, "Conference Camp Readied for the Summer," *Gospel Evangel*, May–June 1960, 15.
106. Ibid. Camp Amigo was renamed Amigo Centre in 1995 as its programs expanded beyond conventional camping.

Chapter 7: The Priesthood of All Believers

1. Note dated October 17, 1957, Russell Krabill collection (HM 1-599), box 69, folder "J. C. Wenger notes and letters," MCUSAA–Goshen.
2. Bergthal Mennonites were a Russian immigrant group, originating in the Bergthal colony, that settled in Manitoba in the 1870s. In subsequent years they broke into several groups, including one that affiliated with the General Conference Mennonite Church.

3. While the term "the priesthood of all believers" did not originate with the Anabaptists, the concept has been central to the Anabaptist faith since its inception in the sixteenth century. Anticlericalism was a major force in the religious and political reform movements that included Anabaptism.

4. James T. Patterson, *Grand Expectations: The United States, 1945–1974*, Oxford History of the United States, vol. 10 (New York,: Oxford University Press, 1996), vii.

5. Keim, *Harold S. Bender*, 464; Steven M. Nolt, "From Bishop to Bureaucracy: Observations on the Migration of Authority," *Vision: A Journal for Church and Theology* 5, no. 2 (Fall 2004): 17.

6. Harold S. Bender, "Priesthood of All Believers," *Mennonite Encyclopedia*, vol. 4 (Scottdale, PA: Mennonite Publishing House, 1959).

7. "The 1954 Conference Sermon," Harold S. Bender collection (HM 1-278), box 101, folder 3, MCUSAA–Goshen.

8. Keim, *Harold S. Bender*, 337.

9. Indiana-Michigan Mennonite Conference, *Report of the Annual Sessions of the Indiana-Michigan Mennonite Conference, June 6, 7, 1956*, 19.

10. Attending the 1952 Amsterdam retreat were Irvin Horst, John W. Miller, Paul Peachey, Cal Redekop, David Shank, Orley Swartzentruber, and John Howard Yoder—all Goshen College alumni. Despite its longevity, Concern was never a formal organization and participation was fluid. For an overview, see J. Lawrence Burkholder, "Concern Pamphlets Movement," *Mennonite Encyclopedia*, vol. 5 (Scottdale, PA: Herald Press, 1990).

11. Quoted in Keim, *Harold S. Bender*, 456.

12. C. Norman Kraus and John W. Miller, "Intimations of Another Way: A Progress Report," *Concern: A Pamphlet Series* 3 (1956): 8.

13. Carolyn to Wilma, September 30, 1955, Carolyn Hertzler collection (HM 5-3), file cabinet 2, drawer 1, folder "K-Groups, College Mennonite, 1955," MCUSAA–Goshen.

14. Ibid.

15. Dave Jackson and Neta Jackson, *Glimpses of Glory: Thirty Years of Community* (Elgin, IL: Brethren Press, 1987), 35.

16. Kraus and Miller, "Intimations of Another Way," 15–16.

17. Jackson and Jackson, *Glimpses of Glory*, 32–34; Schlabach, "History," 55–56.

18. Jackson and Jackson, *Glimpses of Glory*, 34.

19. Ibid., 37–41.

20. Ibid., 81–82.

21. J. C. Wenger to Virgil Vogt, November 8, 1962, Indiana-Michigan Mennonite Conference collection (II-5-1), box 3, folder 34, MCUSAA–Goshen.

22. Nolt, "From Bishop to Bureaucracy," 15, 22; Harold S. Bender, "Bishop," *Mennonite Encyclopedia*, vol. 1 (Scottdale, PA: Mennonite Publishing House, 1955).

23. William Wickey to Floyd F. Bontrager, April 23, 1966, Indiana-Michigan Mennonite Conference collection (II-5-2), box 3, folder 12, MCUSAA–Goshen.

24. Harold S. Bender, "South Central Conference," *Mennonite Encyclopedia*, vol. 4 (Scottdale, PA: Mennonite Publishing House, 1959).

25. Indiana-Michigan Mennonite Conference, *Report of the Annual Sessions of the Indiana-Michigan Mennonite Conference* 1964, 18.

26. Indiana-Michigan Mennonite Conference executive committee to Clarence Troyer, December 20, 1947, Indiana-Michigan Mennonite Conference collection (II-5-2), box 2, folder 33, MCUSAA–Goshen.

27. Mary Handrich and Willard Handrich, interview by author, June 21, 2006, Grand Marais, MI, recording in author's possession.

28. Indiana-Michigan Mennonite Conference executive committee to Clarence Troyer, December 20, 1947, Indiana-Michigan Mennonite Conference collection (II-5-2), box 2, folder 33, MCUSAA–Goshen.

29. Willard Handrich to Indiana-Michigan Conference Executive Committee, January 23, 1958, Indiana-Michigan Mennonite Conference collection (II-5-2), box 2, folder 33, MCUSAA–Goshen.

30. Handrich and Handrich interview.

31. Ibid.

32. Simon Gingerich and J. C. Wenger, "Report of Investigative Visit to Grand Marais, Michigan," July 20, 1961,Indiana-Michigan Mennonite Conference collection (II-5-2), box 3, folder 33, MCUSAA–Goshen.

33. Norman Weaver to J. C. Wenger, January 19, 1962; and Wenger to Weaver, February 6, 1962, both in Indiana-Michigan Mennonite Conference collection (II-5-1), box 3, folder 33, MCUSAA–Goshen.

34. Pigeon Mennonite Church Council to Indiana-Michigan Mennonite Conference Executive Committee, May 19, 1962; and Indiana-Michigan Mennonite Conference Executive Committee to Pigeon Mennonite Church, June 27, 1962, both in Indiana-Michigan Mennonite Conference collection (II-5-2), box 3, folder 8, MCUSAA–Goshen.

35. Black binder "Ministerial Committee," Indiana-Michigan Mennonite Conference collection (II-5-12), MCUSAA–Goshen.

36. Ibid.

37. "Report of the Annual Sessions of the Indiana-Michigan Mennonite Conference, July 30–August 2, 1964," 17.

38. Galen Johns to Bill Wickey, December 8, 1969, Indiana-Michigan Mennonite Conference collection (II-5-1), box 3, folder 16, MCUSAA–Goshen.

39. Leonard Gross, "Bethany's Vigorous Birth," in *Hearing Our Teacher's Voice: The Pursuit of Faithfulness at Bethany Christian Schools, 1954–2004* (Goshen, IN: privately published, 2004), 71.

40. Galen Johns to Brethren, February 27, 1970, J. C. Wenger collection (HM 1-337), box 22, folder 27, MCUSAA–Goshen.

41. Russell Krabill, "Radio—To Spread the Gospel," *Rural Evangel*, September–October 1947, 3.

42. Herbert L. Osborne, "History of the Mennonite Church in Fort Wayne, Indiana, 1903–1953" (unpublished manuscript in Mennonite Historical Library, Goshen, IN), 22.

43. Indiana-Michigan Mennonite Conference, *Report of the Annual Sessions of the Indiana-Michigan Mennonite Conference* 1954, 11.

44. J. C. Wenger to C. F. Yake, January 26, 1949, Indiana-Michigan Mennonite Conference collection (II-5-2), box 1, folder 2, MCUSAA–Goshen.

45. C. Joseph Martin, "Mennonite Church Discipline Based on the Practices of the Mennonite Churches of Indiana-Michigan and Ohio & Eastern" (research paper, Goshen Biblical Seminary, 1960), 8.

46. Indiana-Michigan Mennonite Conference, *Report of the Indiana-Michigan Church Conference* 1946, 3.

47. "Meeting of the Conference Executive Committee with the Bishops of Indiana-Michigan Mennonite Conference, North Goshen Mennonite Church, February 23, 1949," Indiana-Michigan Mennonite Conference collection (II-5-2), box 1, folder 2, MCUSAA–Goshen.

48. Mennonite General Conference, *Mennonite General Conference Report, August 26–30, 1953* (Scottdale, PA: Mennonite Publishing House, 1953), 81–82.

49. Reproduced in J. C. Wenger, *Dealing Redemptively with Those Involved in Divorce and Remarriage Problems* (Scottdale, PA: Herald Press, n.d.), 20.

50. Ibid., 22.

51. Clarence Troyer to Ezra Beachy, March 24, 1953, Indiana-Michigan Mennonite Conference collection (II-5-1), box 4, folder 7, MCUSAA–Goshen.

52. Irene Bechler to "Mother, Dad, all," March 12, 1951, private collection; Bechler and Bechler interview. The matter of receiving divorced people as Ninth Street Mennonite Church members apparently never was problem after that initial occurrence. Mennonite Board of Missions general secretary J. D. Graber, who had a more welcoming stance, would succeed Tobe Schrock as Ninth Street bishop.

53. J. C. Wenger, *Dealing Redemptively*, 26.

54. Ibid., 27.

55. "Report of Study Committee on Divorce and Remarriage," n.d., Indiana-Michigan Mennonite Conference collection (II-5-1), box 4, folder 8, MCUSAA–Goshen.

56. Anson Horner to committee, March 18, 1955, Indiana-Michigan Mennonite Conference collection (II-5-1), box 4, folder 7, MCUSAA–Goshen.

57. J. D. Graber to Ezra Beachy, January 27, 1955, Indiana-Michigan Mennonite Conference collection (II-5-1), box 4, folder 7, MCUSAA–Goshen.

58. Harold S. Bender to Anson Horner, December 14, 1954, Indiana-Michigan Mennonite Conference collection (II-5-1), box 4, folder 7, MCUSAA–Goshen.

59. Indiana-Michigan Mennonite Conference, *Report of the Annual Session of the Indiana-Michigan Mennonite Conference* 1956, 12–13.

60. M. M. Troyer to Galen Johns, March 20, 1954, Indiana-Michigan Mennonite Conference collection (II-5-2), box 2, folder 29, MCUSAA–Goshen.

61. Charles Haarer to Executive Committee of Indiana-Michigan Mennonite Conference, December 7, 1957; and Galen Johns to Bro. Haarer, March 4, 1958, both in Indiana-Michigan Mennonite Conference collection (II-5-2), box 2, folder 33, MCUSAA–Goshen.

62. Indiana-Michigan Mennonite Conference, *Report of the Annual Sessions of the Indiana-Michigan Mennonite Conference* 1951, 7; Indiana-Michigan Mennonite Conference, *Report of the Annual Sessions of the Indiana-Michigan Mennonite Conference* 1952, 8.

63. Ira S. Johns to J. L. Stauffer, July 16, 1945, Indiana-Michigan Mennonite Conference collection (II-5-2), box 2, folder 14, MCUSAA–Goshen.

64. D. A. Yoder to John C. Wenger, February 6, 1948, Indiana-Michigan Mennonite Conference collection (II-5-2), box 2, folder 16, MCUSAA–Goshen.

65. Ibid. Conservative Mennonites often cited the Church of the Brethren, an Anabaptist group that was more acculturated than the Mennonite Church, as a primary example of a once-nonconformist people that had gone astray. They had a sizable population in areas of Mennonite concentration, such as Elkhart County.

66. "Report of the 1949 Conflict at Olive Mennonite Church," compiled in 2002, Olive Mennonite Church collection (III-14-8), box 1, MCUSAA–Goshen.

67. Prairie Street minister J. S. Hartzler was ordained in 1881, twenty-six years before Yoder. He died in 1953.

68. J. C. Wenger, *Glimpses of Mennonite History and Doctrine* (Scottdale, PA: Herald Press, 1959), 162.

69. Jackson and Jackson, *Glimpses of Glory*, 79.

70. J. C. Wenger to J. E. Gingerich, March 14, 1950, Indiana-Michigan Mennonite Conference collection (II-5-2), box 2, folder 20, MCUSAA–Goshen.

71. Indiana-Michigan Mennonite Conference, *Report of the Annual Sessions of the Indiana-Michigan Mennonite Conference 1958*, 4.

72. J. C. Wenger to O. S. Hostetler, August 17, 1960, J. C. Wenger collection (HM 1-337), box 9, folder 28, MCUSAA–Goshen.

73. *Guidance for Church Weddings*, published by the Indiana-Michigan Mennonite Conference Christian Workers Conference, 1955, Indiana-Michigan Mennonite Conference collection (II-5-1), box 2, folder 4, MCUSAA–Goshen.

74. J. C. Wenger to J. D. Graber, June 9, 1958, Indiana-Michigan Mennonite Conference collection (II-5-2), box 3, folder 30, MCUSAA–Goshen.

75. Titus Morningstar, "Beginnings of the Plato Mennonite Church," *Gospel Evangel*, November–December 1951, 6.

76. Percy J. Miller, "A Message from the Secretary," *Gospel Evangel*, November–December 1951, 4.

77. Mrs. Clarence Yoder [Delilah Miller Yoder], "The Challenge of Being a Pastor's Wife," *Gospel Evangel*, January–February 1955, 4.

78. Indiana-Michigan Mennonite Conference, *Report of the Annual Sessions of the Indiana-Michigan Mennonite Conference 1953*, 6.

79. Maggie Glick to "Dear Friend," December 3, 1957, Indiana-Michigan Mennonite Conference collection (II-5-1), box 3, folder 30, MCUSAA–Goshen.

80. Untitled document, March 2, 1951, Indiana-Michigan Mennonite Conference collection (II-5-2), box 2, folder 21, MCUSAA–Goshen.

81. Ibid.

82. Clarence Troyer, *The Mennonite Church in the Upper Peninsula*, 12.

83. "Report of the Special Committee on a Separate Michigan Conference, March 10, 1952," Indiana-Michigan Mennonite Conference collection (II-5-1), box 4, folder 12, MCUSAA–Goshen.

84. Ezra Beachy to Ivan Weaver, October 19, 1956, Indiana-Michigan Mennonite Conference collection (II-5-1), box 4, folder 13, MCUSAA–Goshen.

85. Ezra Beachy to the Special Committee for a Separate Michigan Conference, undated, Indiana-Michigan Conference collection (II-5-1), box 4, folder 11, MCUSAA–Goshen.

86. James Troyer interview.

87. Wayne Wenger to Russell Krabill, July 23, 1957, North Goshen Mennonite Church collection (III-14-19), box 3, folder 3, MCUSAA–Goshen.

88. "Final Report of the Voting of the Michigan Congregations," June 2, 1952, Indiana-Michigan Mennonite Conference collection (II-5-1), box 4, folder 12, MCUSAA–Goshen.

89. Indiana-Michigan Mennonite Conference, *Report of the Annual Sessions of the Indiana-Michigan Mennonite Conference* 1952, 6.

90. "On a Separate Michigan Conference," undated, Indiana-Michigan Mennonite Conference collection (II-5-2), box 2, folder 33, MCUSAA–Goshen.

91. "Tally of the Mich. Mennonite Ministers," December 20, 1955, William Wickey collection (HM 1-716), box 1, folder 5, MCUSAA–Goshen.

92. 1957 Ministers Meeting (Michigan) notes, William Wickey collection (HM 1-716), box 1, folder 5, MCUSAA–Goshen.

93. Indiana-Michigan Mennonite Conference, *Report of the Annual Sessions of the Indiana-Michigan Mennonite Conference* 1958, 4–5.

Chapter 8: A New Look

1. Borntreger, *History of the First Settlers*, 8. Isaac Schmucker's ordination was technically the first for Indiana-Michigan when he became bishop of the Amish Mennonite group in 1843. But having previously been made a minister in Ohio, he was already in congregational ministry.

2. Licensing is a temporary credential for new pastors. After a period of time, usually a couple of years, the pastor is then eligible for ordination, which is permanent (unless voluntarily relinquished or revoked due to some transgression).

3. Irene Smucker, "Wilma Bailey's Search," *Purpose*, January 1977, 1–3.

4. Leland D. Harder to Ronald Krehbiel, Russell Mast, Walter Neufeld, Harris Waltner, James Waltner, Kenneth Bauman, John Esau, and Joe Richards, April 20, 1978, Indiana-Michigan Mennonite Conference collection (II-5-2), box 3, folder 20, MCUSAA–Goshen.

5. Myron A. Marty, *Daily Life in the United States, 1960–1990: Decades of Discord* (Westport, CT: Greenwood Press, 1997), 20.

6. Wuthnow, *Restructuring of American Religion*, 115.

7. Paul Toews, *Mennonites in American Society, 1930–1970: Modernity and the Persistence of Religious Community*, Mennonite Experience in America, vol. 4 (Scottdale, PA: Herald Press, 1996), 239; Leo Driedger and Donald B. Kraybill, *Mennonite Peacemaking: From Quietism to Activism* (Scottdale, PA: Herald Press, 1994), 62, 124–31.

8. Matthew 5:39.

9. Quoted in Driedger and Kraybill, *Mennonite Peacemaking*, 126.

10. Black binder "Ministerial Committee," Indiana-Michigan Mennonite Conference collection (II-5-12), MCUSAA–Goshen.

11. "Message to District Conferences from Mennonite General Conference," August 23, 1963, Indiana-Michigan Mennonite Conference collection (II-5-1), box 3, folder 36, MCUSAA–Goshen.

12. I am indebted to Andy Brubacher-Kaethler for introducing me to the distinctions between "countercultural" and "anticultural" for the Mennonite context.

To be sure, the relationship between faith and culture, for Mennonites or any religious group, is of such complexity that it can't be adequately addressed here.

13. Niles Slabaugh to Galen Johns, May 7, 1955, Indiana-Michigan Mennonite Conference collection (II-5-2), box 2, folder 30, MCUSAA–Goshen.

14. Indiana-Michigan Mennonite Conference, *Reports of the Annual Sessions of the Indiana-Michigan Mennonite Conference* 1968, 57.

15. Schlabach, "History," 29, 68–73; Gladys Beyler, Areta Lehman, and Lucille Swartzendruber, interview by author, September 19, 2012, Goshen, IN, recording in author's possession.

16. Beyler, Lehman, and Swartzendruber interview.

17. Board of Elders to the Congregation, memorandum, March 3, 1972; and College Mennonite Church Congregation Business meeting, April 5, 1972, both in College Mennonite Church collection (III-14-1.9), box 6, folder 59/7, MCUSAA–Goshen.

18. Marlin Jeschke, interview with author, Goshen, IN, August 14, 2007.

19. Ibid.

20. Schlabach, "History," 65–66.

21. Edna Beiler and Melvin King, "A Study of the Prayer Veil as Viewed by the College Mennonite Church," (research paper, Goshen College, 1968), 18–20.

22. Executive Committee minutes, March 21, 1973, Indiana-Michigan Mennonite Conference collection (II-5-2), box 1, folder 18, MCUSAA–Goshen.

23. Findings Committee to Indiana-Michigan Ministerial Committee, December 23, 1959, Indiana-Michigan Mennonite Conference collection (II-5-1), box 3, folder 30, MCUSAA–Goshen.

24. Secretary's notebook, Indiana-Michigan Mennonite Conference collection (II-5-1), box 2, folder 24, MCUSAA–Goshen.

25. Your Pastor, Elders and Church Council to Dear Brothers and Sisters in Christ, September 3, 1961, First Mennonite Church (Fort Wayne, Ind.) collection (III-14-22), box 1, folder 4, MCUSAA–Goshen.

26. Simon Gingerich to J. C. Wenger, Paul M. Miller, Howard Zehr, and Harold S. Bender, October 18, 1961, Indiana-Michigan Mennonite Conference collection (II-5-1), box 3, folder 32, MCUSAA–Goshen.

27. R. C. Laurie Mitton to John C. Wenger, November 18, 1962, Bethany Christian Schools collection (II-5-8), box 1, folder "Correspondence 1960–1963," MCUSAA–Goshen.

28. Ibid.

29. J. C. Wenger to R. C. Laurie Mitton, November 22, 1962, Bethany Christian Schools collection (II-5-8), box 1, folder "Correspondence 1960–1963," MCUSAA–Goshen.

30. Richard Benner, "South Side Fellowship Formed," *Gospel Evangel*, March–April 1966, 13.

31. Susan Fisher Miller, *Culture for Service*, 239.

32. Schlabach, "History," 76–79.

33. "Practicing a Common Life Together," *Gospel Evangel*, March–April 1976, 1–3.

34. While a group of university students and their spouses initiated what became First Mennonite Church in Indianapolis in 1953, the congregation was largely driven by and composed of alternative service workers in the city. See chap. 6.

35. Black binder "Ministerial Committee," Indiana-Michigan Mennonite Conference collection (II-5-12), MCUSAA–Goshen.

36. Ann Arbor Mennonite Fellowship 1967 directory, Ann Arbor Mennonite Fellowship collection (III-22-16), MCUSAA–Goshen.

37. Evie Shellenberger and Wallace Shellenberger, interview by author, September 14, 2006, Paoli, IN; "Professionals Practice Practical Christianity," *Gospel Evangel*, January–February 1976, 1; Sanford Eash, "Paoli Fellowship Worships and Serves," *Gospel Evangel*, June 1979, 1.

38. *Mennonite Yearbook and Directory*, 1961–81 (Scottdale, PA: Mennonite Publishing House).

39. Schlabach, "History," 99.

40. Dorothy Yoder Nyce to Ministry Team at College Mennonite Church, February 5, 1977, College Mennonite Church collection (III-14-1.3e), box 1, folder 3, MCUSAA–Goshen.

41. College Mennonite Church actually commissioned all congregational members, an action that generated some internal criticism. See Schlabach, "History," 102–3.

42. Dale Schumm to Russell Krabill, November 5, 1973, Indiana-Michigan Mennonite Conference collection (II-5-13), box 1, folder 6, MCUSAA–Goshen.

43. Homer E. Yutzy to Dean Brubaker, June 27, 1976, Indiana-Michigan Mennonite Conference collection (II-5-13), box 1, folder 8, MCUSAA–Goshen.

44. Homer E. Yutzy to Vernon Bontreger, June 17, 1976, Indiana-Michigan Mennonite Conference collection (II-5-13), box 1, folder 8, MCUSAA–Goshen.

45. Dean M. Brubaker to Homer Yutzy, June 22, 1976, Indiana-Michigan Mennonite Conference collection (II-5-13), box 1, folder 15, MCUSAA–Goshen.

46. Harold Bauman to Arnold Roth, March 20, 1981, Indiana-Michigan Mennonite Conference collection (II-5-2), box 3, folder 22, MCUSAA–Goshen.

47. Study responses, Indiana-Michigan Mennonite Conference collection (II-5-13), box 2, folder 40, MCUSAA–Goshen.

48. Robert J. Baker, "Conference Sounds," *Gospel Evangel*, September 1981, 1; "Report of the Indiana-Michigan Mennonite Conference," *Gospel Evangel*, October 1980, 10.

49. Church Life Commission minutes, December 13, 1979, Indiana-Michigan Mennonite Conference collection (II-5-13), box 1, folder 2, MCUSAA–Goshen.

50. Roy K. Yoder to Church Life Commission, July 21, 1980, Indiana-Michigan Mennonite Conference collection (II-5-13), box 2, folder 40, MCUSAA–Goshen.

51. "Persons and Places," *Gospel Evangel*, March 1984, 9.

52. John Steiner to thirteen AMBS students, January 18, 1977, Indiana-Michigan Mennonite Conference collection (II-5-13), box 2, folder 1, MCUSAA–Goshen.

53. Wuthnow, *Restructuring of American Religion*, 228.

54. John H. Mosemann, "Congregational Life in Change," *Gospel Evangel*, October 1980, 1.

55. Driedger and Kraybill, *Mennonite Peacemaking*, 84–86.

56. See chap. 7.

57. Schlabach, *War, Peace, and Social Conscience*, 367–84.

58. Questionnaire on Peace and Social Issues, Indiana-Michigan Mennonite Conference collection (II-5-13) folder 6, MCUSAA–Goshen.

59. Daniel Slabaugh to J. B. Shenk, Ray Horst, Marion Lehman, and Melvin Leidig, January 11, 1968. Russell Krabill collection (HM 1-599), box 64, folder "Ind.-Mich. Conference Various Reports and Papers," MCUSAA–Goshen.

60. Flier in Russell Krabill collection (HM 1-599), box 64, folder "Ind.-Mich. Conference Various Reports and Papers," MCUSAA–Goshen.

61. Susan Fisher Miller, *Culture for Service*, 229, 239.

62. Etril J. Leinbach to Galen Johns, July 18, 1969, Indiana-Michigan Mennonite Conference collection (II-5-2), box 3, folder 15, MCUSAA–Goshen.

63. "Facts concerning April 5 'Take-Over' at College Church," College Mennonite Church collection (III-14-1.3c), box 7, folder "John Mosemann Pastor File, 1968–1982," MCUSAA–Goshen.

64. "Surprise Takeover at GC Service," *Goshen News*, April 6, 1970, 1–2.

65. Schlabach, "History," 92.

66. "Facts concerning April 5 'Take-Over' at College Church," College Mennonite Church collection (III-14-1.3c).

67. Questionnaire on Peace and Social Issues, Indiana-Michigan Mennonite Conference collection.

68. See "Taking It to the Church" in Melissa Miller and Phil M. Shenk, *The Path of Most Resistance* (Scottdale, PA: Herald Press, 1982), 43-52.

69. See "A Time for Nonconformity and Adventure" in Miller and Shenk, *The Path of Most Resistance*, 131-148. "Reports of the Annual Sessions, Indiana-Michigan Conference of the Mennonite Church, July 29–August 1, 1971," 15.

70. Eli Hochstedler, "I Went to Jail," *Mennonite*, June 30, 1964, 433–34.

71. Betty Jean Wicker to LeRoy and Irene Bechler, April 2, 1957, private collection.

72. Ibid.

73. "Breakthrough in Racial Understanding Experienced in Indiana," *Gospel Evangel*, July–August, 1972, 11.

74. Unfortunately, most white Mennonites didn't share the activist ethos being pushed by African Americans and Latinos, which caused significant tension within the church. See Shearer, *Daily Demonstrators*; and Felipe Hinojosa, *Latino Mennonites: Civil Rights, Faith, and Evangelical Cultures* (Baltimore: Johns Hopkins University Press, 2014). They are two essential works on the development of racial and ethnic diversity among American Mennonites.

75. Levi Keidel, *The History of Fairhaven Mennonite Church, 1954–1998* (n.p., n.d.), 6–7; J. C. Wenger, *Mennonites in Indiana and Michigan*, 269.

76. Galen Johns to Arnold Cressman, August 3, 1979, Indiana-Michigan Mennonite Conference collection (II-5-20), box 5, folder 36, MCUSAA–Goshen.

77. J. C. Wenger to conference executive committee and conference examining committee, July 9, 1964, Indiana-Michigan Mennonite Conference collection (II-5-1), box 3, folder 37, MCUSAA–Goshen.

78. Bechler and Bechler interview.

79. Statement Adopted by the Ninth Street Church, Saginaw, June 7, 1964, Ninth Street Mennonite Church collection (III-2-3), folder "Church Records 1973–1974," MCUSAA–Goshen.

80. J. C. Wenger to Nelson Kauffman, July 15, 1964, Indiana-Michigan Mennonite Conference collection (II-5-1), box 3, folder 27, MCUSAA–Goshen.

81. Russell Krabill to Vernon Bontreger, Galen Johns, O. H. Hooley, and John D. Zehr, September 11, 1965, Indiana-Michigan Mennonite Conference collection (II-5-2), box 3, folder 12, MCUSAA–Goshen.

82. By the late 1960s, more than two hundred thousand Latinos were annually coming to the Midwest and Great Lakes regions for seasonal work. See Samuel Shapiro, "Hispanics" in *Peopling Indiana: The Ethnic Experience*, ed. Robert M. Taylor and Connie A. McBirney (Indianapolis: Indiana Historical Society, 1996), 206.

83. Paul and Alta Erb, "Confidential report on Nurture for Growth visits to Ind.-Mich. churches, Jan.–Dec. 1965," Indiana-Michigan Mennonite Conference collection (II-5-12), box 3, folder 4, MCUSAA–Goshen.

84. Peace and Social Concerns Commission minutes, April 22, 1971, Indiana-Michigan Mennonite Conference collection (II-5-15), box 1, folder 1, MCUSAA–Goshen; Roy K. Yoder to Indiana-Michigan Mennonite Mission Board, February 8, 1971, Indiana-Michigan Mennonite Conference collection (II-5-15), box 1, folder 4, MCUSAA–Goshen.

85. Ben Noll, "Pine Manor Was Probably the Catalyst: The Challenge of Speaking for Migrant Workers in Goshen, Indiana, 1969–1971" (research paper, Goshen College, 2009), 1.

86. Ibid., 7–9.

87. Hinojosa, *Latino Mennonites*, 128.

88. Rafael Falcon, *The Hispanic Mennonite Church in North America, 1932–1982*, trans. Ronald Collins (Scottdale, PA: Herald Press, 1986), 118–19.

89. John D. Yoder, "Church Growth Brings Demands for Space," *Gospel Evangel*, May 1987, 1, 3.

90. Teofilo Ponce, "Templo Menonita de la Hermosa," *Gospel Evangel*, December 1985, 3.

91. See Gerald Derstine, *Following the Fire* (Bradenton, FL: Christian Retreat Gospel Crusade, 1980). Mennonite Church officials in 1977 formally apologized to Derstine for the discipline.

92. Charles Haarer to J. C. Wenger, January 10, 1963, Indiana-Michigan Mennonite Conference collection (II-5-1), box 3, folder 35, MCUSAA–Goshen.

93. Roy S. Koch, letter to the editor, *Gospel Herald*, February 20, 1968, 158.

94. Harold L. Mast to Roy S. Koch, February 20, 1968, Indiana-Michigan Mennonite Conference collection (II-5-13), box 1, folder 16, MCUSAA–Goshen.

95. Susan Fisher Miller, *Culture for Service*, 276; Becky Bontrager Horst, "A Struggle for Identity," in *Hearing Our Teacher's Voice: The Pursuit of Faithfulness at Bethany Christian Schools, 1954–2004* (Goshen, IN: privately published, 2004), 101.

96. Susan Fisher Miller, *Culture for Service*, 276–277.

97. John S. Steiner to John Mosemann and Vernon Bontreger, October 18, 1977, Indiana-Michigan Mennonite Conference collection (II-5-13), box 2, folder 1, MCUSAA–Goshen.

98. Dean Brubaker to Russell Krabill, July 5, 1975, Indiana-Michigan Mennonite Conference collection (II-5-13), box 1, folder 15, MCUSAA–Goshen.

99. Roy S. Koch to Pastors Who Attended the Sharing Conference at Rich Valley, July 11, 1971, Indiana-Michigan Mennonite Conference collection (II-5-13), box 1, folder 18, MCUSAA–Goshen.

100. "Tongues among Us," *Gospel Evangel*, January–February 1972, 4–5.

101. John S. Steiner to Church Life Commission, August 24, 1977, Indiana-Michigan Mennonite Conference collection (II-5-13), box 1, folder 10, MCUSAA–Goshen.

102. Galen Johns to Ernest Zilch, September 30, 1983, Indiana-Michigan Mennonite Conference collection (II-5-20), box 7, folder 23, MCUSAA–Goshen.

103. John Bender, "Reconciliation Spreads to the U.S.," *Christian Living*, December 1985, 9.

104. Ibid.

105. Ted Maust, "For a Brief and Shining Moment," *Mennonite Historical Bulletin*, October 2012, 5–10.

106. Church Life Commission minutes, January 3, 1974, Indiana-Michigan Mennonite Conference collection (II-5-13), box 1, folder 1, MCUSAA–Goshen.

107. Church Life Commission minutes, October 10, 1973, Indiana-Michigan Mennonite Conference collection (II-5-13), box 1, folder 1, MCUSAA–Goshen.

108. Peace and Social Concerns Commission minutes, January 25, 1986, Indiana-Mennonite Michigan Conference collection (II-5-15), box 24, folder 5, MCUSAA–Goshen.

109. Marian E. Hostetler, "Refugee Resettlement in Indiana-Michigan," *Gospel Evangel*, March 1980, 3.

110. Indiana-Michigan's emphasis of the spiritual over the physical was not necessarily indicative of the Mennonite Church as a whole. Nationwide, there were a number of hospitals, orphanages, senior citizens' homes, and other social services under either denominational or local auspices, some of them dating to the late nineteenth century.

111. See Matthew 25:34-40.

112. See Vernon H. Neufeld, ed., *If We Can Love: The Mennonite Mental Health Story* (Newton, KS: Faith & Life Press, 1983), chaps. 2 and 8.

113. Robert Hartzler, "The Oaklawn Psychiatric Center," *Gospel Evangel*, May–June 1959, 15; J. C. Wenger to Indiana-Michigan ministers, January 12, 1962, J. C. Wenger collection (HM 1-337), box 23, folder 21, MCUSAA–Goshen.

114. See John Bender, *Greencroft Roots* (Goshen, IN: privately published, 1997).

115. Elizabeth Anderson, *Pathfinders for God at Comins* (privately published, 1984), 22, 27.

116. By this time, Central District Conference had for several decades been capitalizing on the expertise found in Indiana-Michigan. The featured speaker at Central District's 1959 annual assembly was Goshen College president Paul Mininger, addressing "The Church's Place in Higher Education." Four years earlier, Harold S. Bender spoke at an evening service at Eighth Street Mennonite Church.

117. Louis R. Blok to J. B. Shenk, November 7, 1966, Indiana-Michigan Mennonite Conference collection (II-5-15), folder 2, MCUSAA–Goshen.

118. James Troyer interview.

119. See Schlabach, *War, Peace, and Social Conscience*, chap. 7.

120. James Troyer interview.
121. Lowell Detweiler, *The Hammer Rings Hope: Photos and Stories from Fifty Years of Mennonite Disaster Service* (Scottdale, PA: Herald Press, 2000), 43.
122. *South Bend Tribune* special edition, April 25, 1965, 2A, Palm Sunday Tornado collection (HM 3-1), MCUSAA–Goshen.
123. Detweiler, *Hammer Rings Hope*, 46–47.
124. Mennonite Disaster Service is a U.S. and Canadian inter-Mennonite organization that responds to natural and human-made emergencies. It traces its origins to 1950 when members of Hesston Mennonite Church and Pennsylvania Mennonite Church in Kansas created the Mennonite Service Organization as a way to apply the Civilian Public Service ethos in peacetime. The idea spread to other locales, and in 1955 Mennonite Central Committee assumed binational oversight. MDS became a separately incorporated organization in 1993. See Detweiler, *Hammer Rings Hope*, 45.
125. Leon Farmwald, interview by author, date unknown, Nappanee, IN.
126. Galen Johns to Indiana-Michigan pastors, April 15, 1965, Indiana-Michigan Mennonite Church collection (II-5-2), box 3, folder 11, MCUSAA–Goshen.
127. Galen Johns, "Barn Raising—Another Method," *Gospel Evangel*, May 1991, 5.
128. Paul and Alta Erb, "Confidential Report," 5, 9, Indiana-Michigan Mennonite Conference collection (II-5-12), box 3, folder 2, MCUSAA–Goshen.
129. Ora Wyse to Ralph Stahly, April 10, 1969, Indiana-Michigan Mennonite Conference collection (II-5-2), box 3, folder 15, MCUSAA–Goshen.
130. Daniel Kauffman to John S. Steiner, March 17, 1977, Indiana-Michigan Mennonite Conference collection (II-5-13), box 2, folder 1, MCUSAA–Goshen.
131. Roy S. Koch notebooks, 1970–71 and 1971–72, Indiana-Michigan Mennonite Conference collection (II-5-13), box 1, folders 26 and 27, MCUSAA–Goshen.
132. Roy S. Koch notebooks, 1970–71, Indiana-Michigan Mennonite Conference collection (II-5-13), box 1, folder 26.
133. Harold D. Myers, Harry Schrock Jr., T. E. Schrock, Daniel Zook, and Emanuel J. Hochstedler to Indiana-Michigan Executive Committee, December 2, 1969, Indiana-Michigan Mennonite Conference collection (II-5-2), box 3, folder 16, MCUSAA–Goshen.
134. Maynard Hoover, "Operation Bootstrap," Indiana-Michigan Mennonite Conference collection (II-5-2), box 3, folder 4, MCUSAA–Goshen.
135. Paul Horst to Galen Johns, April 14, 1966, Indiana-Michigan Mennonite Conference collection (II-5-2), box 3, folder 11, MCUSAA–Goshen.
136. Paul and Alta Erb, "Confidential Report," 2.
137. Emanuel J. Hochstedler, Floyd J. Bontrager, Menno L. Beachy, Eli Gingerich to Ind.-Mich. Mennonite Conference, January 23, 1972, Indiana-Michigan Mennonite Conference collection (II-5-13), box 1, folder 19, MCUSAA–Goshen.
138. J. C. Wenger, ed., *Mennonite Handbook, Indiana-Michigan Conference* (Indiana-Michigan Mennonite Conference, 1956).
139. Wenger, *Mennonite Handbook*, 100.
140. Salem Mennonite Church quarterly business meeting minutes, December 16, 1975, Salem Mennonite Church collection (III-14-25), box 1, folder 5, MCUSAA–Goshen. The first Mennonite Central Committee relief sale was held in Pennsylvania in 1957 to raise funds for the inter-Mennonite relief and

service agency, and the idea quickly became popular across the United States and Canada. That Salem would no longer participate in an event that was broadly popular among groups ranging from the Old Order Amish to the mainstream General Conference Mennonite Church is a telling commentary on the congregation's attitude toward not just Indiana-Michigan but all Mennonites.

141. Indiana-Michigan Mennonite Conference executive committee minutes, September 7, 1972, Indiana-Michigan Mennonite Conference collection (II-5-2), box 1, folder 18, MCUSAA–Goshen.

Chapter 9: Binding and Loosing

1. Galen Johns to Hubert and June Schwartzentruber, February 18, 1984, Indiana-Michigan Mennonite Conference collection (II-5-20), box 7, folder 19, MCUSAA–Goshen.
2. Galen Johns to congregations not represented at 1981 annual assembly, September 16, 1981, Indiana-Michigan Mennonite Conference collection (II-5-20), box 5, folder 46, MCUSAA–Goshen.
3. Fred Kniss, *Disquiet in the Land: Cultural Conflict in American Mennonite Communities* (New Brunswick, NJ: Rutgers University Press, 1997), 6.
4. Delegate Questionnaire 83, Indiana-Michigan Mennonite Conference collection (II-5-20), box 6, folder 7, MCUSAA–Goshen.
5. The headquarters for the Mennonite Church General Board moved from Scottdale, Pennsylvania, to the Chicago area in 1971.
6. Cynthia A. Valdez Litwiller, "Women in Church Leadership in the Indiana-Michigan Mennonite Conference" (research paper, Goshen College, 1997), 55.
7. Sherm Kauffman to Gene and Mary Herr, March 23, 1988, Indiana-Michigan Mennonite Conference collection (II-5-20), box 7, folder 30, MCUSAA–Goshen.
8. Wuthnow, *Restructuring of American Religion*, 104; Stephen Ainlay and Fred Kniss, "Mennonites and Conflict: Re-examining Mennonite History and Contemporary Life," *MQR* 72, no. 2 (April 1998): 137.
9. Regarding war taxes, see Harold S. Bender, "Taxation," *Mennonite Encyclopedia*, vol. 4 (Scottdale, PA: Mennonite Publishing House, 1959); and Donald D. Kaufman, "Taxes," *Mennonite Encyclopedia*, vol. 5 (Scottdale, PA: Mennonite Publishing House, 1990). Anabaptists have a long record of opposition to paying taxes to fund warfare, dating back to sixteenth-century Europe. In America, Mennonites first objected to war taxes during the American Revolution. During the Vietnam War, Mennonites and other conscientious objectors began more systematically opposing war taxes. Some withheld the percentage of their income taxes designated for the military, while others withheld a token symbolic amount. Many conservative Mennonites opposed such civil disobedience, seeing it as yet another instance of the church straying from traditional nonresistance.
10. Much has been written about the cultural and political ascent of evangelical Christianity, including the religious right, in the United States during the last decades of the twentieth century. For example, see William Martin, *With God on Our Side: The Rise of the Religious Right in America* (New York: Broadway Books, 1996); and Linda Kintz and Julia Lesage, eds., *Media, Culture, and the Religious Right* (Minneapolis: University of Minnesota Press, 1998).

11. John H. Mosemann, "Congregational Life in Change," *Gospel Evangel*, October 1980, 1.
12. Budget working paper, Indiana-Michigan Mennonite Church collection (II-5-4), box 1, folder 22, MCUSAA–Goshen.
13. James Troyer interview.
14. J. Lorne Peachey, "Berne Consultation Focuses on Biblical Authority, Integrity of Leadership, Influence of Humanism," *Gospel Herald*, April 14, 1981, 296–97.
15. See George R. Brunk II, *A Crisis among Mennonites: In Education, in Publication* (Harrisonburg, VA: Sword and Trumpet, 1983).
16. Dean Brubaker to Art Good, Earl Eberly, Wayne Goldsmith, and Joe Swartz, March 18, 1983, Don Blosser collection (HM 1-167), box 1, folder 1, MCUSAA–Goshen.
17. John Roth, "Numerous Factors in MacDonalds' Resignation," *Goshen College Record*, March 21, 1980, 1.
18. Art Good to Indiana-Michigan Conference, March 18, 1985, Indiana-Michigan Mennonite Conference collection (II-5-20), box 7, folder 25, MCUSAA–Goshen.
19. J. Lorne Peachey, "Berne Consultation Focuses on Biblical Authority."
20. The Stonewall Riots of June 1969, after New York City police raided a gay bar in Greenwich Village, are often cited as a turning point in the rise of same-sex orientation from subculture status.
21. Kevin Linehan, "A Pastoral Response to Homosexuality," *Gospel Herald*, June 14, 1977, 476. In the twenty-first century, homosexuality had been expanded to include bisexual and transgendered people. But as a divisive issue confronting Indiana-Michigan Mennonite Church and the rest of the Mennonite Church starting in the 1970s, it was just homosexuality, or more specifically, sexual relations between individuals of the same sex. The words *homosexuality* and *homosexual*, while prominent at the time, have since fallen out of favor; in their place, I use terms such as *same-sex sexual relations* and and *LGBT* (lesbian, gay, bisexual, transgender) *individuals*.
22. For more on the history of gays and lesbians in the Mennonite Church and General Conference Mennonite Church, including Indiana-Michigan Mennonite Conference, see Melanie Zuercher and Lin Garber, *Historical Perspectives*, Welcome to Dialogue Series, vol. 2 (Welcome Committee, 2001).
23. Willard S. Krabill, "Homosexuality: Time to Break the Silence," *Goshen College Record*, February 15, 1980, 3.
24. "Delegate report—Bethlehem 83—Wes Culver," Indiana-Michigan Mennonite Conference collection (II-5-20), box 6, folder 9, MCUSAA–Goshen.
25. Julianna Bontrager, "Seminar on Homosexuality Recovery Scheduled," *Gospel Evangel*, October 1983, 7.
26. JPSC August 27, 1983, minutes, Indiana-Michigan Mennonite Conference collection (II-5-20), box 5, folder 22, MCUSAA–Goshen.
27. Mary Lehman Yoder, "Homosexuality: A Congregational Story," presentation to First Mennonite Church, Indianapolis, IN, 1992, folder "Homosexuality 1989–90" in Assembly Mennonite Church office files, Goshen, IN.
28. Before gays and lesbians could legally marry, some same-sex couples chose to have an ersatz wedding, a public ceremony conducted by clergy where the

partners declared their love and commitment to each other. *Covenanted union* was one of the terms used to describe their subsequent relationship.

29. Southside Fellowship Congregational Council minutes, October 24, 1992; and December 17, 1992, both in Southside Fellowship office files, Elkhart, IN.

30. Mennonite Church congregations expelled for welcoming gays and lesbians were Ames (Iowa) Mennonite Church by Iowa-Nebraska Mennonite Conference, 1988; Germanton Mennonite Church, Philadelphia, Pennsylvania, by Franconia Mennonite Conference, 1997; Rainbow Mennonite Church, Kansas City, Kansas, by South Central Mennonite Conference, 1998; and Atlanta (Ga.) Mennonite Fellowship by Southeast Mennonite Conference 1998. Illinois Mennonite Conference placed under discipline, but did not expel, Oak Park Mennonite Church, Chicago, Illinois, and Maple Avenue Mennonite Church, Waukesha, Wisconsin, both in 1995. Also in 1995, the Northern District Conference of the General Conference Mennonite Church discontinued financial support of a church plant in Saint Paul, Minnesota, because of its position on gay and lesbian members.

31. Charlotte Holsopple Glick to Sherm Kauffman, Don Delagrange, and Marion Hostetler, January 5, 1995, D-5 box 5, folder "Consultation of Conference Leaders on Issues Regarding Homosexuality, January 6–7, 1995, Camp Mack, Milford, Indiana," Indiana-Michigan Mennonite Conference office, Goshen, IN.

32. Southside Fellowship Congregational Council minutes, May 6, 1993, Southside Fellowship office files, Elkhart, IN. Southside was also a member of the General Conference Mennonite Church's Central District Conference. The congregation made the same request for guidance of them and also received no response. But Central District never took any disciplinary action against Southside.

33. Sherm Kauffman to Willard Roth, November 19, 1993, brown binder, Southside Fellowship office files, Elkhart, IN.

34. "Southside Fellowship Congregational Meeting, November 21, 1993," D-5 box 5, folder "Homosexuality," Indiana-Michigan Mennonite Conference office, Goshen, IN.

35. Marlin Miller to Mark Weidner, Sherm Kauffman, and Vern Preheim, February 14, 1994, D-5 box 5, folder "Homosexuality," Indiana-Michigan Mennonite Conference office, Goshen, IN.

36. "Minutes of the 1994 Indiana-Michigan Mennonite Conference."

37. Jay Miiller and Michigan Avenue Mennonite Church to Indiana-Michigan Executive Committee, August 10, 1994, D-5 box 5, folder "Executive Committee MCGB, Homosexuality Consultation 1/6–7/95," Indiana-Michigan Mennonite Conference office, Goshen, IN.

38. Steve Thomas to staff and Executive Committee of the Indiana-Michigan Mennonite Conference, May 18, 1995, Southside Fellowship office files, Elkhart, IN.

39. Statement by Elkhart Area Council of Pastors, February 9, 1995, red binder, Indiana-Michigan Mennonite Conference office, Goshen, IN.

40. Brent Liechty, "A Harvest of Thistles," February 27, 1995, Southside Fellowship office files, Elkhart, IN.

41. Don Delagrange to Executive Committee, Ministry Staff, Delegates and Congregations, February 16, 1995, Southside Fellowship office files, Elkhart, IN.

42. Russ Leinbach to "Brother or Sister in the Lord," June 6, 1995, Southside Fellowship office files, Elkhart, IN.

43. J. Lorne Peachey, "Indiana-Michigan Conference Asks Congregations to Reaffirm Purdue 87 Statement on Homosexuality," *Gospel Herald*, July 18, 1995, 10.

44. Ibid.; "Delegates Approve Accountability Process, Speak to Southside," *Gospel Evangel*, September 1995, 2.

45. Anonymous to Indiana-Michigan Mennonite Conference, undated but received September 19, 1995, D-5 Box 5 Homosexuality, folder "Conference/Executive Committee Agenda, Homosexuality Issue," Indiana-Michigan Mennonite Conference office, Goshen, IN.

46. Stanley Green to John and Leona Brandeberry, Lloyd and Loretta Troyer, and Wilbur and Mary Jane Miller, October 4, 1995, D-5 box 5 Homosexuality, folder "Conference/Executive Committee Agenda, Homosexuality Issue," Indiana-Michigan Mennonite Conference office, Goshen, IN.

47. Gene Troyer to Don Delagrange, October 16, 1995, D-5 box 5, folder "Conference/Executive Committee Agenda, Homosexuality Issue," Indiana-Michigan Mennonite Conference office, Goshen, IN.

48. Untitled document, dated January 29, 1996, D-5 box 5, folder "Homosexuality—FM Indy Process," Indiana-Michigan Mennonite Conference office, Goshen, IN.

49. Gerald Good to Southside Fellowship, June 11, 1996, D-5 box 5 Homosexuality, unlabeled red folder, Indiana-Michigan Mennonite Conference office, Goshen, IN.

50. "Report from the Task Force of IN-MI Conference Executive Committee Assigned to Meet with Southside Fellowship Representatives," October 21, 1998, brown binder, Southside Fellowship office files, Elkhart, IN.

51. James Waltner and Tom Gunden to Don Delagrange and Indiana-Michigan Mennonite Conference executive committee, March 20, 1996, D-5 box 5, folder "Homosexuality—FM Indy Process," Indiana-Michigan Mennonite Conference office, Goshen, IN.

52. Arienne Johnson, "Southside's Scandal: Discerning Authority beyond Homosexuality between Indiana-Michigan Mennonite Conference and Southside Fellowship, 1993–2003" (research paper, Goshen College, 2010), 34.

53. Southside Fellowship congregational meeting, September 29, 1996, pink binder "Southside Fellowship Self Study, 1998–1991," Southside Fellowship office files, Elkhart, IN.

54. "Revised Proposal Report and Request for Counsel" in 1997 Indiana-Michigan Mennonite Conference annual reports, B-39. In Mennonite Historical Library, Goshen, IN.

55. Don Blosser to Sherm Kauffman, July 23, 1997, box C-1, blue three-ring binder "Executive Committee Agenda, March 1997–June 2000," Indiana-Michigan Mennonite Conference office, Goshen, IN.

56. "Report from the Task Force of IN-MI Conference Executive Committee Assigned to Meet with South Fellowship Representatives," October 21, 1998, brown binder, Southside Fellowship office files, Elkhart, IN.

57. Brian D. Arbuckle to Church Life Commission, Executive Committee, and Conference Delegates, memorandum, June 26, 2001, file "Arbuckle, Brian D.," in Central District Conference office, Goshen, IN.

58. Brian D. Arbuckle to seventy-six addresses, email re. "Asking Questions," June 19, 2000, in folder "Arbuckle, Brian D.," in Central District Conference office, Goshen, IN; February 16, 1999, MennoLink post (subject: "Credentialing of Ministers"); Arbuckle to CLC, Executive Committee, and Delegates, memorandum, June 26, 2001. All in Central District Conferene office, Goshen, IN.

59. The other ordained Indiana-Michigan signatories of the "Open Letter" advertisement were Sylvia Shirk Charles, pastor at Waterford Mennonite Church, Goshen; Karl Shelly, pastor at Assembly Mennonite Church, Goshen; and retirees Willis Breckbill and Weyburn Groff. The advertisement appeared in *Mennonite Weekly Review*, February 17, 2000, 7.

60. Laurie L. Oswald, "Indiana-Michigan Network Wants Reform," *Mennonite Weekly Review*, February 10, 2000, 1. While it claimed not to be a splinter group but a renewal and reform movement within the conference and denomination, Evangelical Anabaptist Network participants came largely from congregations that had withdrawn or would withdraw.

61. J. C. Wenger, *Mennonites in Indiana and Michigan*, 204.

62. Michigan Church Life Committee to Indiana-Michigan Church Life Commission, January 3, 2000, Indiana-Michigan Mennonite Conference files, box C-1, binder "Ministry Team," Indiana-Michigan Mennonite Conference office, Goshen, IN.

63. Sherm Kauffman, interview by author, August 2, 2012, Goshen, IN, recording in author's possession. That Schrauger wanted to pull Fairview out of Indiana-Michigan was hardly a secret in the conference.

64. Fairview Mennonite Church to Indiana-Michigan Executive Committee, April 4, 2002, Indiana-Michigan Mennonite Conference files, box C-1, binder "Ministry Team," Indiana-Michigan Mennonite Conference office, Goshen, IN. Despite Fairview's new independent status, some members still kept their conference and denominational identities, even to the point of attending Mennonite Church USA conventions as far away as San Jose, California, in 2007. Schrauger, meanwhile, left Fairview after a short, contentious pastorate and eventually left Christianity. In 2007, his oldest son, a U.S. soldier in Iraq, nearly died from injuries incurred in combat. Soon afterward, Schrauger's two teenage sons were killed in an auto accident. These tragedies helped steer him toward atheism. "Extreme Makeover," Center for Inquiry website, accessed March 14, 2013, http://www.cfimichigan.org/pastevents/event/w-lecture-081011.

65. Indiana-Michigan Mennonite Conference Church Life Commission to Conference Executive Committee, undated, box C-1, binder "Indiana-Michigan Executive Committee Agenda August 2000–May 2004," Indiana-Michigan Mennonite Conference office, Goshen, IN.

66. "Indiana-Michigan Conf. Leader Dies," *Mennonite Weekly Review*, February 11, 1999, 3.

67. The magnitude of the John Howard Yoder saga is only starting to be revealed as of this writing. As part of a process of truth telling and repentance, Mennonite Church USA and Anabaptist Mennonite Biblical Seminary in 2014

invited historian Rachel Waltner Goossen to document Yoder's conduct and the church's handling of it. As part of her research, she was able to gain access to archival files that had long been sealed and unavailable to the public. The result of her work was "'Defanging the Beast': Mennonite Responses to John Howard Yoder's Sexual Abuse," published in the January 2015 issue of *Mennonite Quarterly Review*, the first comprehensive examination of what may be the greatest travesty in five centuries of Anabaptist Mennonite history. For her arduous, groundbreaking work after decades of silence, Goossen deserves my—and the church's—immeasurable gratitude.

68. Ruth Elizabeth Krall, *The Elephants in God's Living Room*, vol. 3, *The Mennonite Church and John Howard Yoder, Collected Essays* (unpublished manuscript, 2013) at www.ruthkrall.com, 72. The General Conference Mennonite Church was also dealing with its own spate of ministerial sexual misconduct cases.

69. See Church Life Commission records in Indiana-Michigan Mennonite Conference collection (II-5-20), box 10, folder 1C, MCUSAA–Goshen.

70. See chap. 7.

71. The distinction between Goshen Biblical Seminary and Mennonite Biblical Seminary, which together composed Associated Mennonite Biblical Seminaries (later renamed Anabaptist Mennonite Biblical Seminary), is critical in the John Howard Yoder saga. Because he was a GBS employee, the problem did not include MBS.

72. Willard S. Krabill, "Sexuality," *Mennonite Encyclopedia*, vol. 5 (Scottdale, PA: Mennonite Publishing House, 1990).

73. Rachel Waltner Goossen, "'Defanging the Beast,'" 10; Ruth Krall, comp., "John Howard Yoder: An Annotated Timeline," Enduring Space website, last amended January 15, 2015, accessed August 4, 2015, http://ruthkrall.com/recommended -reading/john-howard-yoder-an-annotated-timeline-amended-2015/; Soli Salgado, "Yoder Case Extends to Notre Dame," *National Catholic Reporter*, June 19–July 2, 2015, 15; untitled, undated document [1992?] from Carolyn Holderread Heggen and Martha Smith Good, Rachel Waltner Goossen on John Howard Yoder collection (HM 1-49), box 1, folder 1, MCUSAA–Goshen.

74. Goossen, "'Defanging the Beast,'" 11.

75. Ibid., 24–25.

76. Ibid., 29.

77. Ibid., 25.

78. Jamie Pitts, "Anabaptist Re-Vision: On John Howard Yoder's Misrecognized Sexual Politics," *MQR* 89, no. 1 (January 2015): 162.

79. Goossen, "'Defanging the Beast,'" 31.

80. Ibid., 46–47.

81. For an example of such impressions, see Rachel Waltner Goossen, "Campus Protests and John Howard Yoder, 1985–1987," *Mennonite Life* 69 (2015), accessed August 7, 2015, http://ml.bethelks.edu/issue/vol-69/article /campus-protests-and-john-howard-yoder-1985-1997/.

82. Yoder advocated for Mennonites to develop relations and work with other Christian bodies. He often represented Mennonite interests in ecumenical settings and even held positions with the National Council of Churches and

World Council of Churches, even though the Mennonite Church was a member of neither group. As a result, Yoder traveled widely, speaking and teaching in non-Mennonite contexts, which also brought him into contact with more women. See Mark Thiessen Nation, *John Howard Yoder: Mennonite Patience, Evangelical Witness, Catholic Convictions* (Grand Rapids, MI: Wm. B. Eerdmans, 2006).

83. Charlie Cooper to Rachel Waltner Goossen, email, June 28, 2014, Rachel Waltner Goossen on John Howard Yoder collection (HM 1-49), box 1, folder 13, MCUSAA–Goshen.

84. Ruth Krall, "John Howard Yoder: An Annotated Timeline"; Salgado, "Yoder Case Extends to Notre Dame."

85. Krall, "John Howard Yoder: An Annotated Timeline."

86. Walter Sawatsky to Ross Lynn Bender, email, October 18, 2004, in "AMBS and John Howard Yoder," 9–10, Ross Bender website, posted August 18, 2013, accessed August 4, 2015, http://rossbender.org/AMBS-JHY.pdf.

87. Goossen, "'Defanging the Beast,'" 50.

88. Tom Price, "Theologian Cited in Sex Inquiry," *Elkhart Truth*, June 29, 1992, B1.

89. Loren Johns to Walter Sawatsky and Ross L. Bender, email, October 18, 2004, in "AMBS and John Howard Yoder," 11, Ross Bender website, posted August 18, 2013, accessed August 4, 2015, http://rossbender.org/AMBS-JHY.pdf.

90. Charlie Cooper to Rachel Waltner Goossen, email, June 28, 2014, Rachel Waltner Goossen on John Howard Yoder collection (HM 1-49), box 1, folder 13, MCUSAA–Goshen.

91. Goossen, "'Defanging the Beast,'" 47.

92. See chap. 2, n. 36. John K. Stoner, a Mennonite minister and peace activist, at the time argued against the traditional understanding of Matthew 18, which was Yoder's stance, in addressing the allegations against the theologian. Stoner, and others, said Matthew 18 assumes a relative balance of power between the two parties, which was certainly not the case in the Yoder situation. See Goossen, "'Defanging the Beast,'" 53–54.

93. Tom Price, "Church Slow to Explore Rumors against a Leader," *Elkhart Truth*, July 14, 1992, B1.

94. Goossen, "'Defanging the Beast,'" 51. In 2013, Herald Press began including a statement in all books authored by John Howard Yoder acknowledging his abusive conduct; see www.mennomedia.org/?Page=7904.

95. Johns to Sawatsky and Bender email, in "AMBS and John Howard Yoder," 11, Ross Bender website.

96. Harold and Ruth Yoder to John Howard Yoder, July 22, 1991, Rachel Waltner Goossen on John Howard Yoder collection (HM 1-49), box 1, folder 5, MCUSAA–Goshen.

97. Linda Gehman Peachey, "Naming the Pain, Seeking the Light: The Mennonite Church's Response to Sexual Abuse," *MQR* 89, no. 1 (January 2015): 115.

98. Marlin Miller to Vic Stoltzfus, March 20, 1991, Rachel Waltner Goossen on John Howard Yoder collection (HM 1-49), box 1, folder 5, MCUSAA–Goshen.

99. Kimberly Cott, "Yoder Disinvited to Conference," *Bethel Collegian*, March 5, 1992, 1.

100. Goossen, "'Defanging the Beast,'" 68.

101. "Price Told the John Howard Yoder Story," *The Mennonite*, October 2013, 45.

102. Edna F. Bontrager, letter to the editor, *Gospel Herald*, August 25, 1992, 4.

103. Carolyn Holderread Heggen to Mary Mishler, June 28, 1996, Rachel Waltner Goossen on John Howard Yoder collection (HM 1-49), box 1, folder 2, MCUSAA–Goshen.

104. Ibid.

105. Stanley Hauerwas, *Hannah's Child: A Theologian's Memoir* (Grand Rapids, MI: Wm. B. Eerdmans, 2010), 243–45.

106. A "safe plan" refers to procedures to prevent further incidents by an individual, such as requiring his office door to remain open or observers making sure he remains visible so he couldn't slip away and potentially commit more abuse.

107. Goossen, "'Defanging the Beast,'" 68–71.

108. Ibid., 66. Goossen reports that the Accountability and Support Group had suggested that Yoder make continual contributions to the restitution fund, possibly a percentage of his income. But he rejected the idea in favor of a one-time donation.

109. Gordon Dyck to Sherm Kauffman, July 17, 1995, Indiana-Michigan Mennonite Conference collection (II-5-19), box 1, folder 4, MCUSAA–Goshen.

110. "Questions Victims Want RGW's [*sic*] Investigation and Report to Address," June 4, 2014, Rachel Waltner Goossen on John Howard Yoder collection (HM 1-49), box 1, folder 5, MCUSAA–Goshen.

111. John Howard Yoder, *The Fullness of Christ: Paul's Vision of Universal Ministry* (Elgin, IL: Brethren Press, 1987), 10.

112. Goossen, "'Defanging the Beast,'" 59, 63.

113. Gordon Dyck to Sherm Kauffman, Atlee Beechy, and John Howard Yoder, March 20, 1996, Indiana-Michigan Mennonite Conference collection (II-5-19), box 1, folder 4, MCUSAA–Goshen.

114. "Disciplinary Process with John Howard Yoder Draws to a Close," *Gospel Evangel*, July-August 1996, 8.

115. Barbra Graber to Duane Sider, December 27, 1996, Rachel Waltner Goossen on John Howard Yoder collection (HM 1-49), box 1, folder 1, MCUSAA–Goshen.

116. "Progress Report of the John H. Yoder Accountability and Support Group to the Church Life Commission," May 15, 1994, Indiana-Michigan Mennonite Conference collection (II-5-19), box 1, folder 2, MCUSAA–Goshen.

117. That Yoder believed he was prevented from apologizing is evident in a number of discipline-related documents, including his own letters and memos. For example, see John Howard Yoder to George R. Brunk III, January 14, 1997, Rachel Waltner Goossen on John Howard Yoder collection (HM 1-49), box 1, folder 1, MCUSAA–Goshen. At his appearance at Eastern Mennonite Seminary, Yoder spoke "openly of his actions and his desire for healing for the people he had hurt" but did not actually apologize. Ted Grimsrud, "A Faithful Teacher in the Church," *Mennonite*, March 3, 1998, 9. The recording of Yoder's presentation has apparently been lost.

118. Goossen, "'Defanging the Beast,'" 61.

119. John Howard Yoder task force to Prairie Street Mennonite Church Elders, IN-MI Mennonite Conference Church Life Commission, June 26, 1992,

Indiana-Michigan Mennonite Conference collection (II-5-19), box 1, folder 6, MCUSAA–Goshen.

120. Anne Yoder to Gordon Dyck, April 1, 1996, Indiana-Michigan Mennonite Conference collection (II-5-19), box 1, folder 9, MCUSAA–Goshen.

121. George R. Brunk III to Sherm Kauffman, January 15, 1997; and Sherm Kauffman "proposed letter" to Brunk, February 13, 1997, both in Indiana-Michigan Mennonite Conference collection (II-5-19), box 1, folder 4, MCUSAA–Goshen.

122. John Bender to Leonard Gross, email, April 22, 2013.

123. Dan Shenk, "Friends, Family Pay Respects to Yoder," *Elkhart Truth*, January 4, 1998, A6.

124. Paul and Alta Erb, "Summary of Observations," Indiana-Michigan Mennonite Conference collection (II-5-12), box 3, folder 2, MCUSAA–Goshen.

125. John H. Mosemann, "Congregational Life in Change," *Gospel Evangel*, October 1980, 3.

126. Executive Secretary's Report to the Executive Committee, January 15–April 15, 1992, Indiana-Michigan Mennonite Conference collection (II-5-20), box 11, folder 4, MCUSAA–Goshen.

127. "Good-Bye Braves! BCHS to Change School Mascot," *Gospel Evangel*, November 1992, 6.

128. Litwiller, "Women in Church Leadership," 44–45.

129. Showalter was the second woman to become president of a Mennonite college. About six months earlier, Lee Snyder took office at Bluffton College, a General Conference Mennonite Church school.

130. Russell Krabill, "Bethlehem '83 Delegate Report," Indiana-Michigan Mennonite Conference collection (II-5-20), box 6, folder 9, MCUSAA–Goshen.

131. Dual-conference congregations were those that, before the creation of Mennonite Church USA, were members of both the General Conference Mennonite Church and Mennonite Church. So Waltner's Illinois pastorate provided him Mennonite Church experience before moving to Goshen.

132. Silverwood Mennonite Church, formerly Silver Street Mennonite Church, of Goshen, Indiana, split from Clinton Frame Mennonite Church in 1892 and soon afterward planted daughter congregations Topeka (Ind.) Mennonite Church and Eighth Street Mennonite Church, Goshen. In the 1920s, Pleasant Oaks Mennonite Church, formerly Warrant Street Mennonite Church, split from First Mennonite Church in Middlebury, Indiana, and Comins (Mich.) Mennonite Church broke from Fairview (Mich.) Mennonite Church, while Nappanee's First Mennonite Church, formerly West Market Street Mennonite Church, in Nappanee, Indiana, withdrew from Indiana-Michigan. See chap. 4. Similar Central District Conference congregations can also be found in Ohio.

133. Charles Buller to Indiana-Michigan Executive Committee, August 12, 1998, box C-1, blue three-ring binder "Executive Committee Agenda, March 1997–June 2000," Indiana-Michigan Mennonite Conference office, Goshen, IN.

134. Indiana-Michigan Mennonite Conference, *Indiana-Michigan Mennonite Conference Annual Reports* 2001, B42–B43.

135. The Canadian members of the Mennonite Church and General Conference Mennonite, both binational denominations, were able to move more quickly

after the 1995 merger decision and formed Mennonite Church Canada in 1999, three years before Mennonite Church USA was inaugurated.

136. Indiana-Michigan Mennonite Conference, *Confer*, July–August 2001. While both denominations officially approved the merger, for legal reasons, each Mennonite Church area conference also had to decide independently whether to join the new denomination.

137. Laurie L. Oswald, "Great Lakes Merger Proposal Falls Short," *Mennonite Weekly Review*, October 18, 2001, 1.

Epilogue: Relations at the Crossroads

1. See Rachel Nafziger Hartlzer, *No Strings Attached*.

2. Rachel Nafziger Hartzler, email to author, March 15, 2013.

3. Rich Preheim, "Two Indiana-Michigan Congregations Reinstated after Homosexuality Discipline," *Mennonite*, July 1, 2003, 23.

4. Melvin Paulus and Simon Knepp to Indiana-Michigan Mennonite Conference, undated but received October 29, 2001, Indiana-Michigan Mennonite Conference files, box C-1, binder "Ministry Team," Indiana-Michigan Mennonite Conference office, Goshen, IN.

5. "Transformation Letter," Transformation Letter website, posted February 3, 2014, http://transformationletter.blogspot.com. Groups also submitting critical letters were congregational leaders from Franconia, Franklin, Lancaster, New York, Ohio, and Virginia conferences of Mennonite Church USA. The denominational executive board also received a flood of letters from individuals.

6. Kelli Yoder, "Church Leaves Indiana-Michigan," *Mennonite World Review*, July 7, 2014, 11; "Departing Congregations," Indiana-Michigan Mennonite Conference website, posted June 2, 2015, http://im.mennonite.net/2015/06/02 /departing-congregations/. The withdrawing congregations were Clinton Brick, Clinton Frame, Pleasant View, and Iglesia Menonita del Buen Pastor, all of Goshen, Indiana; Germfask, the mother congregation in Michigan's Upper Peninsula; Naubinway (Mich.) Christian Fellowship; Rexton (Mich.) Mennonite Church; and Stutsmanville Chapel, Harbor Springs, Michigan, which was the only one of the group not represented in the letter to the Mennonite Church USA Executive Board. Curiously, the Indiana-Michigan executive committee had previously recommended that Stutsmanville withdraw because of the congregation's lack of conference participation and lack of commitment to the peace position. "Stutsmanville Chapel Withdrawal," Indiana-Michigan Mennonite Conference website, posted June 2, 2015, http://im.mennonite.net /wp-content/uploads/2015/06/Stutsmanville-Chapel-Withdrawal.pdf.

7. See chap. 1.

8. Kelli Yoder, "Church Leaves Indiana-Michigan."

9. Kelli Yoder, "With a Name and New Leaders, Evana Group Moves Ahead," *Mennonite World Review*, April 27, 2015, 1.

10. Emily Pfund, "Two More Churches to Leave Conference," *Elkhart Truth*, June 25, 2015, 1.

11. Kelli Yoder, "Indiana-Michigan Cites Goshen Pastor's 'Variance' for Same-Sex Ceremony," *Mennonite World Review*, April 27, 2015, 21.

12. Pfund, "Two More Churches."

13. At least three ministers in Mennonite Church USA and its predecessor denominations had earlier been disciplined for conducting same-sex marriage ceremonies.

14. Dan Miller, interview by author, June 16, 2015, Goshen, IN.

15. As originally approved, Indiana's Religious Freedom Restoration Act declared that the state "may not substantially burden" the freedom of religious expression by "an association, a partnership, a limited liability company, a corporation" as well as by individuals and religious organizations. See Indiana General Assembly, "Religious Freedom Restoration Act S. 568" (2015), https://iga .in.gov/legislative/2015/bills/senate/568.

16. Ted Koontz, a former colleague of John Howard Yoder at Associated Mennonite Biblical Seminaries, offered demon possession as a possible explanation for Yoder's conduct. Goossen, "'Defanging the Beast,'" 76–77.

17. Anabaptist Mennonite Biblical Seminary, "AMBS Statement on Teaching and Scholarship Related to John Howard Yoder," approved April 30, 2012, accessed August 8, 2015, https://www.ambs.edu/about/documents /AMBS-statement-on-JHY.pdf.

18. Rich Preheim, "AMBS on Abuse: 'We Failed You'," *Mennonite World Review*, March 30, 2015, 1.

19. Much has been written about such developments in "post-denominational" Christendom. A recent sociological examination of Mennonite Church USA is Conrad L. Kanagy, *Road Signs for the Journey: A Profile of Mennonite Church USA* (Scottdale, PA: Herald Press, 2007).

20. The connections with the entire world and their faith implications are recognized in Mennonite Church USA's confession of faith: "Human beings have been made for relationship with God, to live in peace with each other and to take care of the rest of creation." Article 6 in Mennonite Church and General Church Mennonite Conference, *Confession of Faith in a Mennonite Perspective* (Scottdale, PA: Herald Press, 1995), 28.

21. See Perry Bush, *Peace, Progress, and the Professor: The Mennonite History of C. Henry Smith* (Harrisonburg, VA: Herald Press, 2015).

22. Psalm 103:17a.

Bibliography

Primary Sources

Archival Collections

The Mennonite Church USA Archives on the Goshen (Ind.) College campus (MCUSAA–Goshen) is the official repository for the historical records of Indiana-Michigan Mennonite Conference and its member congregations. The archives also houses the official collections of the Mennonite Church agencies and related organizations, plus personal papers of many individuals who were instrumental in Indiana-Michigan's faith and life. All that makes the archives a historical goldmine and the place where I was able to do the vast majority of my research. The MCUSAA–Goshen collections cited in this book are:

Ann Arbor Mennonite Fellowship (III-22-16)
Bechler, LeRoy (HM 1-723)
Bender, Harold S. (HM 1-278)
Christophel, Allen B. (HM 1-319 SC)
Coffman, John S. (HM 1-19)
College Mennonite Church (III-14-1)
Fairview Mennonite Church (III-2-7 SC)
First Mennonite Church, Fort Wayne (III-14-22)
Funk, John F. (HM 1-1)
Goossen, Rachel Waltner on John Howard Yoder (HM 1-49)
Gross, Leonard, oral interviews (HM 6-241)
Hartzler, J. E. (HM 1-62)
Hartzler, J. S. (HM 1-3-3)
Hassan, W. Richard and Hazel Nice Hassan (HM 1-876)
Hershberger Guy F. (HM 1-171)
Hertzler, Carolyn (HM 5-3)

Home and Foreign Relief Commission (VII-1-1)
Indiana-Michigan Mennonite Conference (II-5). An extensive collection that includes Indiana-Michigan Mennonite Mission Board as well as minutes, correspondence, reports, photos, and more from Indiana-Michigan delegate assemblies, commissions, committees, and a multitude of other conference organizations.
Indiana State Council of Defense (HM 8-22)
Krabill, Russell (HM 1-599)
Leo Mennonite Church (III-14-38)
Mast, J. N. (HM 1-331 SC)
Mennonite Board of Education (V)
Mennonite Board of Missions History Project (HM 6-81)
Mennonite Church Peace Problems Committee (I-3-5.1)
Mennonite Mutual Aid Association [Everence] (XII-9)
Meyer, Jacob C. (HM 1-44)
Miller, Payson (HM 1-670)
Mininger, J. D. (HM 1-11-2)
Ninth Street Mennonite Church (III-2-3)
North Goshen Mennonite Church (III-14-19)
Oesch, W. W. and Elva Garver (HM 1-428)
Olive Mennonite Church (III-14-8)
Osborne, Chester C. and Eva Osborne (HM 1-915)
Palm Sunday Tornado (HM 3-1)
Prairie Street Mennonite Church (III-14-2)
Salem Mennonite Church (III-14-25)
Sherk, David Regarding Wisler Schism (HM 1-84 SC)
Slagel, Vesta Zook (HM 1-403)
Smid Family (HM 1-86)
Steiner, Menno S. (HM 1-33)
Sykes, Constance (HM 4-111)
Wenger, J. C. (HM 1-337)
Wickey, William (HM 1-716)
Yellow Creek Mennonite Church (III-14-3)
Yoder, D. A. (HM 1-314)
Yoder, S. C. (HM 1-162)
Zion Mennonite Church (III-22-25)

I also utilized collections in several other archives:

Mennonite Church USA Archives, North Newton, Kansas—Allan Teichroew World War I collection

Bluffton (Ohio) University Archives and Special Collections— C. Henry Smith collection (MS 1)

Elkhart County Historical Society, Bristol, Indiana—Elkhart County Council of Defense collection (1978.075)

Indiana-Michigan Mennonite Conference, Central District Conference, Assembly Mennonite Church, and Southside Fellowship graciously allowed me access to more recent materials still in their offices. Irene and LeRoy Bechler of Goshen, Indiana, also gave me access to documents in their possession pertaining to African American Mennonites.

Author Interviews and Correspondence

Bechler, Irene, and LeRoy Bechler. Interview by author. October 2, 2013, Goshen, IN.

Bender, John. Email to Leonard Gross. April 22, 2013.

Beyler, Gladys, Areta Lehman, and Lucille Swartzendruber. Interview by author. September 19, 2012, Goshen, IN.

Farmwald, Leon. Interview by author. Date unknown, Nappanee, IN.

Friesen, Luella. Interview by author. September 18, 2012, Goshen, IN.

Handrich, Mary and Willard Handrich. Interview by author. June 21, 2006, Grand Marais, MI.

Hartzler, Rachel Nafziger. Email to author, March 15, 2013.

Jeschke, Marlin. Interview by author. August 14, 2007, Goshen, IN.

Johns, Galen. Interview by author. June 2, 2006, Goshen, IN.

Kauffman, Sherm. Interview by author. August 29, 2012, Goshen, IN.

Kreider, Robert S. Email to author, May 10, 2006.

Livermore, J. D. Interview by author. June 21, 2006, Germfask, MI.

Mark, George. Interview by author. June 16, 2006, Elkhart, IN.

Miller, Carol. Interview by author. March 24, 2006, Elkhart, IN.

Miller, Dan. Interview by author. July 16, 2015, Goshen, IN.

Miller, Lois. Interview by author, June 22, 2006, Engadine, MI.

Shaum, Esther. Interview by author. June 22, 2006, Engadine, MI.

Shellenberger, Evie, and Wallace Shellenberger. Interview by author. September 14, 2006, Paoli, IN.

Troyer, James. Interview by author. June 23, 2006, Manistique, MI.

Works Cited

Ainlay, Stephen and Fred Kniss, "Mennonites and Conflict: Re-examining Mennonite History and Contemporary Life," *Mennonite Quarterly Review* 72, no. 2 (April 1998): 121–39.

Amish Heritage Committee. *Amish and Mennonites in Eastern Elkhart and LaGrange Counties, 1841–1991.* Goshen, IN: privately published, 1992.

Amish Mennonite Conference of Indiana and Michigan. *Constitution, Rules and Discipline of the Amish Mennonite Conference of Indiana and Michigan.* N.p., 1905.

Anabaptist Mennonite Biblical Seminary. "AMBS Statement on Teaching and Scholarship Related to John Howard Yoder." Approved April 30, 2012. https://www.ambs.edu/about/documents/AMBS-statement-on-JHY.pdf.

Anderson, Elizabeth. *Pathfinders for God at Comins.* Privately published, 1984.

Baker, Robert J. "Conference Sounds." *Gospel Evangel,* September 1981.

Bartholomew, H[enry] S. K. *Elkhart County, Indiana, in World War I.* Goshen, IN: privately published, 1924.

———. *Pioneer History of Elkhart County.* Goshen, IN: privately published, 1930.

———. *Stories and Sketches of Elkhart County.* Nappanee, IN: privately published, 1936.

Beachy, Leroy. *Unser Leit: The Story of the Amish.* Millersburg, OH: Goodly Heritage Books, 2011.

Bechler, LeRoy. *The Black Mennonite Church in North America, 1886–1986.* Scottdale, PA: Herald Press, 1986.

———. "Saginaw Service Unit." *Gospel Evangel,* September 1949.

———. "Summer Activities at Saginaw." *Gospel Evangel,* September–October 1951.

Beddington, David W. *The Dominance of Evangelicalism: The Age of Spurgeon and Moody.* Downers Grove, IL: InterVarsity Press, 2005.

Beiler, Edna, and Melvin King. "A Study of the Prayer Veil as Viewed by the College Mennonite Church." Research paper, Goshen College, 1968. In Mennonite Historical Library, Goshen, Indiana.

Bender, Harold S. *The Anabaptist Vision*. Scottdale, PA: Herald Press, 1944.

————. "Bible." In *Mennonite Encyclopedia*, vol. 1, edited by Harold S. Bender and C. Henry Smith. Scottdale, PA: Mennonite Publishing House, 1955.*

————. "Bishop" In *Mennonite Encyclopedia*, vol. 1, edited by Harold S. Bender and C. Henry Smith. Scottdale, PA: Mennonite Publishing House, 1955.*

————. "Fundamentalism." In *Mennonite Encyclopedia*, vol. 2, edited by Harold S. Bender and C. Henry Smith. Scottdale, PA: 1956.*

————. "In Time of Peace Prepare for War." In *Christian Doctrine*, supplement, *Gospel Herald*, April 21, 1932.

————. "Krimmer Mennonite Brethren." In *Mennonite Encyclopedia*, vol. 3, edited by Harold S. Bender and C. Henry Smith. Scottdale, PA: 1957.*

————. "Priesthood of All Believers." In *Mennonite Encyclopedia*, vol. 4, edited by Harold S. Bender and C. Henry Smith. Scottdale, PA: Mennonite Publishing House, 1959.*

————. "South Central Mennonite Conference." In *Mennonite Encyclopedia*, vol. 4, edited by Harold S. Bender and C. Henry Smith. Scottdale, PA: Mennonite Publishing House, 1959.*

————. "Taxation." In *Mennonite Encyclopedia*, vol. 1, edited by Harold S. Bender and C. Henry Smith. Scottdale, PA: Mennonite Publishing House, 1955.*

————. *Two Centuries of American Mennonite Literature: A Bibliography of Mennonitica Americana, 1827–1928*. Goshen, IN: Mennonite Historical Society, 1929.

————. "Washington Center Mennonite Church." In *Mennonite Encyclopedia*, vol. 4, edited by Harold S. Bender and C. Henry Smith. Scottdale, PA: Mennonite Publishing House, 1959.*

Bender, John. *Greencroft Roots*. Goshen, IN: privately published, 1997.

————. "Reconciliation Spreads to the U.S." *Christian Living*, December 1985.

Bender, Lynn. "The Yellow Creek Mennonite Settlers: A Study of Land and Family." *Mennonite Quarterly Review* 46, no. 1 (January 1972): 70–83.

Benner, Richard. "South Side Fellowship Formed." *Gospel Evangel*, March–April 1966.

Bixler, J. K. "Women's Spiritual Service in the Church." *Gospel Herald*, January 17, 1929.

Bontrager, Edna F. Letter to the editor. *Gospel Herald*, August 25, 1992.

Bontrager, Erie E. "Zion Congregation." *Rural Evangel*, November 1938.

Bontrager, Julianna. "Seminar on Homosexuality Recovery Scheduled." *Gospel Evangel*, October 1983.

Borntreger, John E. *A History of the First Settlers of the Amish Mennonites and the Establishment of Their First Congregation in the State of Indiana: Along with a Short Account of the Division Which Took Place in This Church.* Topeka, IN: privately published, 1988.

Brenneman, Daniel. "A Visit—Thoughts and Suggestions in Relation to a Reunion." *Herald of Truth*, January 1867.

Brenneman, Timothy. "Reminiscences of J. F. Funk." *Mennonite Historical Bulletin*, July 1948.

Brenneman, Wayne. "Daniel Brenneman: The Birth of a Church." *Reflections*, Summer 1993.

Brunk, George R. "Evils of a Fractional Gospel." *Rural Evangel*, January 1937.

Brunk, George R., II. *A Crisis among Mennonites: In Education, in Publication.* Harrisonburg, VA: Sword and Trumpet, 1983.

Brusewitz, Carl F. "The Mennonites of Balk, Friesland." *Mennonite Quarterly Review* 30, no. 1 (January 1956): 19–31.

Burkholder, J. Lawrence. "Concern Pamphlets Movement." In *Mennonite Encyclopedia*, vol. 5, edited by Cornelius J. Dyck and Dennis D. Martin. Scottdale, PA: Herald Press, 1990.*

Burkholder, Jared S. and David C. Cramer, eds. *The Activist Impulse: Essays on the Intersection of Evangelicalism and Anabaptism.* Eugene, OR: Pickwick Publications, 2012.

Bush, Perry. "Military Service, Religious Faith and Acculturation: Mennonite G.I.s and Their Church, 1941–1945." *Mennonite Quarterly Review* 62, no. 3 (July 1993): 261–82.

———. *Peace, Progress, and the Professor: The Mennonite History of C. Henry Smith*. Harrisonburg, VA: Herald Press, 2015.

Byers, N[oah] E. "Missionary Work in the Foreign Field." *Herald of Truth*, October 1, 1897.

Center for Inquiry. "Extreme Makeover." Accessed March 14, 2013. http://www.cfimichigan.org/pastevents/event/w-lecture-081011/.

Christophel, Harold. "A New Church Building at Battle Creek." *Gospel Evangel*, March–April 1954.

Coffman, Barbara F. *His Name Was John: The Life Story of an Early Mennonite Leader*. Scottdale, PA: Herald Press, 1964.

Coffman, John S. "The Spirit of Progress." Pts 1–3. *Young People's Paper*, February 29, 1896; March 14, 1896; March 28, 1986.

Cott, Kimberly. "Yoder Disinvited to Conference." *Bethel Collegian*, March 5, 1992.

C. S. *Herald of Truth*. May 1865.

Derstine, Gerald. *Following the Fire*. Bradenton, FL: Christian Retreat Gospel Crusade, 1980.

Detweiler, Lowell. *The Hammer Rings Hope: Photos and Stories from Fifty Years of Mennonite Disaster Service*. Scottdale, PA: Herald Press, 2000.

Driedger, Leo, and Donald B. Kraybill. *Mennonite Peacemaking: From Quietism to Activism*. Scottdale, PA: Herald Press, 1994.

Dunbar, Willis Frederick. *Michigan: A History of the Wolverine State*. Grand Rapids, MI: Wm. B. Eerdmans, 1965.

Dyck, Cornelius J., ed. *An Introduction to Mennonite History*, 2nd ed. Scottdale, PA: Herald Press, 1981.

Eash, Marvin. "The Clinton Frame Split of 1892." Research paper, Goshen College, 1964. In Mennonite Historical Library, Goshen, Indiana.

Eash, Sanford. "Paoli Fellowship Worships and Serves." *Gospel Evangel*, June 1979.

Eastern Amish Mennonite Conference. *Report of the Eastern Amish Mennonite Conference from the Time of Its Organization to the Year 1911*. Sugarcreek, OH: privately published, 1911.

Edmunds, R. David. *The Potawatomis: Keepers of the Fire*. Norman: University of Oklahoma Press, 1978.

Eyman, Henry. "From Kent Co., Michigan." *Herald of Truth*, May 1878.

Falcon, Rafael. *The Hispanic Mennonite Church in North America, 1932–1982*. Translated by Ronald Collins. Scottdale, PA: Herald Press, 1986.

Fretz, J. Winfield, and Harold S. Bender. "Mutual Aid." In *Mennonite Encyclopedia*, vol. 3, edited by Harold S. Bender and C. Henry Smith. Scottdale, PA: Mennonite Publishing House, 1957.*

Funk, George. "A Visit." *Herald of Truth*, March 1865.

Funk, John F. "My Journey to Ohio—Conference." *Herald of Truth*, June 1867.

———. *Warfare: Its Evils, Our Duty*. Markham, IL: privately published, 1863.

Gates, Helen Kolb, John Funk Kolb, Jacob Clemens Kolb, and Constance Kolb Sykes. *Bless the Lord O My Soul: A Biography of John Fretz Funk*. Scottdale, PA: Herald Press, 1964.

Gingerich, Melvin. *Mennonite Attire through Four Centuries*. Breinigsville: Pennsylvania German Society, 1970).

———. "The Mennonite Women's Missionary Society." *Mennonite Quarterly Review* 37, no. 3 (July 1963): 113–25.

———. "Research Notes: Jantz-Jontzen-Johnson-Yontz and Smith." *Mennonite Quarterly Review* 33, no. 4 (October 1959): 347–48.

———. "Rural Life Problems and the Mennonites." *Mennonite Quarterly Review* 16, no. 3 (July 1942): 167–73.

———. *Service for Peace: A History of Mennonite Civilian Public Service*. Akron, PA: Mennonite Central Committee, 1949.

Gollner, Philipp. "Against the Warlike Churches: The Mennonite Sunday School Conflict in Civil War America." Master's thesis, University of Chicago, 2010. Electronic copy in author's possession.

Goossen, Rachel Waltner. "Campus Protests and John Howard Yoder, 1985–1987." *Mennonite Life* 69 (2015). http://ml.bethelks.edu/issue/vol-69/article/campus-protests-and-john-howard-yoder-1985-1997.

———. "'Defanging the Beast': Mennonite Responses to John Howard Yoder's Sexual Abuse." *Mennonite Quarterly Review* 89, no. 1 (January 2015): 7–80.

———. *Women against the Good War: Conscientious Objection and Gender on the American Home Front, 1941–1947*. Chapel Hill: University of North Carolina Press, 1997.

Goshen College Record. "Synopsis of Inaugural Address." November 1913.

Goshen Daily News-Times. "Erect Flag Pole and Fly Flag at College." April 27, 1918.

———. "Mennonites Devise Bond Buying Plan." September 14, 1918.

Goshen Democrat. "Rev. D. D. Miller Says Reports Are Exaggerated." September 25, 1918.

Goshen News. "Surprise Takeover at GC Service." April 6, 1970.

Gospel Evangel. "Breakthrough in Racial Understanding Experienced in Indiana." July–August, 1972.

———. "Delegates Approve Accountability Process, Speak to Southside." September 1995.

———. "Disciplinary Process with John Howard Yoder Draws to a Close." July–August 1996.

———. "Good-Bye Braves! BCHS to Change School Mascot." November 1992.

———. "Persons and Places." March 1984.

———. "Practicing a Common Life Together." March–April 1976.

———. "Professionals Practice Practical Christianity." January–February 1976.

———. "Report of the Indiana-Michigan Mennonite Conference." October 1980.

———. "Teofilo Ponce Family." January–February 1971.

———. "Tongues among Us." January–February 1972. *Gospel Herald*. "Field Notes." August 30, 1917.

———. From the editor. "The Meetings in Indiana." August 25, 1944.

———. "Minutes of the Ninth Annual Meeting of the Mennonite Board of Missions and Charities Held Near Newton, Kans., May 18–20, 1915." July 1, 1915.

———. "Our Indiana Meetings." September 6, 1917.

Grimsrud, Ted. "A Faithful Teacher in the Church." *The Mennonite*, March 3, 1998.

Gross, Leonard. "Bethany's Vigorous Birth." Chap. 1 in *Hearing Our Teacher's Voice: The Pursuit of Faithfulness at Bethany Christian Schools, 1954–2004*. Goshen, IN: privately published, 2004.

———. "Conversations with Elizabeth Bender IV." *Mennonite Historical Bulletin*, July 1986.

———. "The Doctrinal Era of the Mennonite Church." *Mennonite Quarterly Review* 60, no. 1 (January 1986): 83–103.

Hammel, Bob. *Hoosiers Classified: Indiana's Love Affair with One-Class Basketball*. Indianapolis, IN: Masters Press, 1997.

Harms, Orlando. *Pioneer Publisher: The Life and Times of J. F. Harms*. Winnipeg, MB: Kindred Press, 1984.

Hartzler, J. S. *Mennonites in the World War, or Nonresistance under Test*. Scottdale, PA: Mennonite Publishing House, 1921.

Hartzler, Levi. "Conference Camp Readied for the Summer." *Gospel Evangel*, May–June 1960.

Hartzler, Rachel Nafziger. *No Strings Attached: Boundary Lines in Pleasant Places: A History of Warren Street/Pleasant Oaks Mennonite Church*. Eugene, OR: Resource Publications, 2013.

Hartzler, Robert. "The Oaklawn Psychiatric Center." *Gospel Evangel*, May–June 1959.

Hauerwas, Stanley. *Hannah's Child: A Theologian's Memoir*. Grand Rapids, MI: Wm. B. Eerdmans, 2010.

Herald of Truth. "Amish Mennonite Conference." June 15, 1891.

———. "Foreign Mission Work." November 15, 1898.

———. "From Germany." April 1870.

———. "The Mennonites in Russia. A Visit from There." August 1872.

———. "Our New Home." May 1867.

———. "The Present Number." February 1873.

———. "To the Readers of the Herald." November 1865.

Hershberger, Guy F. *The Mennonite Church in the Second World War*. Scottdale, PA: Mennonite Publishing House, 1951.

———. "Mennonite Relief Commission for War Sufferers." In *Mennonite Encyclopedia*, vol. 3, edited by Harold S. Bender and C. Henry Smith. Scottdale, PA: Mennonite Publishing House, 1957.*

———. *War, Peace, and Nonresistance*. Scottdale, PA: Herald Press, 1981.

Hertzler, Daniel. "Twenty Years, Ten Churches: A Report on the Mennonite Churches in Michigan's Upper Peninsula." *Christian Living*, December 1958.

Hertzler, Silas. "Long Green Amish Mennonite Church." In *Mennonite Encyclopedia*, vol. 3, edited by Harold S. Bender and C. Henry Smith. Scottdale, PA: Mennonite Publishing House, 1957.*

———. "Mennonite Parochial Schools: Why Established and What They Have Achieved." In *Proceedings of the Seventh Annual Conference on Mennonite Cultural Problems*, 68–79. Hillsboro, KS, 1949.

Hinojosa, Felipe. *Latino Mennonites: Civil Rights, Faith, and Evangelical Cultures*. Baltimore, MD: Johns Hopkins University Press, 2014.

An Historical 75th Anniversary Publication. Elkhart: Indiana Conference of the United Missionary Church, 1958.

History of Elkhart County, Indiana, Together with Sketches of Its Cities and Biographies of Representative Citizens. Chicago, IL: Chas. C. Chapman, 1881.

Hochstedler, Eli. "I Went to Jail." *Mennonite*, June 30, 1964.

Hoffman, Wanda Kauffman. *Brick by Brick: The Story of Clinton Brick Mennonite Church, 1854–2004*. Goshen, IN: privately published, 2004.

Homan, Gerlof D. *American Mennonites and the Great War, 1914–1918*. Scottdale, PA: Herald Press, 1994.

———. "The Burning of the Mennonite Church, Fairview, Michigan, in 1918." *Mennonite Quarterly Review* 64, no. 2 (April 1990): 99–112.

———. "Niles M. Slabaugh's Ordeal in 1918." *Mennonite Historical Bulletin*, October 1989.

Hoover, Amos B. *The Jonas Martin Era*. Denver, PA: privately published, 1982.

Horsch, John. *The Mennonite Church and Modernism*. Scottdale, PA: Mennonite Publishing House, 1924.

———. *Modern Religious Liberalism: The Destructiveness and Irrationality of the New Theology.* Scottdale, PA: Fundamental Truth Depot, 1921.

———. *Is the Mennonite Church of America Free from Modernism?* Scottdale, PA: 1926.

———. *What Ails Our Seminaries?* Scottdale, PA: Fundamental Truth Depot, 1920.

Horst, Becky Bontrager. "A Struggle for Identity." Chap. 3 in *Hearing Our Teacher's Voice: The Pursuit of Faithfulness at Bethany Christian Schools, 1954–2004.* Goshen, IN: privately published, 2004.

Hostetler, Amos O. *Emma Mennonite Church since 1969.* Privately published, n.d.

Hostetler, John A. *God Uses Ink: The Heritage and Mission of the Mennonite Publishing House after Fifty Years.* Scottdale, PA: Herald Press, 1958.

Hostetler, Marian E. "Refugee Resettlement in Indiana-Michigan." *Gospel Evangel*, March 1980.

Howard-Miami Mennonite Church. *History of Howard-Miami Mennonite Church.* Greentown, IN: privately published, 1999.

Hutchison, William R. *The Modernist Impulse in American Protestantism.* Cambridge, MA: Harvard University Press, 1976.

Indiana General Assembly. "Religious Freedom Restoration Act, S. 568." 2015. https://iga.in.gov/legislative/2015/bills/senate/568.

Indiana-Michigan Mennonite Conference, *Confer*, July–August 2001.

———. *Constitution and Discipline of the Indiana-Michigan Mennonite Conference.* N.p., 1909.

———. *Constitution, Rules and Discipline of the Indiana-Michigan Mennonite Conference, 1915.* N.p. [1915?].

———. "Departing Congregations." Posted June 2, 2015. http://im.mennonite.net/2015/06/02/departing-congregations/.

———. *Minutes of the Indiana-Michigan Mennonite Conference, 1864–1929.* Compiled by Ira S. Johns, J. S. Hartzler, and Amos O. Hostetler. Scottdale, PA: Mennonite Publishing House, [1929?].

———. "Stutsmanville Chapel Withdrawal." Posted June 2, 2015. http://im.mennonite.net/wp-content/uploads/2015/06/Stutsmanville-Chapel-Withdrawal.pdf.

J. E. S. "Clinton Frame Congregation." *Rural Evangel*, January 1938.

Jackson, Dave, and Neta Jackson. *Glimpses of Glory: Thirty Years of Community*. Elgin, IL: Brethren Press, 1987.

Johns, Galen. "Barn Raising—Another Method." *Gospel Evangel*, May 1991.

Johns, Ira S. "Colonization as a Factor in Rural Missions." *Rural Evangel*, October 1, 1921.

Johnson, Arienne. "Southside's Scandal: Discerning Authority beyond Homosexuality between Indiana-Michigan Mennonite Conference and Southside Fellowship, 1993–2003." Research paper, Goshen College, 2010. In Mennonite Historical Library, Goshen, Indiana.

Juhnke, James C. "Mennonite Church Theological and Social Boundaries, 1920–1930: Loyalists, Liberals, and Laxitarians." *Mennonite Life*, June 1983.

———. *Vision, Doctrine, War: Mennonite Identity and Organization in America, 1890–1930*. Mennonite Experience in America, vol. 3. Scottdale, PA: Herald Press, 1989.

Kanagy, Conrad L. *Road Signs for the Journey: A Profile of Mennonite Church USA*. Scottdale, PA: Herald Press, 2007.

Kauffman, Daniel. *Fifty Years in the Mennonite Church*. Scottdale, PA: Mennonite Publishing House, 1941.

———, ed. *Mennonite Cyclopedic Dictionary: A Compendium of the Doctrines, History, Activities, Literature and Environments of the Mennonite Church, Especially in America*. Scottdale, PA: Mennonite Publishing House, 1937.

Kauffman, Jess. *A Vision and a Legacy: The Story of Mennonite Camping, 1920–80*. Newton, KS: Faith & Life Press, 1984.

Kaufman, Donald D. "Taxes." In *Mennonite Encyclopedia*, vol. 5, edited by Cornelius J. Dyck and Dennis D. Martin. Scottdale, PA: Herald Press, 1990.*

Keidel, Levi. *The History of Fairhaven Mennonite Church, 1954–1998*. N.p., n.d.

Keim, Albert N. *Harold S. Bender, 1897–1962*. Scottdale, PA: Herald Press, 1998.

King, C. C. "Detroit as a Mission Field." *Rural Evangel*, July 1, 1927.

Kintz, Linda, and Julia Lesage, eds. *Media, Culture, and the Religious Right*. Minneapolis: University of Minnesota Press, 1998.

Klingelsmith, Sharon. "Women in the Mennonite Church, 1900–1930." *Mennonite Quarterly Review* 54, no. 3 (July 1980): 163–207.

Kniss, Fred. *Disquiet in the Land: Cultural Conflict in American Mennonite Communities.* New Brunswick, NJ: Rutgers University Press, 1997.

Koch, Roy S. Letter to the editor. *Gospel Herald*, February 20, 1968.

Krabill, James R. "Jonas S. Hartzler (1857–1953): The Makings and Methods of a Peacemaker." Research paper, Goshen College, 1973. In Mennonite Historical Library, Goshen, Indiana.

Krabill, Russell. "Radio—To Spread the Gospel." *Rural Evangel*, September–October 1947.

———. "With Our Youth." *Gospel Evangel*, July–August 1955.

Krabill, Willard S. "Homosexuality: Time to Break the Silence." *Goshen College Record*, February 15, 1980.

Krabill, Willard S. "Sexuality." In *Mennonite Encyclopedia*, vol. 5, edited by Cornelius J. Dyck and Dennis D. Martin. Scottdale, PA: Herald Press, 1990.*

Krall, Ruth Elizabeth. *The Elephants in God's Living Room.* Vol. 3, *The Mennonite Church and John Howard Yoder, Collected Essays.* Unpublished manuscript at www.ruthkrall.com, 2013.

———, comp. "John Howard Yoder: An Annotated Timeline." Enduring Space website. Last amended January 15, 2015. http://ruthkrall.com/recommended-reading/john-howard-yoder-an-annotated-timeline-amended-2015/.

Kraus, C. Norman. "American Mennonites and the Bible." *Mennonite Quarterly Review* 41, no. 4 (October 1967): 309–29.

Kraus, C. Norman, and John W. Miller. "Intimations of Another Way: A Progress Report." *Concern: A Pamphlet Series* 3 (1956).

Lederach, Paul M., and Harold S. Bender. "Winter Bible Schools." In *Mennonite Encyclopedia*, vol. 4, edited by Harold S. Bender and C. Henry Smith. Scottdale, PA: Mennonite Publishing House, 1959.*

Lehman, James O., and Steven M. Nolt. *Mennonites, Amish, and the American Civil War.* Baltimore: Johns Hopkins University Press, 2007.

Liechty, Joseph, and James O. Lehman. "From Yankee to Non-resistant." *Mennonite Quarterly Review* 59, no. 3 (July 1985): 203–47.

Lind, Ethel. "Biography of J. S. Hartzler." Research paper, Goshen College, n.d. In Mennonite Historical Library, Goshen, Indiana.

Lind, Hope Kauffman. *Apart and Together: Mennonites in Oregon and Neighboring States, 1876–1976.* Scottdale, PA: Herald Press, 1990.

Linehan, Kevin. "A Pastoral Response to Homosexuality." *Gospel Herald*, June 14, 1977.

Litwiller, Cynthia A. Valdez. "Women in Church Leadership in the Indiana-Michigan Mennonite Conference." Research paper, Goshen College, 1997. In Anabaptist Mennonite Biblical Seminary library, Elkhart, Indiana.

MacMaster, Richard K. *Land, Piety, Peoplehood: The Establishment of Mennonite Communities in America, 1683–1790.* Mennonite Experience in America, vol. 1. Scottdale, PA: Herald Press, 1985.

Mann, Cleo. "Indianapolis Our Samaria." *Gospel Evangel*. March–April 1954.

Madison, James H. *The Indiana Way: A State History.* Bloomington: Indiana University Press; Indianapolis: Indiana Historical Society, 1986.

Marsden, George M. *Fundamentalism and American Culture.* 2nd ed. New York: Oxford University Press, 2006.

Martin, C. Joseph. "Mennonite Church Discipline Based on the Practices of the Mennonite Churches of Indiana-Michigan and Ohio & Eastern." Research paper, Goshen Biblical Seminary, 1960. In Mennonite Historical Library, Goshen, Indiana.

Martin, Rufus, and Thelma Martin. *They Had a Vision: A Guide to Some of the Early Mennonite Pioneers in the Yellow Creek Area, Elkhart County, Indiana.* Goshen, IN: privately published, 1995.

Martin, William. *With God on Our Side: The Rise of the Religious Right in America.* New York: Broadway Books, 1996.

Marty, Myron A. *Daily Life in the United States, 1960–1990: Decades of Discord.* Westport, CT: Greenwood Press, 1997.

Mast, Cheryl. *Amigo Centre: In Harmony with God and Nature.* Sturgis, MI: Amigo Centre, 2007.

Maust, Ted. "For a Brief and Shining Moment." *Mennonite Historical Bulletin*, October 2012.

McLellan, Dave, and Bill Warrick. *The Lake Shore and Michigan Southern Railway*. Polo, IL: Transportation Trails, 1989.

The Mennonite. "Price Told the John Howard Story." October 2013.

Mennonite General Conference. *Mennonite General Conference Report, August 18-24, 1943*. Scottdale, PA: Mennonite Publishing House, 1943.

———. *Mennonite General Conference Report, August 23–26, 1949*. Scottdale, PA: Mennonite Publishing House, 1949.

———. *Mennonite General Conference Report, August 26-30, 1953*. Scottdale, PA: Mennonite Publishing House, 1953.

———. *Proceedings of Mennonite General Conference Including Discussions Leading to Its Origination*. Scottdale, PA: Mennonite Publishing House, 1921.

———. *Prophecy Conference: Report of Conference Held at Elkhart, Indiana, April 3–5, 1952*. Mennonite Publishing House, 1953.

Mennonite Church. "The Real Facts about the Attitude of the Mennonite Church on the Issues of the Late War." *Mennonite Yearbook and Directory 1921*. Scottdale, PA: Mennonite Publishing House.

Mennonite Church and General Conference Mennonite Church. *Confession of Faith in a Mennonite Perspective*. Scottdale, PA: Herald Press, 1995.

Mennonite Church USA and Mennonite Church Canada. *A Shared Understanding of Church Leadership: Polity Manual for Mennonite Church Canada and Mennonite Church USA* [working document]. Harrisonburg, VA: MennoMedia, 2014.

Mennonite Historical Bulletin. "Research Source." July 1947.

Mennonite Weekly Review. "Indiana-Michigan Conf. Leader Dies." February 11, 1999.

Mennonite World Conference. *Proceedings of the Fourth Mennonite World Conference*. Akron, PA: Mennonite Central Committee, 1950.

Mennonite Yearbook and Directory for 1923–40 and 1961–1981. Scottdale, PA: Mennonite Publishing House, published annually.

Miller, Ernest E. "The Use of the Radio among the Mennonites of the Indiana-Michigan Conference." *Mennonite Quarterly Review* 14, no. 3 (July 1940): 131–48.

Miller, Ivan J. "Somerset County." In *Mennonite Encyclopedia*, vol. 4, edited by Harold S. Bender and C. Henry Smith. Scottdale, PA: Mennonite Publishing House, 1959.*

Miller, Melissa, and Phil M. Shenk. *The Path of Most Resistance.* Scottdale, PA: Herald Press, 1982.

Miller, Percy J. "A Message from the Secretary." *Gospel Evangel,* November–December 1951.

Miller, Susan Fisher. *Culture for Service: A History of Goshen College, 1894–1994.* Goshen, IN: privately published, 1994.

Mishler, Dorsa, and Russell Krabill. *The Prairie Street Mennonite Church Story, 1871–1996.* Elkhart, IN: privately published, 1996.

Morningstar, Titus. "Beginnings of the Plato Mennonite Church." *Gospel Evangel,* November–December 1951.

Mosemann, John H. "Congregational Life in Change." *Gospel Evangel,* October 1980.

National Park Service. "Indianapolis Union Railroad Station." Accessed March 15, 2013. http://www.nps.gov/nr/travel /indianapolis/unionstation.htm.

Nation, Mark Thiessen. *John Howard Yoder: Mennonite Patience, Evangelical Witness, Catholic Convictions.* Grand Rapids, MI: Wm. B. Eerdmans, 2006.

Neff, Christian. "James, Epistle of." In *Mennonite Encyclopedia,* vol. 3, edited by Harold S. Bender and C. Henry Smith. Scottdale, PA: Mennonite Publishing House, 1957.*

Neff, Christian, and Harold S. Bender. "Conference." In *Mennonite Encyclopedia,* vol. 1, edited by Harold S. Bender and C. Henry Smith. Scottdale, PA: Mennonite Publishing House, 1955.*

Neff, Christian, and Lena Mae Smith. "Deaconess." In *Mennonite Encyclopedia,* vol. 2, edited by Harold S. Bender and C. Henry Smith. Scottdale, PA: Mennonite Publishing House, 1956.*

Neufeld, Vernon H., ed. *If We Can Love: The Mennonite Mental Health Story.* Newton, KS: Faith & Life Press, 1983.

Noll, Ben. "Pine Manor Was Probably the Catalyst: The Challenge of Speaking for Migrant Workers in Goshen, Indiana, 1969–1971."

Research paper, Goshen College, 2009. In Mennonite Historical Library, Goshen, Indiana.

Noll, Mark A. *A History of Christianity in the United States and Canada*. Grand Rapids, MI: Wm. B. Eerdmans, 1992.

Nolt, Steven M. "From Bishop to Bureaucracy: Observations on the Migration of Authority." *Vision: A Journal for Church and Theology* 5, no. 2 (Fall 2004): 14–24.

———. *A History of the Amish*, 2nd ed. Intercourse, PA: Good Books, 2003.

North, Homer F. "A Resolution Passed at Our Last Annual Meeting." *Rural Evangel*, September 1941.

Norton, Mary Beth, David M. Katzman, Paul D. Escott, Howard P. Chudacoff, Thomas G. Paterson and William M. Tuttle Jr. *A People and a Nation: A History of the United States*. 2nd ed. 2 vols. Boston: Houghton Mifflin, 1986.

Osborne, Chester C. "Fernland Congregation." *Rural Evangel*, January 1941.

Osborne, Herbert L, comp. *History of the First Mennonite Church in Fort Wayne, Indiana, 1903–1978*. Fort Wayne, IN: privately published, 1978.

———. "History of the Mennonite Church in Fort Wayne, Indiana, 1903–1953." Unpublished manuscript, n.d. In Mennonite Historical Library, Goshen, Indiana.

———. "Howard and Miami Counties Mennonites and Amish." Research paper, Goshen College, 1948. In Mennonite Historical Library, Goshen, Indiana.

Oswald, Laurie L. "Great Lakes Merger Proposal Falls Short." *Mennonite Weekly Review*, October 18, 2001.

———. "Indiana-Michigan Network Wants Reform." *Mennonite Weekly Review*, February 10, 2000.

Pannabecker, Samuel F. *Ventures in Faith: The Story of Mennonite Biblical Seminary*. Elkhart, IN: privately published, 1975.

Patterson, James T. *Grand Expectations: The United States, 1945–1974*. Oxford History of the United States, vol. 10. New York: Oxford University Press, 1996.

Peachey, J. Lorne. "Berne Consultation Focuses on Biblical Authority, Integrity of Leadership, Influence of Humanism." *Gospel Herald*, April 14, 1981.

―――. "Indiana-Michigan Conference Asks Congregations to Reaffirm Purdue 87 Statement on Homosexuality." *Gospel Herald*, July 18, 1995.

Peachey, Linda Gehman. "Naming the Pain, Seeking the Light: The Mennonite Church's Response to Sexual Abuse." *Mennonite Quarterly Review* 89, no. 1 (January 2015): 111–28.

Pfund, Emily. "Two More Churches to Leave Conference." *Elkhart Truth*, June 25, 2015.

Pitts, Jamie. "Anabaptist Re-Vision: On John Howard Yoder's Misrecognized Sexual Politics." *Mennonite Quarterly Review* 89, no. 1 (January 2015): 153–70.

Ponce, Teofilo. "Templo Menonita de la Hermosa." *Gospel Evangel*, December 1985.

Prater, Rosella. *Mennonite Stirrings in America's Playland*. Naubinway, MI: privately published, 1987.

Preheim, Rich. "AMBS on Abuse: 'We Failed You'." *Mennonite World Review*, March 30, 2015, 1.

―――. "Cooperation's Harvest: The Growth of Inter-Mennonite Relations on 55 Acres." *The Mennonite Historical Bulletin*, October 2008.

―――. "Two Indiana-Michigan Congregations Reinstated after Homosexuality Discipline." *The Mennonite*, July 1, 2003.

Price, Tom. "Church Slow to Explore Rumors against a Leader." *Elkhart Truth*, July 14, 1992.

―――. "Theologian Cited in Sex Inquiry." *Elkhart Truth*, June 29, 1992.

Raber, Clara S. Jennings. *Special Handling: An Autobiography*. Privately published, 1994.

Reedy, Orlin. "The History of the North and East Goshen Sunday Schools." Research paper, Goshen College research paper, 1932. In Mennonite Historical Library, Goshen, Indiana.

The Revelation of Barbara Stutzman, Deceased, to All Mankind (n.p., n.d.).

Rheinheimer, Laura. "Close to the Center, Far from the Heart: The Experiences of Mennonite Veterans of World War II from the Indiana-Michigan Conference." Research paper, Goshen College, 2005. In Mennonite Historical Library, Goshen, Indiana.

Rich, Elaine Sommers. *Mennonite Women: A Story of God's Faithfulness, 1683–1983.* Scottdale, PA: Herald Press, 1983.

Ringenberg, John. "Letter from Lock, Ind." *Herald of Truth,* July 1864.

Ringenberg, William C. "Development and Division in the Mennonite Community in Allen County, Indiana." *Mennonite Quarterly Review* 50, no. 2 (April 1976): 114–31.

Rittenhouse, Charles. "An Interview with John F. Funk." *Mennonite Historical Bulletin,* October 1984.

Ross Bender website. "AMBS and John Howard Yoder," 9–11 [PDF]. Posted August 18, 2013. http://rossbender.org/AMBS-JHY.pdf.

Roth, John. "Numerous Factors in MacDonalds' Resignation." *Goshen College Record,* March 21, 1980.

Roth, Willard. "J. D. Graber Leaves Mission Legacy." *Gospel Herald,* February 7, 1978.

Rural Evangel. "A Change of Name." September–October 1947.

———. "Depression and Spirituality." March 1933.

———. "Echoes from the Field." January 1935.

———. "Editorial." October 1, 1929.

———. "Editorials." July 1936.

———. "Editorials." March 1935.

———. "Editorials." March 1937.

———. "Editorials." November 1933.

———. "Editorials." November 1940.

———. "Editorials." September 1933.

———. "Editorials." September–October 1945.

———. "Gleanings from the Conference Secretary's Report of the Congregations." July 1928.

———. "How Can I Be a Missionary in My Home Community?" July 1, 1922.

———. "A Mission Outpost for Every Congregation." March–April 1956.

———. "The Radio." May 1934.

————. Untitled. May–June 1944.

————. "Voluntary Service under District Mission Board." November–December 1952.

Salgado, Soli. "Yoder Case Extends to Notre Dame," *National Catholic Reporter*, June 19–July 2, 2015.

Salzman, Vinora Weaver. *Day by Day, Year by Year*. Elkhart, IN: privately published, 1982.

Sault Ste. Marie Convention and Visitors Bureau. "History of the Soo Locks." Accessed March 15, 2013. http://www.saultstemarie.com /soo-locks-46/.

Sawatsky, Rodney James. "The Influence of Fundamentalism on Mennonite Nonresistance, 1908–1944." Master's thesis, University of Minnesota, 1973. In Mennonite Historical Library, Goshen, Indiana.

Schlabach, Theron F. *Gospel versus Gospel: Mission and the Mennonite Church, 1863–1944*. Scottdale, PA: Herald Press, 1980.

————. "History." Chap. 1 in *College Mennonite Church, 1903–2003*. Goshen, IN: privately published, 2003.

————. "Nineteenth-Century Humility: A Vital Message for Today?" *Mennonite Historical Bulletin*, January 2002.

————. *Peace, Faith, Nation: Mennonites and Amish in Nineteenth Century America*. Mennonite Experience in America, vol. 2. Scottdale, PA: Herald Press, 1988.

————. "War, Peace, and Nonresistance (1944): Background, Genesis, Message." *Mennonite Quarterly Review* 80, no. 3 (July 2006): 293–35.

————. *War, Peace, and Social Conscience: Guy F. Hershberger and Mennonite Ethics*. Scottdale, PA: Herald Press, 2009.

Schmucker, Tobe. *Beacon of Hope: The Story of an Inner-City Rescue Mission*. South Bend, IN: privately published, 1991.

Schrock, Elden Ray. *100th Anniversary Edition of the History and a Pictorial Directory of the First Mennonite Church, Nappanee, Indiana*. Privately published, [1975].

Scott, Stephen. *An Introduction to Old Order and Conservative Mennonite Groups*. Intercourse, PA: Good Books, 1996.

Shank, C. A. "Mission Board Request." *Rural Evangel*, July 1934.

Shapiro, Samuel. "Hispanics." In *Peopling Indiana: The Ethnic Experience*, edited by Robert M. Taylor and Connie A. McBirney, 198–223. Indianapolis: Indiana Historical Society, 1996.

Shearer, Tobin Miller. *Daily Demonstrators: The Civil Rights Movement in Mennonite Homes and Sanctuaries*. Baltimore: Johns Hopkins University Press, 2010.

Shenk, Dan. "Friends, Family Pay Respects to Yoder." *Elkhart Truth*, January 4, 1998.

Sherk, David. "A Letter from Canada." *Herald of Truth*, June 1864.

Sherk, Harold J. "I-W Service." In *Mennonite Encyclopedia*, vol. 3, edited by Harold S. Bender and C. Henry Smith. Scottdale, PA: Mennonite Publishing House, 1956.*

Shetler, Sanford G. "The Mennonite Church Today." *Gospel Herald*, August 11, 1944.

Showalter, Anna. "The Rise and Fall of the Young People's Conference, 1918–1923." *Mennonite Historical Bulletin*, January 11, 2011.

Simons, Richard S., and Francis H. Parker. *Railroads of Indiana*. Bloomington: Indiana University Press, 1997.

Smith, C. Henry. *Mennonite Country Boy*. Newton, KS: Faith & Life Press, 1962.

Smith, C. Henry, and E. J. Hirschler, eds. *The Story of Bluffton College*. Bluffton, OH: privately published, 1925.

Smith, Tillman R. "Apostolic Christian Church of America." In *Mennonite Encyclopedia*, vol. 1, edited by Harold S. Bender and C. Henry Smith. Scottdale, PA: Mennonite Publishing House, 1955.*

Smith, Willard H. *Mennonites in Illinois*. Scottdale, PA: Herald Press, 1983.

Smucker, Irene. "Wilma Bailey's Search." *Purpose*, January 1977.

Smucker, John R. "One Hundred Years of a Mennonite Presence in Fort Wayne, Indiana." Unpublished paper, 2004. In Mennonite Historical Library, Goshen, Indiana.

Snyder, Ben, ed. *The Ministry of Dean Hochstetler, 1974–2005*. Privately published, 2010.

Sprunger, Eva F. *The First Hundred Years: A History of the Mennonite Church in Adams County, Indiana, 1838–1938*. Berne, IN: privately published, 1938.

Steiner, Elno. "History of the Indiana-Michigan Mennonite Mission Board." Research paper, Goshen College, 1951. In Mennonite Historical Library, Goshen, Indiana.

Stoltzfus, Grant. *Mennonites of the Ohio and Eastern Conference from the Colonial Period in Pennsylvania to 1968.* Scottdale, PA: Herald Press, 1969.

Swartley, Mary. "She Has Done What She Could." Paper presented to Michiana Anabaptist Historians, October 26, 2002. In Mennonite Historical Library, Goshen, Indiana.

Swartley, Willard M., and Donald B. Kraybill, eds. *Building Communities of Compassion: Mennonite Mutual Aid in Theory and Practice.* Scottdale, PA: Herald Press, 1998.

Time. "The Tobacco Road Gang." February 19, 1945.

Toews, Paul. "Fundamental Conflict in Mennonite Colleges: A Response to Cultural Transitions." *Mennonite Quarterly Review* 57, no. 3 (July 1983): 241–56.

———. *Mennonites in American Society, 1930–1970: Modernity and the Persistence of Religious Community.* Mennonite Experience in America, vol. 4. Scottdale, PA: Herald Press, 1996.

Transformation letter website. "Transformation Letter." Posted February 3, 2014. http://transformationletter.blogspot.com.

Troyer, Clarence. *The Mennonite Church in the Upper Peninsula.* Nappanee, IN: Evangel Press, 1986.

Troyer, J. D. "Correspondence." *Herald of Truth*, March 1, 1886.

Troyer, James L. "History of the Wildwood Mennonite Church." Research paper, Goshen Biblical Seminary, 1968. In Mennonite Historical Library, Goshen, Indiana.

Troyer, Ora. *Fairview Mennonite Church.* Fairview, MI: privately published, 1990.

Umble, John S. *Goshen College, 1894–1954: A Venture in Christian Higher Education.* Goshen, IN: privately published, 1955.

———. "John S. Coffman as an Evangelist." *Mennonite Quarterly Review* 23, no. 3 (July 1949): 123–46.

Unruh, John D. *The Plains Across: The Overland Emigrants and the Trans-Mississippi West, 1840–60.* Urbana: University of Illinois Press, 1979.

Weaver, Chester. "Fundamentalism and the Followers of Menno."
    Paper presented at the Anabaptist Identity Conference, March
    12–14, 2015. Electronic copy in author's possession.
Weaver, Edwin L. *Holdeman Descendants: A Compilation of the
    Genealogical and Biographical Record of the Descendants of
    Christian Holdeman, 1788–1846*. Nappanee, IN: E. V. Publishing
    House, 1937.
———. "The Stronger Congregations and the Unchurched Rural
    Communities." *Rural Evangel*, November 1, 1930.
Wenger, J. C. *Anniversary Celebration Clinton Frame Mennonite
    Church, 1863–1988*. Goshen, IN: privately published, 1988.
———. *Dealing Redemptively with Those Involved in Divorce and
    Remarriage Problems*. Scottdale, PA: Herald Press, n.d.
———. *Glimpses of Mennonite History and Doctrine*. Scottdale, PA:
    Herald Press, 1959.
———. "Jacob Wisler and the Old Order Mennonite Schism of 1872
    in Elkhart County, Indiana." Pts. 1 and 2. *Mennonite Quarterly
    Review* 33, no. 2 (April 1959): 108–31; 33, no. 3 (July 1959):
    215–40.
———, ed. *Mennonite Handbook, Indiana-Michigan Conference*.
    Indiana-Michigan Mennonite Conference, 1956.
———. *The Mennonites in Indiana and Michigan*. Scottdale, PA:
    Herald Press, 1961.
———. *North Goshen Mennonite Church*. Goshen, IN: privately
    published, 1986.
———. "Schleitheim Confession." In *Mennonite Encyclopedia*, vol. 4,
    edited by Harold S. Bender and C. Henry Smith. Scottdale, PA:
    Mennonite Publishing House, 1959.*
———. *The Story of the Forks Mennonite Church*. Privately pub-
    lished, 1982.
———. *The Yellow Creek Mennonites: The Original Mennonite
    Congregations of Western Elkhart County*. Goshen, IN: privately
    published, 1985.
Wenger, Wayne. "Developments and Trends in Our Summer Bible
    Schools." *Rural Evangel*, March–April 1950.

Wuthnow, Robert. *The Restructuring of American Religion: Society and Faith since World War II.* Princeton, NJ: Princeton University Press, 1988.

Yoder, Edwin J. "Northern Peninsula of Michigan." *Rural Evangel,* March 1935.

———. "Northern Peninsula of Michigan." *Rural Evangel,* September 1934.

Yoder, Elwood. *The Bishop's Letters: The Writings, Life and Times of Virginia Mennonite Bishop Martin Burkholder, 1817–1860.* Harrisonburg, VA: Shenandoah Valley Mennonite Historians, 2011.

Yoder, Genevieve Friesen. "The History of Maple Grove Mennonite Church, Topeka, Indiana." Research paper, Goshen College, 1935. In Mennonite Historical Library, Goshen, Indiana.

Yoder, Holly Blosser. *The Same Spirit: History of Iowa-Nebraska Mennonites.* Freeman, SD: privately published, 2003.

Yoder, Ida, ed. *Edward: Pilgrimage of a Mind.* Wadsworth, OH, and Irwin, PA: privately published, 1985.

Yoder, John Howard. *The Fullness of Christ: Paul's Vision of Universal Ministry.* Elgin, IL: Brethren Press, 1987.

Yoder, John D. "Church Growth Brings Demands for Space," *Gospel Evangel,* May 1987.

Yoder, Jonathan. *Jungle Surgeon.* Goshen, IN: privately published, 1986.

Yoder, Kelli. "Church Leaves Indiana-Michigan." *Mennonite World Review,* July 7, 2014.

———. "Indiana-Michigan Cites Goshen Pastor's 'Variance' for Same-Sex Ceremony." *Mennonite World Review,* April 27, 2015.

———. "With a Name and New Leaders, Evana Group Moves Ahead." *Mennonite World Review,* April 27, 2015.

Yoder, Marie. "The Balk Dutch Settlement near Goshen, Indiana, 1853–1889." *Mennonite Quarterly Review* 30, no. 1 (January 1956): 32–43.

Yoder, Mrs. Clarence [Delilah Miller Yoder]. "The Challenge of Being a Pastor's Wife." *Gospel Evangel,* January–February 1955.

Yoder, Nathan E. "Mennonite Fundamentalism: Shaping an Identity for an American Context." PhD diss., University of Notre Dame, 1999. In Mennonite Historical Library, Goshen, Indiana.

Yoder, Paton. "Joseph Yoder: Amish Mennonite Bishop." Paper presented to Michiana Anabaptist Historians, April 1, 2000. In Mennonite Historical Library, Goshen, Indiana.

———. *Tradition and Transition: Amish Mennonites and Old Order Amish, 1800–1900.* Scottdale, PA: Herald Press, 1991.

Yoder, Paton, and Silas J. Smucker. *Jonathan P. Smucker: Amish Mennonite Bishop.* Goshen, IN: privately published, 1990.

Yoder, Paton, and Steven R. Estes. *Proceedings of the Amish Ministers' Meetings, 1862–1878.* Goshen, IN: Mennonite Historical Society, 1999.

Yoder, Raymond Mark. "The Story of Daniel J. Johns' Life." Research paper, Goshen College, 1935. In Mennonite Historical Library, Goshen, Indiana.

Yordy, Eric. "The 1922 Investigation of Bishop Jacob K. Bixler: The Preservation of Conservatism." Research paper, Goshen College, 1993.

Zinn, Howard. *A People's History of the United States, 1492–Present.* New York: HarperPerennial, 1995.

Zook, Daniel. "The Mission Station in Battle Creek." *Gospel Evangel,* July–August 1953.

Zook, Ellrose. "Mennonite Publishing: A Church Institution." Unpublished manuscript, n.d. Paper copy in author's possession.

Zook, J. Kore. "Blountstown Tidings." *Gospel Evangel,* November–December 1957.

Zuercher, Melanie, and Lin Garber. *Historical Perspectives.* Welcome to Dialogue Series, vol. 2. Welcome Committee, 2001.

Asterisks denote *Mennonite Encyclopedia* entries, which, in addition to the print version, can be found at the website of the *Global Anabaptist Mennonite Encyclopedia Online,* www.gameo.com. The online version is continually updating existing articles and adding new ones.

Index

Grand Marais Mennonite Church, 182,
204–6
Great Awakenings, 50, 61
Great Depression, 142, 153–56
Great Lakes conference, 298
Greencroft, 254–55, 265
Groesbeck, Alex, 111

H

Haarer, Charles W., 212, 248
Haarer, William H., 94
Hamilton County, Indiana. *See* Arcadia,
Indiana
Handrich, Bruce, 206
Handrich, Mary, 205
Handrich, Willard, 204–5; 254
Harder, Eva, 77
Harder, Leland, 224
Harms, John F., 71
Hartford, Tyler, 302
Hartzler, Harold, 229
Hartzler, John E.: evangelist, 93–94;
Goshen College president, 114–16,
120, 189; Mennonite Church-General
Conference Mennonite Church
relations, 184; Ohio Mennonite
Conference, 122
Hartzler, Jonas S.: Bender, Violet, 126;
Elkhart Institute congregation, 87, 90;
Elkhart Institute, 75; Great Depression,
154; Mennonite Church General
Conference, 76; Mennonite-Amish
Mennonite merger, 79, 97, 100; min-
isterial education, 221; *Rural Evangel*
editor, 150, 153; World War I, 105, 107
Hartzler, Mamie, 152
Hartzler, Raymond L., 132, 134
Hauerwas, Stanley, 288
Haw Patch Amish Mennonite Church.
See Maple Grove Mennonite Church
Heath Street Mennonite Church, 179
Heatwole, Lewis J., 90
Heller, Henry D., 90
Heller, Perry, 149, 151
Hendricks, Gerhard, 29
Herald of Truth: 15; Coffman, John
S., 86; *Gospel Herald*, 92; move to

Elkhart, 49; opposition to, 50; origins,
56, 63; Russian Mennonite immigration, 69; Sunday schools, 63
Herald Press: 285–86
Herold der Wahrheit, 49; 50, 56, 63,
68–69
Hershberger, Guy F.: Burkholder, J.
Lawrence, 240; Civilian Public Service,
169; Community Life Committee,
175; Goshen College, 157–58, 166;
labor unions, 175–76, 256; Mennonite
Mutual Aid, 163–64; Mennonite World
Conference, 186; multicultural aware-
ness, 178; urban summer service units,
181; *War, Peace, and Nonresistance*,
172–73
Hershberger, Rollin, 108
Hershberger, Virgil, 206, 280
Hershey, T. K., 149
Hertzler, Silas, 191
Hesston College: alternative to Goshen
College, 118, 165; Bechler, LeRoy, 178;
Bender, Harold S., 157; Enss, Gustav,
159; Mennonite Board of Education,
342n7; Yoder, Edward, 158
Hildebrand, Vic, 250
Hillsdale College, 75
Hively Avenue Mennonite Church, 188,
295
Hochstedler, Eli, 242
Hochstedler, Jim, 242
Hochstetler, Dean, 297
Hochstetler, Jonas, 223
Hoffer, Isaac, 59–60, 61
Holdeman, Amos, 29
Holdeman, Anna, 30
Holdeman, Christian, 29
Holdeman, Christiana Buzzard, 29, 51
Holdeman, Frederick, 52
Holdeman, George, 29, 30, 51
Holdeman, John, 29, 52
Holdeman, Jonas, 52
Holdeman, Joseph, 29
Holdeman Mennonite Church: Bixler,
Jacob K., 119; conference assembly
host, 33, 109; Holdeman, Christiana
Buzzard, 29; Mennonite Church

Biblical Seminary, 166; leadership and change, 195–96, 214–16; Smoketown conference, 267; Vogt, Virgil, 201–2; weddings, 216; women in ministry, 237; Yoder, John Howard, 290

Wenger, Wayne J., 211, 259

Wertz, Edwin, 105

West Africa, 305

West Liberty, Ohio, Amish Mennonite Church, 41

West Market Street Amish Mennonite Church. *See* West Market Mennonite Church

West Market Street Mennonite Church, 37, 41, 44, 81, 131–32

Western Amish Mennonite Conference, 41, 72, 319n59

White Cloud Mennonite Church, 135, 183, 260

Widdis, Albert W., 111

Wiebe, Peter, 195–96

Wildwood Mennonite Church, 144, 146–47, 258

Wilson, Woodrow, 102

Winona Lake statement, 239

winter Bible schools, 221

Wisler, Jacob, 10, 25, 50, 55, 58–68

Wisler Mennonite Church, 61, 119–20

Witmarsum Theological Seminary, 121–22, 334n82

Wittrig, Paul and Effie, 147

women: credentialing, 223–24; disempowerment, 152–53; gender equality, 241; leadership roles, 213, 234–35, 258, 265, 294–95; pastor's wives, 139, 216; "testifying," 64. *See also* sewing circles *and* democratization

World War I, 101–13 passim, 158–59, 330n16

World War II, 163–64, 166–73, 186, 191, 197. *See also* Civilian Public Service

Wyse, Ora, 145–46, 259

Y

Yale Divinity School, 75

Yantzi, Mark, 251–52

Yellow Creek Mennonite Church, 33; 1917 Mennonite Church General Conference, 104; adult singles gathering, 216; baptism and communion services, 33; Clinton Brick Mennonite Church, 31–32; Great Depression, 154; Mennonite-Amish Mennonite relations, 42; origins, 25, 316n11, 318n32; preaching outposts, 30; voting, 151. *See also* Brenneman, Daniel, Funk, John F., *and* Wisler, Jacob

Yellow Creek statement, 104, 108

YMCA, 45, 54, 101, 109, 112

Yoder, Amzie, 247

Yoder, Anne, 288–91

Yoder, D. A., 73, 164, 173, 183, 212–14

Yoder, Delilah Miller, 216

Yoder, Edward, 157–58, 160

Yoder, Edwin J. and Mary, 135–36, 142

Yoder, Fyrne and Jonathan G., 149

Yoder, Harold and Ruth, 286

Yoder, Harvey N., 94

Yoder, John Howard, 200, 282–91, 303–5, 362n67, 363n82

Yoder, John K., 43

Yoder, John M., 94

Yoder, Loretta and Richard, 234

Yoder, Ray F., 261

Yoder, Roy K., 238

Yoder, S. S., 131–32

Yoder, Samuel, 90

Yoder, Sanford C.: 1944 Mennonite Church General Conference, 174; 1948 Mennonite World Conference, 186; Bender, Harold S., 157; conference sermon, 212; First Mennonite Church, New Bremen, New York, 183; Gingerich, Loren, funeral, 184

Yoder, Tillie, 178

Yoder, Walter, 186

Yontz, Andrew and David, 70

Young People's Conference, 129, 157

Ypsilanti State Hospital, 170

Yutzy, Homer, 236–37

Z

Zehr, Howard, 242, 252

Studies in Anabaptist and Mennonite History Series

Series editor Gerald J. Mast; with editors Geoffrey L. Dipple, Marlene G. Epp, Rachel Waltner Goossen, Leonard Gross, Thomas J. Meyers, Steven M. Nolt, John D. Roth, Theron F. Schlabach, and Astrid von Schlachta.

The Studies in Anabaptist and Mennonite History Series is sponsored by the Mennonite Historical Society. Beginning with volume 8, titles were published by Herald Press unless otherwise noted.

1. Harold S. Bender. *Two Centuries of American Mennonite Literature, 1727–1928*. 1929.
2. John Horsch. *The Hutterian Brethren, 1528–1931: A Story of Martyrdom and Loyalty*. 1931. Reprint, Macmillan Hutterite Colony, Cayley, Alberta, 1985.
3. Harry F. Weber. *Centennial History of the Mennonites in Illinois, 1829–1929*. 1931.
4. Sanford Calvin Yoder. *For Conscience' Sake: A Study of Mennonite Migrations Resulting from the World War*. 1940.
5. John S. Umble. *Ohio Mennonite Sunday Schools*. 1941.
6. Harold S. Bender. *Conrad Grebel, c. 1498–1526, Founder of the Swiss Brethren*. 1950.
7. Robert Friedmann. *Mennonite Piety Through the Centuries: Its Genius and Its Literature*. 1949.
8. Delbert L. Gratz. *Bernese Anabaptists and Their American Descendants*. 1953.
9. A. L. E. Verheyden. *Anabaptism in Flanders, 1530–1650: A Century of Struggle*. 1961.

10. J. C. Wenger. *The Mennonites in Indiana and Michigan.* 1961.
11. Rollin Stely Armour. *Anabaptist Baptism: A Representative Study.* 1966.
12. John B. Toews. *Lost Fatherland: The Story of Mennonite Emigration from Soviet Russia, 1921–1927.* 1967.
13. Grant M. Stoltzfus. *Mennonites of the Ohio and Eastern Conference, from the Colonial Period in Pennsylvania to 1968.* 1969.
14. John A. Lapp. *The Mennonite Church in India, 1897–1962.* 1972.
15. Robert Friedmann. *The Theology of Anabaptism: An Interpretation.* 1973.
16. Kenneth R. Davis. *Anabaptism and Asceticism: A Study in Intellectual Origins.* 1974.
17. Paul Erb. *South Central Frontiers: A History of the South Central Mennonite Conference.* 1974.
18. Fred R. Belk. *The Great Trek of the Russian Mennonites to Central Asia, 1880–1884.* 1976.
19. Werner O. Packull. *Mysticism and the Early South German-Austrian Anabaptist Movement, 1525–1531.* 1976.
20. Richard K. MacMaster, with Samuel L. Horst and Robert F. Ulle. *Conscience in Crisis: Mennonites and Other Peace Churches in America, 1739–1789.* 1979.
21. Theron F. Schlabach. *Gospel versus Gospel: Mission and the Mennonite Church, 1863–1944.* 1980.
22. Calvin Wall Redekop. *Strangers Become Neighbors: Mennonite and Indigenous Relations in the Paraguayan Chaco.* 1980.
23. Leonard Gross. *The Golden Years of the Hutterites: The Witness and Thought of the Communal Moravian Anabaptists during the Walpot Era, 1565–1578.* 1980. Rev. ed., Pandora Press Canada, 1998.
24. Willard H. Smith. *Mennonites in Illinois.* 1983.
25. Murray L. Wagner. *Petr Chelcický: A Radical Separatist in Hussite Bohemia.* 1983.
26. John L. Ruth. *Maintaining the Right Fellowship: A Narrative Account of Life in the Oldest Mennonite Community in North America.* 1984.

27. C. Arnold Snyder. *The Life and Thought of Michael Sattler.* 1984.
28. Beulah Stauffer Hostetler. *American Mennonites and Protestant Movements: A Community Paradigm.* 1987.
29. Daniel Liechty. *Andreas Fischer and the Sabbatarian Anabaptists: An Early Reformation Episode in East Central Europe.* 1988.
30. Hope Kauffman Lind. *Apart and Together: Mennonites in Oregon and Neighboring States, 1876–1976.* 1990.
31. Paton Yoder. *Tradition and Transition: Amish Mennonites and Old Order Amish, 1800–1900.* 1991.
32. James R. Coggins. *John Smyth's Congregation: English Separatism, Mennonite Influence, and the Elect Nation.* 1991.
33. John D. Rempel. *The Lord's Supper in Anabaptism: A Study in the Theology of Balthasar Hubmaier, Pilgram Marpeck, and Dirk Philips.* 1993.
34. Gerlof D. Homan. *American Mennonites and the Great War, 1914–1918.* 1994.
35. J. Denny Weaver. *Keeping Salvation Ethical: Mennonite and Amish Atonement Theology in the Late Nineteenth Century.* 1997.
36. Wes Harrison. *Andreas Ehrenpreis and Hutterite Faith and Practice.* 1997. Copublished with Pandora Press Canada.
37. John D. Thiesen. *Mennonite and Nazi? Attitudes among Mennonite Colonists in Latin America, 1933–1945.* 1999. Copublished with Pandora Press Canada.
38. Perry Bush. *Dancing with the Kobzar: Bluffton College and Mennonite Higher Education, 1899–1999.* 2000. Copublished with Pandora Press U.S. and Faith & Life Press.
39. John L. Ruth. *The Earth Is the Lord's: A Narrative History of the Lancaster Mennonite Conference.* 2001.
40. Melanie Springer Mock. *Writing Peace: The Unheard Voices of Great War Mennonite Objectors.* 2003. Copublished with Cascadia Publishing House.
41. Mary Jane Lederach Hershey. *This Teaching I Present: Fraktur from the Skippack and Salford Mennonite Meetinghouse Schools, 1747–1836.* 2003. Published by Good Books.

42. Edsel Burdge Jr. and Samuel L. Horst. *Building on the Gospel Foundation: The Mennonites of Franklin County, Pennsylvania, and Washington County, Maryland, 1730–1970*. 2004.

43. Ervin Beck. *MennoFolk: Mennonite and Amish Folk Traditions*. 2004.

44. Walter Klaassen and William Klassen. *Marpeck: A Life of Dissent and Conformity*. 2008.

45. Theron F. Schlabach. *War, Peace and Social Conscience: Guy F. Hershberger and Mennonite Ethics*. 2009.

46. Ervin R. Stutzman. *From Nonresistance to Justice: The Transformation of Mennonite Church Peace Rhetoric, 1908–2008*. 2011.

47. Nathan E. Yoder. *Together in the Work of the Lord: A History of the Conservative Mennonite Conference*. 2014.

48. Samuel J. Steiner. *In Search of Promised Lands: A Religious History of Mennonites in Ontario*. 2015.

49. Perry Bush. *Peace, Progress, and the Professor: The Mennonite History of C. Henry Smith*. 2015.

50. Rich Preheim. *In Pursuit of Faithfulness: Conviction, Conflict, and Compromise in Indiana-Michigan Mennonite Conference*. 2016.

The Author

Rich Preheim is a freelance writer, blogger, and historian who has spent more than thirty years working in and around the Mennonite church. He was director of the Mennonite Church USA Historical Committee and Archives for seven years. He previously was a writer for Mennonite Central Committee and a reporter and editor for *Mennonite World Review* and *The Mennonite*. As a freelancer, Preheim's articles on Mennonites have appeared in the *New York Times*, *Washington Post*, *Christian Century*, *Sojourners*, and elsewhere.

A native of Marion, South Dakota, Preheim earned a bachelor's degree in history from Bethel College, North Newton, Kansas, and a master's degree in journalism from Indiana University, Bloomington. He and his wife, Leanne Farmwald, live in Elkhart, Indiana, where they are members of Hively Avenue Mennonite Church. His congregational involvements have included preaching, leading worship, working as congregational historian, and serving on numerous commissions and committees.

CPSIA information can be obtained at www.ICGtesting.com
Printed in the USA
BVOW06s0237120516

447750BV00006B/27/P